Harry Greene's

COMPLETE DIY PROBLEM SOLVER

Harry Greene's
COMPLETE DIY PROBLEM SOLVER

LAWPACK

First published in 2003 by
Law Pack Publishing Limited
76–89 Alscot Road
London SE1 3AW
www.lawpack.co.uk

A catalogue record for this book is available
from the British Library

Text and line drawings ©2003 Harry Greene
Design ©Law Pack Publishing
Designed and typeset by
Bookcraft Ltd, Stroud, Gloucestershire

For details of photograph copyright owners see
Acknowledgements page
ISBN 1 904053 28 9

Printed in the Czech Republic

Foreword

I first met Harry when Joan Littlewood cast us in 'Make Me An Offer' in 1960. We were pretty hard-up actors, so delighted to be in this West End Musical. During the run his wife Marjie, who was also in it, invited me to their beautiful home in North London. I was amazed to hear that he had done it all himself! But then, he had been trained in design and architecture! I had just bought my first tiny house with a mortgage and asked Harry if he'd like to work his magic on it.

On a very limited budget, he turned a two-up-two-down cottage into a palace! So inspiring was it that it immediately got featured in a glossy magazine, which resulted in offers coming in from other media folk. He later designed and worked on a second home for me. This also got publicity, so his design and construction career flourished and Harry stopped being an actor. He concentrated on his television DIY presenting instead.

Harry is the only person in the UK to have been awarded the highest accolade by the DIY Industry in the twentieth century – DIY Personality of the Year. I am really delighted to have been asked to write this Foreword for his latest book and pleased if, earlier on, I helped promote his extraordinary talent.

Sheila Hancock

Harry's anecdotes ... from the homes of celebrities

Nina Myskow

TV celebrity journalist Nina Myskow says I saved her from a flood when I was called in to advise at her North London home. She was great at reglazing but had to be stopped from banging nails into loose floor boards. Underneath we found water pipes and electric cables!

Liz Carling

Ladies are much better at reading safety instructions. The installer of my water feature for actress Liz Carling was just leaving when she said, 'Hold on, these rubber rings should be protecting the cable as it goes through the metal!'

Julie Goodyear

It was fun working at Julie Goodyear's farm-house in Lancashire despite the rain. One day a call went up for the lads laying slabs, 'Tea up and Eccles cakes.' I looked from the site office at Julie plodding along with a tray, one wellington boot on and the other stuck in the mud a yard behind!

Sharron Davies

Sharron Davies was in her gym every day that I worked at her home. She is also brilliantly organised and had researched safety in the home before I got there! Brochures on burglar alarms, fire alarms and door locks, amongst others, were on the table when I arrived – plus tea and cakes!

Patsy Palmer

Don't be fooled! Patsy Palmer is not like her 'Eastenders' persona. Flat-pack furniture had to be assembled quickly and the blokes complained about the Allen keys hurting their fingers. Patsy said, 'Harry, pop that (a hex driver) into the cordless screwdriver.' Using it she was quicker than everybody!

Sian Lloyd

I offered sound advice to Sian Lloyd when working at her country home in Wiltshire. She had drilled into a wall to hang a picture, but struck a rising main. I joked, 'So you suffered a wet front and a deep depression, Sian!' She loved the pun and the present of a pipe-and-cable detector I gave her.

Peter Baldwin

One memorable project was Peter Baldwin's house and garden in North London. A magazine photographer was due on the Monday. We worked late the Friday before but left the work unfinished. By Monday the shed was glazed and varnished and the fencing completed by Peter himself, a great DIYer.

Neil Morrissey

When Neil Morrissey played the dopey, Sammy the Chamois window cleaner, he asked me to design his kitchen. Neil's outlook, at odds with his TV persona, prophetically said, 'Harry, I'm a great believer in positive thinking, I believe in myself and I'm convinced everything will fall into place'. Now he's a national treasure and a caring children's charity worker!

Barbara Windsor

I designed and installed an office in a spare bedroom for Barbara Windsor. During decorating, she laughed as she recalled the 'hysterical time trying to stick a border over wallpaper.' Barbara said, 'Next morning it looked like Christmas decorations.'

Sid Owen

We called Sid Owen 'the level boss' when renovating his garden at his Cambridgeshire home. Having a break from his busy 'Eastenders' schedule he loved working with the lads. But Sid is an exacting personality and demanded high standards. He was always ready with a joke – and his spirit level!

Philippa Forrester

After working at Philippa Forrester's West London home, I know why she is a good investigative TV journalist. She just wants to learn! Philippa loves old oak and wanted some beams in my kitchen design. She treated the woodworm, smoothed, polished and helped install the eighteenth-century beams.

Huw Higginson

Part of my brief at the home of 'The Bill's' Huw Higginson was to find an easy-to-install burglar alarm system. As manufacturers are now more aware of DIYers' needs, this was not difficult. A wireless system is remarkably effective and meets the necessary criteria. Huw found it simple!

Craig Fairbrass

A designer should be flexible since a scheme can grow as it progresses. Tiling at Craig Fairbrass's house was like that. Elke, his wife, had views about the bathroom and steam room tiling. Her choice of size, colour and layout blended with the overall scheme and 'Eastender' Craig was delighted.

Jono Coleman

DJ Jono Coleman just loves everything about life. He is a gregarious character and told me that he was brought up to eat barbecued meals, which is why I was being fêted with a 'Jono Special' when working with him at his London home. 'Hygiene and safety, though, are paramount,' he said.

Paul O'Grady

Wallpaper stripping was seen on TV with Lily Savage! I taught Paul O'Grady (Lily) different DIY tasks on a series of 'The Big Breakfast'. Lily's 'you are going to see some stripping' and 'well, wallpaper stripping can be exciting too!' was followed by the proper demonstration!

Les Dennis

Les Dennis forgot what I had told him about turning off the water at the mains before replacing a tap washer – and flooded his kitchen! He now knows that instructions must be followed in all DIY tasks.

Gregor Fisher

Gregor Fisher is not only a great character actor, but a character with pride in his inventiveness. During the installation of a large pond in my garden design at his manse in Scotland, he designed innovative features and demonstrated how to build them. A man of many talents including DIY!

Malandra Burrows

I drove to the lovely country home outside Leeds of 'Emmerdale's' Malandra Burrows to find an accomplished DIYer, who didn't mind getting her hands dirty. Over the following weeks, it proved to be as true as my theory 'that most ladies read and learn every instruction on every product'.

Lisa Maxwell

I found Lisa Maxwell to be the perfect novice DIYer as she'd never used hand or power tools. Intuitively she said, 'If you don't mind I'll spend time reading and learning the instructions before installing the mortice lock!' She did a brilliant job, as was seen on my TV series.

Julian Ballantyne

Many viewers contact me to say how they value Harry's expertise and DIY skills. I have it at first hand: people would pay to be in my unique position learning from the popular DIY Guru every week for ten years!

Ruth Langford

Elegant TV presenter Ruth Langford had a garden of builders' rubble behind her new home in South London. Soon her stylish outfit was replaced by denims, to work with the makeover lads! She said 'I'd like stargazer lilies, cream petunias, buddleia and bamboo, clematis and catalpa and furniture only from sustainable forests please Harry!' She'd had her first garden as a teenager!

Gillian Taylforth

I was restoring the garden of actress Gillian Taylforth's detached house in Hertfordshire. We had an area of decking laid for playing, dining and entertaining. Gillian saw a workman on his knees applying waterproofing. 'Use a roller,' I heard her shout. He did and finished in record time!

Sarah Greene

Over a period of a year my daughter, Sarah, was seen weekly with me on my DIY series, TVam's 'Dream Home'. She was really working! She proved that you don't have to be big and tough to accomplish most DIY jobs like concrete mixing, tamping, drilling and pumping silicone treatment for rising damp!

Paul McKenna

There was no influence on me designing the kitchen at hypnotist Paul McKenna's home! A down-to-earth man, he saw the sense of doing preparatory work himself. With guidance he stripped wallpaper and hacked off old tiles, making it ready for me to do the tiling – a real team effort!

Sir David Steel

Teaching Sir David Steel to plaster was easy. On my series 'DIY Challenge' he was charming and very talented. He picked up the tricks of the trade quickly, using the float to get a fairly good finish. His comment, 'Of course it was easy, that's not called a "steel" float for nothing, you know!'

Laura Greene

Children can develop talents influenced by parental example. My daughter, currently National Geographic Today anchor in Washington, also studied furniture making. Her DIY work in her own flat has been seen on TV. With proper guidance on tools and their uses DIYers can blossom!

Shaun Williamson

Actor Shaun Williamson is an enthusiastic DIYer and is always willing to learn. He said, 'We have to be fast learners on 'Eastenders' and I assimilate information quickly.' He demonstrated this by learning new painting techniques, as I saw when working at his home on my designs.

Max Bygraves

I was a corporal in Max Bygraves's first film 'Charlie Moon', instructing him and the squaddies. Forty years later I'm instructing him about electricity on my 'DIY Challenge' TV series. With a demonstration plug the size of a TV set in his arms, he said, 'Harry I've never been given such a big plug. I wish I could say the same for the plugs I got in my long, long career!'

John Altman

As the hard man of 'Eastenders', John Altman's character is the egomaniac with a taste for power. But that's worlds away from the sensitive lover of classics I met. So his first request for his new garden in his South London home was not a surprise: 'I'd like four statues, Harry, based on Greek sculptures!'

Nicola Duffet

One of my designs in the home of actress Nicola Duffet incorporated her idea of a four poster bed. The decorative drapes then had to be reflected in the paint technique applied to the walls. A base colour and a lightly applied sponged, paler colour satisfied Nicola and a magazine home editor!

Toyah Wilcox

One lady who has impressed me with her capacity to tackle the planning and preparatory work of any DIY building job is actress and singer Toyah Wilcox. I was asked to help at her Worcestershire home and was delighted to find a very professional approach to her DIY – a salutary lesson for all!

Harry Greene

Introduction

This definitive COMPLETE DIY PROBLEM SOLVER is dedicated to all you enthusiastic DIYers, who I think of as my great big circle of friends. We all have a common bond because we aim for the same goal: self-sufficiency. I have been pioneering DIY on TV since January 1957, when I devised and presented the very first 'hands-on' DIY programme on TV in the UK. My credits in the *TV Times* read: 'HARRY GREENE being HANDY AROUND THE HOUSE'. Wobbly sets and cumbersome cameras didn't help, but I was doing what I loved: communicating. (In the commercial breaks I would become another character to sell some product or other: the dishevelled early morning tea drinker in a dressing gown for Lyons Quick Brew, then the suave gent removing five o'clock shadow with the Remington Razor!) It was great fun and a great way of broadening my TV experience.

Trained in Engineering, Architecture and Interior Design, I ran my own building company for more than 30 years and learned all trades by becoming a mate to the sub-contractors that I hired! Communicating ideas and actually being seen carrying out all trades in the 46 years of DIY on television has given me an incredible insight into the needs of DIYers nationwide.

Harry's first TV DIY show in 1957: 'Harry Greene being Handy Round the Home'.

And now in my 80th year I've completed ten years of weekly, live DIY shows with QVC, The Shopping Channel, 46 years of DIY on TV, radio and in the publishing media and 50 years appearing on TV. I have been lucky enough to have acted with a lot of the 'greats' in more than 40 films, been in hundreds of TV dramas and plays and to have designed and worked in the homes of more than 30 media celebrities. Communication has been part of my lifestyle for as long as I can remember and this book is the direct result of talking into a personal recorder. The mini-cassettes were despatched to Betty Robinson (a real gem on a computer with a whimsical ear for a technical phrase!), then emailed to the publisher to be laid out in 'spreads' with my DIY pictures and my own illustrations, covering over 130 common DIY problems around the home and garden.

So now make practical use of your own personal PROBLEM SOLVER. Carry me around with you to solve the nagging problems in the trouble spots. In every home, in fact in practically every room, you can find a problem to be solved, something cracked, chipped or broken. To put things right is often a simple matter, but it is easier to avoid the problem! A cracked tile, a dripping tap, squeaking stairs or a blocked drain – there are more, many more, as you'll find out within! But doing a good DIY job will make you feel happier because your home will look better, it will have a longer life and it should increase in value.

Enjoy your DIY, but stay safe, remembering my catchphrase coined more than 40 years ago: 'SAFETY FIRST, DIY SECOND'. My first woodwork teacher, CB Thomas, always said, 'proceed with circumspection Greene'. That's another good catchphrase, worth remembering too...!

Harry Greene

Harry Greene

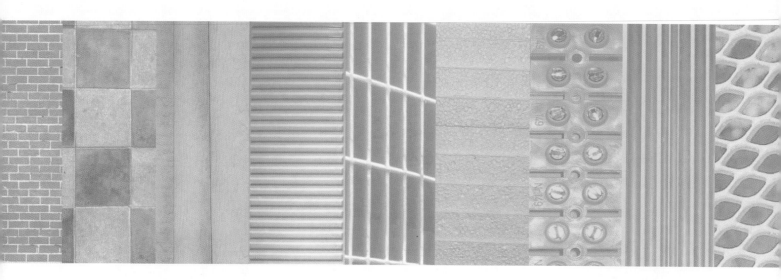

Photograph acknowledgements

The author and publisher would like to thank the following for their generous help in making available photographs for reproduction in this book:

For the products
(page number and position: r = right
l = left, t = top, c = centre, b = bottom)

ABAC 83, 84tl
Andy Sandy 211br
Artur Fischer (UK) Limited 194bl,
  194cl, 195b, 195c
Aston Trading Ltd 120
Bradstone 65 all, 78 all
Clear Group 123
Crown Paints 112tl, 113tl, 113bl, 114tl
Forest Garden plc 81
GET plc 87tl, tc
H&R Johnson Tiles 138c, 138b, 139r, 140t,
  140b, 141 all, 143br
HSS Hire Service Group PLC 273bl
Hozelock 92
Imperial Home Decor 130, 132b
Kährs UK Ltd 153l
Knauf UK 177
L G Harris & Co Ltd 103, 110r, 111, 118, 119r,
  120, 128bl, 128br, 128cl, 128cr, 132t, 136r
Lotus Water Garden Products 98t
MER Pruducts Ltd 270
MK Electric 242 both, 245t
Richard Burbidge 201 all, 157
RMC Specialist Products 110l, 116, 117, 118
Russell Perry 12
SK Enterprises 103
TCL Supplies Ltd 139l

For the celebrities
Maureen Barrymore	Liz Carling
Tony Davies	Julian Ballantyne, Harry Greene (back cover)
Sarah Dunn	Sarah Greene
Amanda Fearle	Sheila Hancock
Funky Beetroot Celebrity Management Limited	Patsy Palmer, Shaun Williamson
Nicky Johnston	Philippa Forrester, Paul O'Grady, Gillian Taylforth
Francis Loney	Nina Myskow
Andy McCartney	Lisa Maxwell
Johnny Mans Productions Ltd	Max Bygraves
Chris Monaghan	Les Dennis
Fatimah Namdar	Toyah Wilcox
National Geographic	Laura Greene
The *Sun*	Neil Morrissey, Sir David Steel
SUNDAY *Magazine*	Malandra Burrows, Sharron Davies, Nicola Duffet, Craig Fairbrass, Huw Higginson, Ruth Langford, Sian Lloyd, Paul McKenna, Sid Owen, Barbara Windsor
Ian Watson	Gregor Fisher

All other photographs © Harry Greene

Contents

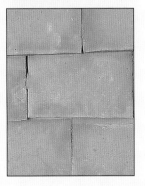

Roofs Chimneys

The flaunching holding the pots to the stack has cracked and no longer seals the joint. Rainwater has penetrated to cause larger cracks where ice has expanded to open up the joints even more.

Flaunching cracks
Small cracks in the flaunching can be repaired with exterior mastic. However, loose pots and crumbling mortar can lead to rainwater penetration and even falling pots! Take immediate action and reflaunch a new pot. Hack off the old mortar and carefully remove the pieces with a rope and bucket. Use a stack scaffolding tower. SAFETY FIRST, DIY SECOND!

Fixing new pots
Clean off the tops of the bricks. Repoint the stack. Place pieces of slate around the flue opening to support the pot. Spread the flaunching mortar over the top of the chimney and smooth it into a dome using a trowel. This shape will throw off any rainwater.

Pots Chimney pots are usually the topmost part of the structure of a house and therefore most vulnerable to all weathers. However, because we are somewhat removed from them, we are not too bothered by moss, a stain or a slightly leaning pot. Look more closely with a pair of binoculars (this is a good DIY tip for scanning the whole of the roof) and you'll get a clearer picture of a potential danger area. Do it annually in the summer, it's more pleasant and easier to work on any part of the roof when it's a longer day! But do remember my catch-phrase, it can help you to work on a roof with circumspection: SAFETY FIRST, DIY SECOND.

A chimney pot is an important element in the construction of a stack. Designed to prevent downdraught and smoky rooms, a pot safely discharges smoke and gases that are carried by hot air into the atmosphere. The pot is safely secured to the top of the stack by flaunching – a mortar mix of one part cement, one part lime

Bad flaunching joining pot to stack. Bad patching to spalling bricks and pointing. Growth allowed to flourish on stacks encourages damp.

and five parts fine builder's sand. This has to be maintained in good condition with no cracks and a smooth surface so that no growth is allowed to harbour damp. The inherent danger then is a build-up of frost, which can split the mortar. This makes larger cracks which allow more rain penetration and the possible dislodging of the pot as the flaunching breaks off.

Solid mortar can be left, but hack off the loose pieces and widen cosmetic cracks with a bolster chisel. Have someone below to check on safety and falling debris. Clean off soot stains and apply a coating of PVA as a binding coat for the mortar mix. A mortar plasticiser can be used instead of lime in the mix. It makes it easier and quicker to work in difficult areas and produces a very smooth finish.

If you're confident enough to tackle a roofing job, all the necessary safety equipment, ladders and lightweight scaffolding can be hired locally. These come with full instructions and these are essential reading. Even, if you have somebody else to reflaunch the pots, it is always a good idea to have this information and the knowledge of what is involved. This goes for any repair on any part of the roof so then you become your own DIY roof-repair supervisor!

Keep a roof repair kit handy.

Brickwork

Get a close-up view of the brick courses of the chimney stack using your binoculars. If you see staining, lichen, or discoloured pointing, these problems can be solved by repointing those affected lines of mortar. With safety in mind work out how best to repair the pointing, making use of a hired scaffolding tower, a hooked roof ladder and a stack tower. Make a procedure list, a tool list and materials list. The essential tools for repointing are a plugging chisel and hammer for hacking out perished mortar, a pointing trowel and a hawk. Make a hawk by fixing a handle centrally under a piece of ply about 23 cm (9 in) square, to hold the mortar. Scoop off a slice with your trowel to slide it into the raked joints. To finish, angle the trowel to form a weather-struck joint sloping downwards. Shape all the vertical joints first, then the horizontals to give a full sweep along the line. This will look very professional, but will also give a weatherproof finish to the repointed chimney stack.

Chimney flashing

The design of the weatherproofing, where the pitch of a roof meets the side of a stack, gives a permanent protective covering. The rear of the stack is also protected by a 'gutter' flashing brought around the sides to protect the stepped flashing. An apron-type cover flashing is then dressed into the mortar course and falls down flat to protect the upstand.

Stepped flashings are dressed into the mortar courses at the sides. These cover the 'soakers' which are separate pieces of lead laid as tiles and turned up against the stack. The front 'apron' is dressed into the mortar course and turned around the sides to be covered and protected by the stepped flashing. The slates or tiles are laid last to cover the soakers and the top edge of the front apron.

Lead apron

Often the place where rain-water penetrates into an attic in front of a chimney stack. This is caused by the top edge of the protective lead apron dislodging from the mortar course. Usually this piece of lead is bedded into the mortar joint two courses above the slope of the roof. It is then dressed either side of the stack, lapped by the side stepped-flashing and by the tiles or slates. This gives a permanent weathered finish to the roof covering. However, time and the contrasting weather conditions can cause problems! The lead apron will last for years, so to fix the problem first hack out the pointing that has been securing the top edge of the lead. Then hold the apron in place in the raked joint with small rolled pieces of lead (a worker's trick of

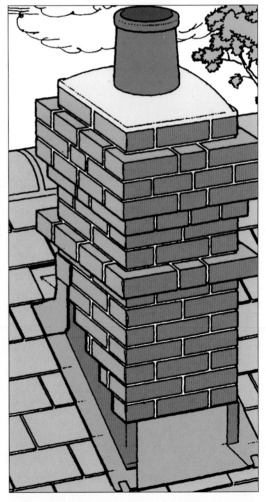

Flashing

It is essential that a stack is protected by mortar, pointing and flashing from its base to the top of the pot. The drawing shows a typical stack arrangement and how it should look if kept properly maintained. Regularly sweep the flue to guard against fires and to help the upward draught.

An example of stepped flashing in good condition, effectively sealing the joint between the sloping roof and the parapet wall.

Make no mistake too about the weight of chimney pots! They are heavier than they look. So you'll need help. And a rope to hold and to hoist. Hack off all the old flaunching with a bolster chisel and a club hammer. Lift off each piece carefully and place into a sack securely tied to the chimney scaffolding. It's always easier to carry away the old pot in pieces, especially if it's already cracked or broken, but they do make attractive garden ornaments if still in one piece!

Once the pot is removed you'll probably find a square hole about 23 cm × 23 cm (9 in × 9 in) with a lot of soot around. Clean it all off before coating the top surface with a PVA mix. Then cover the top of the brickwork with your mortar mix, gently lower the new pot centrally and start the flaunching. Where it touches the pot, make it at least 10 cm (4 in) high to slope down to all the edges smoothly.

Check your roof with binoculars for damaged tiles, timber sag, leaning stacks.

the trade). Repoint using the small trowel and the mix as above. If the lead has distorted anywhere or is not totally covering, use a brush-on DIY roof repair treatment. This seals and adheres and is instantly effective.

Stepped flashing
Stepped flashing looks to most people like an attractive decoration at the side of a chimney where it meets the slope or pitch of the roof, but if this clever design is not maintained in good order rainwater will pour into attics. Hidden underneath the length of lead with the cut triangular shapes are separate lead pieces called soakers. Usually, if there is a leak problem, it is only necessary to refit the top of the stepped flashing into the mortar joints. Any other problem areas of which you may have a doubt can be treated with a DIY roof repair treatment. These come with full details of their uses and coverage on the label.

Fixing new pots
The essential consideration when confronted with the problem of fixing a new pot is that the replacement is exactly the same dimensions as the old one.

Fixing new pots
Clean off the tops of the bricks. Repoint the stack. Place pieces of slate around the flue opening to support the pot. Spread the flaunching mortar over the top of the chimney and smooth it into a dome using a trowel. This shape will throw off any rainwater.

Cement fillets

Sealing cracks A party wall that separates two houses in a terrace often extends above the pitched roofline. It extends about 60 cm (2 ft) above the roof and is capped with coping stones. In Edwardian houses particu-

Cement fillets
Use a cartridge gun and exterior mastic to repair cracks simply.

If the cement fillet has perished in parts, simply follow the line of the original but, before applying the mortar, apply a coat of diluted PVA.

larly, an alternative to lead flashings was to seal the gap between the slope or pitch of the roof and the vertical wall with a cement fillet. This triangular shape mortar fillet extended about 7.5 cm (3 in) on to the roof and 7.5 cm (3 in) up the wall. The mix was of one part lime, one part cement and five parts fine builder's sand. To get good adhesion the mix was kept sloppy and this also enabled the builder to get a very smooth surface with a steel float. The fillet was sloped and smooth as it was essential that no rainwater remained to freeze in very cold weather.

In the UK all building materials suffer the hazards of extremes, that is, very cold in the winter and hot in the summer. These extremes of temperatures, combined with soakings in wet weather and drying winds in the autumn, can all contribute to a great deal of movement, expansion and contraction in building materials and the fabric of a house. However, mortar and cement are rigid and immoveable.

Whether the cement fillet has been applied against a chimney stack or an exterior wall, there are inherent problems in maintaining a waterproof joint. At the first sign of a crack appearing in the surface of the cement fillet, it is essential that this is rectified immediately. If rainwater is allowed to penetrate even a tiny crack, it can creep by capillary action on to the rafters or purlins to cause wood rot. In winter time water which remains in the crack can, in very cold weather, freeze and expand to make a wider gap and break the adhesion between the

A cement fillet between the pitch of a roof and a parapet wall is no substitute for stepped flashing. The cement fillet is rigid so movement in the roof timbers always causes fractures and attic leaks.

mortar and the tile or wall. In bad weather it is possible for lumps of mortar to become dislodged and dangerously fall to the ground.

Bearing in mind the hazards of working on a roof, make certain that you have covered every safety check. A hooked ridge ladder is ideal for tackling this repair problem. In an unconverted attic, check with a torch for tell-tale water stains on rafters, purlins or even on the bedroom ceiling joists closest to the wall. Look on the brickwork for streaked stains then try to trace the source. With the torch switched off it is possible to see daylight through problem cracks.

If the problem is not tackled the bedroom ceiling could show stains or even bulging plasterboards with spoilt decorations on the walls. Another result of water ingress is that it creeps behind wallpaper, eventually showing as mould on the surface of the paper. This is not to be confused with condensation, which is also covered in this book. Many successive problems could result from not having spotted a hairline crack in the cement fillet.

Apply a coat of diluted PVA solution after hacking out the loose mortar. This will ensure extra good adhesion of the new mortar to the roof tiles and to the wall. Remember that wet cement is very heavy to handle, especially on a sloping roof, so carry up only half a bucketful at a time. And do have a helper at ground level. Apply a new section of the fillet by building up the thickness and allowing each level to cure before the next coat is applied.

If you only see cosmetic cracks across the cement fillet or between the fillet and the wall there is a good alternative to sealing the cracks. This is especially so if the bulk of the mortar fillet is sound and solid. Firstly, run the tip of an old screwdriver along the crack. Then, fill with a sloppy mix of sand, cement and lime using diluted PVC instead of water. Once this is cured and set, an application of a brush-on DIY roof repair treatment will ensure a long-term weatherproof joint. This sealant will adhere to the tiles (or slates), the cement fillet and the brickwork.

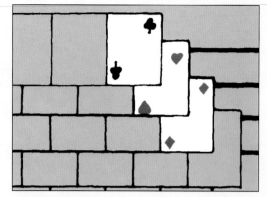

Tiles and slates

Replacing With the aid of a pack of cards I'll show you how easy it is to understand the simple but very effective method of overlapping tiles or slates to make a roof watertight! Lay out the cards as illustrated in the sketch and you will see that this particular system is a double lap cover. Most of the slate-covered roofs dating from Victorian times have this system. As you can see only a third of the card (or slate) is actually exposed as two-thirds is covered by successively laid slates. The sides are touching rather than being overlaid. Battens are nailed to the rafters to support each row or course of tiles. The battens are very precisely positioned so as to give support in three positions for each slate. Then, the slates are either nailed or hooked to the battens. This is the system for most pitched (or sloped) roofs and understanding this construction method makes it easier to fix problems. This applies to your own DIY work or to supervising others.

There is also a single-lap system, but this is usually used with clay or concrete tiles. Here, tiles are hooked over each other at the top and at the sides to make the waterproof seal. They are profiled or shaped to lock into each other, enabling them to do this.

Ordinary clay tiles are also used as a double-lap covering, but usually they are literally hung on to the tiling battens by their preformed nibs at the top end of the back of the tiles. These are the easiest of roof covering to restore. Tiles can be lifted out without disturbing the surrounding ones which just lower back into position, so replacing a broken or damaged tile takes only minutes. Ensure that replacement tiles match in style, colour and size.

The V-roof construction popular in Victorian times can cause problems caused by sagging timbers if they are of too small a cross-section. Note the solid timbers, wide valley gutter and generous overlap of flashings. Begin by dressing the lead of the new valley-gutter at the lowest point and overlap as you go higher. Plenty of overlap of all protective material ensures no future damp problems.

Replacing tiles
The drawing shows how tiles are laid onto the roof with properly spaced battens. Take a pack of cards and lay them out as shown to familiarise yourself with a fairly simple method of laying.

Removing tiles
Tiles can be removed easily by lifting out singly and prising up the tiles above the damaged one with a trowel. Lift the tile over the tiling batten which supports it. The tile hangs on the batten by nibs or pegs. Pull out any nails with a slate ripper. A replacement tile can be pushed up until the pegs hook over the batten.

Creasing tiles overhang the gable end to protect the wall and the supporting timbers.

These tiles have been re-bedded in a strong mix of one part cement to five parts sand. The face must be smoothed flat in line with the edges of the tiles to ensure no ingress of water. Note that every other creasing tile is larger than a standard tile and is in fact called a 'tile-and-a-half'. This gives a staggered joint to every other course of roof tiles.

Solve the problem of obtaining matching tiles for restoration and repair by scouring reclamation and demolition yards. All sorts and types are available: Georgian, Victorian, Edwardian and modern.

The full tile to the left of the rafter perfectly illustrates a proper tiling arrangement. Two tiles give protection from the weather. Roof tiles cover a span of three battens.

Insert two wooden pegs either side of the tile to be replaced. Slide the tile into place and hook it over the tiling batten.

Slate replacement

Slate replacement is slightly more tricky because it involves the use of a slate ripper. This flat steel tool slips under the damaged slate and, with the hook end in position, the holding nail is drawn downwards under the slate, which is then released and removed. Two nails hold each slate. Sometimes the ripper will cut through the nail rather than remove it. With the batten exposed, nail a strip of lead to it long enough to fold back over the bottom edge of the replacement slate. This effectively holds it in position. Plastic clips are available as an alternative fixing and these come with full instructions.

Tiling a roof is a precise craft, because only the correct spacing of battens will ensure total weathering of the building. By creating the proper measurement between battens you get row upon row of tiles or slates in correct alignment and spacing.

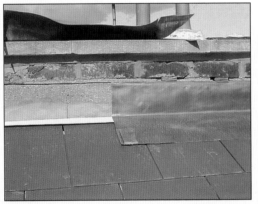

Cut a slot either in the mortar course or above it to take the lead apron flashing. Initially, hold it in place with lead wedges, then point with mortar.

Ridge tiles

At the top of the roof is the ridge. This is where the two pitches meet. In order to weatherproof that meeting point a clever but simple method of sealing is to bed inverted v-shaped or half round-shaped ridge tiles into mortar. The original lime mortar used

If neglected, ridge tiles and the mortar joint in between will soon loosen to allow rainwater to creep onto important roof timbers. Re-bed the tiles to stop rot weakening the roof structure.

by the builders often breaks down and crumbles. You can spot this easily with binoculars. If damp is present there will also be growth, moss or lichen, which is a sure sign that timbers underneath will be suffering the effects of water penetration.

Re-bed the tiles with a mix of one part cement, one part lime and three parts fine builder's sand. This time though use a stiff mix, but do dampen the tiles before laying on a bed of mortar that follows the outline of the old lime mortar. Fill in the hollow end of each successive ridge tile that you have to relay with mortar. Finish by smoothing away excess mortar and carefully pointing the joints between the ridge tiles.

Re-bedded hip tiles cemented to overlapping roof tiles giving complete protection. The tiles are properly aligned to throw rainwater into the gutter which has been resealed at the elbow. A hip tile-hook supports the whole corner renovation.

Cutting and fixing slates

Replacing a slate on an old roof once often involved matching with a larger slate that has to be cut to size. A worker would chop with a trowel along a line on a supported slate, but an easier, quicker and more accurate cut is made with a cutting disc. These multi-purpose pliable discs are available as an accessory held by an arbor fixed in the chuck of an electric drill. Remember SAFETY FIRST, DIY SECOND, so wear safety goggles, mask and gloves. Slates can be brittle, especially old ones, but they are also easy to handle, cut and drill. A positive approach means a successful DIY job accomplished!

Solve the problem of breaking roof tiles by using a powered masonry saw but you must plug it into a residual current device for your safety. Note the protective guard and the baulk of timber keeping the tile in place. Keep your foot away from the saw.

A peg-tiled roof on a timber-clad building is part of our heritage and should be preserved! Great craftsmanship went into the work. This example in Essex shows neglect over a long time.

Tiles

Tiles are more difficult to remove and replace if they have interlocking edges. The secret is to lift and insert wedges in the tiles either side of the damaged ones. Some tiles have a deeper interlocking system, so the only way to solve the problem of removing and replacing one, is to lift and support as many as necessary of the surrounding tiles. Use the 10 cm (4 in) angle-grinder to cut a tile, but remember to wear protective gear.

This is how tiles should look when properly spaced for expansion. Tiling battens are nailed to the rafters to give the correct coverage of each tile, as successive tiles are nailed or hung on 'nibs'.

Flat roofs

Millions of homes in the UK have a flat felt roof either over a porch, a shed, a garage or an extension. Statutory regulations are strict relating to the construction of felt coverings on roofs and these are adhered to by reputable builders. However, even though the regulations are designed to ensure that the fabric of the building is safe and watertight, felt deteriorates over a long period. In extremes of temperatures, especially in hot weather when the sun's rays degrade the bitumen and mastic coverings, splits and blisters occur. Chippings are often spread over the surface to reflect the UV rays of the sun and so protect the felt.

The construction of a flat felt roof is simple but effective. Joists support the boards to which the felt is fixed. Ceiling boards are nailed to the underside of the joists in the room. Thermal and damp barriers should be in the gap and ventilation is an important factor to prevent the build-up of condensation. Layers of felt covering are laid flat on the boards. The top one is usually a coded mineral felt. Sometimes a job of this nature can be skimped and it is difficult to investigate whether or not good professional building practice has been carried out. If not, there can be degeneration of materials and the need for problem-solving.

Moisture, through condensation, or even that carried in the air, can cause movement, twisting and warping in timber. The drying out of the ends of the joists can cause shrinkage. Heat causes the bitumen to creep if it is not protected. Two important factors are involved in achieving a sound roof construction: the builder's knowledge and expertise, and the materials used. However, we then have a responsibility for the maintenance of the roof surface. Often it's a case of out of sight and out of mind! But we are visibly shaken when a stain appears on the ceiling and the drip-drip of rainwater requires the quick remedy of a bucket or bowl.

This is what a properly constructed flat felt roof should look like! Chippings reflect UV rays and coping stones protect the walls. An overhang of felt helps to shed rainwater into the gutter and lead flashing covers the wall–roof joint.

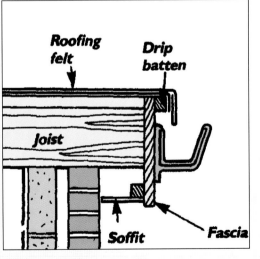

Eave construction

The diagram shows the construction of a closed-eave over a cavity wall. The building fabric is protected from the weather by the roof overhang, the fascia and the soffit. Note that the roofing felt overhangs the back edge of the gutter.

In the past, the solution has been a quick brush-on of the 'black stuff', but only a temporary repair is affected. Proper preparation has been neglected, the mastic will lose its adhesion and out it comes again. Further deterioration will then require a builder's full roof repair job involving hefty costs.

Now, however, brush-on DIY roof repair treatments are available as the perfect solution. These are the DIY answer to any roof leak and the great thing is that they can be applied even in the rain! These products are formulated especially for the DIYer and although the skill factor is minimal, the finish is utterly professional. This will remain so even though it is to be subjected to ageing, the action of the sun, and freezing and thawing cycles. The great thing is that the problem is solved immediately that any sign of a leaking roof appears indoors. Think 'safety' when climbing on to a roof, even a single-storey extension, especially in the rain.

Repairing leaks

Any roof problems can be solved using DIY roof repair treatments whether the building material is lead, zinc, felt, aluminium, steel, galvanised sheet metal, concrete, tile, glass, wood, brick, concrete, hard PVC, asphalt or bitumen.

Clean off all debris, chippings and growth from a flat roof. Wash it down to neutralise. Follow the instructions to cover completely after making any necessary repairs.

A sealing compound will give many years of renewed life to a flat zinc roof. It is easily applied as a DIY application, but take care to work safely!

Ribs are part of the construction of some flat roofs, where the sheets of roofing material overlap. The ribs run in the direction of the 'fall' and have an inverted 'U' cover strip. Splits running along a rib must be sealed with a self-adhesive tape and sealant.

Flat felt roofs have a number of advantages, not least the low cost and relatively speedy installation. The water-repellent nature of felt may seem an ideal flat roof covering, but neglect it at your peril. Calling in a roofing contractor could involve resurfacing with hot bitumen or tars and prove to be very costly.

Manufacturers have long been aware that roofs on commercial buildings have been better served than domestic roofs. A specially formulated liquid has been traditionally used, which, when applied and cured, forms a continuous weatherproof sheet roof covering, like a membrane. Nowadays, manufacturers of DIY products are much more aware of the needs of the DIYer and are spending more time and resources on design and development. Brush-on DIY roof repair treatments can also be used on caravans, balconies, zinc roofs, stacks, and, in fact, on any roofing material. They have a compound that is easy to apply with a brush to adhere to any material on a whole roof or as a patch repair, say to a blister that is letting in rain water. Their elasticity allows them to be spread easily. They have terrific strength properties and a long shelf life, they are durable and UV-resistant, and are the ideal problem-solver for flat roof problems. Brush off all growth and chippings which are not necessary before applying the treatment. Use a fungicidal liquid if there is any growth present, but use water to clean off and to neutralise it afterwards. If a split is letting in water, use large-headed galvanised clout nails to refix before applying the treatment. Blisters must be cut with a trimming knife into a star shape so that clout nails will hold down the four corners flat. If deep puddles are forming in depressions in the felt, fill in the depressions with a strip of felt and mastic. Cover them with the DIY roof treatment. This prevents the puddles freezing in the winter which could cause more splitting problems.

If the felt roof has any upstands that are leaking, apply a DIY roof treatment to the suspect joints of freestanding vents, valley gutters and stacks.

Lastly, remember my catch phrase – SAFETY FIRST, DIY SECOND – and the obvious rules applying to health and safety when working on a roof – use a secured ladder at the correct angle, which is 30 cm out for every 120 cm up the wall (1 ft out for every 4 ft up), wear suitable clothing including protective gloves, and your helper must keep children away.

Flat roofs – leaks and splits
The ideal problem-solver for leaking roofs or vents on a flat roof – even on the metal parts – is a DIY roof repair treatment.

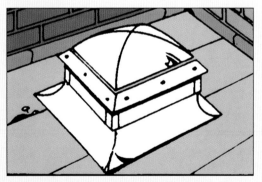

Flat roofs – blisters and cracks
First cut all the blisters with a cutting knife to form a cross. Use felt nails to hold down the corners. Apply a DIY roof repair treatment.

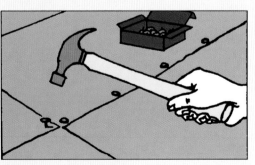

Flat roofs – splits at seams
Where seams have opened to let in rainwater, force in a DIY roof repair treatment. Use clout nails to hold down the felt. Apply another coat of the roof repair treatment.

Flat roofs – leaks in upstands
These often need extra protection. When the lead or felt fails, apply a coat of a DIY roof repair treatment to make an instant repair.

Corrugated roofs

In the early part of the twentieth century, corrugated roofs were used not only on sheds, outbuildings, farm buildings, garages and commercial buildings, but also on low cost domestic houses. There are roofs still built of this construction all over the country. Unfortunately many were laid with asbestos corrugated sheets. At that time there was not the outcry against the common use of asbestos in the building trade. Not so much was publicised about the possible hazards of the dangerous fibres used in its fabrication. In recent years we've learnt more of its dangers. For this reason specially licensed teams will demolish and remove any asbestos corrugated roofing in any part of the country. These specialist firms have to comply with stringent health and safety regulations when dealing with asbestos including dampening, stripping, encapsulation and safe disposal, so it is not in anyone's best interests to cut, drill, break up or remove corrugated asbestos sheets, no matter what colour the sheets may be. Myths have grown up about one colour being safer than another. It will remain a myth! Check, however, with a knowledgeable builder if you are not sure because you could have asbestos fibres to deal with.

Corrugated sheets for roofing come in all sorts and types of materials including iron, steel, aluminium, bitumen, plastic and polycarbonate. Each has its own properties, particular uses and advantages, but each also has its own problems. Some are difficult to cut, others difficult to handle. All, however, supply a need for speedy fixing and a low cost to purchase compared with traditional forms of roof covering.

Corrugated iron Used mainly on barns, farm buildings and low-cost commercial properties, these sheets, which can be 2.5 m to 3 m (8 ft to 10 ft) long, are fixed to horizontal timbers laid to support them. The corrugations carry rainwater in the channels very efficiently, even at a low gradient. Holes are drilled through the convex curve, that is the tops of the corrugations, to fix them to the purlins. Special galvanised serrated nails with large heads hold

A fine example of straight cut eaves, extensive ridge cover and a matching hip (angled corner joint) cover-strip, giving total protection to a large area of corrugated roof.

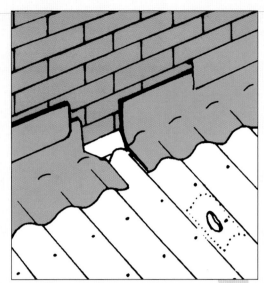

Sealing a corrugated iron roof

There are three sealing methods:

Traditionally, lead flashing was dressed over the corrugations with its top edge laid flat 15 cm (6 in) above and onto the wall. It was then let into a mortar course and packed with cement mortar to totally seal the system.

The right-hand side of the drawing shows a special fixed-shape plastic unit which is covered and sealed at the top by an apron. This unit can be purchased in many contours to fit most corrugations.

On the left-hand side of the drawing the unit is sealed at the top by a proprietary brand of building sealing tape, available at all DIY stores.

Use self-adhesive scrim to repair a hole. Cover the hole about 50 mm (2 in) all around. Use a proprietary brand of exterior mastic or DIY roof repair treatment to cover the repair.

Replacing corrugated roofing

Remove the old nails and slide out the damaged sheet. Use a wood block to hold up the side where the new sheet will slide under. Drill holes to match the existing fixing points, making sure that they are in the 'peaks' and not in the 'valleys'. Match the flashings if they exist.

A hole in a corrugated roof can be repaired with a kit of self-adhesive tape and a sealing compound. The repair is then stronger than the roof itself!

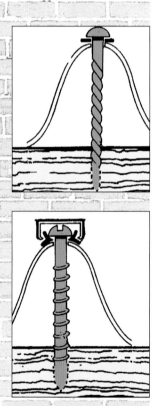

Corrugated roof fixings
The screw and the screw nail (which is driven in with a hammer) are the two most common fixings. The screw has a backing soft washer and a push-on protective cap. The nail also has a washer but take care not to drive it too far and damage the roofing sheet.

the sheets in position. Some nails have a curved plastic washer which guards against rain penetration. Corrugated strips of foam are now available to push into the lower ends of each sheet as a form of weather and pest excluder. Each successive sheet is laid to overlap at the sides to give a continuous watertight covering. At the lower end water runs into the gutter.

If the roof is a traditional pitched type, a covering is necessary at that point where each slope meets at the ridge. This can be a preformed ridge tile or a long flat-topped ridge fixture with corrugated sides to lap the corrugated sheets. A brilliant new cutting tool is available that even cuts across the corrugations. This is a drill attachment with a safety cutting device that makes light and easy work of cutting through heavy gauge metal and other roofing materials.

Check the size of the corrugations if you are replacing a sheet that may have rusted and perished in places. The standard size profile is 32 mm (1½ in). Also check if the sheets are fixed with nails, screws or hooked bolts. The bolts also come with protective plastic washers and caps.

One of the problems with corrugated iron roofing sheets is the risk of rust. They are subjected to a great deal of rain in this country so it's essential to think in terms of long-term protection. At the first sign of rust, remove it with wet-and-dry abrasive sheets or more easily with a disc attachment held in an electric drill. For your own safety always plug a power tool into an RCD (residual current device) when working out of doors. This will cut the power instantaneously if anything goes wrong, so you cannot be harmed. Once you are back to the metal, use a bitumen-based coat to prime the repair. Finish with a topcoat to match. Remember that you are dealing with a ferrous metal so do not use water-based paint.

If you are confronted with a hole to repair and do not want to replace the sheet, there is an easy DIY solution to this problem. Self-adhesive rolls of 5 cm (2 in) and 15 cm (6 in) webbing come with tins of some DIY roof treatments.

This is a strong reinforced material that will safely cover the hole. Apply a coating of the treatment over the webbing extending about 5 cm (2 in) past the hole. You now have a permanent repair. If the repair is to a corrugated roof that is termed a 'lean-to', that is, the top ends supported on a timber against a wall, a corrugated apron-cover moulded exactly to fit the corrugated sheets will cover the gap at the wall. Then apply a self-adhesive aluminium-backed tape to seal the top edge of the cover to the wall. You might find an apron of lead let into a mortar course to protect the top edge of the cover. If this is loose at the wall, it's easy to hold the lead in position in the raked out mortar course with small lead wedges before repointing with mortar.

Corrugated iron and steel sheets for roofing are fabricated with a coating of zinc for protection. This is applied by dipping into hot zinc. It should be ready immediately for painting to match the existing sheets. Sometimes it is easier to paint before carrying it up to roof height. But do be careful to check the exact positions of fixing holes before drilling. Any chips in the zinc surface from handling or transporting can be primed with zinc phosphate primer, but take the usual precautions.

Aluminium sheeting This sheeting usually comes with a square profile but is very 'whippy' when handled, especially in windy conditions. This is of course a non-ferrous metal so will not rust nor corrode, and even in the worst of weathers it will not need to be painted for protection. It really is a versatile roofing material for small outbuildings, extensions, garages, etc.

Aluminium sheeting may, after many years, become dull and grey. Sometimes tiny white crystals appear on the surface. It is very simple to remove and clean up the sheets using white spirit with wet-and-dry abrasive paper. This cleans up the surface but don't rub too hard to get back to the metal. Clean up the residual particles with a soft cloth dipped in white spirit, then give it a coat of zinc phosphate primer. Never use any paint with a lead content on aluminium.

Walls   Rendered

Traditional house exteriors change from county to county in Britain. From brightly painted fronts in Cornwall to flint in Hampshire, wood cladding in Norfolk to artistically decorated stucco in Essex. Intricately combed patterns on rendered elevations applied with care are still unblemished today. A testament to good preparation, materials and creative ability.

Render has been a common finish to the external walls of domestic buildings for the past hundred years. This roughcast finish was much favoured by designers of middle of the range housing. Builders liked it because it was easy to apply and made a solid brick wall impervious to rainwater penetration. It gave a quick method of house construction because a 23 cm (9 in) solid brick wall was easier and quicker to build than a cavity wall. When an exterior wall had dried out, it was prepared for the first of two coats of render. The first was a mix of one part cement, one part lime and six parts sand which was applied with a float and then straightened with a long batten drawn down the wall. Finally, it was 'combed' with a wooden batten which had protruding nails to mark it and thus 'key' the wet render. After drying out, a sloppy mix of one-and-a-half parts cement, half part lime, two parts crushed stone and three parts sand was made up. This was applied with a laying-on trowel but not smoothed. The crushed stone gave the wall the roughcast appearance typical of houses of the time. Interestingly, in the 1920s and 1930s it was usual to use horsehair as a binding agent to help adhesion.

Apply a water-repellent to outside walls to prevent water penetration.

Most householders personalised their rendered walls with a favourite colour to harmonise with doors and windows. If the render is old and shows signs of lichen or other growth, then it is imperative to do two things before painting. Firstly, thoroughly clean off the residue of sulphurs and grime from years of pollution. A jet gun will save time and effort. One with a compressor giving 9 bar pressure is best, but take care to protect the glazing with sheets of ply or similar. Secondly, use a stabilising solution to cover the whole of the wall. The undercoat is applied when the wall has dried out. It is always best to wait for a spell of fine weather before painting outside. The two enemies to exterior painting are damp and dust, so avoid a wet and very windy day. Hire a scaffolding tower, which comes with instructions on how to use it. Pay special attention to the safety precautions.

If the exterior coating on your wall has a pebble-dashed render finish, this would have been applied with a hand scoop. Pea shingle was mixed with the sand and cement and thrown with a scoop on to the coat of cement render while it was still wet. The coloured tiny pebbles remained exposed and created an attractively coloured and textured wall finish.

Cracks   The skill of the worker was an all-important factor in the long-term effectiveness of the render. If there was not good preparation, loss of adhesion and 'blown' areas of the render caused cracks to appear. Rainwater was then drawn in by capillary action soaking the brick-work and causing deterioration of the mortar joints. This shows up on the inside walls as

Mortar render is applied to a wall to offer protection against the weather. Attempting to cover serious cracks with emulsion paint traps moisture behind the render. It will freeze in winter and expand the cracks even more!

Pebble-dashed surfaced wall showing signs of water penetration caused by breakdown of horizontal DPC under top bricks. Clay tiles laid flat, form the DPC and the top header course is of hard engineering bricks. Without an effective DPC rainwater will cause a lot of damage.

A totally neglected Victorian stuccoed façade. This is where it is essential to hire a lightweight scaffolding tower. Anchor it to the building for safety.

damp patches and ruined decorations. An annual inspection of the walls is essential to offset this possibility and even the tiniest hairline crack in the render is enough to start the damp creeping into the fabric of the wall. Also look at areas where hooks or nails have been hammered in to the walls. Rainwater pipe fixings often cause cracking in the render. An inexpensive DIY damp detector is a boon in all households.

Repair cracks in render with mortar to stop water penetration and damage.

Perished render   Hack off any suspect patches of render right back to the brickwork. Take care though not to disturb the sound render but only take out perished or blown render back to the edges of solid render. This gives an area to be re-rendered. Brush off all debris and apply a coat of diluted PVA, remembering to include the chopped edges. When dry, create a matching render mix and apply with a trowel. If the area is painted, match with a fresh coat of paint.

Treat cracks the same way by chopping out loose material, ensuring that the crack is wide enough to take the newly-mixed render. It is best to undercut a crack at either edge, that is, to make a wedge-shaped crack, wider at the back of the crack. This ensures that the new render, when cured or hardened, makes a key to prevent it falling out.

At the very first sign of a hairline crack in exterior render it is essential to rake out the crack. Use a mastic filler or a lime mortar mix to match the existing, otherwise penetrating rain will cause 'blown' patches.

Re-rendering   The first essential task when tackling a re-rendering job is to set up a scaffolding plank platform or hire a lightweight tower. You cannot work up a ladder because both hands have to be free. If you are tackling a whole wall that has a damp problem, it needs to thoroughly dry out before starting the job. So choose the time for action carefully.

If the wall is a 23 cm (9 in) solid brick wall and has been affected by penetrating damp through the mortar courses, hire a dehumidifier to help extract the moisture from the inside wall. Re-rendering the exterior wall will give a continuous, impervious coating and will protect the wall from further damp problems.

With all the old render hacked off, let the outside wall have 3 or 4 days of drying-out time. Apply a coat of diluted PVA and let that dry. Perished pointing must be hacked out with a plugging chisel. Repoint where necessary. Don't be too fussy about a struck joint because the slight indentations in the mortar courses will help key the first coat of cement render to the wall. The easiest, quickest and most effective cement-finish coating to apply for a professional look is called Tyrolean. The machine which holds the render mix is called a Tyrolean cranking machine. The mix is literally sprayed on to the wall by cranking the machine's handle. A finely textured wall finish is achieved which looks very much like a stipple finish on interior plaster. Most tool hire shops stock this machine.

Mask all windows, doors, gutters and downpipes. Work in only small areas at a time, so that the masking material can be moved each time to the area being sprayed. Good adhesion is assured because it is a wet mix being sprayed on to a dry render undercoat, and overlapping is good because there is no chance of missing a patch or applying it too thinly where areas meet.

Protection   Nowadays there are paint systems to suit all situations, which is why an exterior cement-based paint has been formulated for outside walls. This is a multi-coat system. It comes with full instructions and can be applied by brush, pad or roller. The first coat

A perfect example of the restoration of a rendered, double-gabled elevation. The render must not continue down over the damp proof course. This will prevent rising damp creeping into the walls.'

Renewed exterior render can be finished to match the existing. For a smooth, almost stucco finish, you'll need to draw a straight-edge over the surface guided by temporary battens. Then 'polish' the surface with either a wooden float or with a steel float which will give a smoother finish.

Walls can suffer from unsightly organic growth depending on whether the sun and wind can dry them out. Walls that are too protected will remain damp. Remove growth with a wire brush and treat with an inhibitor.

Render (1)

A suspect area of render will sound hollow when tapped. Hack it out to a solid surface and solid edges. Apply a coat of diluted PVA, especially to the edges.

Render (2)

Use a hawk to hold a small amount of mortar (a mix of five parts of sand to one part of cement – not sloppy to prevent sagging). Glide the mix on to the wall with a steel float. Fill small areas at a time, working towards the edges to key it.

Render (3)

Use a straight-edge batten to level the mortar mix. Fill any hollows as you go. Match the existing surface texture when the mortar is almost dry.

is a stabilising coat, followed by the undercoat, and finally your choice of coloured top coat. There is even an impressive fourth coat of transparent protective liquid which can be sprayed or brushed on.

The alternative to painting, if the original colour of the render is to be kept, is to use a sealant. There are many proprietary brands on the market with similar claims for sealing exterior walls and maintaining the original colour. One is actually labelled as a 'water repellent'. This is guaranteed to protect the wall from water penetration providing the wall is in good repair.

Moss If moss, lichen or any other growth is seen on an exterior wall, it is probably the result of moisture being held on the wall. This in turn suggests cracks or perished mortar joints. Scrape off all signs of the growth and thoroughly brush down with a stiff hand brush. The use of a wire brush is not recommended because it could leave wire bristles in or on the wall. Any covering of these wires with cement or paint is going to cause a breakdown of the protective coat later on through rust. This could lead to a whole sequence of damp problems, frost problems and eventually damp inside the wall. After carrying out any necessary repairs to the wall or to the mortar course and after removal of the growth, use an antifungal spray to cover the whole area to prevent further growth.

Moss

Moss and lichen will grow on rendered or plain brick walls if the conditions are right. Remove with a wire brush and stabilise before applying a coat of water-repellent.

Timber-clad

A good example of expertly installed exterior wall cladding. Horizontal cladding is simply fixed to an exterior wall with secret nailing or secret steel fixings. Once installed, protect it with two coats of wood preservative and two of exterior varnish. Don't forget to reapply the protection periodically!

Most timber problems outside the house are the result of poor preparation. The preparatory work is perhaps as important as any part of a job. In the last century builders and carpenters in Essex and Kent knew a thing or two about preparation. The timber-clad houses in these counties had as much care and attention given to them as the Elizabethan timber houses of the sixteenth and seventeenth centuries, when the timber was not kiln-dried but dried naturally over a period of years after being sawn by hand into planks. Oak was found in abundance and these houses now exhibit the robust and iron-like qualities of this matured wood.

Different parts of the country have different climatic problems to contend with and every timber surface is subject to blistering heat which can distort paint and wood, to frost and ice which can split open timber joints and to driving rain penetrating the fabric of the house causing rot. The South-West suffers salt-borne driving wet winds, the hills of Wales and Scotland are often hung with a grey mist, industrial towns in the North-East have suffered

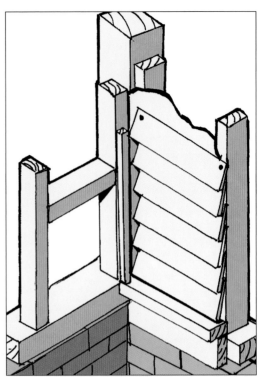

Timber frame wall construction (1)

A typical construction of the inside corner of a timber-framed and timber-clad Victorian house. It is based on long-established building practices which are still in use today. A structure is built on main supporting corner posts. It is similar to a stud partition with a timber wall plate and a header.

Cover mouldings protect the ends of the feather-edge cladding. Felt or 'building paper' sheets provide weatherproofing.

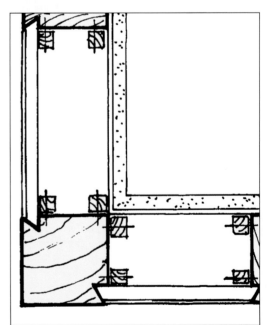

Timber frame wall construction (2)

An external corner showing the main post, the intermediate posts, the fixing fillets (battens) and the external rendering on laths. Posts are tarred or painted black, and the panels between them are painted or decorated with a pattern.

damaging pollutants since the industrial revolution, but everywhere the common problems of woodworm, dry rot and wet rot exist if the timber has not been properly prepared and maintained. Even though a coat of paint looks fresh, it doesn't mean to say that problems aren't hidden beneath the gleaming surface. The outside of your house probably deserves more attention than it gets!

Protection

Years ago a supporting timber or post that was to be subjected to possible contact with damp would have had its end sealed by charring it with fire. Today, we enjoy the benefits of pre-treated timber. This has been subjected to a non-toxic strong preservative applied under extreme pressure to give it a long life free of rot and worms. The building industry has used these techniques for years, but now DIYers can go to a timber merchant and buy pre-treated timber. We can now get pre-treated fencing panels, timber for garage walls and for exterior cladding. Unfortunately, a lot of the timber around the outsides of our homes, that is, doors, window frames, decorated boards, fascias, gable end boards, wooden steps, balconies and gates, suffers from not being pre-treated.

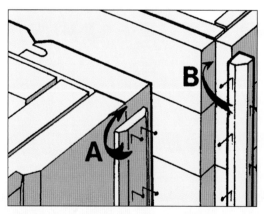

Exterior wood cladding

The cladding joint method and cover boards are of utmost importance whether it is used as a single skin to cover a shed or garage or as part of a timber-framed house. The tiniest crack or gap will let in rainwater, which by capillary action gains access to the structural timber causing rot. This is particularly so at joints and corners of a clad building. After an exterior flexible mastic has been applied as a bead to cover all the exposed joints, paint or seal to protect the timber.

External corner joints need a vertical cover board (A). Horizontal cladding meeting at a corner (B) must have a tight fitting batten shaped, glued and pinned, or screwed into place.

Treatments

Manufacturers have invested a great deal of money and time into research developing stains, varnishes, primers, and durable top-coatings, which prevent moisture penetration and resist UV rays. Other treatments are moisture-permeable, which means that they let the wood breathe, allowing moisture to escape but at the same time giving a weather-resistant coating. Different products are available to suit different timber finishes. Exterior woodwork comes under attack not only from weather pollutants but also from spores carried in the air that result in a fungus growth which eats into the wood.

If timber is damp or if there are signs that the paint coating is being pushed away from the wood, the problem has to be solved immediately. Blisters are the direct result of poor preparation, so it is essential to allow exterior timber to dry out completely before applying paint. Moisture or resin would be drawn out of the timber but has nowhere to go. The result is that the paint loses its adhesion and is pushed into a blister.

All new exterior wood, including posts and cladding, could in the future suffer from wet rot if not properly protected. There is now a three-part paint and repair system to cure damp. The protective treatment comes in a range of colours too.

Modern microporous stains and preservatives are suitable as a long-lasting exterior wood treatment. Whether you are using softwood or hardwood doesn't matter. The stains and paints in this range produce a protective film on the wood which contains the microscopically small pores, and allows the wood to breathe out water vapour naturally. It means that vapour pressure does not build up beneath the film of paint. As temperature changes the wood treatment remains flexible, expanding and contracting with the natural movement of the timber. The build up of the impervious film on the surface of the timber makes it ideal for exterior woodwork when moisture might result in an attack of wet rot.

All exterior timber used in the construction of sheds, fencing, garages, cladding, chalets and conservatories needs protecting. A compressor with a spray gun is ideal for use with paint, preservatives, wood stains and colourants.

Timber will lose its strength if it is unprotected even for one season. It will turn grey and crumble the following season and, once the rot sets in, expensive replacement is the only option.

Wet rot Wet rot can only occur in timber that has been neglected and allowed to imbibe a high moisture content. Often it creeps and develops behind a coating of paint where two adjacent parts of timber have opened up allowing rainwater to get in by capillary action. The lower joints of a door frame or the bottoms of garage doorposts are typical of areas to check for peeling paint and spongy wood underneath. You might find black or dark brown brittle wood crumbling under the chisel. This is dried-out wet rot, not to be confused with dry rot. Hack out or saw off the offending timber. Then treat the whole area with a reputable brand of wet rot liquid treatment. Give the area a good soaking, especially the end grain of wood that is likely to be exposed.

Replace with pre-treated matching timber or fill any small holes with a two-part wood repair kit. Obviously take care when using flammable solvent wood preservers. Gloves, goggles and a proper respirator mask are essential and keep windows open for ventilation if working indoors.

Dry rot Dry rot is mostly found attacking wood in dark, badly ventilated and damp areas inside the house. If you see strands looking like cotton wool creeping over wood and brick-work, a serious dry rot problem is present and should be solved straightaway. These strands could easily migrate from an attack in exterior woodwork because they are able to penetrate through walls of brick or stone along the lines of the mortar. It could be that timber on the outside of, say, a bay window has been attacked and is affecting the joist just inside the window causing the floor to bounce when walked on. If there is no apparent evidence of dry rot outside, check by lifting a floorboard just inside the bay window. If the floor joists are supported within the walls or on a dwarf wall adjacent to the window, check the ends of the timbers which might have fine grey strands running over them. If there is evidence of brown and brittle cracked timber either in the floorboards or the joists, check if the wood has split into cube-like shapes or if there is a mushroom-like growth present. This advanced form of dry rot produces reddish spores, which are thrown off to float and infect surrounding areas including brick or stone. Any timbers on the outside of the wall adjacent to the attack will then show signs of mycelium. These strands will then migrate to attack surrounding exterior timber posts, cladding, door frames, window frames and any supporting timbers, for example, timber lintels within the wall structure. When you expose any exterior timber cladding or cover piece, also check for a strong fungus smell akin to mushrooms which will be a further indication of dry rot. This is the most insidious form of timber destruction and needs prompt problem-solving.

If the attack is widespread, get in a specialist firm. All the affected timber and an area

Check all the timber in your home and treat it if necessary. Woodworm in any part of a timber-framed or wood-clad building must be treated immediately. If it's extensive, the wood must be removed and burned. Replace the wood only after treating the area to within 1m (3ft) of the infestation. A DIY treatment is fine for a small local attack.

See pages 204–8 for details and pictures of wet rot, dry rot and woodworm.

surrounding it must be removed, bagged and handled carefully so as not to spread the spores. Even plaster has to be chopped away if the strands have grown behind it. For minor attacks it is possible to solve the problem with a proprietary brand of chemical dry rot treatment. This can be brushed or sprayed on by a high-pressure jet. The best method is to use a compressor and spray, this will ensure that the atomised spray gets beyond the affected area and penetrates the end grain of adjacent timber. Any walls that are suspect also need to be treated. In this case drill holes angled downwards inside and out, so that the liquid can soak into the wall. The drill holes will be sealed if the wall has to be replastered, otherwise seal each hole separately. You will need to replaster with a zinc oxychloride plaster after the wall has completely dried out. Only use pre-treated timber for replacing the rotted wood. Always remember SAFETY FIRST, DIY SECOND, so use full protection when dealing with preservative liquids. A respirator mask is essential at all times.

Woodworm

A small area peppered with the flight holes of wood beetles does not necessarily threaten the structure of a building. The back of an old wardrobe might show signs of beetle infestation but this problem is easily

solved with a DIY woodworm eradicating kit. However, a timber surface that has shallow channels joining each other suggests that the inner wood has been eaten away. Obviously this is more serious and replacement of the affected timber is an absolute necessity. Cut out all affected timber and go just beyond the area to offset further spread of the wood boring larvae. Woodworm eggs are laid in or on the timber by the beetle and the larvae feeds upon and bores through the wood leaving a network of holes. An insecticide preservative in a spray can comes with the DIY kit together with a small-bore plastic tube for inserting into the exit holes where the attack is minimal.

You might spot tell-tale holes in timber lintels or any other unpainted areas. Sometimes you will find a fine dust, like fine sawdust, under the area of infestation. This 'frass' will indicate that the woodworm larvae are active, and since they can be growing and boring into the wood for up to three years, they need to be tackled as a matter of urgency.

Treatment

You might spot indications of woodworm activity in the structural timbers of very old buildings, but the activity is not limited to old timbers. Newer timber in buildings, which has not been treated or painted, can be susceptible to beetle attack. If the attack is extensive and threatens the stability of that part of the building, a specialist firm can be contracted to deal with the infestation. If you only find a small area needing treatment then it is quite simple to solve the problem yourself. Check the extent of the infestation and work out the area of wood to be removed and replaced. If you have a compressor and a spray gun, the problem is easily solved by only having to purchase the necessary amount of solvent-free, water-based woodworm eradicator. Compressors come with all the accessories needed to solve this problem. This non-flammable liquid has a low odour, is not noxious and will not harm surrounding parts of the exterior of the building. Hire a long-handled lance to reach difficult areas and remove some cladding boards if necessary to get to the back of the supporting timber studs and noggins.

Brickwork

Brick bonding

Take a close look at the brick walls in your area and you will be surprised to see so many variations in how they were laid! In order to get a solid and permanent wall, good adhesion of the brickwork construction to the mortar course is obtained by a particular 'bond' The is 'stretcher' bond is the most commonly used today to clad the exterior of timber-framed houses.

English bond. This bond forms a very solid construction but was not generally favoured in earlier building work because its alternating courses of 'stretchers' and 'headers' tend to produce a distinctive linear look. This was not to the liking of Victorians. However, even though it is slower to build than, say, a 'stretcher' bond, it is now used extensively because it provides a densely bonded construction.

Stretcher bond. This is a favourite of bricklayers. The vertical joints, or 'perpends' are aligned alternately in courses giving a solid construction to a wall. It is used in cavity wall construction.

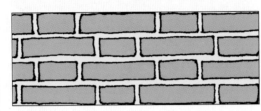

Flemish bond. This is usually found in solid 23 cm (9 in) walls where it is important that a 'header' bonded the whole thickness of a wall. 'Stretcher' bricks are laid alternately with 'header' bricks to form an extremely strong construction.

Garden wall bond. This type of construction economises on 'headers' by alternating three courses of 'stretchers' with one of 'headers'. It is often used for decorative purposes. The 'headers' are actually half-bricks (half-bat).

Bricks

(A) The surfaces of a brick are called 'brick faces'. The four different faces are the 'stretcher' (the long narrow face), the 'header' (the end of a brick), the 'frog' (the indent for receiving mortar which helps bonding) and the 'flat' (the bedding face). The brick is laid with the 'flat' face upwards if it is the top course of a wall, otherwise lay the bricks with the 'frog' face upwards.

(B) A brick that has been chopped in half across its width is called a 'half bat'. It is used within a wall to fill in near the end of a wall, or in a single thickness garden wall as a 'header'.

(C) In both Flemish and English bond walls, it is necessary to split and insert a brick lengthways to get a natural staggered joint at the end of a wall – a 'Queen closer'. This is built in as the penultimate brick before the wall terminates, or turns a corner, with the 'header'.

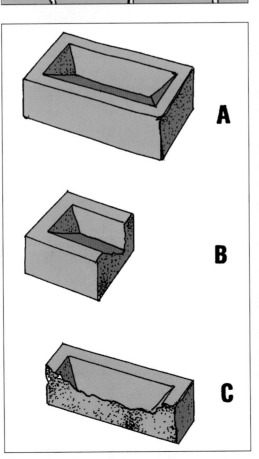

The restoration of a Victorian front elevation has been successful by replacing spalling bricks with matching bricks from a reclamation yard and repairing the sliding sash windows.

Brickwork and pointing must be protected. Perished pointing and delaminating bricks can dangerously weaken the stability of a wall.

Chopping a brick in half

Use safety goggles and gloves. Secure the brick between battens and two wedges tightly hammered into the positions shown. Mark the cut line and use a DIY powered angle-grinder to score along the line to a depth of about 20 mm (³/₄ in). A few taps with a bolster chisel and club hammer will successfully split the brick.

Laying the half-brick

Drill and chop out half the spalled brick. Cut a matching brick in half. Spread mortar into the opening. Butter the top of the half-brick and gently ease it into the opening. Match the pointing and brush of any excess mortar when it has almost dried. Apply a water repellent when completely dry.

Spalling

We should all be aware of the quality of the bricks used in the construction of our homes. Many speculatively built houses had different bricks at the rear elevation from those in the front. At the back of the house raw brickwork was typical because of cost, even if the front was stuccoed or rendered. The colour and physical properties of bricks varied from different parts of the country. Yellow London Stock bricks are totally different to the hard red brick originating around Lancashire. Many houses in the South have an oatmeal-coloured facing brick, while in Staffordshire a deep blue brick is commonly found. This is all because the clays in different parts of the country have different constituents and can be fired at different temperatures.

Bricks that look darker in a wall than the surrounding bricks have been over-fired to be harder than the rest. These will not suffer weathering as much as the lighter coloured ones. The latter will be prone to deterioration caused by driving rain saturating the softer surface. Later, frost will cause the brick surface to 'burst' or delaminate as the water trapped inside freezes and expands. This is unsightly but, more importantly, the brick loses its outer surface and the softer clay core is then exposed to further weathering. This problem confronted me when I was building an exterior door opening in the kitchen I had designed for former Tomorrow's World presenter Philippa Forrester. Adjacent to the door were bricks that needed to be replaced because of spalling. Luckily we found a demolition yard that stocked matching bricks.

Treatment

You will need a power drill, with a hammer action and a 12 mm masonry bit, plugged into an RCD indoors. With safety in mind, wear protective goggles, a dust mask and

Replacing a corner brick

Clean out the corner opening and chop away all traces of old mortar. Dampen all the faces and spread mortar on the sides and bottom of the opening. Butter a brick on the top and slide it into position, lining it up properly. Match the pointing and when dry use a colourless water repellent over the whole wall.

gloves. Set the depth gauge to 50 mm (2 in) and drill a series of holes close enough to help break up the front half of the brick with a bolster chisel and club hammer. Use the chisel to slice through the front half of the brick and chop into the surrounding mortar. The front half of the brick is now ready to be replaced by a matching brick cut in half along its length. A DIY powered angle-grinder with a cutting disc is ideal for this job. Anchor the brick in position between battens fixed to a board. Push wedges in to hold it fast. Cut through both sides of the brick to meet in the middle.

Be sure that the new half brick is mortared into place with the face out. Mix the mortar in proportions of one part cement, one part lime and six parts washed sand. Colourants can be added if you need to match pointing. Dampen the whole of the opening with a diluted PVA mix to help adhesion of the brick and the mortar. Trowel the mortar into the opening and squeeze in the half brick. Fill in the gaps around the brick before striking the pointing shape to match the existing bricks. Once the mortar is dry and hard, clean off the whole wall and apply a coat of clear water-repellent. This treatment will allow the wall to expel any trapped moisture but will prevent further ingress from rain water. There should be then no further spalling problems to solve.

Chop with a 'hand-protected' bolster chisel to chip concrete or cut bricks.

A new wall showing early signs of salts migrating to the outside surface. Don't be tempted to wash off efflorescence, it'll be reabsorbed into the wall with the washing liquid. Just keep rubbing it with dry sackcloth.

Efflorescence

Efflorescence is a white powdery deposit often found on exterior walls particularly of new brickwork. All clays contain soluble salts from the earth and these can still be active in bricks even after firing. Under certain conditions the salts migrate to the surface of the bricks and can look unsightly if they occur on a large area of newly built houses. The chemical reaction of clay with mortar and rainwater can be the cause. When the brick surface dries out, the salts are deposited. If old brickwork is subjected to an unusual amount of rainwater, the same crystalline deposits will occur. The salts actually are harmless and will in time disappear but you can help by rubbing them off occasionally with rough sacking.

If anyone suggests the old myth of brushing with diluted vinegar or using a bleach, ignore this advice! Any form of liquid application will dissolve the crystals but immediately the liquid will be sucked back into the brickwork for the crystals to reappear later. If the wall is already decorated or you have plans to paint it, wait until the wall is completely dry. At that stage only paint with a primer that is alkali-resistant. This will help neutralise the effects of the efflorescence allowing you to apply a masonry paint which will let the wall breathe.

Perished mortar

When scanning the brick wall of a house you can often see patches of deeper grey pointing. This indicates that perished mortar is underneath and that too strong a mix has been applied over it without good knowledge of the principles of pointing. There is absolutely no point in using a strong cement mix in the hope that it has more adhesion and is stronger. Pop an old screwdriver into the edge and bits will fly out exposing perished mortar only millimetres from the brick surface.

Perished mortar must be raked out to a depth of 10–20 mm (½–¾ in). Much of it will have fallen out in time due to water and erosion, which breaks down the constituents of the mortar mix. Frost is a great enemy of mortar. The tiny crack between the original mortar and the adjacent brick will allow rainwater penetration. This in turn will freeze and expand to push out the mortar, which is the less strong of the two elements. When this happens in an area that is difficult to see, it will lead to a lot of water seeping through the wall. You can check at a window opening reveal if the wall is a 23 cm (9 in) solid wall. A cavity wall will still be affected by damp but it will take longer to manifest itself on the inside wall. The water will fall inside the cavity to affect the bottom of the

Weather damaged bricks show signs of laminating and the mortar is perished. Even though the lead flashing is sound, it is not sealed into the joint, allowing rain water to creep inside by capillary action.

wall inside or it will migrate to an inside wall by capillary action along one of the many metal wall-ties that are built into each skin of the cavity wall to help stabilise it.

Another problem that perished mortar can cause is the rotting of joist ends of suspended wooden floors, especially those on the ground floor. In low-cost housing construction, it was considered normal building practice to house the joist ends in small pockets left open in the brickwork. In walls that were only 23 cm (9 in) thick, it meant that only half a brick thickness separated the vulnerable joist ends from the outside air moisture or attack by rain water along a perished mortar course. This could lead to rotting of the joist ends and a bouncing floor! If joists are spongy, check the exterior pointing. You will have to replace the joists locating the ends on to galvanised steel hangers built into the brickwork and, of course, repair the exterior pointing.

Repointing
This is not as daunting as it might appear. There are myths that have grown up about trades such as pointing that once had a mystique about them. Solve one simple DIY problem and you'll be moving on to the next with more confidence. Look at any elevation of your home and you'll probably discover a small area of brickwork that needs repointing. As with any job that is new to you, consider carefully the safety factors and make a materials and tool list. Pointing is actually an easy art to acquire and very rewarding because the results will be there for years to come.

Joints between bricks deteriorate before the bricks suffer any damage. If the joints show signs of decay or the pointing has perished, act as soon as you can. Structural movement in a building can cause mortar to crack so don't ever be surprised to find that a problem has occurred that has to be solved, and with a little common sense, a minimum of tools and

instructions to follow, it's easy and gives a great deal of satisfaction.

Use a safe platform and wear protective gear. If necessary hire a scaffolding tower with a safe platform from which to work. Rake out the area to repoint with a plugging chisel (or ordinary cold chisel) and a club hammer to a depth of about 12 mm (½ in). Try not to use a claw hammer because the constant banging of the head on to a steel chisel will round it. This will be dangerous. Use the hammer for its designated purpose, which is banging in nails. Leave a squared-off recess between the bricks otherwise the new mortar might fall out. Brush out all debris and dampen the bricks and recess with water before repointing.

Repointing (1)
Hack out to a depth of 20 mm (¾ in) all the perished pointing with a plugging chisel and a club hammer. Take care not to chip the bricks. Brush off all the grit and debris. Use a bag of ready-mixed mortar especially formulated for pointing. Mix as recommended on a mixing board.

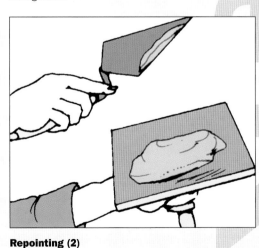

Repointing (2)
Put a small amount of mortar onto the hawk and thinly spread one edge of it outwards so that you can pick up a 'finger' on the back of the trowel.

Only use a 'plugging' chisel to hack out perished pointing to a depth of 150 mm (6 in).

A good example of raking out perished pointing. Repointing the verticals before horizontals.

Repointing (3)
Dampen a small area to be repointed. Hold a hawk with a small amount of mortar close to the work. Take a slice of mortar on a trowel and feed it into the joints – the vertical ones first. Trim off the excess and then shape the joint to match that already there. When it has dried completely, spray or brush on a protective coat of water repellent.

Smooth pointing with a dowel drawn down all verticals first, then horizontals.

Mix just enough mortar to use in one session. Each mix should be in exactly the same proportion of sand, cement and lime to the previous mix to maintain the colour of the mortar throughout the whole of the repointing job. Mix dry on a clean dry surface one part cement, one part lime and six parts washed builder's sand. When the constituents are thoroughly mixed scoop out a hollow in the centre and add water gradually. Continue to add and mix until you find it easy to pick up a trowel full and then slide it easily off the trowel. If the mix is too watery it will slip out of the raked joints. If the batch has dried out before you have finished repointing one small area, throw it away. Adding water will weaken the mix because the structure of the mortar will be changed.

Use a hawk, (that is, a square of ply about 300 mm × 300 mm (12 in × 12 in) with a handle centrally placed underneath) to hold a fistful of mortar. Form a small pyramid and with the back of the pointing trowel facing away from you take a slither of mortar, about 12 mm (½ in), from the lower edge of the pyramid. Tilt the trowel to keep the mortar uppermost and gently ease it into the vertical recesses first. Try out a patch of about 300 mm × 300 mm (12 in × 12 in) to start. Force the mortar into the uprights first, then the horizontals. Strike all the verticals, then as you strike with the trowel along the length of the line, the vertical pointing will be cleanly cut. There are many types of joints, for example 'flush', 'tooled', 'recessed', etc., but a 'weathered' joint is the easiest and is created by pushing the trowel blade into the top of the joint and striking it along at an angle. This successfully throws off rainwater. However, you have to match the existing joint when patch pointing. When the mortar is almost cured but still

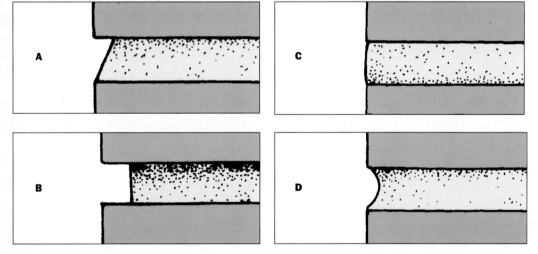

Mortar joints

Lime mortar was common in Victorian houses. This made the mortar slightly more elastic and tolerant to small changes in structural and thermal changes as it did not crack. However, if it was not properly prepared, it would eventually lose its adhesion and crumble. A problem we have to solve today.

Nowadays, we use a cement mix of one part cement to four parts sand, and add a plasticiser. However, for restoration work use a lime mortar mix of one part lime, one part cement and six parts sand.

A. Weather-struck joints. This is an efficient joint which easily throws off rainwater. It is formed with a pointed trowel. 'Strike' all the verticals first, followed by the long horizontals to give a continuous sloping profile.

B. Raked (recessed) joints. This is more impressive than the weather-struck joint. It gives a more defined overall pattern to a wall but it is not as effective at throwing off water which tends to settle on the lower 'flat' of the joint. The mortar is compressed with a jointing tool or a piece of metal shaped to fit.

C. Flush joints. This joint gives a flat uninteresting appearance. Scrape off all the excess mortar flush with the surface, then stipple gently into the mortar joints using a brush. This slightly 'disturbs' the surface texture by exposing the sand aggregate.

D. Rubbed joint. This joint is achieved by dragging a bent tube along the joint to get a recessed curve – verticals first, then horizontals. You'll more clearly see the shapes of all the edges of the bricks if you use this joint.

Correct gaps left in hacked out mortar courses after removal of perished pointing. Repoint the verticals first, then the horizontals – all to be 'bagged' flush with existing mortar.

'green', brush off unwanted mortar with a fine brush. Excess mortar at the lower edge of the horizontal joint can be neatly removed with a 'Frenchman' (this is simply a piece of metal with the tip bent at right angles). When slid along a guiding batten, it trims off the residual mortar to make a clean neat edge giving a professional finish to your DIY repointing job.

Protective coating

Before applying any protective coatings to a brick wall, get the preparation work out of the way and you'll be half way to solving this DIY problem. For example, any rust stains from a leaking iron gutter or rainwater pipe can be cleaned off with a steel brush before priming with an aluminium spirit-based sealer. If this is not done and the wall is to be painted, the stains will breathe through. If, on the other hand, the original look and colour of the bricks is to be retained, colourless water-repellent liquids are available to make the wall impervious to rainwater without changing the look or colour. This special preparation will allow the wall to breathe, that is, any moisture in the wall will be allowed to dry out, yet the wall remains protected. A compressor with a long lance spray is the best and quickest method of applying the solution. Mask all areas to stop the atomised spray from getting on to doors and windows. Some sealants have a dye which dissipates when it dries on the wall. This makes it easier to cover every inch of the wall. Using a compressor and spray makes this a very enjoyable way of solving this particular DIY problem.

Use a piece of sacking to gently rub off all excess mortar level with the facing bricks. It is a very quick and easy method of obtaining a weatherproof joint but does not give a very decorative finish to brickwork.

Decorative recessed pointing is easily achieved with a 12 mm (½ in) batten drawn between the bricks. This removes excess mortar to give a 10 mm (⅜ in) depth joint. The disadvantage is that rainwater can sit on the horizontal ledge of each course.

This is the most effective 'struck' pointing joint for throwing off rainwater. The water is shed from top to bottom of a wall without penetration.

Check any area where you suspect damp, especially if you see a tidemark. Use an inexpensive DIY damp meter called a protimeter to give the extent and degree of dampness.

Damp course

The results of rising damp in the walls of a house are far from pleasant. It can be seen, felt and smelt. There are several causes of rising damp and often the problem could have been avoided if one was aware of certain principles of building. When the foundations of a house have been laid and the brick walls are beginning to rise, it is a laid down building regulation to insert an impervious layer of material, the damp-proof course (DPC), 15cm (6in) above the outside ground level. Nowadays, it is common practice to lay a bitumen-based material or a specially formulated plastic material on to a bed of mortar before continuing the brickwork. This strip has to be the same width as the wall, so as to prevent any damp from the ground getting into the main wall. In the nineteenth century the DPC was likely to be a layer of overlapping slate.

If there are signs of damp rising from about 30cm to 90cm (1ft to 3ft) inside, it is pretty certain that either no barrier exists or most likely that one has broken down or collapsed. The source of rising damp in the soil or subsoil underneath the wall is moisture content, decaying plant material, salts, nitrates, chlorides, and soil-living animals. Damp showing on the inside walls is therefore a dilute solution of various materials including nitrates and chlorides. As the damp dries out inside the room, salt deposits are left behind because they cannot evaporate. These salt deposits on wallpaper and in the plaster form the basis for diagnosis of rising damp by a specialist firm.

Air vents built into the outside walls of a house with suspended wooden floors must be left completely clear. Air must be allowed to freely circulate in the void to prevent damp and wood rot.

Earth bridging the damp-proof course
As a nation of garden lovers we find ways of piling earth against a wall. But beware! The damp-proof course (DPC) is an integral part of the house structure preventing rising damp. Earth piled above the DPC will cause damage to the wall and decorations.

The exterior wall of a house that shows obvious signs of a broken down damp proof course will have problems inside! A DIY solution is to inject a silicone fluid under pressure. Your local hire shop will have the tools and give advice.

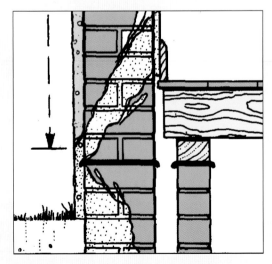

Rendered wall bridging the damp-proof course
Stucco or render on an external wall can be attractive and protective. But it must stop above the DPC, otherwise damp will rise into the wall causing damage to it and the interior of the building.

Salts carried in water from the soil are hygroscopic, which means that they absorb water from the atmosphere and form a solution. The surface of the wall then becomes susceptible to the slightest humidity in the atmosphere, so not surprisingly the dampness will show up unexpectedly on some days and will disappear just as puzzlingly.

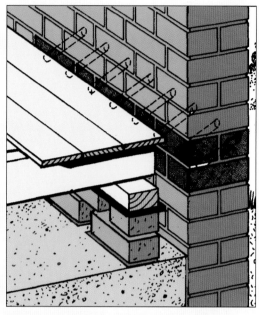

Silicone injection to overcome rising damp
A DIY application that creates a permanent barrier to rising damp is to inject a silicone solution. The materials and pressure tools can be hired, but carefully read all the instructions before switching on the compressor.

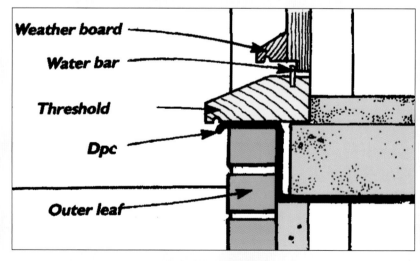

Front door threshold
The door threshold is protected from the weather by a water bar and a weather board. The damp-proof course under the concrete base runs up and under the threshold to prevent rising damp.

Rising damp Another indication of rising damp is the tidemark at a given height above the floor level around the room. If one wall is dry it is probably because it is a stud wall resting on the floor joists and not in contact with the ground. An inexpensive DIY damp meter is available which allows you to monitor the damp conditions around every room. It's useful too for confirming penetrating damp at a high level, which could be because of perished pointing.

Each year you might be tempted to buy bags of compost and topsoil to build up borders around the house. Without realising it, potential problems occur if you build up the soil over the level of the damp-proof course (DPC). Remember that this is just 15 cm (6 in) above ground level so any soil in contact with the bricks above that is going to permanently feed moisture through and into the walls. This is then seen on the inside walls as spoiled decorations and blown plaster. Similarly a patio or path built at the side or back of the house above the level of the DPC will be a source of damp from the outside brickwork through to the inside walls.

Sometimes the cause of rising damp can only be discovered by removing a brick at DPC level from outside. By inspection through the hole you can discover whether mortar has been allowed to drop inside a cavity to a height above the damp course. Carelessness by the original bricklayers often results in apparent inexplicable signs of dampness inside the room at floor level even though the DPC is still sound. The droppings of mortar can build up and can be high enough to cause a bridge above the DPC. Laying a solid floor, without prior knowledge, will cause a similar problem if it is laid at the wrong level.

If earth reaching the DPC is the cause of rising damp, this problem is solved by digging down to 15 cm (6 in) below the level of the DPC. This is not too difficult to spot because the mortar course is slightly wider there. External rendering could be another problem if it's carried down over the level of the DPC. Just chop it back to slightly higher than the level of the DPC to solve the problem.

If no DPC exists, or if rising damp persists because of a breakdown of the system, the problem can be solved by injecting a water-repellent silicone solution. This used to be the province of the builder, but all the tools and materials can now be hired by the DIYer. Full instructions come with the compressor, the container of silicone solution, the pump, hoses and probes. A powerful hammer drill with long masonry bits come as standard. Drill holes about 10cm (4in) apart, angled down and in a line along the wall just above the DPC level. Insert the probes into the holes and pump the silicone in to saturate the wall. The bricks imbibe the silicone solution and it spreads to make a continuous barrier across and along the wall. Full safety instructions come with the kit and should be strictly adhered to.

through the walls. Without the asphalt there would be no guarantee of a water-resistant construction. The nominal measurement of having the DPC in the walls at 15cm (6in) above outside ground level was to ensure that ground water or rainwater splashing back against the walls did not penetrate above that height. So whatever the construction of the inside ground floor, timber or concrete, the essential component to stop rising damp damaging the structure of the walls is a DPC.

You can often check from the outside of the brick wall at 15cm (6in) above ground level whether a slate or asphalt DPC has been built in. It was found that even though slates over-lapped to give a continuous barrier, movement in a building or just the age of the slates caused

Inserting a damp-proof course – suspended wooden floors
Drill holes about 150mm (6in) above ground level but below the suspended wooden floor. Pump in a silicone fluid that creates an impervious barrier.

Inserting a damp-proof course – solid floors
A concrete floor should have a damp-proof membrane beneath it, but if there isn't one in the wall or there is rising damp, insert a silicone barrier just above the floor level. Drill a series of holes 100 mm (4in) apart and sloping down at 30°. Follow the instructions that come with the hired equipment.

These descriptions of damp problems and their solutions have only referred to brick walls and suspended wooden floors but there is another problem related to brick walls and solid concrete floors. The Victorians successfully solved the problem of damp rising up walls and through concrete floors by laying a 15mm (½in) contin-uous layer of asphalt over the concrete floor and

crumbling leading to a breakdown of the DPC. However, with the foregoing instructions for a DIY application of inserting a silicone DPC, you'll be celebrating the successful completion of the job in much less time than anticipated. Remember that this is one of those DIY jobs where the essentials are minimal expertise, sound common sense and a calm approach!

Parapet walls

An old-established lean-to roof of thick Welsh slates, still in good condition. The parapet wall needs repointing and the joint flashing is leaking.

A parapet wall is an external extension of a constructional wall of any house. It can be sloping, as on a pitched roof such as an extension of the party wall separating two houses in a terrace, or it can rise above the front elevation wall, especially in a Victorian terrace, to conceal a V-shaped pitched roof. In this latter instance the two slopes of the roof meet at the middle of the house. A valley gutter runs at right angles to the front elevation and you will often see an outlet or spout centrally located about 90 cm (3 ft) below the top of the front parapet wall. The simplest type of roof supported by a parapet wall is the 'lean-to' or shed-type roof. The rafters lean against the parapet wall which extends upwards another couple of feet. The lower ends rest on a timber wall plate bedded on top of the wall but low enough to give the correct 'fall' for weather protection. Only small spans are considered for this construction because the outward thrust could push out the parapet wall.

Look at a flat roof extension and you'll probably find a low parapet wall surrounding it on three sides. Usually brick-built parapet walls have to be protected mainly from water penetration from the top. However, it was common practice to build in a series of tiles laid flat to protrude to form a 'drip'. These tiles, called creasing tiles, are specially made to form a weatherproof course so that rainwater is thrown away clear of the wall. Alternatively, the final stone component used to prevent rain washing out joints between bricks on top of the parapet wall is a wide stone coping. This is usually of a non-absorbent stone about 10 cm (4 in) wider than the wall with its top surface smoothed. Where it projects either side of the wall it has a groove or throating on its underside to allow rainwater to drip clear of the wall. Nowadays concrete coping stones have replaced natural stone but it is essential to lay a bituminous felt DPC on a bed of mortar under the coping stones to reduce the risk of damp entering the mortar

Bedding new copings on existing parapet wall showing felt DPC in position and hacked off old render, ready for repair.

course which can cause possible frost problems in extreme weather conditions.

Repointing Parapet walls are vulnerable to all types of weather, including rain from every direction, because they are exposed on both sides and ends. It is imperative that adequate protection is provided to prevent rainwater entering the inner walls of the house to cause further damage. Check whether you're dealing with a 23 cm (9 in) solid brick wall or a 33 cm (13 in) cavity wall. With a cavity wall, a continuous DPC is laid at an angle inside the cavity to prevent ingress of rainwater to the inside walls. The 23 cm (9 in) solid wall has a simple DPC laid across the width of the wall. However, both constructions depend upon conscientious work by the bricklayer otherwise a break in the pointing is going to give future problems.

When mortar has perished between coping stones high on a roof, it is difficult to spot the danger signs. Check the condition of all suspect parts every summer using a pair of binoculars.

If there is the slightest sign of perished pointing, discolouring of the mortar, or moss or lichen growth, then immediate action is needed. These indications are serious and to solve the problem of potential damage to the structure of the wall or to interior decorations, repointing is necessary. Hack out all signs of perished pointing especially where DPCs have been inserted. Carefully check the mortar course under coping stones. This holds and seals continuous flashing over an upstand or 'skirting' that covers the joint at a flat roof junction. Remember that coping stones, flashings and DPCs are only as good as the protective mortar joints between

them, so rake out to at least 15 mm (½ in), then repoint. Small lead pellets can be used to hold in the flashing if necessary. Use one part cement, one part lime and six parts washed builder's sand to get a pliable mortar mixture. Push the mix deep into the recesses and strike a weather joint, sloping to throw off rainwater.

Parapet walls, being high and exposed, suffer more from weathering than lower walls. There is high likelihood of a rendered wall at parapet height showing signs of cracks or loss of adhesion to the substrate (the raw bricks).

If you're working from a flat roof on the inside wall, it's fairly safe. The outside of the wall, however, is a different proposition and thought has to be given to the safety aspect. Hire a safe lightweight tower from a reputable hire firm and ask for full instructions for putting it up and for working at height. Look at their illustrated brochure and get help in deciding on the size and type of scaffolding that suits your task. Tall towers need to be braced with 'outriggers', that is, angled corner pieces. Importantly, the lightweight tower has to be level to be safe, so once the lower section has been assembled, level it with the help of a spirit level and the adjustable feet. Platforms can be erected at whatever height they are needed and inside the scaffolding uprights. Never, ever, climb the outside of the frame as this is highly dangerous. Place the scaffolding boards at the top to make a safe working platform with a guard rail. Essentially, for your own safety and for those on the ground, don't ignore the kickboards all around. You don't want to accidentally kick a tool off the unguarded platform.

Now secure the platform with ropes tied to large ringbolts either into the masonry, which is the best, or into the fascia board. When building up the sections and arriving at the intermediate platforms, leave a space for the ladders so that you have continuous easy access to the top. When working from a platform never overreach, as with ladders, and if you're not used to working at heights always have another person at the base to do the mixing and carrying, and to keep an eye open for the unexpected!

Parapet walls (cavity)

Coping stones (A) bedded on to a cavity wall need a piece of slate (B) to bridge the cavity. A continuous DPC prevents any rainwater running down the inside of the walls (C). This is laid at an angle. Flashing (D) is dressed over the upstand or skirting of the roof covering (E) to continue the protection.

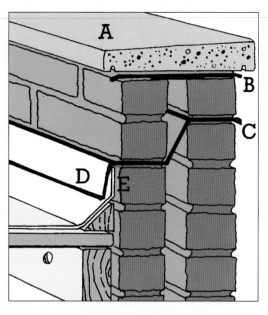

Parapet walls (solid brick)

Parapet walls are protected at the top by coping stones (A). These are vulnerable because they are exposed at both sides. It is imperative that adequate protection is provided to prevent rainwater entering the inner walls of the house. Ensure that a continuous DPC is laid under the coping stones (B). Where a flat roof is built over an extension there must be a 'skirting' or upstand (C) of roof covering covered by a DPC (D) in the form of flashing (E).

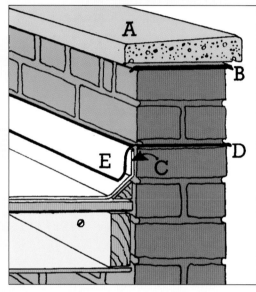

In this section look up the sections on repointing rendered walls. They give all the necessary information on the step-by-step instructions for mixing the ingredients for mortar and how to solve the problems of perished pointing and damaged render.

If there's a breakdown of the DPC that bridges the two brick skins of a cavity wall, there is a risk of water shedding to the inside lower walls of the house. The illustration shows exactly how a coping stone protects the top of the parapet wall and how the angled DPC is let in. If the coping stone becomes loose, then it has to be rebedded on a mortar mix, having first removed all the old mortar. If the DPC has failed, top courses need to be removed in order to replace the angled DPC. The drawing helps explain what is involved. Repointing of the joints must be carefully undertaken so no gaps are left.

When lifting off parapet coping stones, take great care to number them and replace them in the same position. Take care where you stack them as they can be cumbersome and heavy. A few on top of the platform are OK, but too many are not! Clean off the backs of the stones and prepare the bricks with a bed of mortar. Any flashings let into a mortar course, say dressed over an upstand of a flat roof, must be treated as described in the section on 'Flat Roofs'. Always think SAFETY, especially wear protective gear including safety goggles, a dust mask and gloves. If you use a powered angle-grinder for cutting stones or bricks plug it into an RCD indoors, which will cut the power immediately if a fault occurs so you cannot be harmed.

Roof joint You could find a flat roof covered in any one of a number of roofing materials. These include felt, zinc, copper, lead and asphalt. Whatever the roofing sheets are made of, where they abut a surface like a parapet wall, they're turned up against the brickwork and masked by a flashing inserted into a mortar course. The upstand is fixed into a course and the flashing (usually zinc) goes into the course above to give total cover to the upstand and therefore protecting the joint to the roof.

Most DIY stores now stock a bitumen-based self-adhesive roll of flashing. Some come with an aluminium facing to protect it from the elements. The bitumen is pressed (it can be warmed if it is not pliable) on to the top of the upstand and tight to the brickwork to give a watertight joint. This material has done a great deal to make our DIY tasks easier and cheaper to solve. This sealing problem has been simplified by developments in the building industry but remember that any job one undertakes is only as good as the devotion we put into it. However, time is on our side and we're solving problems in our own homes!

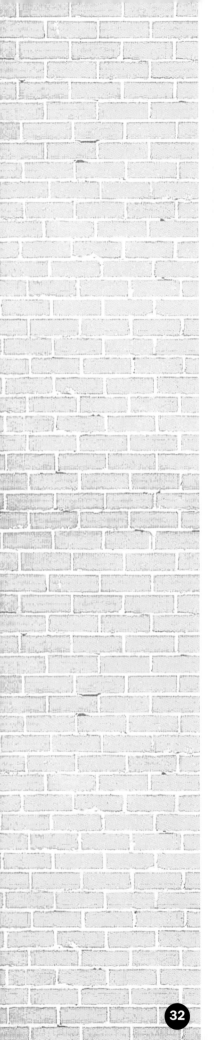

Sills

There are two main factors to consider in order to solve any problems with sills: the materials used and the method of insulation. Sited at the foot of the door and window openings is the wood or stone sill. In solid brick or masonry external walls, sills are usually of stone cut longer than the width of the window opening. Rainwater sheds off the sloping top which projects in front of the brick surface. At the lower front edge underneath is a groove about 15 mm (½ in) in from the front edge. This ensures that the shed rainwater drops to the ground from the edge and does not run back to where the sill is embedded in the wall. This joint, if it has been neglected, is the spot where potential damp troubles occur. An exterior silicone waterproof sealant is the answer to that common problem. Use a cartridge of mastic in a skeletal gun and squeeze the mastic into the joint to give a continuous and flexible seal. The mastic comes coloured to match the building materials or painted surfaces. The technique is simple and similar to the application of silicone sealant around a bath. Constant pressure on the trigger and slow steady progress in the movement gives a good-sized continuous bead. Use a wet spatula to seal it to the wall and to smooth the surface.

The Victorians also made use of a cheaper sill installation. The stone sill was made equal to the width of the window opening and not built into the reveals (the window sides). These were cheaper to install than the conventional sill but less durable because shed rainwater could seep into the exposed vertical joints at either end. Whereas a built-in stone sill was liable to cracking from movement or settlement, the 'slip' sill didn't suffer cracks so much. The top surface usually sloped down to help discharge rainwater. In good constructional building work a groove for a metal water bar was also incorporated in the stone sill's top surface. This stopped water seeping back through any gap between the top of the stone sill and the bottom edge of the wooden window sill.

Paint In Victorian times, much of the exterior stonework, like sills and lintels over the windows, was painted because the stone used was soft and porous. Even now this causes us problems when paint might be neglected and rainwater allowed to soak through flaking paint into the porous stone sill. Gloss paint is impervious and so makes an excellent protective coat against not only rain but also chemical pollutants and frost. Most manufacturers produce an exterior paint with a long life especially formulated for masonry.

Traditionally Victorian sills were meant to be painted. This adds distinctive decorative features and gives contrast to an otherwise featureless front wall of standard brick. However, for practical reasons it is important to keep a check on the condition of vulnerable parts of one's home. Horizontal areas like sills are subject to harsh weathering and need more attention than other surfaces. Rake out any loose cement and look for mould or growth. Remove the raked-out debris and brush on a fungicidal solution to prevent further attack by moss or lichen. Blisters or flaking paint can be easily removed with a scraper. Fill in cracks with a proprietary exterior filler and wait for it to cure before sanding smooth. Prime, undercoat and paint before using a matching mastic sealant along and around all joints between the sill and the surrounding brickwork.

Door sills Sills under external doors, if not of stone construction, are made from a hardwood. The profile is designed to stop ingress of shed water but also to stop wind and rain from being blown in underneath. A metal, galvanised, rain-bar is often let into a groove and needs to be properly maintained to remain effective. If for some reason the bar is missing or loose, it needs to be replaced. They can be readily purchased. Allow the wood to dry completely before banging the new one into place. Never directly strike the metal with a hammer! Use a scrap of timber resting on its length to knock the bar into place. If necessary use one of the new cartridge metal to wood adhesives in the groove if the bar is too loose.

Wood rot

A wood repair kit strengthens and reinforces decayed wood. The hardener binds and hardens the wood around the hole in readiness for the filler, which neither shrinks nor cracks. Protect the surrounding wood by inserting wood preservative tablets into drilled holes.

Rot Check all round the sill for signs of water penetration, loose cement or wood rot. If a wooden window sill or a door sill shows signs of rot, it is probably wet rot. The problem is easily solved with a three-part wood repair kit. Neglected exposed wood eventually turns grey and the surface loses its texture and lustre in parts. In the worst spots, it becomes soft and spongy. It is these areas that need to be hacked out back to solid wood and treated with colour-less wood hardener solution. This is a quick-drying liquid with a resin that binds and hardens the surrounding decayed fibres of the wood. The two-part filler is resin-based to provide a very tough repair that can be drilled, screwed, sanded, planed and painted. It bonds and adheres to the surrounding wood but is flexible enough to move with the wood's natural expansion and contraction. Its life is probably longer than the wood itself because it doesn't shrink, crack, split or fall out. As with all timber treatments be sure that the wood has time to dry out so that the moisture content is not excessive. Further protection is afforded by the insertion of wood preservative pellets pushed into pre-drilled holes. Then cover the holes with a wood filler or pieces of dowel. If moisture enters the wood in this area the pellets are activated and preservative is released to protect the wood.

Preservatives A wooden sill has to be preserved and protected, providing it is still sound, even if it you have solved a problem of rot or fungal attack. Sufficient preservative solution can be brushed or sprayed on to the wood to prevent fungal attack, rot or even insect attack. The more preservative that the wood takes in and the greater the depth of its penetration, the more effective it will be. Most preservatives are carried in an organic solvent, which enables them to penetrate easily and readily into timber, giving a high degree of efficiency. They are ideal for DIY application by simple methods: brushing, dipping or spraying. Most are reinforced by the addition of a water repellent to the preservative compound. This slows down the rate at which wood gets wet. Keeping timber sills dry not only helps preservation but, more importantly, helps control

Poor workmanship and no maintenance can cause the problems seen here. The timber sill and the architrave have never had a protective coat and so retain moisture leading to rotting. The lead flashing is poorly cut and dressed at the side joints allowing at weathering at the gaps. However the front apron is a good length.

It is not good practice to try to solve a rot problem in exterior timber by using plaster filler and paint! A long-life repair can be done with a three-part epoxy-resin repair kit.

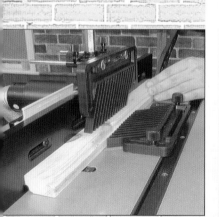

Timber used in the construction of buildings is powerfully strong, firm and will last for years – if protected! Neglect it and soon it will crumble in your hands. Sills, particularly, need three coats of wood-preservative to prevent rot setting in and total collapse.

Safely guide a timber sill on a router bench to cut the nosing and the back tongue.

Note that the hands are kept well clear. A guide is used to push the sill, non-return flexible clamps prevent 'kick-back' and an extractor hose removes all debris.

movement thereby reducing the irritating nuisances of doors and windows sticking or leaving gaps at the sills.

Replacing a wooden sill
When a window is made the sill is the heaviest piece of timber in the construction and is an integral part of the frame. Some sills have a galvanised metal water bar inserted and all types have a particular profile that is fairly standard. Make a note of the end profile and the length of the sill before ordering a new one. Replacement sills are available at most timber stores.

Start in the morning on a dry day so that you get the job finished the same day! As you remove the old sill, note that there will be weatherproofing or damp-proofing inserted. Saw through the sill in two places near the uprights to cut it free and so that the centre part can be levered free first. Make the cuts angled out at the front so the piece slips out because it is cut narrower at the back and wider at the front. Carefully free the two remaining sections by levering, trying not to hammer which might move the uprights of the timber frame. Without disturbing the frame, which is securely fixed to the reveals, completely clean the corners of debris and any fixings. If you are not certain of the profile, use the centre-piece to get a match. Again, treat all the cut ends, when cleaned, with preservative containing a fungicidal additive. Use a mastic gun to apply the bead of sealant everywhere that the new sill is in contact with the frame and the brickwork. You might find it easier to replace the sill from the inside but it does depend on the construction detail. You must check whether the bottom ends of the side members of the existing window frame need to be sawn through at the base. If you do this you will also need to cut the new sill at both ends to fit around the framework. Glue and screw the component parts and seal totally with an exterior silicone mastic. Cartridges of coloured mastic are available so that you can match your existing decor.

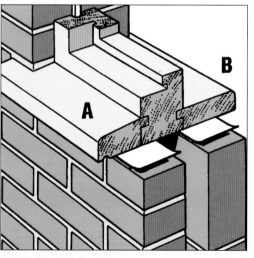

Replacing windows

A – exterior sill. B – interior sill.

Both sills are wooden and part of the structure of the window frame. This illustration will help you to make repairs or fix a replacement window. Note the essential damp-proof material under both sills.

Repairing an outside windowsill

First remove all flaking paint using a hot air gun and spoke shave. Make sure to use a residual current device when working outside with powered tools. Wear protective goggles and gloves.

This stone sill and the door have been allowed to deteriorate over the years with disastrous results. The sill has lost all its protective mortar pointing so frost will continue to open up the joints.

Stone sill If a stone sill has not been protected by a seal or by paint, it will deteriorate and delaminate with bits falling off periodically. If the sill is still solidly built in and is sound beneath the flaking top, repair it! Use a bolster chisel and a club hammer to remove the top layer of flaking stone. You might find it easier to use a hammer drill and masonry bit to drill down about 20 mm (³/₄ in) over the whole of the area of the sill to help ease the chiselling. Remove just a quarter of the thickness of the sill and level it. Remove all dust and give it a coat of diluted PVA to help seal the surface and also to help the new mortar mix adhere to it. Cut pieces of wood to fix temporarily to the sill so that the new mortar is set to the same shape and size as the original sill. Slightly slope the top of the sill down from the back. The mortar mix should be one part cement, five parts builder's sand with a water-repellent additive. The mortar will set in two days but can still be 'green' when you can remove the wooden slats that make up the 'former'. Allow the mortar to thoroughly cure before painting it to match the existing sill.

If a stone sill has a few minor cracks, the problem is easily solved with one of the many proprietary brands of filler on the market. A quick-setting ready-mixed mortar is already waterproofed and is applied with a filler knife. Rake out the cracks and undercut to provide a key by making the bottom of the hole wider than at the surface. Dampen with a diluted PVA mix before applying the quick-drying mortar. Use a wet soft brush before it cures, which can be minutes, to get a smooth, flush finish. Sand the whole top surface before repainting with an exterior quality paint system.

exterior

Doors and windows

A totally neglected sash window showing how weathering can wreck unprotected paint, putty and timber.

With a powered planer plugged into a residual current device you can safely work outside to plane small amounts off a window frame to make it fit. Prime immediately to offset any danger of moisture attacking the wood.

Frames

We are all presented with problems of protecting the exterior of our homes whether we live in the countryside, in a polluted town centre or at the seaside. Every surface of the outside of our homes is subject to the UV rays of the sun, which distort paint on wood and cause blisters. Frost and ice can split open timber joints of a window frame or even the

Rotten door posts (1)
If a door post (for a garage, shed, outbuilding, etc.) is not protected the bottom will rot, especially if it is in contact with the earth. Soak a post by standing it in a bucket of preservative before fitting. If the remainder of the post is sound, cut only the rot away, then trim the post into a splice joint.

Rotten door posts (2)
Cut a replacement base for the post from a length of timber that has been pretreated and has a long-life guarantee. Mark the cutting positions from a template traced around the side of the existing post. Cut as shown. Dig a hole large enough to slide in the overlength replacement and pour in concrete. Apply an exterior silicone sealant between the spliced sections before securing the pieces together with post bolts.

brickwork to which a window frame is attached. Add to this sulphur, salts and pollutants and you begin to see why the exterior surfaces of our homes need care. They probably need more attention and protection than they get. Often it's a case of providing more than the ordinary stain or gloss to protect doors and window frames. Fortunately, there are now high-quality coatings available formulated for specific uses. These provide the solution to the problems of sealing, staining and protecting.

Manufacturers now pre-treat timber used in the exterior construction of our homes with a preservative forced in under pressure. We are often confronted with a problem that has been building up over a very long period. If the property is Edwardian or Victorian, and if parts have not been properly protected, we suffer the consequences. However, most problems can be solved with the aid of newly formulated products with a DIYer in mind. These preservatives, varnishes, stains, primers and unique durable top coatings, which prevent moisture penetration and resist the UV rays of the sun, make problem-solving so easy. The top coatings allow the wood to shrink, expand and contract, providing a lasting protective coating which bonds with the wood. They are also resistant to cracking, peeling or flaking. They are ideal for timber that is built in against masonry like window and door frames.

Rot Typically a wooden frame is exposed to rainwater being shed on to it from above and any defects already there will precipitate wet rot. There is now a three-part paint and repair system to cure damp. Hack out all the soft wood back to the sound timber. Apply the 'hardener' liquid to the affected parts and beyond. Allow it to dry out before applying the 'filler'. This is specially formulated to give a tough, rot-resistant finish, which can be moulded and sanded to the background shape. Small pellets are then inserted into the predrilled holes around the affected area. Wood filler covers the pellets and seals the holes. These pellets are, over the years, slowly imbibed by the surrounding wood to give it permanent protection from further damp attack.

Removing rotten wood
Allow the wood to dry thoroughly. Remove all soft timber back to a solid edge. Clear out all the debris.

Hardening the surrounding timber
Saturate the exposed timber with the 'hardener' solution. Be sure to wear gloves. Leave to dry. Clean the brush afterwards with thinners.

Filling the hole
Fill the hole with the mixed filler. Match the shape and profile of the frame. Allow to cure, then sand flat. Paint or stain to match.

Loose frames If a frame loosens there is more than one problem to solve. The brickwork to which it is fixed must be repaired (see the section on Brickwork). The seal between the wooden frame and the brick reveal has to be renewed. When a house was built, it was common practice to continue the mortar pointing into the gap between the brickwork and the timber frame. However, settlement and movement, however small and imperceptible, will cause rigid cement mortar between two different building materials to crack. Eventually it falls out leaving cracks and holes through which rainwater will penetrate. Remember that even the tiniest hairline crack across a cement fillet or pointing can give access to water through capillary action. Unfortunately, over a period of time, this will be seen on an inside wall, which is a nuisance that nobody wants to experience. The solution to this problem is to use a seal to protect that vulnerable gap. A builder will use a cartridge and gun with a flexible mastic sealant for one of the last jobs to complete a present-day house under construction. All window frames and all door frames have this protective treatment.

Sealing the frame to the opening

If a problem occurs in an old type of dwelling, the cost and ease of solving the problem is within everyone's grasp. Make certain that brickwork is repaired or repointed, loose filler or cement is removed and debris brushed away. Apply the mastic in a continuous bead and smooth with a wet spatula. Alternatively, after the bead has been applied, use a spray bottle of tap water to dampen the bead and smooth with an old knife blade or the back of a spoon handle.

The upper edge of a window frame is also vulnerable because most windows do not have a drip on the outside wall. Rainwater from all the wall area above the window will run down to continue its course along the top reveal or soffit to the top of the frame. If the seal is broken it should spur you into action to repair it immediately. This is a sort of forgotten area when most damage can be done to the internal structure and decoration. Rainwater can seep in

Loose frames
Fischer frame fixings are designed to be hammered into a wooden frame and brickwork. The plug is an integral part of the holding device and stays in the wood and wall.

Sealing a wooden frame to brickwork
Stop water penetrating a window or door frame by applying a mastic sealant. Apply this with a cartridge gun. Any joint between brickwork and timber is vulnerable to water penetration because timber moves and brick and stone does not.

for ages to cause rot problems in the window frame, only to be discovered when paint blisters and soft fibrous wood is discovered beneath.

Sliding sash windows Sliding sash windows are less often used in house construction these days, however, they were commonly used in the nineteenth and early twentieth centuries. Many of us still have to contend with problems of wear in older window frames. In this type of window, the sashes slide vertically and are counterbalanced by weights hung on sash cords. The weight system is hidden in a box built into the sides of the window frame. From the front of the frame it is not apparent that heavy iron bars are going up and down every time the window is opened. The rope and pulley working over the years is bound to wear and the rope needs to be replaced as soon as it shows signs of fraying.

Seal the cracks between a frame and brickwork with a mastic sealant gun.

Sash cords   Never just replace the one that is broken or worn. It's always worth doing both. The box which houses the sliding sashes is not the mysterious assembly of pulleys, ropes, pocket pieces and hidden weights that it seems. Once you've taken one apart, you will find it is simple to understand the problem of sash cord replacement.

Prise off the staff beads, which form a sort of picture frame around the sliding sashes. They hold in the sashes but are not so tight as to stop them moving freely. As they are mitred at the tops and bottoms, you will need to first spring the uprights out from the centre. Oval nails are used to hold them in place. You might find that releasing one upright staff bead is enough to ease a sash out. The cord is secured in a groove in the side of the sash by clout nails, which are easily extracted. To get at the weights, first ease out the pocket piece. Work from the bottom, because the top of it is usually chamfered (sloped) to wedge it back in position.

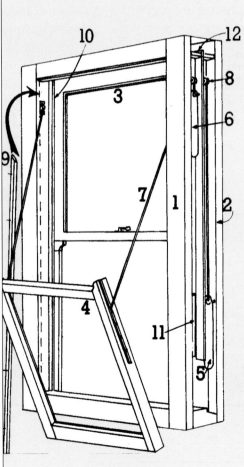

Sliding sash windows
The component parts of a vertical sliding sash window are: (1) inner lining; (2) outer lining; (3) top sash; (4) lower sash; (5) top sash weight; (6) lower sash weight; (7) cord; (8) pulley; (9) staff bead; (10) parting bead; (11) pocket; and (12) parting slip (separating the weights).

Thread the new cord over the pulley at the top and down the box to the pocket opening. If you find it difficult, drop down a 'mouse' (any small weight) on a piece of string, to pull through the sash cord. This is then knotted to the weight and nailed at the right length to the groove in the sash. This deals with the upper windows.

If the cord is broken on the lower sash, remove the wooden bead that separates the two sashes at the centre. This wooden parting bead has to be removed entirely to allow both sashes to come out. Then proceed as above. Try to prise off each of the timbers, which are relatively small in sections, in one piece so that you don't have to buy replacements. See the illustration for details of a sash window configuration.

Modern sliding sash windows usually have spiral balances with no box frames to cause problems. The manufacturers have designed them to be able to replace the traditional system of heavy weights and pulleys. The simple torsion spring and spiral rod are contained in a metal tube so the small section unit can be housed in a groove cut into the sash stile or side member in the window frame. The pair of balances is made to match the dimensions and the weight of the sashes. They are nationally available through builders merchants. Full fitting instructions come with the spiral balances. Fixings are provided for attaching the top to the frame's side and the spiral to the bottom of the sliding sash. The torsion spring can be tensioned to allow the sash to slide properly by simply unhooking the rods from the fixture and turning the rods once or twice before rehooking.

Rust   A casement window is the simplest form of window opening. It can hang on hinges at the side, top or bottom. wrought-iron casements were produced throughout the nineteenth century and in the early part of the twentieth century. These were favoured by house designers and builders because there was little movement in the metal to cause rattling in windy weather, a flaw to which wooden windows were susceptible because of shrinking and swelling. In the 1920s they were superseded

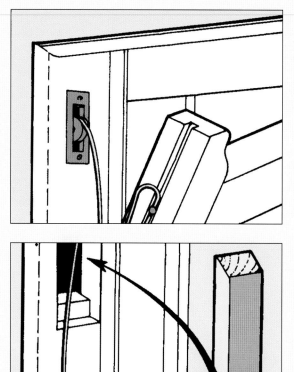

Sash window pulleys
The pulleys must be kept free from paint and dirt. Oil them occasionally to keep them running freely. The cord is fixed into a groove cut into the side of the sash but the top nail fixing must be lower than the centre of the pulley measuring from the top of the pulley stile (in which it is fixed).

Replacing a sash window cord
Remove the pocket piece after lifting out the parting bead from its groove. This gives access to the weight. Some pocket pieces are screwed into place so take care not to split the wood if paint or filler has been used to hide the screw heads. Mark the pocket pieces, left and right. Also, label the inner and outer sash weight as these sometimes differ.

by steel windows. Then came problems of rust and anyone with metal casement windows built into a house after the 1920s would have to solve this problem. Ferrous metals (iron and steel) are attacked by a combination of moisture, oxygen and carbon dioxide. The corrosion, in the form of rust, will show up on any metal where the protective coating has worn away. Paints will protect metal windows from rust penetration but the need for primers is paramount. A metal window frame should be removed from its timber surround if it is to be satisfactorily restored after rust has appeared. The frames are held in place by lugs at the sides of the frame or by screws through the frame itself. Remove the holding screws or saw through them between the metal and wooden frames. You will probably find rust at the back of the metal as well. Sand blasting, one of the best methods of getting rid of rust, will reveal gleaming metal. A DIY compressor and air pressure unit with a sand-blasting gun give a marvellous result. One can be hired inexpensively for a weekend.

If only a small amount of rust is seen, use a chemical liquid or gel stripper and either wire wool or a wire brush. A wire cup brush in a drill will shorten the time if you can get to the trouble spot easily. Wear protective clothing, goggles and, especially, gloves. Clean off with white spirit to neutralise the surface ready for the primer. Use a primer that has a rust inhibitor as a constituent. An alternative is to use a proprietary rust jelly which combines with the rust and becomes inert. The jelly is from the phosphoric acid family and forms inactive iron phosphate. Whichever method you choose to solve the rust problem, be sure to read the instructions because unless you are conscientious and do a thorough job you are wasting time and effort. Don't forget – GOOD PREPARATION IS HALF A JOB DONE SUCCESSFULLY! Brush or spray the finishing coats of metal paint to match the existing.

Coating We are all aware that the fronts of our homes create a lasting impression. Cosmetic applications are the easiest to attain, whether the front elevation is painted, stained or the beauty inherent in the grain of the wood protected by a transparent seal. Look through the protective finishes available for exterior wood in manufacturers' brochures, which are continually being brought up to date with new developments in paints and protective decorative coatings for exterior wood. When applying an oil-based finish on window frames, rub down the bare wood to get a clean, grease-free, flat surface. Wipe with a clean lint-free rag dipped in white spirit. Apply the primer, which must be compatible with the subsequent coats, to seal the timber and form a good solid base for the undercoat. Gently rub down with fine wire wool or fine sandpaper. Apply two coats of undercoat, rubbing down after the first coat is totally dry and hard. Always check the instructions on the tin and never let the paint drip down to cover the label. The directions will tell you what solvent to use for thinning and for cleaning brushes, as well as specifications related to drying and recoating times. The top oil coat will now give you a mirror-like finish that repels rainwater and which will not harbour grime caused by pollutants.

Windows

Fittings   Casement window fittings for wooden sashes include a 'peg-stay' which holds the sash in the open position. The sash, when open, is subject to wind pressure, so the pin fixed to the sill or frame will suffer movement. The stay has a series of holes to allow a graduated opening of the window. There are several causes for problems. Movement of air causes the sash to rock, the wooden corner joints of the sash will then weaken, the hinges will be under a lot of undue pressure and the stay screw fixings possibly loosen. Constant checks must be made. Larger windows are obviously going to suffer more.

Joints   If a corner joint needs attention, drill two holes through the mortise and tenon joint after compressing with a sash clamp. Glue in dowels, trim and seal. Check hinges for movement. If any screws are loose or continue to turn without biting, use a slightly larger screw of the same length or glue in plugs to make the screw hole smaller. Ensure that all the screws are driven well home into the countersunk hole in the hinge leafs. If the casement binds at the hinge side, unscrew the frame hinge leaf to insert a 'cardboard' shim. This pushes the sash a small amount away from the frame. If the frame binds at the handle side, deepen the hinge recess to bring the sash closer to that side. It may be necessary also to plane a little off a stile (side member) but if you need to plane the top or the bottom of the sash, always plane in from either side so you don't split the end grain of the side stiles.

Rattles   Movement or rattle in a closed casement window could be caused by a loose 'cockspur' fastening. This is the most common form of a closing and holding handle for a casement window. The cockspur plate is fixed to the sash and the striking plate fixed to the frame. In older houses the end of the handle ended in a delightfully curved spiral or swirl. The simplest method of solving the problem of a rattling sash is to move the striking plates slightly away from the sash. This will pull the sash closer to the frame rebate and will stop

movement. A foam self-adhesive draught strip will also help to prevent rattles if the gap is excessive. Stick it to the rebate against which the window closes on three sides but on to the frame on the hinge side.

A sliding sash that rattles when closed is easily put right. The tools you need are a claw hammer, a chisel and pincers. The top sash slides between the frame at the back and a parting bead in the centre. The lower sash slides between the parting bead and a stop bead at the front. This stop bead continues right round the frame and is about 20 mm (¾ in) square, mitred at the corners. It is easily removed because it is not glued in place but held by oval nails. Over the years, wear in the sashes and the beads results in rattling sashes, so to compensate for this movement merely move the stop bead closer to the sashes to close up the gap. Also check that the gap at the meeting point of the two sashes, where you will find them chamfered, is not too wide.

Different types of sliding sash fasteners have been designed over the years but the two original and best fasteners are still available. One of the most familiar is a latch which operates horizontally, instead of vertically like a door latch. A metal bar swings through a quarter-circle to engage in a 'keep' fitted to the top of the lower sash. The fastener draws the sashes together by the swinging of the metal arm into the curved slot and the tightening of the thumbnut on the finely threaded screw. The circular nut operates against this curved lug fitted to the lower sash and gives added security against possible forcing from the outside.

The 'Fitch' fastener is also an traditional design. A small hollowed helical leaf-shaped cam is fastened to the top of the meeting rail of the lower sash. A 'bent-finger' hook is fitted to the bottom of the upper sash. When they come together and the cam is swung under the hook, the two sashes are drawn together horizontally, forcing them up and down to prevent draughts and rattle at the meeting point and at the top and bottom of the sashes. Make sure that nobody pushes at the centre rail to raise the

Cracks in putty at the lowest edge will lead to rot – so rake out and re-putty.

After each side has been completed into the corners, the mitres form quite naturally. When you reach the final stage, excess bits of putty will come away by drawing a damp brush lightly over the putty.

Reglazing more than one pane of glass in a window that is not on the ground floor should be done with the sash removed. Hack out the glass and tacks using gloves and goggles, then prime the frame.

With a small ball of putty run a bead along the recess to form a bed for the glass.

lower sash because this will loosen the corner joints. The best way is to fix two hook sash lifts either side of the bottom rail. These make opening of the window easy and safe.

Putty Perished putty and its replacement are the most common problems on the exterior of any window. Old putty also causes the most trouble because water can seep behind the it and into the timber. Solving the problem is fairly simple but care is needed if you're working at a height.

The first indication that something is wrong is minute cracks running across the putty. You'll be amazed at how easy it is to prise out little squares of putty which have perished and lost their adhesion. New putty will adhere to glass better when the glass has been cleaned with methylated spirits.

Putty is never ready to use straight from the container. In a new tub there'll be oil floating on the top of the putty. Thoroughly work the putty with your hands so that it has no lumps but also is not too oily. Glaziers like to knead their putty, rather like dough, on a plank of clean wood. If it's too oily and is sticking to your fingers try rolling it out on a newspaper. Thoroughly clean and scrape out any residue in the small areas that need new putty. If the wood is bare, prime it. When dry, press a small amount of putty firmly into the gap. Keep moistening your fingers to prevent the putty sticking to them. Use a putty knife or a clean filling knife to smooth the putty to match the existing slope. Dip a soft, clean brush into water and smooth it in even strokes over the putty to help get a professional finish. You'll be amazed at how this smoothes out irregularities and seals the putty to the glass and to the wood.

Reglazing If the pane of glass to be replaced is not at the ground floor level, you will be faced with working on a safe scaffolding tower. Alternatively, a better idea could be to unscrew the casement window to work inside the house. In the past, glazing hasn't been counted as a DIY repair job. With the availability of safe, lightweight towers, glass cut to

Removing a broken window pane
Criss-cross the glass with tape to try and hold it together. Carefully remove all shards wearing goggles and heavy duty gloves. Clean out every bit of old putty and prime the bared wood.

size by suppliers and ready prepared putty in small tubs, you can now get professional results yourself.

Your first reglazing job should ideally be on an easily accessible ground floor window. You'll need a chipping chisel or hacking knife, a hammer, pincers, some sprigs, a putty knife, a small brush and some water. Common sense, minimal expertise, and a tub of good quality putty will get you off to a good start! Then you'll need some safety accessories: goggles and gloves, together with a container for the broken glass. I always criss-cross masking tape over a pane of glass before tapping it out. In this way the centre should come out in one piece. If it's a small pane of glass in an older type house, the glazing bars are probably lightweight so use extra caution. As you clear the old putty you'll find tiny nails called sprigs. Pull them out with your pincers. Use a quick drying primer to prepare the wood for the putty, but do let it dry completely.

Glass Glass can be cut to size at most suppliers. Take the measurement of the opening with you and get the glass cut 3 mm (⅛ in) smaller on each measurement than the opening. If, however, you are cutting the glass yourself, make sure it's the same thickness as the existing piece and take into account the thickness of the cutter against your straight

Exterior

edge. Score with a glass gutter, place match-sticks under either end of the scored line and gently press each side to snap it along the score. Take a piece of putty the size of a golf ball, and make it pliable. Press the putty gently in the rebate of the opening to make a cushion to take the glass. It should be about 3mm (⅛ in) after the glass is squeezed gently against it. Only press at the edges. Replace the sprigs, one to each side. Take care tapping in the sprigs

because if you tap too hard the sprig could go right through the glazing bar to hit the next pane of glass and break it.

Now you have to form a triangular fillet on the outside of the glass. With thumb and forefinger work the putty along one edge at a time and strike it smooth with your putty knife to form a bevel. You'll soon get the knack of joining the mitred corners together, and the great thing is that you can go on practising until you get it right. If the putty begins to stick to the knife, wet it. The excess putty squeezed on the inside of the glass is easily cut away with the edge of the putty knife. Wait for a skin to form on the surface of the putty before painting, which is essential to protect it from weathering. Never leave putty unprotected.

Metal windows   There are two differ-ences in the procedure for reglazing metal windows. Special metal casement putty must always be used and glazing clips instead of sprigs are used to hold the glass in position. As you remove the old putty, you will find the s-shaped clips clamped into a hole in the frame and sprung around the pane of glass. The special metal putty has the same properties as putty for wood so use the same techniques to prepare and apply it.

The year 2002 saw sweeping new legislation relating to glazing and windows. Part 'L' of the Building Regulations requires that all replace-ment windows and fully glazed doors are double glazed with special insulating glass. Home extensions and conservatories have to comply with the same regulations. The regula-tions do not apply to replacing a broken pane. However, if you consider replacing a small vulnerable window and frame in, say, a rear WC, then it would be advisable to consult with the Local Council Building Regulations Department. The reason for this is that the new rules could possibly affect you if at any time you were to sell your house. In future the searches of the buyer's solicitor will include a request for a certificate proving that any replacement glazing installed after April 2002 complies with the regulations.

Applying the putty
Apply putty that has been 'worked' so that it has no lumps and is pliable. Press the putty into the frame in a continuous strip or 'bead', ensuring that it is firmly bedded between the wooden frame and the glass.

Smoothing the putty
Use a putty knife or narrow scraper to pull the putty, gently but firmly, at an angle. Keep it in a straight line in touch with the wood and the glass. A brush dipped into water and stroked along the angle gives a clean seal.

Sealing putty to glass
A very effective method to prevent getting paint on to glass is to use masking tape, but it is essential to seal the putty to the glass by leaving a gap of 1.5 mm (¹/₁₆ in) between the tape and the putty. Remove the tape before the paint is fully dry.

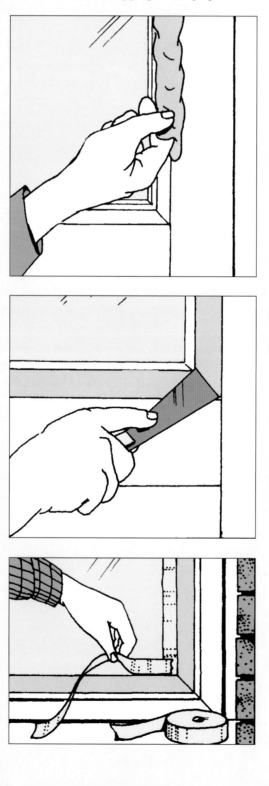

Dormers

Attic windows Natural light is provided in an attic or loft space converted to a habitable room by either a dormer window, a conventional window built into a gable end, or a roof light. Dormers project from the roof space and are framed up when the roof structure is erected. In a conversion the window framing becomes an integral part of the timber construction. Regency houses favour the wagon-head dormer for lighting top-storey rooms contained in a mansard roof behind a parapet. However, the two most common dormers to be found in Victorian and later houses are those with a small pitched roof or a flat roof. The fronts of the dormers terminate at the eaves on the front of the slope of the roof. Without scaffolding these are difficult to maintain and repair. The advantage of a Regency dormer is that it is accessible along a walkway behind the parapet wall. The frames and sashes are the same construction and therefore have similar problems to those in lower windows. (See the sections on Windows.) However, because the dormer windows are higher in the building they are obviously subjected to more weathering, and being exposed on three sides makes them more vulnerable. Check for rain penetration not just at the front of the frames but around the sides too. Cover boards protect the joint between the window frame and the constructional timber. Extra cover is then provided at the side of the dormer windows sometimes by hung slates, hung tiles, treated boards or metal sheets. Whatever the joint, it needs extra protection.

Rot Sometimes the vertical seal between two timbers on the sides of a dormer window will have broken down allowing rainwater to penetrate. This in turn could lead to wet rot. A simple solution to solve the problem of the breakdown of a seal between the two materials, whether between timber and timber or between timber and slates, is to use a strip of bitumen-based felt. Ensure that the surfaces, to which the aluminium-faced bitumen strip is to be applied, are completely dry. The bitumen can be slightly warmed to ensure that it has good adhesion. If

Two new dormers have been designed to overcome any planning problems and successfully blend in with the existing sliding sashes. Consult with your local Building Control Officer if you plan such a conversion.

These dormers have withstood the vagaries of the British weather! They are beautifully designed and crafted with stone mullioned windows, moulded stone window rain-drips, stone cheeks, decorative copings and diamond patterned leaded glazing – a testament to the inventive talents of early English builders.

Unlike most modern dormers, built simply and quickly, Victorian gables were built with consideration for the design of the whole house. Walls and roofs were solidly built and an integral part of the main structure.

Strip the flashing and the surrounding tiles to cure the problem of damp in an attic room cause by a rotten sill and a frame with a poor overlap of flashing at the sill corner. Lift the front apron to check the side cover flashings extend under the front apron.

Missing eaves tiles give problems in the attic and on top of the rear wall. The perished apron flashing allowing ingress of rainwater to rot timbers. There is insufficient overhang of front dormer roof so rainwater is shed on to tops of casement windows.

Rainwater is damaging attic timbers causing rot and spoiling decorations in a bedroom.

any of the timber shows signs of being grey or soft and spongy then wet rot has probably occurred and has to be treated accordingly. Remove all rotted timber and treat the surrounding timbers with a preservative that has a fungicide additive. Then use a wood hardener where the spongy wood was removed. A filler of resin and hardener is best to fill any holes. Use new pre-treated timber to replace the rotted wood and removed timber facings. Seal with paint to match or use a proprietary varnish type paint or sealer. Complete the job with exterior mastic sealant on all vulnerable joints.

Where a dormer is capped by a flat roof, it was generally finished with sheet metal, either lead, copper or zinc, laid to a minimal fall. The sheet metal could also be used as the cladding for the sides (cheeks). These triangular side areas were sometimes waterproofed with slate or tile hanging. Sometimes the cheeks are glazed in part to admit more daylight into the attic room. The side glazing is called a 'fixed' light, with no opening features, so these are easier to make watertight.

Perished putty
Casement windows that are difficult to repair or reglaze from the outside can be unscrewed and worked on indoors. Dormer windows, being the highest in the building, require special attention and therefore one has to think SAFETY FIRST, DIY SECOND. It is always easier to remove a casement by unscrewing the hinge leaf at the frame side. In this way you can also improve the screw holding when replacing the sash. Test the screws for 'holding' and if necessary either plug the holes or use a higher gauge screw to give more purchase in the screw hole. Brass screws are better for windows because of the risk of

steel screws rusting and becoming embedded in the timber.

If the putty is perished only in places, don't think of just replacing those patches. Hack out the lot, once the sash is safely indoors. Laying the sash flat on a protective cloth makes it easy to run a putty knife on a horizontal surface, unlike working on a sash in situ where one cannot retain the same pressure on the putty knife, going vertically and horizontally (see paragraph on Putty for details of preparation and puttying of glazed windows).

Reglazing
Original dormer windows in an older style house are constructed of bulky wooden frames and strong, firm glazing bars. The rebate, into which the glass sits, is usually deep enough to take a double-glazed unit so it might be worth considering this added refinement for the thermal and sound insulation of the attic room, and hence the house. We know that heat losses are more from an attic room and especially through a single-glazed window. Glass merchants stock all sizes of double-glazed units or they can be ordered and made to size. You can fit them yourself. Instructions come with the unit, which is simpler to fit than a conventional pane of glass. Expect it to be heavier, of course, but bedding it into a frame laid flat on the floor is not difficult. The extra care that you'll need to think about is because of its extra weight when lifting the reglazed sash to rehang it. Have a practice run with the unglazed lighter sash before you tackle the heavier job!

Skylights
In places where something simpler than a dormer or lantern light was required for giving extra daylight in attic

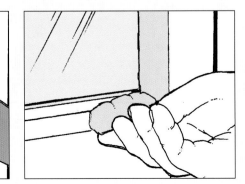

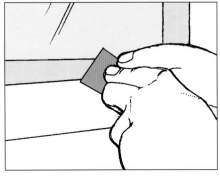

Excellent examples of: (1) a repointed parapet wall; (2) re-bedded coping stones; (3) lead flashing sealing a lean-to roof to a wall; (4) perfectly laid slates; (5) a built-in skylight; and (6) a front lead apron to a skylight.

rooms, the Victorians incorporated skylights or roof lights built into the rafters in the same plane as the pitch or slope of the roof. A rafter was cut to the required length and cross members of the same dimensions formed an oblong opening. A wood lining was fixed to take the frame to which the window sash was then attached. The whole construction was weatherproofed on the outside. The basic design is the same whether or not the skylight was made as a 'fixed' light or as an opening one. The opening mechanism is simply a pair of strong, non-ferrous hinges fixed to the sash head and the timber curb below.

Replacement Prefabricated skylights are available at most timber merchants and DIY outlets. They come in standard sizes and can be fitted very easily into a newly formed opening in the roof or as a replacement for a badly performing older skylight. The instructions for fitting a new skylight are very comprehensive and cover tile or slate roofs and the weather-proofing essential on the outside. Do take care to follow explicitly the fitting instructions, then you'll be proud of your DIY roof problem-solving.

When you want to renew or fit a new skylight, check first with your supplier who is informed and will be helpful at the early stages. The makes generally available are supplied with flashings to match the metal cladding of the sash surfaces. These flashings are available in different profiles compatible with slates, tiles or pantiles (curved). The windows are normally supplied with sealed double glazing already fitted. This of course prevents condensation forming, a problem in attics with single glazing. Designed to fully open, they usually incorporate a vent in the top of the window frame. This can remain open even in the worst rain, yet not allow water penetration.

To substitute an outer worn or damaged skylight with a modern replacement is a job worth tackling and will not disrupt the character of any existing roof pattern. One big difference between older style skylights and modern ones is the hinge position. Nowadays the problem of cleaning and maintenance is solved by the centre pivot hinge, enabling the window to open fully to a vertical position. However, top hung windows are also available but are designed for fitting to a 75° pitched roof. Fortunately skylights can be fitted and fixed from inside the attic, which is safe and easy. Only a basic tool kit and instructions are needed. The one important consideration in positioning and fixing the skylight is if a major timber runs across under the rafters (a purlin). This is an integral part of the supporting timbers of the roof and should not be cut or disturbed. Planning permission is not usually needed to install a skylight but it does depend whether your property is in a conservation area or is a listed building. However, do contact the Building Department of your local Council because you're making a structural alteration and it will be necessary to seek Building Regulation approval.

The final position for the new skylight will depend upon the timber configuration in that part of the attic where you want it located. The bottom of the window should ideally be in line with slates or tiles, as specified by the supplier's instructions, and full or half slates or tiles positioned either side. The dimensions for the full opening, after you've removed battens, felt and rafters, will be in the specification. The new frame minus the glass unit will then fit the opening and is screwed into place. Follow the illustrated instructions to complete the outside weatherproofing with slates or tiles and the full flashing kit. You'll get most satisfaction when you slot the glazed sash into place and see it opening and closing smoothly on its central pivot. All fixing positions are pre-drilled for you. Then comes the small amount of making good on the inside ready for decorations and the pleasure of a problem solved.

A centrally pivoted skylight with a double-locking mechanism. A double-glazed unit is relatively easy to fit because it will come with fully illustrated easy-to-follow instructions.

Soil pipes

Architectural design in this country has improved immeasurably since Edwardian days, mostly because techniques have been modernised but particularly because materials have been developed to make building easier and speedier. For example, only two types of pipe for underground drainage were available to Victorian and Edwardian builders, cast-iron and salt-glazed stoneware pipes.

Although in those days every attempt was made to avoid laying drains below the house for fear of damage to the pipes, in terraced houses it could not be avoided. Damage could be caused by settlement or by subsidence to the pipes that drained from the rear to the front where the main sewer was located in the street. In the best quality work, the drains directly under the house, which perhaps were subject to more distortion, were carried out in cast-iron, giving a very rigid construction, less liable to collapse. However, high costs caused builders to rely instead on encasing stoneware pipes in concrete where they passed below a building. Two manholes were incorporated in this arrangement, one at the rear and one at the front. These gave access for maintenance and rodding.

It's as well to know that older type manholes or interceptors were constructed of only 10 cm (4 in) single skin brickwork. They have always been prone to damage from frost. The top bricks collapse and the seal is then broken. Also, the stoneware pipes had a collar at one end into which the next pipe in line was inserted and then held in position with neat Portland cement or equal parts of sand and cement to give it tremendously rigid joints. This was one of the contributing factors to underground drainage problems, with consequent problems for the integrity of the whole run of pipes and drains. A further problem was found to exist where pipes leaked and saturated that part of the subsoil. All tree roots, and particularly willow, grow towards water. The finest roots, which are found farthest from the tree, can easily enter the pipe through

the smallest of cracks and gaps, ultimately choking the drain.

Another problem can occur where underground drainage pipes leak because of damage. If a leaking drain is not spotted or if it's ignored, the ground becomes more and more marshy and less able to support the foundations of the house. Subsidence problems occur because of soil drying out. Conversely, saturated soil can cause structural damage through 'heave' when too much water is in the ground and has nowhere else to go.

It is neither necessary any longer to run soil pipes above or underground in cast-iron with joints caulked (filled) with lead nor is there need for glazed stoneware pipes with rigid cement joints. The technological development of plastics in manufactured building materials has been phenomenal in recent years. This is particularly so in the plumbing and drainage industry. Robust UPVC (plastic pipes) can be used for mains water but also increasingly for underground drainage. Add to this the flexible joint system of joining pipes together and you have a wonderful improvement all round. Modern adhesives, specially formulated to totally bond plastic to plastic, will give a totally effective leak-proof plumbing run.

In modern building work designers and builders aim to run 10 cm (4 in) soil discharge pipes in ducts inside the house. This obviously prevents attack by pests, pollution and frost. The exterior of a nicely decorated house looks better too without pipes spoiling the overall look.

In some older properties we still see lead or cast-iron soil pipes carrying drainage above ground to the sewer system. When houses are being improved today, it is normal practice to swap cast-iron for light grey UPVC waste pipes, soil pipes and vent pipes. These are generally maintenance-free and have the advantages of being light to handle and that the joints between sections of pipe are made leak-proof with a plastic solvent cement. This cement is formulated to be used only on compatible

UPVC systems. Also a full range of fittings for the different patented systems, including the moulded plastic versions of all accessories, akin to cast-iron drainage, is available at most DIY outlets.

If a cast-iron soil pipe leaks at a joint, check how the collar was caulked. Originally the joint would have been filled with molten lead but if it was jointed to a stoneware socket then cement would have been used. It is difficult to remove lead, especially if working at a height. The easiest and most effective method of sealing a leaking joint is to use a modern proprietary product that can be applied with a brush and which adheres to any building material. These seal immediately even on soil pipes and cure completely in three to four days becoming inert so they are not affected by waste products.

Soil pipe joints
If a leak occurs in a UPVC soil pipe joint, repair it safely from a ladder or lightweight scaffolding tower. Brace a ladder at its base and use a 'stand-off' at the top. This is a device, anchored to the stiles (side pieces) of the ladder, with arms extended to the front to keep the ladder about 30 cm (1 ft) away from the wall and the pipe.

Older joints would have been sealed either with a rubber ring or by bonding the pipe into the socket with solvent cement, so it is unusual for a joint to become loose except by lateral movement of either piece. Make sure that the clamps holding each section are firmly fixed to the wall. If not use new plugs and screws.

Once the pipes are firm and secure, dry the pipes around the joint and make sure nobody runs any water in the system at a point above the repair. Use a solvent cement for hard plastic liberally applied right around the pipe joint. You'll find the plastic softens on both touching surfaces and then bonds into one solid seal ensuring a watertight joint. Follow the instructions so that you allow the correct curing time before running water is allowed to pass the cured joint.

Various soil-pipe bends, including this 135° bend, are available for turns in pipe runs. Make sure that the seals are completely watertight.

Regularly paint a vent pipe. This is a good example of an old iron system that is still functioning properly.

Problems with cast-iron pipes

If you live in a house which was built before the 1940s it is possible that you still have cast-iron soil and waste pipes at the back of your house. One problem that modern house owners have to solve often involves the weight of the soil vent pipe, particularly where the pipe extended past the eaves and the supports have weakened or broken down over the years. Regulations relating to the height of the soil vent pipe above a top opening window are stringent. For obvious reasons the venting of a sewage system has to comply with the regulation that says 'The top of a vent pipe should be at least 1 m (40 in) above the top of any window within a horizontal distance of 3 m (10 ft). The principal purpose of a vent pipe is to allow foul air to escape from the drains in such a position that it cannot enter the building. It should also be fitted with a durable wire or plastic cage which does not unduly restrict the flow of air.'

The importance of a well-supported, airtight, pipe system to carry away waste products to the sewage and drainage system cannot be overstated. If any part of a cast-iron pipe has a fracture or even a hairline crack in it, solve the problem immediately by a temporary repair or by a permanent replacement. If the crack is a

There are many reasons why old iron soil pipes are being replaced with 10 cm (4 in) plastic ones; they are easier to handle, are relatively inexpensive, the joints are simple to fit and they remain watertight. You can even colour them to match the exterior of the house!

Back of iron pipes rust and holes form – card will protect the wall as you paint.

A cast-iron soil pipe carrying waste from the house always has a rodding (cleaning) eye at a 90° elbow.

short vertical one, make a temporary repair with one of the many proprietary tapes or bandages sold for the purpose. Otherwise replace with a UPVC system. When removing the cast-iron pipe you'll need professional help but the replacing job is a DIY application. Make certain that all the pipe clip holes are repaired and sealed. These have been the cause of many penetrating damp problems in the past!

Checking cast-iron pipes There are certain parts of a cast-iron soil pipe system that have to be monitored periodically. For example, the pipe nails that hold the pipe lugs securely to a wall are liable to rust and the wooden plugs can rot and lose their hold. Replace any that show these signs but fill the holes in the wall first and re-drill for new plugs.

cast-iron is prone to rusting especially where it has not been protected by paint. The hidden rear part of a pipe against a wall is the most likely area to be neglected and it is here that rust will attack the metal and eventually cause holes to appear. Soiled water can then spill on to the brickwork. It is only because cast-iron pipes are thick that they last so long but pipes over 100 years old, if not protected, will eventually suffer rust.

A cement joint is usually found at the base of an exterior cast-iron soil pipe. The haunched cement joint is of a strong mix but problems can still arise especially with standing rainwater that freezes. If a crack appears and there is a leak, hack away sufficient cement to be able to form a new watertight cement joint. Use a mix of quick-dry cement but follow the instructions for mixing and curing. Brush the cleared-out joint with diluted PVA before applying the new mix. Protect the cement and only allow water to pass the joint after it has completely cured.

Unblocking Unblocking a cast-iron soil pipe is typically done from the top vent pipe. This is usually above the eaves so there is a safety factor to be considered. The big differ-

ence between unblocking a cast-iron soil pipe and one made of UPVC is that the latter has a series of cleaning eyes built in, whereas the former is solid with no intermediary access. The UPVC pipe will have a large openable cleaning hole into which a long wire auger can be pushed and twisted. To discharge a blockage, keep cranking the handle of the auger which will eventually clear the obstruction. Use a garden hose, preferably with a power jet, to help clear the pipe as far as the inspection cover, where you can check for further problems and take appropriate action. Use a rubber plunger on extending rods for rodding an interceptor trap which can be situated at the mouth of the drain at the outlet end of the manhole, or use an auger with a corkscrew fitting for a straight through channel. After unblocking, always hose the manhole and the surrounding area and use plenty of disinfectant. Remember SAFETY FIRST, DIY SECOND so always use proper protection, it's common sense really!

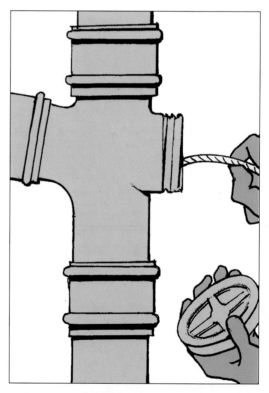

Unblocking a soil pipe
Plastic 100 mm (4 in) soil pipes are easier to clean than older cast-iron pipes. Large cleaning (rodding) eyes are located at strategic positions. Hire a flexible drain auger which has a cranked handle. Wear gloves and protective clothing, and lay protective covers. Use disinfectant. Hose down and run plenty of water through the system to flush.

The drawing shows the component parts of a typical plastic rainwater system.

Gutters – these are supported by brackets screwed to the fascia board. If the rafter ends are left open, the supporting brackets are fixed to the tops or sides as shown.

Rainwater pipes – plastic pipes are held onto a wall by circular clips with a lug and two screw holes. The shoe end sits over a yard gully which is connected to the drainage system.

Rainwater pipes

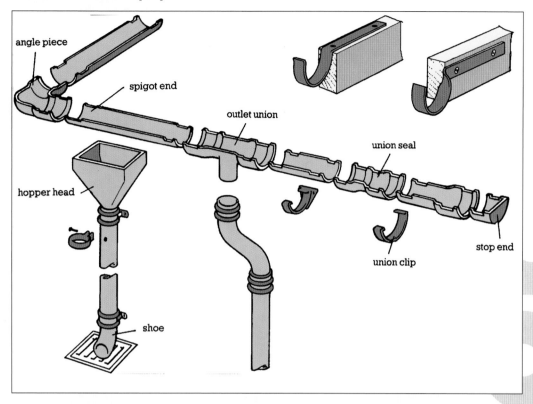

Clear gutters of debris every year and insert a wire basket in the outlet.

On a rainy day it really is amazing how hundreds of litres of water are discharged from a small roof of say 40 m² (50 yd²) into a gutter through an outlet and into a downpipe. Multiply that by say 200 days and it gives an indication of the importance of maintaining a drainage system that stays watertight and efficient. When a house is designed, consideration is given to the size and pitch of the separate parts of a roof. Based on these calculations, the number of gutters, outlets and downpipes is calculated, so any alteration to what is already fixed on your house could affect the performance of successfully discharging even the lightest downpour of rain. Don't be tempted to replace two downpipes either end of a gutter with one central one – you'll get blockages. Adding right-angled bends (or offsets) will slow down the flow capacity and water will build up behind the bend. This can lead to water overflowing on to walls causing damp problems. A rainwater downpipe is an important part of the water discharging process as it carries all the shed roof water to the underground system. It is vulnerable to blockages, which in turn can cause wet walls and penetrating damp problems.

Leaks in UPVC downpipes can be caused by being accidentally struck, by degradation through UV rays of the sun, or by the freezing of water built up through blockages. Leaves are the main cause of blockages, but only if a wire balloon is not used in the gutter stop-end outlet. This prevents leaves entering the outlet and being washed into the downpipe. Regular gutter clearing in the autumn is a MUST. Do not attempt to cement the lengths of downpipe together if an O-ring is an integral part of the spigot and socket joint. UPVC lengths of pipe have a socket at the top into which the bottom end of the upper length sits. Under each socket a circular pipe clip supports the weight of that length of pipe. The reason for this is very important and should not be overlooked. The pipe that sits inside a socket must have an expansion joint of about 6mm (¼ in) to allow for heat expansion in the sun.

At the lower end of a downpipe the rainwater is usually discharged into a yard gully. There are two types of gully built into the system to take both surface water and rainwater from roofs. One is an open gully and here a shoe is used to

Water-butts are inexpensive and easy to link to your rainwater pipe.

throw the water away from the wall and into the gully. The alternative is to fit the downpipe into what is termed a back inlet gully. The square gully with the grating has a separate circular hole behind it into which the spigot end of the downpipe is secured.

Cast-iron   A cast-iron downpipe, on a present day house, is probably a legacy from Victorian days. It is rigid with solid joints, so any building settlement or subsidence could cause problems with broken joints or cracked pipes. Sections of pipe with lugs or 'ears' already cast on to the pipe for fixing each part to the wall were manufactured. Each ear is fixed to a horizontal mortared joint with two 100 mm (4 in) wrought-iron pipe nails. I would recommend totally replacing a cast-iron down-pipe and gutter as soon as deterioration, cracks

or splits are seen. A repair to cast-iron of that age can probably only be a temporary one. Rust build up over a period of time can cause a hole in a cast-iron pipe in a position that it is difficult to spot and it might only become obvious when a nasty brown stain appears behind and around that part of the pipe where there is a problem. This is a notoriously common problem with cast-iron soil and rain-water pipes and arises only because it is diffi-cult to paint when the pipe is so close to a wall. There is a solution to this leaking problem without having to replace a section of the pipe. Paint the rust with a rust-inhibitor jelly which removes and neutralises at the same time. The combined process forms an inert covering which can then be painted with a metal primer to protect the metal. Use self-adhesive webbing and a proprietary mastic coating. This will solve the leaking problem and prolong the life of the cast-iron pipe. To

Cast-iron rainwater pipes become brittle with age and rust appears at vulnerable spots. Emulsion paint has not covered up this cracked and rusty joint or stopped water pouring out. It is best to replace the whole length with manageable plastic pipe.

paint the back of the pipe without getting paint on the wall, hold a piece of stiff cardboard against the wall and move it down to paint each section.

Leaks in UPVC Replacement or repairs of UPVC downpipes is simpler. Just take out the section affected and replace it with a matching piece. All parts are available in DIY outlets. If the repair is a minor one, an easy and effective method of solving the problem is to use a DIY brush-on treatment repair kit or similar. A self-adhesive repair bonding tape usually comes with the compounds. This will cover a split, crack or even a hole. Once the tape is in place, the compound is brushed on and overlaps on to the pipe. It is immediately effective but cures hard in 3–4 days.

An alternative is to use a proprietary can of spray-on mastic. This asphalt preparation will cover cracks and splits but can also be used in conjunction with a patch of glass fibre netting. Spray a coat of mastic around the hole, firm it with the netting, then recoat all the edges to ensure a watertight seal.

Renewing UPVC downpipes You will need to work from a safe ladder or a lightweight scaffolding tower because replacing a UPVC downpipe means starting at the top. At the gutter outlet, measure the distance to the wall from the outlet. Joining the gutter outlet to the downpipe position will mean fitting two offset bends joined by a short length of pipe with a top end socket. This will all depend on the distance from the gutter outlet back to the wall and it is really the amount of eaves overhang that you have to take into consideration. Fix the top length of the downpipe in position with a pipe clip and screws. Always remember SAFETY FIRST, DIY SECOND when drilling into an outside wall. Plug into an RCD indoors. Work safely from a secured ladder or scaffolding tower. Use a masonry bit that is compatible with the plug and screw. Use only rustproof screws. Having measured the distances necessary to make the offset or swan neck, take the pieces to a bench. Lay the three modules for the offset flat on the bench and use

UPVC solvent cement to fix them together. The rest of the pipe joints in the run must not sit tightly together but have a 6 mm (¼ in) expansion joint between the bottom end of a spigot and the shoulder of the socket.

If a hopper-head is needed to receive waste pipes from other sources, treat it as part of the downpipe system. Position it so that the other waste pipes discharge properly into the hopper allowing the rainwater from the roof to run through unhindered.

Colouring UPVC It is possible with a brand new invention to colour-match your UPVC pipes and gutters. The innovative bonded coating comes in a huge selection of colours and is a DIY application. Easy to apply by brush, the third coat gives both a deep colour and a protective coat unaffected by UV rays. It is a revolutionary new water-borne coloured coating for exterior and interior plastics which solves the problem of non-adhesion of ordinary paint on plastic. All residual dirt and grease and other contaminants must be removed with a strong detergent to ensure good adhesion. Always rinse with clean water. Start only on a dry and clean surface. Mask all areas not to be painted. A synthetic tapered brush is best because it gives a smooth surface and there is no loss of bristle. Leave for at least one hour before applying the second coat. When that is dry, sand with 300 grit wet-and-dry paper (just like on a car). Then apply a third coat. Instead of renewing you can save time and money by restyling and colour-matching gutters and downpipes to doors and windows. You'll get a great thrill seeing a magnificent transformation.

Gutters

Guttering is so often a neglected part of the rainwater drainage system of a house and yet it is an integral and essential part of successfully discharging and shedding rainwater from the roof. Badly designed and installed guttering can make a difference between a home that has dry internal walls and one that is continually damp. Peeling paint or wallpaper in bedrooms near

Gutters are there to properly discharge hundreds of gallons of rainwater into the drainage system – when they're in working order! Missing gutters will cause rot in timber-framed buildings and destabilise the ground beneath.

the ceiling are indications either of condensation or of a penetrating moisture problem. If a gutter is not properly aligned at the correct distance from the eaves slates or tiles (as little as 6mm (¼ in) can make a difference), rainwater can and will be thrown on to the wall and not into the gutters. It is essential to follow the guidelines of the original design for the guttering and downpipes. These have been designed with consideration given to the roof area, to the gutter size and to the number of downpipes to safely discharge the maximum amount of rainwater. If the eaves slates have an edge of roofing felt showing underneath and lipped over the guttering, it is there to prevent rainwater being whipped back in high winds which would then cause internal damp problems.

Cast-iron
Cast-iron was used extensively on Victorian and Edwardian houses for gutters and downpipes and you might still have them on your property. They could be a half round section or the more popular Ogee profile that always formed a decorated pattern. Then came a long period of 'ease and speed' of maintenance and installation with plastic so the Ogee profile, except where it has been preserved by house owners sensitive of their heritage, became obsolete. Now, however, this gutter profile is once again in vogue.

The edge of roof slates at the eaves should project about 25mm (1 in) in front of the vertical fascia board (on to which the guttering brackets are fixed). This ensures that shed rainwater falls into the gutter fitted underneath. A lesser projection would allow the water to be blown back below the slates and run down the fascia board on to the wall to cause damp problems.

Unfortunately, there is an inherent defect in cast-iron guttering. The rusting of the flat back plate of the moulding around the fixing nails causes leaks and the eventually collapse of entire lengths of the gutter. Another common problem is the metal putty used to seal the joint between two lengths of gutter. After the putty is applied a small nut and bolt draws the two parts together to squeeze the putty into a watertight seal. Over the years this is obviously going to be vulnerable to degradation.

I've heard it said that one advantage of a solid cast-iron gutter is that a ladder can be leaned against it. Remember though SAFETY FIRST, DIY SECOND – cast-iron can become very brittle, the joint bolts can rust and break and bracket screws weaken over a long period, so play safe and use ladder stays.

Aluminium
For some time there has been a great demand for putting back historically interesting and architecturally correct period details on a house. One of the most interesting developments is to use aluminium to form Victorian Ogee-shaped gutters. Manufacturers saw the need and designed a machine which forms colour-coated strip aluminium to Ogee and other shapes. Obviously, aluminium is thin-walled and has to be respected as such, however it is lightweight and very easy to install.

UPVC
Moulded plastic UPVC guttering is used almost universally in new building work and in the restoration of houses. Standard colours are black, white and grey. Black is probably used the most for various reasons: against the overhang shadow of a roof it disappears and, also, the carbon black constituent of the compound safeguards the plastic gutter against rapid degradation by UV rays. If you are solving a particular replacement problem, don't add to it by ordering a section that is incompatible with the existing piece. Plastic gutters can come in different profiles and sizes with various forms of sealing of the joints. They can be clip-fastened with rubber seals or cemented with solvent. Brackets are usually screwed to the fascia board and the gutter section is squeezed

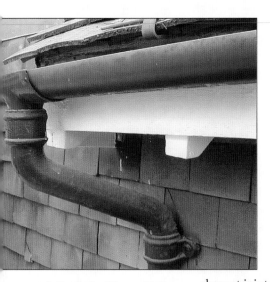

Gutter faults: (1) no rubber seal between gutter and outlet to pipe; (2) badly fitting plastic outlet to cast-iron swan-neck; and (3) gutter bracket 'lug' broken so the gutter has no fixing.

into the top tight-fitting lugs. The eaves gutter system is joined into one long continuous channel that is totally supported on brackets about 90 cm (3 ft) apart. Make sure that its brackets support every joint to ease the pressure on that vulnerable area.

Repairs If a UPVC guttering section has suffered degradation due to neglect or to attack by UV rays, drips begin to show at joints and at splits. The synthetic rubber gaskets formed in the sealed joints can degrade and allow leaks. A build-up of debris and leaves can cause blockages at a running-outlet or at a stop-end outlet. These two outlets, one in the middle of a run and the other at the end, feed rainwater into the socketed pipe. Usually an offset is connected to it and to a straight section fixed to the wall. The offset or 'swan's neck' will have to be of a particular length to fit exactly between the gutter outlet and the vertical pipe because of the eaves overhang. A proprietary brand of self-adhesive repair kit is available to repair splits and cracks in plastic gutters. New gaskets (rubber seals) are available to replace those which are worn or damaged. Instructions are easy to follow and the gasket easy to fit. Special solvent cement successfully bonds two plastic surfaces together to make a watertight seal. Sometimes pipes simply fit into sockets with no adhesive. If a blockage occurs in a gutter outlet

Rainwater has been pouring down the pipe and shedding onto the brickwork. Decorations are spoiled and mortar perished because nobody spotted the disconnection.

and the debris is tight in the offset pipe, use a blockage discharge pressure tool to dislodge the debris through the length of pipe to the gully area, otherwise simply lift off the sections of pipe to hook it out.

Brackets The weight of water in a filled gutter system caused by a blockage can cause brackets to snap. Snow is very heavy and, if it freezes, can block an outlet or build up on a gutter and the supporting brackets. Sometimes, if a fascia board has not been primed and painted, moisture can cause problems particularly where the screws hold the brackets. All plastic gutter brackets have two clip ends. These can be referred to as lips or lugs. If a gutter section is wrongly forced under the clip ends they can snap off, then there is no support and

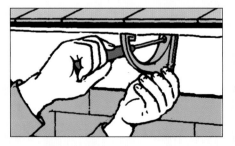

Gutter brackets (1)
All brackets must be in line but have a gradual 'fall' to the outlet. Use a piece of string tied to nails at the ends of the run to get the correct gradient. Fix the brackets at the recommended distance apart. Fix the top screw first and then use a spirit level to make sure it is vertical before fixing the lower screw.

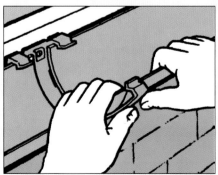

Gutter brackets (2)
All fittings holding or joining new gutters allow for expansion and contraction. When installing a new gutter, make sure that it doesn't pass the insertion depth marked on the fitting.

Gutter brackets (3)
You'll need to fit a downpipe shoe if rainwater is to discharge onto a flat surface or into an open gully. Use a supporting pipe clip to hold the shoe to a standard round section downpipe.

no stability for the gutter. It makes sense to follow the instructions for inserting gutters into the lugs of the brackets. If bracket screws are loose, replace them with larger gauge screws but use non-rust screws or glue in a wooden plug into the screw hole. Use a pilot hole. Replace brackets where necessary and follow the explicit instructions especially regarding compression of the rubber seal. If it's a cold day, here's a tip: slightly warm the brackets so that the clips are more pliable and less likely to snap.

Replacing sections

Fitting together the component parts of UPVC gutters and pipe system is like fitting together the parts of a plastic toy. It is essential to follow the instructions. Gutters come in long lengths with one end slightly wider to allow the next section to fit into it, giving an open socket and a plain spigot system. Always push the back edge of a replacement gutter into the back lug of the bracket first. By pulling up very slightly on the front lug the front of the gutter should clip under it quite easily. When the socket and spigot come together a rubber seal needs to be compressed to make it watertight. Adjust where the two ends meet to leave an expansion joint of, say, 6 mm (¼ in). We've all

heard the creaking of plastic gutters trying to find room to expand on a hot day! Don't let it be one of your problems. If you need to shorten a section, only cut at the spigot end using a magic saw (hacksaw). If a gutter edge needs notches to receive the bracket lugs, measure the positions accurately and file down 3 mm (⅛ in) to the width of the bracket.

There are numerous gutter accessories available. For example, to turn inside and outside corners to get to an adjacent wall, use one of a number of gutter angles from 90°–135°. Another useful accessory is a running outlet section which has a socket at both ends. Use this to install a downpipe at any given position in the gutter run. Simply cut the gutters either side to sit inside the sockets. Again check the profile of the system and only buy compatible types of guttering and accessories. If more than one section is needed, run a length of string between the remaining sections to get the correct 'fall' or gradient. The new brackets must be in line with the existing ones to prevent water standing in a horizontal position. Another great invention is the right-hand (or left-hand) gutter adaptor for joining two different systems together. Often it is necessary to join a plastic half round system to a neighbour's square section of older guttering. This can happen when terraced houses have a common rainwater system that has been changed in part over the years.

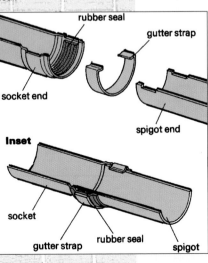

Gutters (1)
After cutting a gutter to length, measure the distance from the end to the position for the strap that clips into the notches.

Gutters (2)
To clip two lengths of gutter together, slide the replacement spigot end into the socket end. The strap will secure the ends tightly to the seal.

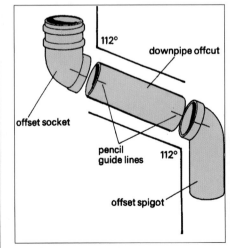

Gutters (3)
An offset socket will fit over the outlet of a gutter. The off-cut of pipe must be measured accurately allowing for the overlap at both ends.

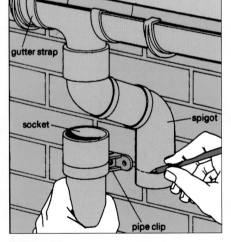

Gutters (4)
Before marking the pipe-clip screw holes, check the overlap of the spigot inside the socket.

54

Waste pipes

All waste water and waste products flow from our homes usually to an inspection manhole just outside the house and then to the main sewers. The largest pipe to be seen outside the house is the soil vent pipe which finishes well above the eaves. This is the ventilation pipe which allows air into the drainage system. Without it, if a lavatory is flushed, for example, the down-rush of waste water would suck the water out of the traps of basins and baths. These traps, or U-bends, are the bends in the waste pipes underneath basins, sinks and baths designed to hold water to prevent unpleasant smells from entering the house and causing a health hazard.

House waste pipes are usually 100 mm (4 in) internal diameter and start at the back of the lavatory. This is connected to the soil pipe (or stack) into which might be connected various other waste pipes from handbasins, baths, etc.

Siphonage   Inspection manholes are constructed where the first soil pipe leaves the house and waste is carried to the next manhole, where there is a change in direction of underground pipework or where another soil waste pipe enters the system. This method of laying pipes in straight lines with interceptors built into the system allows all the pipework to be cleaned by rodding.

The Planning and Building Regulations relating to drainage works are very straightforward. An inspector will always give free advice. The law says specifically what you can and cannot do when installing, laying or altering plumbing and waste drainage. The whole system must undergo a watertight test to the satisfaction of the local inspector. Before the 1960s cast-iron pipes were common and joints were sealed with strong cement. In the mid-1960s Building Regulations were sensibly introduced to the effect that all mains drainage stacks, soil pipes, etc., were to be built and installed within the fabric of the building. This also improved the external appearance by removing unsightly soil and vent pipes from an otherwise attractively

decorated rear elevation. The great advantage of ducting internally is not running the risk of damage by frost in winter conditions.

Often you'll see a two pipe system of waste disposal with a mass of pipes running down a rear elevation of an older but charmingly proportioned house. WCs discharged into the 100 mm (4 in) soil pipe which was kept separate from the waste pipes of sinks, basins, bidets and baths. This system was used until the 1960s and was successful in one major respect, that is, it kept waste seals intact and prevented siphonage. Siphonage is the sucking out of water from the traps and can happen if pipework is not properly designed. This can happen in a single stack system. Another health hazard, that is, the foot of the stack becoming blocked and foul water backing up the pipes, can also be present in a single stack system. All this can be avoided by proper design.

Waste pipes for bathroom handbasins can cause problems because they have the smallest pipe bore and could possibly be full of water in its entire length. This can result in water being siphoned out of the trap so there would be no seal against foul air and gases from the sewage system.

Siphonage can be avoided by a simple device. A piece of pipe connected behind the trap is joined to the main soil vent about 600–1000 mm (2–3 ft) above the highest connection. A building inspector will normally insist on this if the design of the layout suggests possible siphonage.

Blockages   If a blockage occurs in a trap beneath a sink or handbasin, then there are two ways to unblock it quickly. One is to use the very well-established method of a rubber cup on a handle, called a force cup. With a little water in the sink and a cloth held firmly over the overflow hole, push the force cup up and down over the plughole a couple of times. This should give sufficient pressure to dislodge any blockage. A more efficient method is to use a pressure cartridge, an inexpensive device that is non-chemical, non-toxic and gives a very

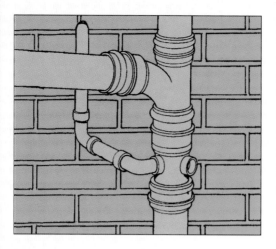

powerful blast of pressurised gas to effectively dislodge the worst blockage by creating waves along the pipe.

Access can be gained to the trap if it is blocked with, say, solidified meat fat poured down the sink after cooking – a very bad habit! As soon as hot fat meets cold water in the trap it will coagulate to form a solid mass. Some traps have a screw-on seal underneath them. Others can be disassembled by unscrewing the compression nuts at the joints. The trap contains water so use a bucket or bowl underneath to catch the residual overflow water.

WCs   If the water level in the lavatory pan rises to the rim when you flush it, there is some sort of obstruction which you'll need to clear. A force cup with a rubber plunger large enough to seal the outlet of the bowl could do the trick. Wear rubber gloves and use disinfectant to carry out this operation hygienically! Alternatively, use a pressure cartridge that has a soft rubber plunger which gives a complete seal by moulding to the shape of the pan outlet.

One or two blasts from the pressurised cartridge invariably clears the problem. Other methods still employed to clear blockages are as follows:

WC auger – this is a handle-controlled coiled-wire device. The handle is cranked and twists the short wire to dislodge a blockage close to the outlet.

Hydraulic pump – this is a hand-operated device that creates a powerful jet which sends the obstruction on its way. It can also create a vacuum to suck the water and the obstruction to the surface.

Drain auger – this is a long, thin coiled small diameter wire that will go through the smallest pipes until it reaches the blockage. The handle is cranked to engage the corkscrew end of the wire in the blockage material so that it can be pulled clear.

Remember that disinfectant and gloves are important commodities in any operation when dealing with WCs and drainage systems. If a WC in a bathroom has to be unblocked you must deal with the handbasin and bath wastes too. Usually the three units discharge into the same soil pipe and can be linked even before the main stack pipe, so there is always the possibility that a wave of pressure in one trap will draw water away from another. Always cover all the overflow outlets to prevent back siphonage in any of them. Run plenty of water into each after cleaning any blockages.

Cleaning eyes   Modern UPVC drainage systems are better designed than Victorian cast-iron ones where exterior soil pipes were difficult to unblock. Newer plastic pipes have a series of cleaning eyes properly placed to enable the clearing and cleaning of obstructions with a drain auger. Where branch pipes (waste pipes from basins, etc.) are attached to a soil pipe boss, there is a cleaning eye enabling an obstruction in that length of pipe to be cleared. The eyes are screwed on to a rubber gasket to prevent any leakage. It's possible to move the obstruction one way or another by a series of pushes and pulls. Use a garden hose to wash out the pipe and use disinfectant in and around the stack.

Keep a bag of rock salt handy to sprinkle on ice formed by dripping pipes.

Traps Most traps under sinks, baths and basins have an access cap or a screwed base which facilitates the clearing and cleaning operation. Three types of UPVC traps are the S-trap, the P-trap and the Bottle trap, and they are all accessible for cleaning. The S-trap has a side or bottom eye, the P-trap has a bottom eye, and a Bottle trap has a large opening at its base to unscrew so that the whole base can be removed. Lavatory pans have either an S-trap, where the pipes go vertically down through the floor, or a P-trap which goes horizontally through the back wall. Before starting the unblocking operation check that the nearest manhole is running clear and is not full of waste water. If it is, you'll need to hire a set of drain rods with attachments. The metre-long rods screw into each other and are extremely flexible. Screw the rubber plunger to the first rod and push it into the manhole outlet; twist the rods clockwise to help discharge the waste water. Don't twist the other way, you'll unscrew the rods! Keep adding extra rods as you go deeper into the sewer pipe. After clearing the blockage use plenty of water to clean up the area before using disinfectant and replacing the inspection cover.

Frost protection Wherever a pipe system that carries water is exposed to the air, it will be vulnerable to frost attack and freezing in winter conditions. Just as we need an overcoat and gloves, pipes need insulation too. Large diameter soil pipes never fill up with water, except when blocked, and so are not exposed to those risks, but small-bore water pipes are vulnerable and need foam lagging. This comes in various sizes to accommodate all pipes and is simply pushed on to the pipe by means of a long slit running its full length. The lagging then closes completely around the pipe.

External pipes, garden taps, etc., must be lagged but not with material that can hold water, it will obviously compound the freezing problem. Pipes that are close to the eaves in an attic must of course be lagged. In fact, all pipes and water tanks in an attic need this attention to prevent freezing and a possible burst. In wintertime, if your house is likely to be empty for a period, even as short as a weekend, put salt in all the traps and in the WC pans to prevent the water freezing and causing a split pipe or a cracked pan.

Frozen water can cause cracks in the cement around the base of a soil pipe. Check it regularly and seal it with exterior mastic.

Boards

Bargeboards

A protective bargeboard covers the vulnerable timbers at a verge on a gable-end wall. The sloping edge of the roof can end flush with the brickwork or extend past it supported by short timbers built into the wall. The drawing shows a typical 'extended' verge showing a straight bargeboard, however, often a highly decorated board is used to provide an attractive finish to a plain end gable.

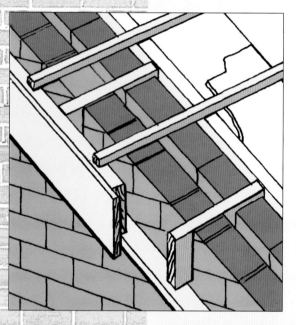

In Victorian times the lavish decoration of a property's exterior became a mark of the house-owner's status. The bargeboard was high up and large enough to be prominently seen, so ideal for artistic expression!

Bargeboards

In Victorian and Edwardian times, bargeboards on the gabled ends of houses were often elegantly carved, but the function of a bargeboard was much more important than just being a decorative feature. The junction of a slated roof with an angled gable is weatherproofed and finished by carrying the slates across the full width of the wall and on to the top edge of the wooden bargeboard. This top edge was carefully lined up with the tiling battens before being screwed into position. A bargeboard was designed to support the edges of the slates, to protect the end grain of all the tiling battens from wet and possibly rot, and to give an attractive finish to the top of the gable wall. Often a carved and moulded bargeboard complemented the intricate and decorative ridge tiles which were also a feature of Victorian roofs. Another function of a bargeboard is to protect the end of the fascia board. Eave slates normally end over a timber fascia board, the end grain being closed off by the gable bargeboard.

Nowadays, the construction of the gable end favoured by builders is somewhat simpler. If a bargeboard is used it is usually a plain board fixed to the end verge rafter. It still protects the tiling battens and supports the verge tiles but is somewhat lost as a decorative feature. A soffit board is fixed to the underside of the verge rafter in line with the front face of the rafter. This enables the bargeboard to be fixed to the rafter and to the front edge of the soffit. The lower edge of the bargeboard should act as a drip by being at least 50 mm (2 in) lower than the soffit.

With all this in mind you can appreciate that to maintain good weatherproofing and to protect vulnerable timbers from possible rot, annual checking is essential. To work at this height means having SAFETY FIRST, DIY SECOND in mind. Preferably work from a hired lightweight scaffolding tower that has foot braces; you must tie it off at gutter height. Knowledge of the roof construction at the gable will help you to check every part that could have problems.

Dry rot   If timber is not protected and is subjected to weathering, problems of rot will eventually have to be solved. The worst scenario is that rainwater might have penetrated in to the darkened void between the last verge rafter and the outer wall and below the roofing felt. Over a period of years these conditions, especially if ventilation is excluded, are conducive to dry rot. It is important that the original design of the gable end is not altered in any way as gable layouts are prone to extreme weather conditions and have to be well maintained. The design of the weatherproofing boards must not be altered. The confined space described, if badly ventilated, encourages dry rot to creep along timbers and even through walls. The white-grey strands grow at a fast rate and spread, destroying timber and causing it to lose its strength. A nasty dank smell of mouldy mushrooms will certainly confirm the presence of this most insidious form of rot. By lifting a few slates or tiles sufficiently to be able to peer in with a torch, you might find mushroom-like fruit bodies inside.

Immediate action is now necessary. All affected timber must be gently removed. Try not to disturb the fruit bodies as you remove them. They can send out a fine dust of reddish spores which settle on adjacent timbers infecting them. Wear protective clothing, a respirator mask and gloves for this operation. This fungus, called mycelium, can be removed and treated by a specialist rot contractor, but if the attack is just detectable it can be a DIY application. After cutting out the affected timber and beyond by about 300 mm (12 in), scrape off and wire brush all the brickwork then use a chemical dry rot treatment, sold in DIY stores. Follow the instructions to get the best possible results. If, however, structural timbers are affected, get advice from a builder.

Wet rot

Wet rot is a condition that affects timber outdoors as well as indoors, unlike dry rot. It needs a great deal of moisture for it to thrive. If moisture has been allowed to attack the end grain of tiling battens or to continually drip on to rafters or joists, wet rot will result. Use a penknife to prod into suspect timbers. Even though a bargeboard might have been painted, if the back was not protected, wet rot can attack it over time. Sometimes you'll see peeling paint and here your penknife test will reveal soft spongy timber underneath. Again, remove all the affected timber, use a DIY brush-on or spray application, getting it well into end grain timber and into jointed sections. If you want to replace a rotted Victorian-style bargeboard, go to your local carpentry workshop with the measurements and a photograph of the existing piece. Be sure to treat the board front, back and edges to protect it fully. Use two lightweight scaffolding towers and get help to replace it – with an expert to guide and help you, at least you'll then be part of the team!

Fixing

The two common verge types differ in that only one has a protective bargeboard fixed to an 'overhang'. A projecting verge has the extra rafter outside the brickwork, whereas a flush verge of a gable end has the last rafter inside the wall. Short pieces of timber of similar cross-section are built at staggered intervals into the sloping top of the gable wall to fix the extra rafter. These are designed to support the extra rafter nailed into the short noggins built into the wall. More support for the rafter comes from the tiling battens when nailed into the top edge of the rafter. Then the bargeboard is screwed directly into the rafter before tiles or slates are fixed in place. Nails and screws used externally must of course be galvanised or rustproof. When working at a height try to use every tool and device available to ensure that you work safely and speedily – for example, a cordless screwdriver is essential.

Protection

To more fully understand the importance of annually inspecting all boards surrounding and protecting the roof and the fabric of the house, look up at houses as you walk along the street. Owners who have neglected maintenance will have lost out on the value of their property and certainly will meet with a problem of trying to save the situation when a decision is forced upon them to get the problem solved. Paint protects but it has to be applied properly prepared. If a bargeboard is damp there is no point in applying paint. If it is flaking, scrape and sand back to the wood. You needn't bare wood where the paint is sound, just lightly sand those areas to give a key to the topcoat. Once the cleaning off and sanding is done, wipe with a cloth and some white spirit then dry the board before applying a primer to the bare area. Apply an undercoat, but sand in between to 'featheredge' the different applications. At joints and end grain make certain that every inch is covered to protect against water penetration. If any joints appear to be vulnerable to water ingress, there is a DIY solution to this particular problem. Exterior flexible mastic comes in a range of colours and can be applied with an inexpensive cartridge gun. It is certainly worth the small amount of extra work while the scaffolding tower is still in place. The added protection will last for years and will prevent joints opening between two adjacent timbers. Don't, however, seal where rainwater is not going to run and harm timbers and where the sealing might cause a ventilation problem by preventing the circulation of air.

See also pages 204–8 for details of rot and worm

Fascia boards

Reaching the eaves
Soffit boards and fascia boards can be reached safely using a ladder or scaffolding tower. Fix a screw eye into the fascia board when working on a small area of it, but never over-reach.

Extension ladder and fixings

It has been calculated that the safe angle to set a ladder against a wall is in the ratio of four to one – for every four feet up a wall the ladder's feet should be one foot out from the wall. Try to get fixings at the top and bottom. If the ladder is on a firm base, hang a bucket of sand from a low rung. If on grass, peg a large board to the ground and securely fix the ladder to this.

I made a very interesting discovery when examining the roof structure at the Wiltshire home of weather presenter Sian Lloyd. I had designed, and was about to install, a full security system and saw something very interesting on the fascia boards. A series of bolted hook eyes held with nuts and washers at the back of the boards had been permanently fixed at intervals around the house. As they had obviously been coated each time the board was painted, it was difficult to spot them at first. Their purpose was a means of safely securing the tops of ladders or scaffolding towers. A great idea and an extra special use for the fascia boards.

A good example of the decoratively exposed ends of rafters, typical of some Edwardian homes. The fascia board and the soffit still do their respective jobs and add to the appeal of this style of building. The eaves void is totally protected.

Light-weight aluminium scaffolding

A scaffolding tower can be hired by the day or weekend. It will be delivered and collected, and comes with easy fitting instructions. Follow these for your safety and for the safety of others working on or near to it. Brace-stabilisers are also available to anchor the feet after locking its wheels.

Fixing Fascia boards have a number of important functions, not least is to support the brackets for a guttering system. In order to do this the board has to be firmly fixed to the vertically cut ends of each rafter and to the wedge shaped fillet used to tilt up the eaves tiles. However, if the rafters do not overhang and are cut flush to the wall, the fascia board is nailed to the vertical cuts and close to the wall. In this way the rafters are protected from the weather. Older buildings used as barns or for storage often had open eaves with no fascia board. Here, the gutter brackets had to be screwed to the sides of the rafters or on to the top edges. However, most domestic dwellings were designed to take fascia boards that were grooved along the back lower edge. This provided a housing for the horizontal board, called a soffit board, which completed the 'box' covering protecting the whole of the exposed rafter ends and voids between rafters. This was also developed to ensure that birds and other animals could not enter the attic or roof void. The joint of the fascia board to the horizontal soffit board, as described above, meant that the routed channel is exposed with no protection from moisture. Often it is at this junction that rot can become evident. Constant exposure to damp air and the possibility of movement in the timber could open the joint. Check for any signs of damp but leave the problem-solving for a dry spell. When the timbers are completely dry then use an exterior mastic as a bead all along the joint, so that the two boards are drawn together and sealed at the joint. Use non-rust countersunk screws at 300mm (12in) intervals and then cover the screw heads with filler before painting. A cordless screwdriver is ideal when working at heights; there is no cable to cause a (tugging) problem. Where a fascia board is fixed to rafters, the ends of which are flush with the outside wall, ventilation is still essential to the roof void. If the board is a tight fit to the wall, the natural undulations in the wall's surface will leave gaps but drilling a series of holes in the fascia board just above the top course of bricks will help solve the problem.

Ventilation Ventilation, through, in and around the area of the roof where condensation could be a problem, is absolutely essential. However, it is necessary to fix fascia boards at places other than the eaves of a pitched roof. Often in a terrace, instead of a continuous gutter with a communal fascia board, separate gables can be seen for each house. This gives a more interesting aspect to the street layout. Some will have a hipped roof where ridge tiles are seen on the sloping intersection. Others will show a valley gutter where the two pitches meet on the main roof. It is at this lower junction that a trough unit is built to throw rainwater into an internal gutter angle, supported by two meeting fascia boards. Where two end grain boards meet can be a problem area unless the boards are sealed and protected against damp penetration. So, be diligent and observant in these vulnerable areas. It's a tricky bit of carpenter's craft to mitre the fascia boards and the component parts that fit together. Protect them to maintain the fabric of the house in good condition.

Fascia boards

This drawing shows the typical roof timber construction at the eaves. Here, rafters are cut flush with the exterior wall. The fascia board is fixed to the ends to protect them and provide support for the gutter. Ventilation to the roof void is provided by vents cut into the fascia board.

In some speculative Edwardian buildings, the rafters were left exposed to be painted as part of the decorative features. The gutter brackets, screwed to either the tops or sides of the rafters, were hidden by the overhang of the tiles.

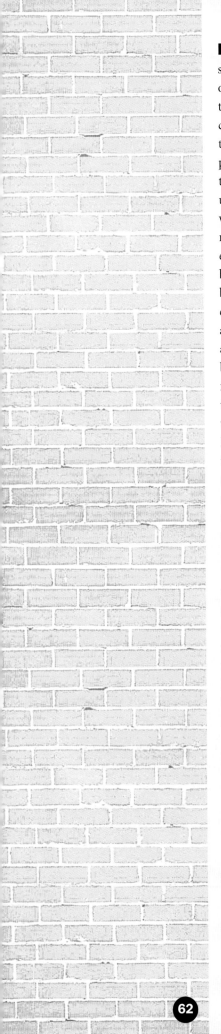

Rear extensions Flat roof rear extensions need to be carefully monitored because of the complex arrangement of the roof structure and its covering. The statutory regulations covering this type of construction are designed to ensure that the building is safe and weatherproof. The construction of the roof is such that the component parts must be carefully measured and cut so that there are no gaps to allow water to leak in whether the timber-framed roof arrangement is for a main roof or a rear extension. One of the important final fixing boards is the fascia board. This is a continuous board around the building perimeter that encloses the roof void, takes the gutter brackets and protects all the structural timbers. Fixed along the upper edges of the fascias are drip battens to which are fixed strips of reinforced felt. These hang down over the battens to throw rainwater into the gutters. Check that the felt is properly positioned to lip the gutter. If not, replace the felt strips by gently heating the top felt layer and easing up the edge to get a new 100 mm (4 in) strip under the top layer of felt. Make sure that the necessary distance allowing the bottom edge to fall over the fascia and into the new gutter is present.

When overhauling the gutter brackets, remove the gutters and unscrew the brackets before repainting the fascia boards. Prior to replacing the brackets, run a bead of exterior flexible mastic along the drip batten joint where it meets the fascia board. If the fascia boards have been there for a long time, check that they do not 'flop' at the bottom edge. Nails or screws used to fix into the end grain of the cut rafters can become loose over a period of time. As long as the rafter ends are sound, drive in long 'superscrews' through a predrilled pilot hole in the fascia board. There is no need to drill into the rafter end, it will accept large gauge screws comfortably. Countersink the head and cover with a wood filler to protect the head of the screw before painting.

Protection All exterior timber on a building must be annually checked and recoated at least every two years. This is essential to keep the timber in prime condition. It is a myth to believe that all painted surfaces have to be stripped before repainting. If the painted surface is sound without blemish, blister or flaking, then it needs only to be lightly sanded to give a key to the new undercoat and topcoat. Always allow the coat of paint to dry thoroughly (check the instructions on the label on the tin) before sanding. If the condition of the paint is exceptionally good, then it is only necessary to apply a topcoat after the light sanding.

Flaking paint and blisters are indications that damp is present underneath the skin of the paint. There are two reasons why this might happen. The previous coat of paint could have been painted over damp timber or there has been penetration subsequent to the last painting job. Whatever the cause it will be necessary to bare the timber either by using a jelly paint stripper, especially on a vertically painted surface, or by simply using a metal scraper, followed by coarse, then fine, glasspaper. It is obviously expedient to use a cordless orbital sanding machine to sand large areas. This will make the job easier, quicker and give a more professional finish. Where bare timber meets sound paint a lot of 'feathering' will be necessary so that there is no obvious join showing through the finished coat. Feathering is a means to obtain a graduated finish from full-bodied paint to nothing. Tackle this type of job when you expect a couple of dry days without wind, remember that the two enemies of paint are damp and dust. Repaint with a compatible primer on the bared surfaces then undercoat. Finally, apply an oil-based top coat. You might find, when renovating exterior timber which might have been neglected in the paint department, that you need to apply two undercoats, but with a difference! The first is applied diluted – check with the instructions on what solvent is recommended for thinning and cleaning brushes and use it for diluting the paint. The second undercoat is called an obliterating coat. This also gives body and depth to the compatible finishing coat.

Soffit boards

Every roof must have ventilation to stop condensation and rot. The accepted principle is to drill holes in the soffit board and insert small, plastic vents.

The pitch angle of a roof is critical in its construction and the bottom ends of the protruding rafters are cut twice to give vertical and horizontal surfaces to which boards are fixed. These two boards, that is, the vertical fascia board and the horizontal soffit board, enclose the opening to the roof void. So that a good fixing is obtained, a groove is routed along the lower edge of the vertical fascia and a rebate is formed along the leading edge of the horizontal soffit board. When brought together a tight fit ensures that the fixing is permanent. The other edge of the soffit is fixed to a batten, and drilled, plugged and screwed along the wall at the appropriate height to hold the soffit horizontal. Hidden timbers must be pre-treated with preserver liquid. If there is no means of ventilation in this arrangement of timbers, condensation will cause rot in the timber and problems with interior decorations. A series of ventilation holes with plastic vents provides a sufficient flow of air to offset this problem. These are fitted at intervals along the centre of the soffit board and need to be maintained with no blockages or debris covering them. If you find no vent holes in a soffit board, it is an easy DIY job to solve what could cause a condensation problem. Small plastic push fit vents suit-

able for the thickness of a soffit board, usually 25 mm (1 in) can be purchased from a builders merchant. After drilling the recommended size of holes, make certain no damp is going to give problems around the bare wood. Use a wood preservative or paint the bare wood with a good wood primer. Allow it to thoroughly dry before inserting the vents.

At the eaves the rafters are fixed to the horizontal wall plate and to the joists. The timber wall plate is flat on the inner skin of a cavity wall and the rafters are notched to fit over the outer top edge of the plate. Some constructions have no need for a soffit board because the fascia board is fixed flat to the outer skin of the cavity wall. This does not give as much protection as that afforded by a fascia and soffit construction. When a soffit is an integral part of the 'cover box', the overhang of the roof has a closed-eaves formation and soffit vents are needed.

A lean-to construction usually has a soffit board fixed to the fascia board and gives the same protection as on the main roof. The difference, however, is that because a lean-to is at the rear of a property, it is deemed to be not as

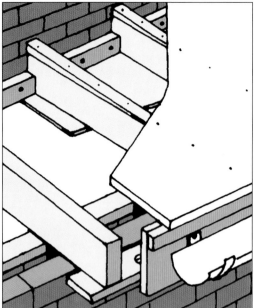

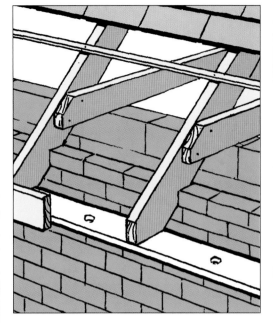

Soffit boards

Rafters are 'tied' by fixing them to the joists which become the fixings for the ceiling. The fascia board in a 'closed eaves' system is fixed to the joist ends and the all important soffit board encloses the void at the eaves. The soffit boards are fixed to both the horizontally cut rafters and to the fascia board which holds the gutter. Ventilation holes in the soffit allow air circulation to the attic to prevent condensation and rot.

important. Therefore it is made more cheaply and sophisticated jointing is dispensed with.

From the illustration of a cut-away, flat-roof construction, you will see that the timbers used are certainly designed to fulfil their roles in the assembled parts. The fascia has a batten at the top front edge to help support the roofing boards and the soffit is butt-jointed to the back of the fascia board. Even if the parts are glued and screwed, it cannot be as permanent a fixture as one where parts are properly jointed together, so it is even more important to keep a check on any movement in the timbers. At the outlet, if there is no sign of a mastic joint

Relaying a flat roof

Statutory regulations cover the construction principles of flat roofs to ensure that the building is safe and weatherproof. The drawing shows a typical construction.

A heavy timber ledger is bolted to the house wall. Joists are notched and fixed to the ledger and to a timber wall plate resting on the cavity wall. Wedge-shaped 'furring' pieces provide the 'fall' or slope. Timber 'decking' is laid on top of the furring pieces with the plasterboard ceiling below. A vertical fascia board, supporting the gutter, and horizontal soffit board enclose the structure. Small vents in the soffit provide ventilation. New felt comes with full instructions for laying. It is essential that the felt overlaps the gutter so that rainwater does not fall onto the top of the wall and cause future problems.

sealant being used, get a cartridge and do the DIY job now. It could save time and expense in the future. Seal the soffit board with a mastic bead to the wall. Go twice over any large inden-tations where a mortar course might be too deep for one application, then seal the soffit on its underside to the bottom back edge of the fascia board. Keep all timbers painted! Check each year and paint at least every two years. Don't skimp by painting around gutter brackets. Remove them – it takes only minutes with a cordless screwdriver and an extension adaptor – then you can check all screw holes too. As this is probably a single-storey back extension, you can work safely on a stepladder. However, it is always much safer to work with a helper. And with SAFETY FIRST, DIY SECOND in mind always place the feet of a stepladder tight against the wall so that any pushing with a screwdriver against a surface will not result in the stepladder toppling.

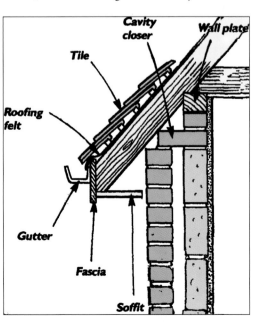

Eave construction

The diagram shows the construction of a closed-eave over a cavity wall. The building fabric is protected from the weather by the roof overhang, the fascia and the soffit. Note that the roofing felt overhangs the back edge of the gutter.

64

Patios

Bases

Often the soft landscaping of lawns and foliage is given priority over the hard landscaping of an attractive patio. Look on a patio as a fair-weather extension to your house and if you have room for one, it can provide an aesthetic, decorative area for socialising and relaxing. It is the ideal place to enjoy the sun and to have a barbecue. Choose the sunniest position which can either be adjacent to the house or in the garden away from the house. If the patio is adjacent to the house there are two golden rules, or really restrictions, to be observed. Firstly, the patio surface must be 150 mm (6 in) below the level of the damp proof course (DPC) of the house. This prevents damp rising inside the house and rainwater bouncing off the patio to soak the wall above the DPC

outside. Secondly, the surface should slope about 1 in 60 (25 mm in 1.5 m or 1 in in 5 ft). This 'fall' ensures adequate drainage away from the house without affecting the stability of your garden furniture. Any repairs, maintenance, alterations or improvements to your patio must in no way affect these two restrictions.

Even though your patio is well designed and shows no apparent signs of problems, there are acknowledged improvements that can avoid potential problems. Trellis and climbing plants are ideal for providing some degree of privacy and give protection on a windy day. Installing a patio tight against the base wall of the house is not a good idea. Differential movement in the patio and in the house foundations can cause problems. One improvement is to dig out a narrow strip of the patio slab and the base, and use pea gravel as an infill. This will remove any future damp problems in the wall and rainwater running down the wall will soak into the ground below the gravel. The strip needs to be only 100 mm (4 in) wide to get a good result.

Lay slabs on five blobs of mortar.

Use a wooden mallet to level the slabs.

Use a spirit level to check the slabs are level.

Fill the joints with a mortar mix for pointing.

When laying concrete for a patio base or any foundation, tamp it properly with a thick plank in order to get it level, compacted and ridged. The ridges make a key for the next stage and provide a non-slip surface for a concrete path.

Patio edging stones must be set on a concrete foundation. A wide patio must be divided into manageable bays and the concrete foundations laid between expansion joints of timber.

Slope a patio – 1 in 60 away from the house and 150mm (6in) below the damp-proof course.

Relaying a base There are traditionally two methods of constructing a patio base depending on its proposed use. For light traffic, that is walking, a wheelbarrow or a small sit-on lawnmower passing to the front lawn, a base of sand on compacted soil is enough. For heavier traffic and more constant use, a base of compacted hardcore of up to 100mm (4in) thick is necessary. If vehicles use the patio, a sub-base of at least 150mm (6in) of well-compacted hardcore, firmed in place with a hired powerful plate vibrator, must be laid. Spread at least 25mm (1in) of sharp sand on top of the base. This should be tamped flat. Lay the slabs on five blobs of mortar, one at each corner and one at the centre. Usually, a fairly dry mix of one part cement to four parts sand is best. Push a dry mix of one part cement to four parts of sand into the gaps between the slabs with a slim baton. Brush away any excess before sprinkling with a watering can to cure the jointed mortar.

Before making any repairs or replacements to your existing patio, it will be necessary to check its construction, taking into account the hardcore, sand, mortar screed, bedding-in mortar and thickness of slabs. Check the type, colour and size of slab and whether it is natural stone or one of the many manufactured slabs. Pre-cast concrete paving slabs are made in many shapes and sizes. A range is cast in moulds to produce various surface finishes. Many resemble natural stone and come in subtle blends of, often quite appealing, colours.

One natural stone slab that has been popular for years is genuine York stone, a fine grain sandstone quarried in Yorkshire and valued for its warm golden hues. It was previously used extensively for pavements all over the UK and second-hand slabs can be obtained from reclamation yards or from some local councils. If you have a patio of York slab and you need to renew a broken slab, there is one difficulty to overcome: slabs come in a variety of thicknesses. Use an angle grinder to cut a slab.

Relaying a base to the correct slope
Note the damp proof course 150 mm (6 in) from ground level. Excavate to the required depth. The dotted line indicates the top of the concrete level. Remove the timbers after the concrete has hardened and cured. A tamping beam is used to force the concrete down and to level it to the correct height.

Patio slopes
Patios, drives and paths all need slopes. Wooden pegs make ideal datum levels. Use two pegs and level them at the correct height for the finished surface. Then use a piece of wood on top of the peg where the slope is to be at its lowest. The thickness of the wood must be the same as the required drop in gradient for the length between the pegs. Knock in the peg until the spirit level shows it is horizontal. The pegs will then give the correct slope for the finished surface. Continue with more pegs to fill the space.

Refixing probably means digging out before compacting the disturbed base on which to drop the trimmed slab. Allow for the mortar joint when cutting the slab. Tamp it in with a club hammer and an off-cut of timber. Any levelling adjustment can be made with sand before the new slab is set on to a bed of mortar. If the original York slabs had a stone sealant to protect from grime and growth, treat the new slab as well. Clean the whole patio with a powerful jet hose, allow to dry and apply the colourless sealant to the whole patio.

Natural stone slabs, like York stone, used for patios or drives must be bedded on a mortar screed because movement will cause the stone to laminate. On patios, it is also advisable to seal the slabs with a proprietary stone sealer.

A path or a drive can deteriorate when rainwater penetrates and loosens the subsoil. Lift and stack every sound stone, keeping the broken stone for hardcore. Hire a compactor to ram the site ready for relaying a mix of the reclaimed and matching new slabs.

With the screed laid to a proper fall, work in small areas, laying each slab on five blobs of mortar. The mortar should be five parts sand/one part cement and not a sloppy mix. Use a spirit level on a long straight-edge to give at least a 50 to 1 gradient. After the slabs have set, brush a dry mortar mix into the joints, then sprinkle with water.

Renewing screed A rocking slab is the first sign that a screed is crumbling. Rainwater will have penetrated the joint and compounded an existing problem which could be a weak mix of cement and sand. In this case, lift all the loose slabs and remove the crumbling screed which is easily lifted out. Do not attempt to reuse what looks like sand, it will have undergone a chemical change and should be thrown away. Lay a batten across the void between two adjacent slabs and dig out sufficient old sand to give you at least 50 mm (2 in) of screed plus the thickness of the slab and a mortar base. Measure this distance from the underside of the batten to get the correct depth. Tamp the disturbed base to get a compacted sub-base for the new screed of one part cement to eight parts of sand. Use the levelling batten to get the refixed slab in a level line with the surrounding slabs, then use a dry mortar mix for the joint and sprinkle water on to start the mortar curing process.

If a large area of screed has deteriorated, the best plan is to stack the slabs after numbering them so that they go back in the same place and pattern. Alternatively, draw the pattern on graph paper for reference. If the renewed screed has an edge that has to be supported, use a long board vertically, held by wooden pegs driven into the ground along a string line in the correct position. Lay screed fairly dry with a mix of 1 to 8. Ram it into the hardcore, making sure that all crevices are filled. Try to start the job on a dry day and in the morning, so that the job can be completed in one go.

You will have discovered that paving slabs are heavy or at least you'll begin to feel the strain after lifting a lot of them. Lift with care to prevent injury, ensuring that your back is straight – it's the legs that should be bent! Start laying at a straight edge, either at the house wall or at a stretched string line along one edge. Having measured the space between the slabs, make a number of wooden spacers. Probably, these will be 6–12 mm (¼–½ in) thick, depending on what was there before. Use an odd bit of wood and the handle of the club hammer to tap each slab into place ensuring

that it is bedded in to the correct depth and level with the surrounding slabs. Keep checking for the right 'fall' with a batten and your spirit level laid on top. Work on one row at a time. Don't risk breaking a slab by banging too hard with the club hammer. At the end of the day you will find that the mortar joints will be passed the 'green' stage and by morning will have set off, permanently locating the slabs in position and preventing ingress of rainwater.

If you want to alter an existing design, don't be averse to leaving out one or two slabs to give room for plants or shrubs. This can alter the existing aspect, but be careful not to provide obstacles, so choose carefully where the spaces should be. You may have to cut the slab to fit. A stone cutter (angle grinder) is the best tool, but it does make the dust fly! And remember SAFETY FIRST, DIY SECOND, so wear gloves, protective goggles and a dust mask, and do it somewhere that is not going to cause a nuisance. Check the wind direction too. When cutting allow for the mortar joint right round the slab. If the slab is thicker than the existing, compensate by lessening the thickness of the screed underneath that particular slab.

Renewing screed

Lay 50 mm (2 in) of screed on to a consolidated sub-base. Tamp level. While it is still wet, set pebbles into the screed and tamp with a baulk of timber and club hammer. When it has almost cured, clean the pebbles with a sprinkle of water.

Lay bedding sand on new solid screed 50–75 mm (2–3 in) thick into which bricks can be set. Hire a plate-vibrator to firm and level the bricks. Sprinkle dry sand into the joints.

Broken slabs (1)
A broken slab can be used for hardcore or saved for a smaller space by trimming off the broken part. Score the surface and the side using a bolster chisel and straight edge.

Broken slabs (2)
Lay the scored slab on sand. Place a wooden off-cut against the scored line, but on the waste side, and a straight batten under the scored line as shown. Bang the top batten with a club hammer. Wear goggles and gloves for safety.

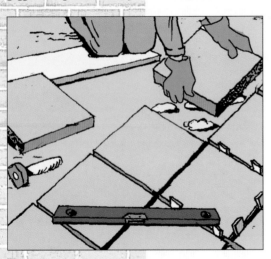

Renewing slabs
Set out the slabs on five blobs of mortar on top of 100 mm (4 in) of hardcore and 75 mm (3 in) of concrete. Use spacers to give a 10 mm (³⁄₈ in) joint. Use the handle of a club hammer to level each slab. Check with a spirit level.

Broken slab   If a patio is old and well matured, the stones will have mellowed and taken on an interesting texture and colour. You will have to search a reclamation yard or 'age' a new slab to match a broken slab. There are various ways of aging a slab. A builders merchant will stock a selection of colourants that can be added to a cement mix. Mixing these with water will tone down any slab, but wait for one to dry before proceeding. Be patient, slabs are usually porous, so the drying out process is slow. After getting a match, use a translucent water sealant to protect the slab so that the colour will remain.

Considerations   If a neglected patio needs to be totally overhauled, there are some prime considerations worth taking account of. After you've lifted all the slabs look at the site afresh. It should provide a sound and flat surface which dries quickly after rain and which should be relatively easy to clean or hose down. Think of the room you will need for chairs and a table, perhaps a sunlounger and a spot for children's toys or a table tennis table. A small pool with water cascading over rocks provides a pleasant touch. This is easily incorporated and can act as a focal point. The link between the house and the garden, probably through patio doors and across the patio, should be a strong one in design terms. Do not make it over-complicated. Too many types of paving can make it look fussy.

If you want to make the patio slightly larger, keep to a straightforward scheme but add a second type of paving, one that reflects the tone and texture of the house perhaps. Try designing your new layout on graph paper, draw it to scale, it will help you to finally decide on your scheme. Once you've relaid the patio it should last indefinitely, so aim for as high a standard as possible. It will certainly add value to your property.

Some influences to take into consideration when relaying a patio are the type and consistency of the soil and the slope of the existing land. Soft ground will need a deeper excavation to obtain a good solid foundation than hard ground. Using lines of string and pegs, mark out the area. Don't throw away any good top soil that you excavate, it will probably be fertile and so could support raised beds to form part of your newly designed patio garden. You can peg out the area by using a levelling batten's straight edge on top of two adjoining pegs, working along the whole area until the pegs which are parallel to the house are level and horizontal. However, the pegs receding from the house will have a fall of about 1 in 60. Don't be tempted to leave the joints unpointed. Rainwater will undermine the screed and future problems will cause slabs to move and wobble. Messy pointing, resulting from too wet a mix, will ruin the appearance of the paving. A builder's tip is to rub a dowel along the mortar joints to give a slight depression. This will give a neat edge to each paving slab and a crisp, professional look to the whole patio.

Renewing patio slabs and laying on dry mix. Raise each slab to the correct level by forcing mix under any low spots. Use a spirit level to get the correct 'fall'. The mortar mix between the slabs is sprinkled using a watering can and then allowed to cure.

Cleaning   It is necessary to clean off all growth, algae, grease and grime every year. The best time is after the autumn leaves have fallen and before the first frost. The most successful method is a power jet, but be careful, it can easily cut through plant stalks! If you use a detergent, hose it to a gully, not on to a flower bed where it can damage plant roots.

Timber patios

Wooden patios

We usually think of a patio in terms of paving slabs but wooden squares make a cheaper and attractive alternative. Different designs are available and you can lay them in different orientations to create your own patterns. Fix the panels on felt strips (to stop rising damp) laid on pretreated timbers The wood squares are pretreated and so are long lasting.

If a timber-decked patio shows signs of wood rot, it is probably because the original timber was not properly prepared. Decking is normally pressure treated with preservative to give at least a guaranteed 20–25 years of life without problems. The timbers are fixed to small section joists with galvanised screws or nails which have been usually fired from a nail gun, so it is easy to remove any timbers that have to be replaced. Most timber yards and DIY outlets stock all the regular patterns and sizes of decking boards. Never bang wood to remove a piece – always prise! It's good building practice. Also it is not necessary to renew a whole piece

of decking that is rotten just at one end. Saw off the rotten end about 250 mm (10 in) past the damage, then treat the whole board with a proprietary brand of wood preserver and stand the end grain in a bowl of the liquid so that it is completely saturated. If a joist or two have spongy ends or show signs of any rot, remove and burn. It is essential to use well-treated timbers and non-rust fixings. Decking is always exposed to the weather, so you need to ensure its durability with a good protective coat of preservative. Make sure that the supporting timber joists are spaced about 400 mm (16 in) apart and use a felt damp proof course (DPC) between the concrete base and the joists. Rainwater drains off decking through the gaps which have been spaced equally over the whole of the patio by the use of a temporary wooden spacer. Some boards are flat but boards with grooves running along their length are better for safety and help drainage. It's a good idea to enclose the patio with a vertical protective board screwed to the sides so that the top edge of the vertical board is level with the top surface of the patio. Finally, never neglect treating the wood to ensure its long life and to eliminate the possibility of future problems. For a natural finish, give the timber patio three coatings of teak oil. A proprietary brand of clear wood preservative is an alternative which also preserves the beauty inherent in the grain of the wood.

Untreated exterior timber will quickly lose its strength and durability. Apply a spray coat of a good quality preservative annually to ensure a long life.

The combination of natural slabs and timber decking makes an attractive patio but don't restrict design to straight lines. Make sure exterior timber is protected with preservative.

Barbecues

Brick-built barbecue – laying a base (1)
Use pegs to hold the boards in place. The compacted hardcore base has 75 mm (3 in) of concrete. A scissor movement with the tamping batten gives the best results.

Brick-built barbecue – laying a base (2)
Start laying bricks at a corner, bedding the first course in 12 mm (½ in) of mortar. Chop the bricks in half with a bolster chisel and a club hammer. Tap all around the brick to incise it first.

DIY barbecues are fun – but never build near flammable structures.

Fire was used by early humans for warmth outdoors and was the only means of cooking hunted food. It has been central to our existence ever since and we still get great pleasure from cooking and eating in the open air. Eating outside is very enjoyable and the aroma of barbecued food arouses the most timid appetite in most of us. There is an enormous range of barbecues available at all garden centres and DIY stores. Some are as basic as a foil tray with a grill, charcoal and a firelighter, to be disposed of after one meal, but a built-in barbecue can be part of the overall design of a garden layout maybe with integral seating and a serving slab. There are also free-standing types, which, being portable, can be moved around to catch the late sun or away from winds.

The location is very important. First of all a barbecue must stand on a firm, solid base, not too far from the kitchen, but not close to any flammable materials such as overhanging trees, awnings, sunshades and umbrellas. A barbecue is designed for outdoor eating so it is inadvisable to use it in a shed or garage. All portable barbecues must be kept indoors in winter after being thoroughly degreased. Rub metal parts with an oily cloth to protect against rust. Barbecues with gas bottles will have full instructions for storing the gas containers safely – adhere to all the safety checks and especially make sure they are not accessible to children.

Brick-built barbecues – laying the first course
Check each brick as you proceed using a spirit level both horizontally and vertically. Scrape off any surplus mortar as you go to save pointing later. Lay the first course as recommended by the barbecue kit supplier.

Barbecue kit
The ideal barbecue for the DIY enthusiast. Components come in kit form with full instructions. Steel 'lugs' are bedded at various heights to support the cinders tray, the coal grid and the cooking grid.

Kettle barbecue

The kettle barbecue is the most common because of its versatility. Use it for roasting, baking, braising and stewing. The cover reflects the heat and cooks the food an all sides.

Free-standing barbecue

This manoeuvrable barbecue is durable and convenient because it folds flat for easy packing in a car. If you pack it away for winter check for signs of rust. Use a rust inhibitor each year to keep it in good condition.

Gas barbecue

This barbecue is easy to light and reaches cooking temperatures in about ten minutes! The heat comes from lava rock imitation coals. Regulate the heat by controlling the gas from standard refillable cylinders.

Your local garden centre will also stock the metal parts necessary to complete the building of a brick-built barbecue. When I taught the entertainer Max Bygraves how to build a brick barbecue, I asked him if he knew anything about bricks – 'I've dropped a few', he said, to everyone's amusement.

You will need about one hundred bricks (available from a demolition yard) and follow the instructions that come with the simple kit purchased from a DIY outlet. You will also need to buy a couple of bags of ready-mix mortar.

Having laid a concrete base (or you can choose a ready-slabbed base) lay the tray from the kit on the ground, put the bricks in place around it and chalk around them. Remove the bricks and spread the mortar between the chalk marks. Lay the first course of bricks with the frog (or recess) up, leaving a 15 mm (½ in) gap between each brick. Keep going with mortar and bricks, bonding the courses as you go. Cutting bricks in half to finish off the corners and edges can be tricky but easy if you lay another brick as a guide across the one you want to cut, then use a bolster chisel and a club hammer. At the recommended height, place the metal lugs for holding the charcoal tray in place in the mortar between the bricks. Place more lugs higher up to hold the cooking tray. Top off with a few more courses but this time the top bricks have the frog down so that you have a flat top to your brick-built barbecue.

Either side of the barbecue and bonded to it you can add brick-built seating and serving slabs. You'll need about three hundred bricks to do this. As this is a 'rustic' design, you can explain away any rough patches as being 'country style'!

When I advised the radio DJ Jono Colman on a suitable barbecue for his family, he pointed out that he came from 'down under' where barbecuing is a national pastime. He said, 'picnicking is second nature to me'. He's a jolly person and we had lots of laughs as we got down to testing six portable barbecues in his beautifully kept large garden. I found a good position to lay a flat base with slabs and his wife provided the chops and sausages! But it was the presenter Chris Tarrant who was also very knowledgeable about barbecues, especially about barbecued flounder steaks which are apparently his favourite! He said, 'Unlike other fish, these stay firm'. Then he gave us his recipe. 'First put the flounder in a dish and marinate for one hour in a mix of white wine, lemon juice, chopped onion, a pinch of powdered cloves and a pinch of cinnamon.' Chris said that the ancient Greeks discovered these sizzling open air feasts but now everyone knows cooking outdoors is fun.

Portable barbecues are available as DIY self-assembly units with full instructions. From the simple bowl type with legs that detach for easy storage to the fantastic wagon-type range with bottled gas, an oven, shelves, a powered roasting spit and a windshield. There's even a stylish terracotta oven barbecue in the shape of a 'beehive'. There is a large selection to choose from so take your time to read all specifications at the store and ask such questions as:

- What is the quality of the metal?
- Will the handles get hot?
- Will the grills sag under heat?
- How long will it take to assemble?
- Is there an automatic gas cut-out device if the flame blows out on a gas barbecue?
- Are wooden slatted shelves pretreated to stop warping?
- Is there a dripping fat collecting drain?

Some handy safety tips to remember:

- Children and pets should never be allowed near a hot barbecue.
- Use long tongs and gloves for serving.
- Use specialist lighters and lighter fuel – never use petrol or methylated spirits.
- Never add fuel to lit coals.
- Grey ash-covered charcoal is very hot – take care when raking – beware of showering ash.
- Don't annoy neighbours with smoke.

- Don't relax with hygiene – so sanitise all surfaces, cooking equipment and cutlery with a taint-free anti-bacterial spray cleanser such as Dettox™. Have warm water and a towel handy for washing your hands. Cover all food – bacteria thrive in warm weather!

Here are some tips for lighting. Use lumpwood charcoal (this is charcoal that comes straight from the kiln), briquettes or handy instant-lighting charcoal, which burns as you apply a lit taper to the bag. Start a lumpwood charcoal or briquette barbecue by spraying on a proprietary brand of lighting fluid and leaving it for at least 30 seconds before lighting it – all the time keeping safety in mind. Bags of charcoal carry instructions on them so please read them, follow them and stay safe. An alternative to using a lighting fluid is to lay firelighter cubes under a pyramid of charcoal and light them with a long taper before adding more charcoal. Now you have at least half an hour to prepare the food and pour the drinks. This is the time that the charcoal takes before it is ready to be gently raked. Once you see that there is an even layer of grey ash covering the charcoal, you're ready to start cooking. Coals should be white and glowing to give an even temperature for cooking.

A barbecued meal should be an event, make sure that it's highly enjoyable and safe. And remember, for your next barbecue, everything needs to be sparklingly clean and hygienic without any sign of the previous feast. This, of course, means a clean-up job after every event!

Paths and drives

The permanent features around the outside of your house, including patios, lawns, paths and drives, will all have been designed and constructed to meet a need. It may well be an aesthetic one. Paths and drives will also have a practical purpose. If their preparation and construction has been scrimped, there will be future problems. We've all heard of the tarmac layer with an amount left over 'which is just enough to give you a new drive' and then, six months later, holes appear and edges crumble, but there's no one to sue.

When the first signs of a breakdown in the mortar between slabs on a drive appear, effect a repair immediately. Vehicular movement will compound the problem and soon the restoration will be major and costly!

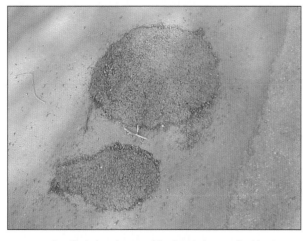

A pothole in a tarmac drive has to be repaired in stages: undercut edges, fill with a proprietary 'cold cure' tarmac and heavy tamp. Otherwise poor patching will look bad and will soon break up to leave another hole.

The essentials when paths and drives are being designed and laid can be summed up very simply. For instance, a path leads a person from one point to another in a chosen direction, straight or curved. It has a solidly compacted base to support a choice of surface finishes, be it York stone, crazy paving, brick on edge, paving slabs, cobbles, gravel or concrete. The path design might encompass a width for two people to walk or for a sit-on lawnmower and must be strong enough to support its designated use. A drive takes heavier traffic, obviously, and will have been constructed taking into consideration important factors like a solid sub-base, a proper gradient or fall in appropriate directions relating to the site of the drive, expansion joints and edging stones. There are two main reasons for protecting the edges: one is to prevent rainwater undermining the structure and the other is to stop the edge collapsing under the weight of a vehicle driven too close to the side of the drive.

Over the years, vulnerable areas of a path will be subjected to a great deal of wear. These areas could be a bend in a path where hurrying and scuffling feet change direction or where a child's bicycle will cause swirls and damage by constant application of the brakes and then immediately

Mixers
A hired portable concrete/cement mixer will save hours of back breaking labour when mixing to lay patio slabs or shed bases. Observe all the rules and regulations for the use of either an electric or a petrol portable concrete/cement mixer.

Wheelbarrows

A builder's barrow is not too expensive and will last for years. You also can hire one. It is indispensable for transporting bricks, tiles, bags of cement, and even mixed cement.

Paths and drives – edges

Protect all path and drive edges with edging stones or by bricks set in concrete. This will stop the edges breaking up, especially in winter. If cracks appear at the edge of a concrete drive, chop back to form a hard edge. Lay a board upright and support it by pegs. Dig out as far as the hardcore and use a PVA mix before filling and levelling with concrete.

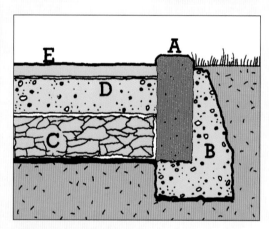

Drive surface with tarmac

The edging stone (A) is set in concrete (B) to form a buttress that protects the drive edge. Well-compacted hardcore (C) is laid to a thickness of 100 mm (4 in) before sand or old plaster is used to bind it. This will support 75 mm (3 in) of concrete (D). Lay and roll the tarmac (E) on top to give a long-lasting and durable surface.

Resurfacing a path or drive

If a tarmac path or drive shows signs of wear or develops potholes it is easy to resurface it or fill the holes with a proprietary brand of cold cure tarmac. (Use fresh bitumen emulsion embedded with stone chippings to resurface a tarmac drive.) To refill a pothole, cut it out to expose the hardcore, paint with the bitumen emulsion supplied, fill with the 'warmed' tarmac and roll it flat. Sprinkle with water from a watering can to keep the roller wet.

Planning paths or drives

Proper planning is essential. Formwork must be laid level with pegs to maintain a good level surface. Check each peg with a spirit level. Compacted soil or, better still, 100 mm (4 in) of hardcore compacted with a plate vibrator, supports the concrete. Work in bays to make the job easier and provide expansion joints. Make a slight fall so that rainwater runs away.

accelerating. Even the passage of time and the changing seasons can cause damage. Moss and fallen leaves hold rainwater which freezes in wintertime. The resultant ice can break up the surface, especially in the mortar between slabs and in fine cracks in a tarmac finish. A constant vigil is essential, particularly in areas that appear to be sound. A minute crack can be overlooked but we are all too aware when a fracture appears because it is large, it is obvious and it calls out for immediate attention. A tiny crack, however, one that is almost indiscernible, will soon have moss growing in it, enlarging it to become a fracture (to some people this might be an attraction, a bit of naturalness in an urban setting). However, be aware, one can be guilty of familiarity, that is of accepting a tiny fault and getting used to seeing it grow, without really noticing, but when it's too late a big repair job will be needed.

Covered paths

After repairing a garden path, why not build an attractive frame for roses or wisteria? Use a fence post auger to make 600 mm (2 ft) deep holes for chestnut or larch posts. Fix the posts with galvanised screws or nails.

Pergola

For a masonry pergola or arbour, set reinforcing rods in a concrete base to support each brick built pillar. The pillars are 2 m (6 ft 6 in) high on a 600 mm × 600 mm (2 ft × 2 ft) concrete base (150 mm (6 in) deep). Bed a pier cap in mortar, then fix the pretreated timbers held with fixing bolts.

Expansion joints Any path with a concrete base that meets a wall should have been constructed with an expansion joint between the concrete and the wall. This should be of compressible material (like pretreated timber) and inserted before the concrete was laid. Often people mistakenly blame builders or landscapers of neglecting to remove these expansion joints when they happen to spot a timber still separating concrete areas. When the separators are removed an exterior mastic is forced into the joint to prevent ingress of water. The joints are there to compensate for the contraction and expansion of concrete paths and to prevent cracking due to temperature changes. If, for example, a manhole happens to be in the middle of a pathway, it is important that expansion joints are inserted around the perimeter of the inspection chamber rim. If the edge of a path or the edge of an expansion joint shows signs of wear or crumbling do not hack out the expansion joint and pour a sloppy mix of concrete into the slot as this will obviously compound the problem and cause headaches when the next frost appears! It is best to use two applications of exterior mastic, applied with a cartridge gun, to solve the problem of water ingress into the expansion joint. The first application will stop just below the level of the surface of the path or drive. The second application will then sit on top of the first but will finish just proud of the surface of the path about 1.5 mm ($^1/_{16}$ in) above it. The flexible

mastic compound will not suffer wear over the years.

Uneven paths When constructing a path it is obviously essential to consider the safety of people who will walk along it. The surface finish must be free of undulations and be skid-proof. If your path has a concrete surface, it will have been finished in one of a number of ways. The method of finishing can give an attractive look to the path especially if one of the available colourants has been added to the mix. The finish might be formed by drawing or pulling a yard brush across the width of the path very lightly to give a series of fine lines. This can look most attractive if the brush is held with the back of the bristles at a low angle so as not to raise a concrete like 'burr' either side of each etched line. Overdoing the brushwork can result in an uneven surface. Another finish is one where small aggregate or a scatter of pebbles is thrown into the wet concrete and tamped gently so that they lay just showing as the surface becomes flattened. Overdoing the tamping can cause water in the mix to be brought to the surface. This is one reason why, when cured (or dry), the concrete can show signs of a powdery finish and an uneven surface.

If an incorrect mix has been used in the concrete, or if the concrete was not completely mixed to an even colour, some sand will form in

After bedding down old mellowed York slabs, decide on the finish. You might decide that your well-trimmed garden is better served with an open grass joint as seen here. The joint will be seeded and trimmed with the lawn.

pockets and cause collapse in parts of the path. This will cause the path to have stability problems, eventually giving an uneven surface. All of these problems can be solved by hacking out the unstable parts and getting back to a solid edge. Prepare the hole by painting with a PVA mix to help adhesion of the new infill. Only mix sufficient to fill the hole or indentations. Use a mix of one part cement, two parts sand and three parts aggregate. Always thoroughly mix dry before adding tap water to get a workable consistency. Never ever use water from ponds or rivers. Match the existing finish with pebbles, a brush finish or a float finish. Cover the patch repair with a damp sack to help the curing process.

Broken edges

All paths should have been constructed at the outset by setting a temporary edging board called formwork. Wooden pegs are first driven in, all along the centre of the path, to get the correct surface height of the concrete. 2.5 cm (1 in) thick planks of a corresponding height are laid along each edge of the path, fixed to wooden pegs along the outside face. Accommodate slow bends with shorter pieces of plank but for tight bends it is necessary to make a series of saw cuts across the board on the outside of the bend. It is essential to know how the path was constructed to solve any problem of a crumbling or broken edge.

An investigation of the crumbling area will reveal what sub-base has been installed, whether it's concrete or compacted hardcore or just sand on clay. Dig out the debris to expose a solid foundation and solid edges ready for the remedial work. Undercut the solid cut edge to form a key with the bottom of the cut edge wider than the top edge. Fix a board tight to the outside of the edge of the path to cover the repair area and 300 mm (12 in) beyond each end. Fix to wooden pegs and tap down until the top is level with the existing path surface. Tamp inside the repair area with the end of a board or timber to compact the sub-base. Tamp in some broken brick or stone to form a foundation for the concrete. Mix sufficient concrete to make one repair at a time. The mix

should be one part cement to two parts sand to three parts aggregate. Providing that the edging timber (formwork) has been pretreated, it can stay in place, but drive in the pegs slightly so that they are covered by whatever is adjacent to the path whether it's soil or grass.

York stone

Match the finish to this repair as close as possible to the existing stone, but because a path is subject to much weathering and maturing, the repair will soon resemble the existing. For a York stone repair to an edge it is good practice to get a thicker slab and to keep the base lower. Cut the stone piece with an angle grinder plugged into an RCD (residual current device) for protection. Allow sufficient clearance for the same mortar joint measurement as that existing. Lay the stone on a continuous bed of mortar rather than just five blobs. This will reduce the chances of rainwater running underneath the stone slab. Point up the joints with the same mortar mix of one part cement to four parts sand. Put a damp sack over the repair to help it set and allow 2–3 days before removing the retaining board. The mortar will still be 'green' enough so as not to disturb the repair. Back up the surrounding ground to support the edge with whatever existed before.

Tarmacadam

For a tarmac repair, buy a small bag of the mix from any builders merchant. The instructions on the pack will help you in the preparation and the laying. This particular problem is easy for the DIYer to solve and there are different coloured packs to help match the existing. Leave in the pretreated edging boards to form a solid support for the tarmac patch. The instructions also tell you what to do if there is a 'puddle' problem, where rainwater remains in lower areas of the tarmac. In essence it will be necessary to bolster chisel the edges of the concave area to give a sharp edge to the indentation. Undercut with the lower edge wider than the top edge to form a key. The pack material is poured in and forced under the edges to bind the repair in the newly formed hole. Tamp fiercely to get a good solid level surface and allow it to set for the recommended time before use.

Drives (1)

Reinstating a drive or relaying a replacement drive when the original has collapsed is not too difficult for the enthusiastic DIYer. Make a scale plan of the area. Dig sufficient soil out to lay hardcore, concrete, mortar screed and your chosen surface finish. Lay the concrete base in bays with expansion joints. Drive in pegs to hold the shuttering boards and for creating a 'fall'. The lowest peg will support a piece of timber (under the long straightedge) to give the correct fall when the spirit level is horizontal. Note the expansion joint where the drive meets the garage.

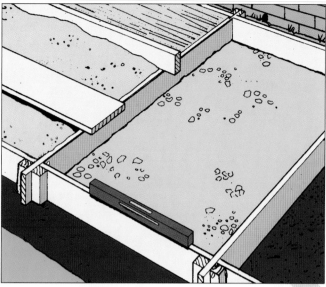

Drives (2)

When laying a concrete drive or a base for a tarmacadam drive, work in bays with pretreated timber forming the expansion joints. Excavate as required. Check that all the boards are vertical, level and have the correct 'fall' away from the house. Having compacted the hardcore and blinding, pour in the concrete ready for tamping. Use a kneeling board and wear protective clothing.

Hire a petrol or electric cement mixer and follow the instructions. Remember SAFETY FIRST, DIY SECOND. Put in half the ballast and half the water, then add the cement and the rest of the mix. After 2–3 minutes you'll get a workable mix which can be poured into a wheelbarrow or straight on to the job for levelling. Keep the machine on level ground and clean out the drum immediately after use.

Leave at least 150 mm (6 in) between the edge of the drive and the wall of a house. This is good for drainage purposes. Keep the concrete damp for 4–5 days to help the curing process. Leave the expansion timbers in place, but trim the ends flush.

Brick Proceed as above allowing for the brick measurement from the surface down to the mortar. Edges of paths of brick should have a more permanent and solid support. Dig a trench and pour foundation concrete into it to a depth sufficient to accommodate a row of either brick on edge or proprietary kerb slabs. Back-up concrete is laid against the outside of the bottom of the edging kerb to act as a buttress. When cured the rest of the repair can be safely carried out without fear of another collapsed edge. Finish by laying the bricks either on sand or on a bed of mortar. Fill the joints to match the existing.

Driveways All of the solutions above refer to drives as well as paths, with one exception – where there is heavy traffic. Here, the base should be concrete on a hardcore sub-base. Whether the surface is then chippings, small pebbles, tarmac or herringbone pattern bricks, problems can be solved very simply by applying one of the new proprietary brands of dry resurfacing treatments. The two most popular are not restricted to builders and can be a DIY application. It is interesting that these products can be used quite separately or in certain circumstances in conjunction with one another.

Repairing or resurfacing The two drive problem solvers in general demand by DIYers are available from most DIY outlets or from builders merchants. They are based on the hot tarmac treatment seen all over the country, laid by a team of experienced operators, who don't seem to be affected by the pungent smell or the heat! Now, we have a DIY cold-cure tarmac which comes in sacks and in colours. Having prepared the area by removing growth and weeds and swept away all loose chippings, debris and dust, read the instructions fully before proceeding. This is essential because it is a step-by-step application to be followed rigorously to get the problem solved in a professional manner. Once the surface has been prepared, a coating of bitumen-emulsion from the kit is painted over the area to be resurfaced. After half an hour it turns black and is ready for the cold-cure tarmac to be spread. Then this has to be compacted with a roller if a large area is to be covered. Keep the roller wet with a sprinkler. Start early morning on a fine dry day and keep the bags in a warm room overnight to help the flow of the cold-cure tarmac. Loose chippings are supplied in the kit (as an alternative finish to the plain tarmac). These are easily scattered on to the surface and rolled into the tarmac before it sets.

You can also resurface areas that are in need of restoration with a selection of stone chippings sprinkled and firmly laid in a generous coating of bitumen-emulsion. This needs to be brushed on to a solid surface of concrete, brick or similar, that is non-absorbent. If one area is particularly badly worn the problem is solved by applying a coat of cold-cure tarmac before finishing with the bitumen-emulsion application and a layer of chippings on top of the cured tarmac. It is also possible to make a more stable surface for vehicles with two applications of the emulsion and chippings. The simple instructions cover all these alternatives so your problems are easily solved.

Setting out with battens and levelling.

Laying 'setts' – stone blocks in a pattern.

Using a hired stone cutter to get exact shapes.

Brushing in dry mix to fill joints.

Fencing

Fence types

There are four main types of timber fence. These are close-boarded (top left); panel (top right, available in different styles); post-and-rail (bottom left); and picket or palisade (bottom right).

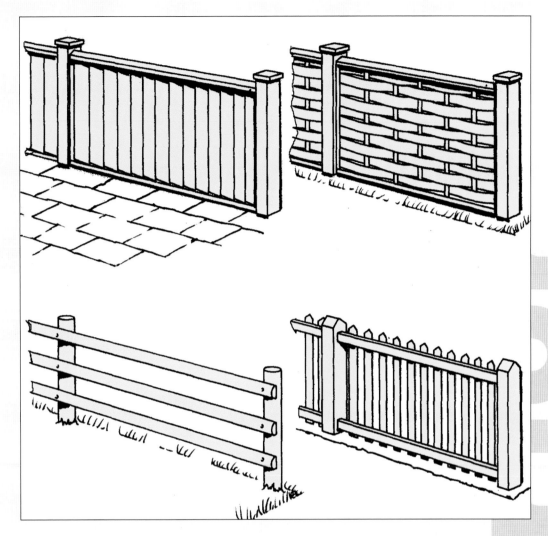

There is a fascinating history to the marking of boundaries of land by banging posts into the ground! From time immemorial posts and rails have staked out a person's claim on a plot of land. Today we think of fencing as being close boarded 6 ft × 6 ft panels bought from the local DIY outlet. Fencing has caused many disputes over boundary lines. Today, more than ever before, if as little as a couple of inches is gained by a reintroduced fence line, litigation is bound to take place! This is because the value of land is sky-high. The moral of this is by protecting your fence, you are protecting your plot.

It is possible now to put up a replacement fence that is virtually maintenance free. Concrete posts set into a concrete base, with concrete strip panels which slide into grooves in the posts, will give total privacy. There is little in the way of

maintenance other than decorative. These fences are windproof and peep-proof. Even though they are more expensive than wooden panels, you can see that you can solve many problems by replacing damaged panels with a concrete fence. When replacing or building a new fence, consult with your local Planning Department, because there are statutory regulations covering all fencing. However, you can build a fence up to 2 m (6 ft 6 in) high without making an application for planning permission. Also check your lease or title deeds to find the exact positioning and delineation of your boundary line. This is most important because any future sale or dispute might be affected by misjudgement. Make certain that any new posts supporting the replacement fence are dug into land on your side of the fence. This is not law but good neighbourly practice.

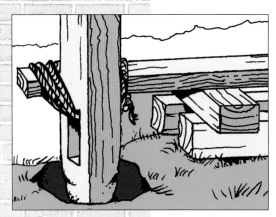

Removing rotten fence posts

Dig a small hole around the post. Use a lever to lift as shown. Place extra blocks under the lever bar as the post is lifted. Burn the rotted wood.

Posts
Rotten posts

Wooden posts rot because usually they are made from softwood and will perhaps have not been pressure treated with a wood preservative. Nowadays manufacturers are much more aware that there is a demand for either hardwood posts or extremely well-prepared softwood posts that have a minimum 20-year guarantee. It's not surprising that posts erected over 20 years ago will sometimes need to be replaced. Another reason that a post rots is that it was not properly 'capped' at the top end to protect the end grain from constant penetration by rainwater. The bottom of the post, just at ground level, will be the part mostly affected by weathering. As in all DIY jobs go for the best material you can afford; in this case, oak posts. In the past post ends were fired or charred to give protection.

Spiked fence post holders

If you have limited space use a metal spiked post holder. Remove the post by levering. Fill the hole and compact it thoroughly. Keep the holder vertical as you drive it in. Use galvanised nails or screws to fix the panel.

Wooden fencing posts and panels must have a frequent spray coating of protective material. Wood preservatives can be brushed, rolled or sprayed and will give a fence a long life, otherwise rot sets in and a costly replacement will result.

Neglect of any exterior timber will start the 'rot' process. Once a wooden gatepost has become loose at its base and is unprotected, the banging gate will loosen it further allowing more rainwater to penetrate.

Stump removal Removing a post end that remains in the ground when the top part has snapped off is simply an application of the lever. Tie a rope around the top of the sound half of the post and to the stump left in the ground. Place a baulk of timber or a stone about 300 mm (12 in) from the stump. Lay the tied post on top of the stone or timber and press the outer end with your foot to apply leverage to the stump. Slowly it will rise as your foot lowers. You might have to dig around the base if the large chunk of concrete remains and pull the lot out by making a higher fulcrum point (stone or timber). If the rope slips up to the stump post anchor it by driving a large gauge screw above the tied rope to stop it slipping. New posts which have been properly treated are available at all garden centres and DIY stores. Refixing a panel is easy, just follow the pattern of the others. If new battens are required, they, too, are readily available. Always use galvanised nails or screws for fixing – these will not rust – but make sure they are not of too heavy a gauge to split the 20 mm × 20 mm (1 in × 1 in) battens which attach the panels to the post.

Use a metal post-holder to successfully replace a fence post. Make sure that you keep it vertical. Buy a spike suitable for the density of the sub-soil so that the fence will withstand high winds.

Replacing posts

If the post to be replaced is at a starting point against a wall, it is probably fixed with a Fischer fixing type post bolt. This should be quite easy to remove with a socket set because the head of the bolt is usually countersunk inside a large drilled hole accommodating a washer and the hexagonal head of the bolt. If the post is loose because of rot, use the blade of a hacksaw to get between the post and the wall in order to saw the bolt shaft in two. Fill the holes with filler or mortar and drill new bolt holes using a masonry drill compatible with the new fixing bolt.

An alternative to fixing wooden posts into concrete is to use a metal spiked post holder. These come in different configurations for different cross-sections of post. The spiked holders come in 600–900 mm (2–3 ft) lengths and are driven into the ground with a sledge hammer. Always check that the post is going to end up vertical, of course.

Posts set in concrete need at least a quarter of their length bedded into the concrete. It's a good idea to let a post rest in a bucket of wood preservative overnight to completely saturate the end that is to be underground. Do it even if the post has been pretreated at source. When the post is surrounded by fresh concrete, use two battens as braces nailed to the post with two pegs driven in at the foot of each support. Check with a spirit level so that you get it vertical. Allow the concrete to cure before removing the braces. The concrete must be piled higher than the ground level and haunched, that is smoothed into a dome shape so that the rainwater is thrown off the base of the post.

Caps

Posts have to be capped to protect the top end grain from water penetration which will cause rot. Overhanging caps supplied with posts have an angled pyramid top to throw off rainwater but these do not totally protect the post end. It is not enough to simply use galvanised nails because there can never be a weatherproof joint. Apply an exterior mastic bead around the top edge of the post before placing the cap in position so that a watertight seal is made when the cap is nailed down. Drill pilot holes the same diameter as the nails to prevent splitting the wooden cap. Alternatively, match an existing metal cap with a similar cap. These are available at DIY outlets. Some posts will have been cut with a pointed top, cut on four bevels to shed rainwater. A single cut will do the same job as a double bevel, but no bevel will equal a capping properly sealed to the top of the post. If trellis panels have been fixed to the tops of the panels, longer posts will have to be used to leave at least 100 mm (4 in) of post showing above the top of the panels.

Replacing fences (1)
Rust proof post clips hold a replacement panel to the post. Smear the top of the post with water-resistant adhesive, then use galvanised nails to hold the post cap. Drive these in at an angle to create a 'key'.

Replacing fences (2)
Spiked post-holders are ideal for making a permanent support for a replacement post. An off-cut of hardwood or a special striking block must be used with a sledgehammer. No tedious digging is involved, no concrete is required, and you can buy shorter posts!

Replacing fences (3)
It is slightly more difficult to erect fencing on sloping ground. You'll need longer posts and each panel must be kept horizontal with a short piece of post showing above each successive panel. Insert gravel boards into the triangular space beneath each panel. Either shape these or dig out the earth to accommodate.

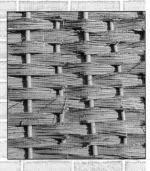

An attractive, long-lasting, interwoven willow fence panel which is peep-proof but allows wind to blow through without resistance – so there is no storm damage!

To help a fence stay upright in bad storms, use panels that allow the wind to blow through but are peep-proof.

There is no fear of gusty winds doing any damage to a fence that has concrete posts, is vertically close-boarded and has three generous coats of wood preservative annually.

Panels

Nowadays, the easiest fence to erect, which is also the cheapest to use as a boundary divider, is the popular, prefabricated 6ft × 6ft panelled fence fixed to robust posts. Larch is predominantly used for the panel strips which can be interwoven, overlapping or shaped into decorative diamonds. Tops of panels can be straight, wavy, convex or concave to give a distinctive and interesting appearance. However, the one fault attributed to some fence erectors is that they can overlook the wind factor. At a particularly windy open space thought must be given to the possibility of wind damage and close boarded fencing panels must remain intact in the fiercest storms. Stronger posts are necessary in this situation, probably hardwood with a cross-section of 100mm × 100mm (4in × 4in). Interlap fencing is often used to combat potential wind damage because the boards are nailed to alternate horizontal rails on either side of the panel. This allows strong winds to pass through the gaps between the upright boards reducing the risk of damage. The fence still gives privacy because the boards overlap.

Panel replacement

If a prefabricated fencing panel becomes damaged, it is very easy to replace. Panels are lightweight, of standard sizes and readily available. Choose a calm day to refix! Prise off the 25mm (1in) square retaining battens from the posts, if they exist, or prise off the panel from the metal brackets on

Setting fence posts in concrete
Ensure that the post is vertical by using a spirit level and hold it with two braces while the concrete sets. Arris rails go into pre-mortised holes in the post. Buy a matching post that has been pressure treated with preservative.

the post. If the posts have not moved, the replacement panel will fit nicely against each post and can be nailed into place. Underneath each panel you may find a stout 150 mm × 25 mm (6 in × 1 in) board fixed lengthways. It is unlikely that this has to be replaced, but it is there to prevent rot affecting the lower rail of the panel. It also gives more protection at ground level. Each end of the board is nailed to 125 mm (5 in) long square battens, called cleats, securely screwed to the post. These are more vulnerable to rot and could be replaced while working on the panel.

Giving the fence and trellis an annual spray coat of wood preservative will give it a much longer life. Using a coloured preservative will also improve the look of the fence.

Replacing feather-edged board fencing

Unprotected feather-edged boards become brittle. Take out the holding nails or drive them in with a nail punch and hammer. Replacement boards must match and be pretreated. Slide the thin edge under the thick edge of the right-hand board. Use galvanised nails through the thick edge.

Feather edge Feather edge close board fencing differs from panel fencing in that it is constructed of feather edge boards nailed vertically to horizontal triangular arris rails in a continuous 3 m (10 ft) run from post to post. The fence is made in situ, the feather edge boards nailed to overlap the preceding board, so it is relatively easy to prise open a few of the boards to extract one that is broken or rotten. The boards come in standard widths of 100 mm (4 in) or 150 mm (6 in) and taper from side to side from 16 mm (⅝ in) to 5 mm (³/₁₆ in). The boards are nailed only through the thick side which holds the thin side of the preceding board in place. Nail about 18 mm (¾ in) from the thick edge but only overlap about 12 mm (½ in). This nailing arrangement is important because all boards move and shrink in time, but the whole fence retains its stability and stays peep-proof. Always treat all timber used for problem solving with a wood preservative.

Trellis panels Trellis panels are useful for training climbing plants and for purely decorative purposes, but they are not strictly for protective fencing. However, they are easy to repair. Constructed of laths of standard width and thickness and a framework of small cross-section softwood, they come in various shapes and sizes. The trellis top to a close boarded fence is normally 1800 mm (6 ft) long × different heights in 300 mm (12 in) steps. Because trellis is not robust, it is good practice to use a powered staple gun to refix laths. A fan shaped trellis is designed to be fixed to a wall to train a climbing plant like a clematis or climbing rose. Sometimes the horizontal members are nailed tight to the wall but this encourages rainwater to sit on the wood. The vertical battens should be against the wall to allow rainwater to run freely behind them. The panels are usually fitted with masonry nails, which are notoriously difficult to drive in without sideways movement which can split the wood. Take the trouble to drill a pilot hole with a masonry bit to a depth of at least half the length of the nail to help keep it straight. Concertina type trellis is popular because it can be made to fit into a given space by expanding or contracting it. It also has the capacity to be slightly curved to bend around a shaped plot. If replacement laths are necessary, ask for cedar as they last longer and are less liable to rot.

Metal As well as fence post spikes, there are many metal accessories available to help solve fencing problems. Check what has been used on your fence before proceeding with any repair. It is always possible to replace plugs and screws holding the first fence post to a wall. Metal expanding bolts come with instructions

Exterior

83

Instead of applying rust remover and scraping for hours, it's far quicker to sandblast rust and grime from iron railings with a compressor.

Gates

Ornamental steel gates and fence panels can be made by a DIY enthusiast using a steel scroll-forming kit or a metalwork former. Your DIY store will have leaflets to help you.

This once elegantly designed Victorian iron gate will last many more years if properly restored. Remove the rust and peeling paint with a compressor and sandblasting gun, before priming and painting.

and are a more permanent replacement. Metal post holders with a square socket and a flat base, are available and can be screwed to a concrete base. Use these to hold a post in a difficult position. Metal angle iron posts successfully hold in tension chain-link fencing. Maintenance is important to prevent rust which, if present, must be treated with an anti-rust preparation before painting metal primer and recoating with metal paint.

When replacing a panel, refix with specially designed metal angle brackets as an alternative to nailing. These are fixed to the sides of the post in three places. To fix, prise flat one side of the bracket, force into place the fence panel, bend back the wing of the bracket and nail into the panel frame.

Gates

Never use metal base supports to replace gate posts. They have to be set into concrete. If a post has rotted and a 1 m (3 ft) wide gate has to be rehung, you will need to dig out the concrete that supports the post. It is very likely that the concrete foundation extends from one post across the width of the gate to the other post, so you will have to hire a powered Kango and use the concrete pieces as hardcore to support the fresh concrete. Remove only enough concrete to enable you to replace with new concrete to support the post. This post should be set at least 600 mm (2 ft) deep and supported in the vertical position with two braces and pegs while the concrete sets. Use a mix of one part of cement to two parts of sand

to three parts of aggregate. Whatever metal latch, strap hinge or automatic latch was used on the gate, it is good practice to replace them when carrying out a problem solving exercise.

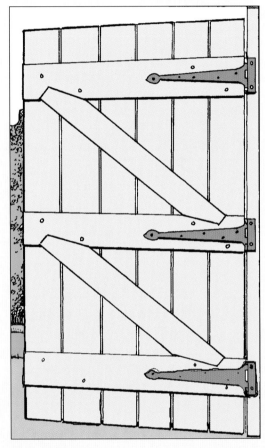

Garden gate

When constructing a garden gate, either for fitting in a fence or in a wall opening, there are some guidelines that must be followed. Use pretreated timber and give the top and bottom end grain an extra soak of preservative before hanging. Three ledges are better than two. Braces must rise from the hinge edge. This close boarded ledged and braced gate has been made from TGV board. Use only zinc-plated screws.

A good example of a simple but attractive galvanised-steel gate and fence. The clean lines of the fence complement the linear slabs and the neat brickwork making a favourable first impression!

A new front gate gives a good impression when approaching a house for the first time. This is a simple, but elegant, cottage-style gate – however, problems lurk! The brace is the wrong way round, so the latch side will drop. Note that braces support from the lowest hinge.

Furniture

Wooden garden furniture, by its nature, will not last as it is subjected to all forms of weathering. For instance, rainwater can cause rot problems if the feet of chairs and tables are allowed to stand in puddles. Depending on the wood used in its construction, garden furniture can be affected by the UV rays of the sun, especially if it's not protected. Whether garden furniture is built with the rustic charm of waney-edged timbers, described in some magazines as cottagey, or with top quality polished hardwood, protection is the keyword for its long life. And maintenance the keyword for retaining durability.

Most problems with garden furniture relate to two potential weak areas. Vulnerable joints showing end grain is the first and metal holding devices the second. Garden furniture is usually purchased in kit form to be assembled at home. If the instructions are not followed implicitly, future problems are bound to arise.

Protection Wood stains with water repellent can be bought for long-term protection and the enhancement of all wooden garden furniture. These restore a richly coloured finish and bond with the wood. If garden furniture has lost its lustre, is absorbing rainwater and has taken on a greyish hue, use a special wood stain which is absorbed into the surface of the timber to eliminate problems such as cracking, blistering or flaking. All of these can occur if the furniture has been sprayed with a film-forming seal. Some wood stains contain specially selected wood preservatives and resins which penetrate to stop fungal attack. The best are formulated to repel water penetration but will allow water vapour to escape in a controlled way. These are 'microporous'. Often we don't read the instructions because we get impatient with the tiny print size. It's a good idea to keep an inexpensive flat magnifier as part of your kit. These come in a plastic case the size of a credit card. Get one and you'll never again feel exasperated at not being able to follow instructions. All specifications on tins and cartons are based on expert technical research and knowledge so they should be read and remembered.

Cover each piece when not in use to extend the life of your garden furniture. Use a waterproof sheet for each piece but allow air circulation to be prevent condensation. From October until March you could even keep them flat if they come in kit form, then, if you have room in a shed or garage, store them in there.

Repair To repair garden furniture, replace any damaged or rotted timber with a piece of exactly the same dimensions and of the same wood type. Wooden tables are usually of the type that have metal brackets holding each leg in position. If a leg is loose it is probably the bracket that is causing the problem. To fix it remove the bolts and screws and check for a bent bracket or for any screws or bolts that need to be replaced or tightened. If the screws are too loose, glue wooden plugs into the holes and drill a new pilot hole. If steel screws have been used, even though they've been protected from direct rain, the moisture in the air will cause them to rust and affect the surrounding wood, making them difficult to remove. Proprietary products are available to solve this problem if the slot or crosshead screw is still sound. Otherwise drill into the centre of the screw with successively larger bits until the hole is clear of metal, then glue in a dowel to fit and start again. The moral is, don't use steel screws on garden furniture!

Remove, back to solid wood, any small areas of rot in wooden garden furniture. Apply a clear solution of wood-hardener before filling with a two part epoxy resin. Some of these come in a thick stick form with the two separate parts visible at its end, the core being a different colour to the outer. Cut off a small section, enough to make the repair. Knead the piece until the two colours have blended into a pale biscuit colour. Force the putty-like substance into the hole and shape it to the original form. It takes a short time to harden and then it can be sanded and coloured to match the original wood. They are brilliant products which can be used to make repairs, to shape broken pieces

Flatpack garden furniture is so well designed, it makes for easy DIY self-assembly. But because it can be left out of doors for long periods, you must protect your investment! Every year wooden furniture should be rubbed down and given two coats of preservative.

and to make lost brackets, and it adheres permanently to any material.

UPVC furniture Plastic patio furniture is now much more popular because it is inexpensive, easily stacked, will not deteriorate under the sun's rays (as in the past) and can be left outside in all weathers. However, because of the long-term degradation of plastic, protection is still important even for a set of inexpensive patio chairs. Despite the fact that it is claimed UPVC garden furniture is maintenance-free, an annual check is essential. A small crack in an armrest, if not repaired, will cause pain if skin becomes trapped. Keep a cartridge of hard-plastic adhesive to make immediate repairs to plastic furniture. Only use an approved adhesive formulated for this purpose.

Millions of sets of UPVC garden furniture are in use in the UK and lots of people would love to be able to colour-match their white chairs and tables to a particular decor. Until recently DIYers tried to solve this problem by using conventional paints which unfortunately do not adhere well to UPVC. This disappointingly results in patches flaking off. Now, however, a new innovative bonding treatment has been invented which is a coloured coating for all UPVC products. It comes in a wide variety of colours and is a simple DIY application.

Plastic garden furniture
This is available in many colours. However, you can transform old furniture with a colour bonding product.

Instructions are quite easy to follow but essentially, as with all DIY jobs, preparation is the key element. It is amazing how much grease and oil we deposit on a armrest just by the repeated action of moving a patio chair. The build up of grease is imperceptible to the eye but is apparent under a magnifying glass. All this has to be removed to give a clean, dry surface for the bonding process to be successful. Brush on at least two applications, allow the first obliterating coat to cure completely before applying the top coat by brushing in the same direction.

Lighting

Lighting can add a touch of theatre to a garden. Cunningly concealed ground spotlights can dramatically alter the ambience of a cluster of bushes in an otherwise dull corner of a garden. By means of a button or a switch, a dimly lit patio is converted into a stage setting for a delightful barbecue supper. But all this comes at a price which is 'SAFETY FIRST'. Exterior lighting has got to be considered with circumspection.

Safety One essential fact must be observed when adding to an existing outside lighting circuit or running an exterior socket for additional standard or table lamps: use a residual current device (RCD). RCDs must be part of any exterior power supply and they are most easily provided by an RCD adaptor. If the circuit is already installed, connected to the main consumer unit with a trip switch or RCD, then no further protection is required. An RCD automatically and instantaneously switches off the power if a fault occurs, such as an earth leakage fault which could give a fatal electric shock. Check that all metal lamp holders and fittings have an earth connection and only use exterior fittings designed for the outside.

Many people fear electricity because of the unknown factors. It is something of a mystery and it can be dangerous. Of course, all this is especially true if you know nothing about even the simplest electrical jobs. Everyone knows that metal and water (or wet materials) are very

At evening a garden is transformed by an illuminated low-voltage stone-effect spotlight. Amusing shapes are available.

By exploiting daylight, and better still, sunshine, these hanging solar lamps will light your garden between the hours of dusk and dawn. A brilliant concept because once you've bought them, there's nothing more to pay. A bonus is that there are no wires to connect so they can be positioned anywhere in the garden by pushing the spike into the ground.

good conductors of electricity and should never be in contact. However, there do exist specially designed and constructed exterior fittings and floating water lights. These are safe to use and present no problems in the installation, provided instructions are followed implicitly.

Solar lights

A small pond with two floating solar lights and a little tinkling fountain is a delight in any garden setting. Solar lighting has come into its own as a safe and attractive source of lighting for a garden path, under trees or for a focal point such as a pond. Attractively designed solar lights with a spiked

base can simply be pushed into the ground anywhere with no fear of damage to flowers or plants and are perfectly safe. There is no direct power source and no cables – the only source being daylight. The unit built into the top of the fitting takes in energy during daylight hours to supply the lighting for dusk and beyond. They come in a variety of shapes and sizes, even as large as a lamp post! The sight of a curved path lit at its edge by a series of diffused glowing amber lights can only be described as magical. These lights are available at most DIY outlets.

Connectors

All exterior electrical fittings and connectors must comply with regulations laid down by the Institution of Electrical Engineers (IEE). The IEE has produced a handbook called 'Guide to Electricity', which every householder should have. Even if you have no desire to repair or install garden lighting, it is essential reading. You need to be familiar with what can and what cannot be done by others, so that the integrity of any circuit installed is protected.

Connectors are used to extend cables. Never use a connector to join two supply cables outside with a connector that is intended only for indoor use. Only use cables and connectors outside that are recommended in the IEE regulations. This is a commitment of responsibility and must be taken seriously. The cable must of course be unplugged from the power source before wiring up the connector. Exterior connectors are heavy duty and fully protected. They come with full wiring instructions which are easy to follow. Make sure that the core wires are fully inserted into the terminals and secured properly. Double check your work before tightening up the connector. Nowhere is it more pertinent to say SAFETY FIRST, DIY SECOND than when dealing with electricity outside the home.

Security

Apart from the aesthetics of having attractive garden lighting, there is the important priority of security. You can fit a passive infra-red (PIR) detector to a porch or patio light at any time. It is an easy matter of

It is absolutely essential that a protected socket is fitted when an electrical supply is needed outside. Notice the thickened cable connector-end ensuring a watertight connection to the sealed socket. This gives protection when a pond pump is wanted.

All electrical fittings used externally must only be those specially manufactured under strict controls. Rainwater and electricity do not mix! Be sure to observe my SAFETY FIRST, DIY SECOND maxim when you fit outside lighting. Follow the maker's instructions regarding fittings, cables, connectors and current breakers. Notice the protected, thickened cable at the connection box.

connecting to the ceiling rose or light fitting connector and running a cable to the small detector. This picks up movement of a person and switches on the light for a predetermined period of time set by a calibrated turn button. However, you can also install a light that has a sensor built in as an integral part of the unit. It can be run from the house lighting circuit by drilling an unobtrusive hole in an outside wall for the cable. Protect the cable with a length of plastic pipe used as a conduit. Connect the fitting to the 1.5 mm cable which passes through the wall to a new 5A four terminal junction box mounted between the floors, (you'll have to lift a landing floorboard if the ceiling rose is in the hall). From the box run a 1.5 mm cable (two-core plus earth) to a new light switch. Turn off the power of that particular circuit. Be certain it's the right circuit by having another person tell you when the light goes out. Flick it a few times at the consumer unit before taping the switch in the off position. Mark it so that nobody else will turn it on. Now run a 1.5 mm cable from the junction box to the ceiling rose, taking care to secure each coloured wire in the terminals with the grub screws. Get professional advice if the circuit is not earthed or you need help to wire the switch. Do not in any event attempt any wiring unless you know exactly what to do. Double check everything that you've done to make certain that the circuit is complete. Only then back-fill holes and refix landing floorboards.

Sockets

Sockets located anywhere outside must be those designed for exterior use and installed by a professional electrician. They must be protected by a residual current device. Plan to fix exterior sockets in a protected location preferably located in a shed or garage, otherwise protect them with a weatherproof, easily opened box. The box can be of the simplest type made of six pieces of marine ply with an overlapping top and a hinged door with a turnkey. Cover the top with a piece of roofing felt or cover the whole box with a coating of a proprietary sealant. Be sure it is rainproof. If, for any reason, an existing outdoor socket is not protected by an RCD, use an RCD adaptor every time that you have to

plug in an appliance. This gives you the same protection and ensures that while using an electrical appliance, for example a lawnmower, you are protected. The protection is such that if by chance you sever the lawnmower cable the power is cut off instantaneously. RCD adaptors are about twice the size of an ordinary plug. The three pins go into a socket outlet and the appliance is plugged into the socket holes on the front of the adaptor. There are push buttons which must be operated each time to check that the adaptor is not turned off and is operational. As an extra protection, while working in the garden using any electrical appliance, always wear rubber-soled boots and rubber gloves, and please remember that not only you but members of your family and others need to be safe when using anything electrical in your garden or home. So, if you're not sure of doing a particular electrical repair, call in a professional electrician but check that he or she is registered with the NICEIC (National Inspection Council for Electrical Installation Contracting).

Fittings

All electrical fittings designed for outdoor use are clearly marked and have a seal of approval. Do not attempt to use any fittings designed to be installed in the home for exterior use. Extra-low voltage lighting can easily be installed outside by a DIY enthusiast by using a low voltage transformer. Providing that you have a protected socket outlet in a garage or well-built shed, you can plug the transformer into a socket and run your lighting cables to a series of lights. The available 13A socket will have been run from the main consumer unit and have been tested after installation, so by plugging the low voltage transformer into it you are doubly protected. Connect the cable that comes with the kit to the two 12V terminals clearly shown on the transformer. Go through the simple instructions carefully and read them again as you proceed through the step by step stages. You'll probably find that you can safely run the cable along a path but keep it safe from sharp edges, people walking on it and certainly from lawnmowers. Any connectors used to run extra cable must be of an exterior waterproof type as described previously.

Garden sheds

Concrete shed base (1)

The principles are the same for laying a slab of concrete for large or small areas. Techniques vary depending on the size of the base. The finished thickness of the cement and the site conditions determine the amount of subsoil that you need to dig out and the depth of hardcore you need to lay.

Dig out at least 150 mm (6 in) of top soil, vegetation and roots over an area that extends beyond the sides of the planned based. For a very large shed or garage dig out at least 230 mm (9 in). Lay 100 mm (4 in) of hardcore, 25 mm (1 in) sand, a damp-proof membrane and 100 mm (4 in) concrete. Set out the timber formwork as shown. A slight fall will allow rainwater to run off, but level the base of the building as you begin the construction.

Concrete shed base (2)

A typical cross-section for a base of a substantial building – 75 mm (3 in) hardcore, 25 mm (1 in) blinding, 25 mm (1 in) sand, 100 mm (4 in) concrete, with a 1000 gauge membrane under the concrete.

Concrete shed base (3)

Mix the concrete as close as possible to the job. Use a plank to wheelbarrow the concrete to the site. Rake the concrete ready for tamping. This important stage gives the finished job strength and durability by expelling air and closing voids. Use a scissor action to get a rippled surface. Finally, use either a wood float to get a lightly textured surface, a soft broom to produce a smooth finish, or a steel float to 'polish' the surface.

As you travel by train through the outskirts of any town, observe the numbers of gardens without a shed. Not many! Delve into the past and you'll find that the well-loved, traditional British garden shed has been around a very long time. And they come in all types and sizes. From the humble 6 ft × 4 ft for a few garden tools, a can of oil and a rickety bench, to the exotic 18 ft × 10 ft Swiss chalet type with an overhanging roof and a wrap-around veranda!

The materials usually associated with the construction of a garden shed include ordinary softwood, square sectioned for the framework and tongue and grooved boards for the flooring, walls and roof. Add a layer of felt to weather-proof the lean-to or pitched roof, and a glazed window and a brace and ledge door to complete the simplest form of shed building. Nowadays, sheds can be purchased in kit form and delivered to your prepared site for easy assembly. Modules are pre-built with tight tolerances so that the screws and bolts slide into place without using force. Instructions come with illustrations to make things easy for the beginner.

Previously, Victorian artisans would build garden sheds with one wall glazed. These would have been used as a greenhouses for growing tomatoes, cucumbers and exotic plants, but also, part was reserved for the storage of tools, a bicycle and a wheelbarrow. Even Beatrix Potter gave Mr McGregor a lovely traditional shed for his tools. Since then, the back garden has been used as the vegetable plot or allotment for the family favourites with more sophisticated additions to sheds developing as time went by. Today, it is not uncommon for sheds to have double-glazed windows, thermally insulated walls and ceilings, and electricity and water laid on.

If a conservatory is beyond your means, at least a nearby glazed shed can house plants and vegetables and be used as a summer-house for relaxation or for a hobby. Traditionally a shed has been more than a store for tools, often and almost universally it has been home to the hobbyist and philosopher, whether it is to turn wood on a simple lathe, to make model aero-planes, to grow chrysanthemums competitively or just to contemplate and write in your favourite armchair!

Your shed will have been erected with consider-ation for a number of factors including the direction of the sun, the proximity of over-

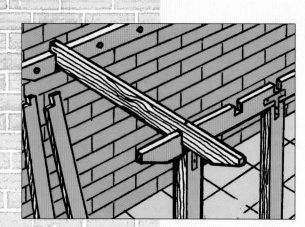

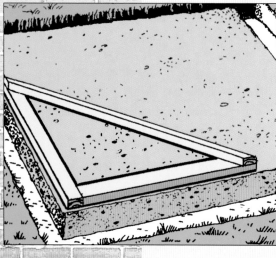

Builders square

Timber builders squares have been used for centuries. Use one to get a perfectly square corner on a concrete base, to square a corner of a room, or to ensure that pergola timbers are square. The secret is to cut the timbers' lengths in the exact ratio of 3 : 4 : 5.

The shed on the left is well constructed and protected at the corners. Three coats of preservative will give it a long life. The shed on the right shows signs of water penetration, the fixings expose bare wood and the tongue and groove boards have loosened.

Use a continuous, protected power cable to a shed – not an extension lead.

hanging trees, protection from prevailing winds and with security in mind. However, the first essential is that the base is firm, flat and stable. It will have been constructed as a concrete pad, which in its simplest form is a very easy DIY job finished in one day. Add 80 mm (3 in) on three sides to the outside measurements of the shed floor and about 90 cm (3 ft) at the front. A simple way to make a calculation for the amount of concrete necessary is as follows. If the shed is 1.8 m × 3 m (6 ft × 10 ft), the base should be 2 m × 4 m (6 ft 6 in × 13 ft) giving room at the front for a hardstanding (decking for an armchair and a table). Now imagine a cube measuring 1 m (3¼ ft) on all sides. Slice it into eight pieces and lay these side by side to give a base measuring 2 m × 4 m (6 ft 6 in × 13 ft) at 125 mm (5 in) thick. A perfect size and thickness for your 6 ft × 10 ft shed with about 2 m × 1 m (6 ft 6 in × 3 ft 3 in) extra hard-standing at the front or back for a water-butt or wheelbarrow. Let's take the above example to calculate what should be excavated for the hardcore and concrete.

Decide first on the height of the top of the concrete above ground. Excavate to a depth to accommodate 100 mm (4 in) hardcore or broken brick and stone plus 125 mm (5 in) of concrete. Boards laid on edge and held in place nailed to wooden pegs must be strong enough to contain the concrete until it has cured. Level the tops of the boards across the shortest distance but allow the boards to fall about 50 mm (2 in) from one end to the other so that rainwater easily sheds off. A simple trick to ensure that each corner of the base is square is to make each diagonal equal. Boards should overshoot at the corners for easy extraction. Once the hardcore is in place, ram it down to compact it, level it, then add sharp sand to 'blind' it (filling all the holes). Concrete can be delivered in bulk but ask for a mix suitable for a pad base for a shed. A cheaper alternative is to hire a concrete mixer and to buy the constituents but this is harder work. The mix should be one part of cement to two parts of sand to three parts of aggregate. For the 1 cubic metre of concrete, as described above, the approximate amounts are 6½ bags of cement, ½ cubic metre of sand and ¾ cubic metres of aggregate.

For a pad 4 m (13 ft) in length I would suggest inserting an expansion joint half way. Use a plank similar to the supporting planks. Drive in nails through the side of the long planks into each end of the dividing plank, dampen the area before pouring in the concrete from a wheelbarrow, but use a scaffolding plank if the ground is soft. Mix and fill as quickly as possible so that the centre board is not distorted, as it has to be removed when the concrete is 'green'. Use the straight edge to tamp down the concrete and to remove high spots, then use a 'sawing' action to level it. You now need to protect it from drying out too soon, from heavy rain and from pets. Three to four days with wet sacking or a polythene sheet over it should solve the problem, but leave it for 8 to 10 days to completely cure. Level your shed floor as you lay it on to the concrete base by compensating with 'furring' pieces or wedges to level the floor joists on the slightly sloping concrete base.

A prefabricated shed is probably given a spray coat of wood preservative when it is manufactured but due to so many pollutants in the air, the action of the sun and the variable weather conditions in the UK, it is no wonder that we get future repair and maintenance problems to solve. When a shed's timbers are subjected to intense heat, distortion occurs and rainwater and frost can split open corner joints. If the timber used in the shed construction was not pressure treated for rot and woodworm then these problems have to be solved. Look through the brochures for wood treatments at your local DIY stores and you'll find many dealing with all problems relating to exterior timber. There are products to suit every timber finish, to combat woodworm, to preserve exterior wood and which give a 10-year guarantee against future attack. There are an assortment of coloured stains which also act as preservers for exterior timber so you can give your shed extra protection and at the same time colour match it to an existing timber construction. Check rotten timbers before you start. Remove and burn these, then replace using galvanised fixings. All door and window furniture should be removed and recoated once every two years, making sure to spray preservative into insertion holes and all end grain. Modern microporous stains and preservatives are suitable for shed treatments and are very long lasting too. These stains have in their composition microscopically small pores, which allow the shed wood to 'breathe' allowing the water vapour to escape quite naturally. This way the vapour does not build up beneath the surface and there is no film to cause splits and blisters as with ordinary oil paint. The wood treatments are flexible so when the sun is out and the wood heats up the wood expands, contracting again when it cools down, so there is a natural movement of the timber components. As these products are specially formulated for bare wood it is a perfect problem solver for treating your favourite garden shed.

A felt roof will have a shorter life than the shed timber so it's worth either renewing or coating it with one of a number of proprietary brands of roofing compound. Some tins of compound, painted on to a 1.8 m × 1.2 m (6 ft × 4 ft) shed roof will give it at least 20 years' extra life. If you renew the felt, cut the felt first then lay it out flat so that it 'settles' and will not curl after clout nailing it to the roof timbers. Use an extra piece to overlap the ridge and use bitumen roofing adhesive only.

Security   Hasps (and padlocks) must be bolted to a shed door and not screwed. A simple door alarm unit is available that is activated if the door is forced open. Window locks which restrict the opening of the latch are inexpensive and easy to fit. Rack-bolts can be fitted to doors and windows for extra security. Security lighting which is wire-less, is another innovative method of deterring a would-be thief. Some lights are activated when someone approaches, others are daylight sensitive and are switched on and off automatically at dusk and dawn.

For outside buildings, sheds and garages, it is of utmost importance to secure the contents, especially if tools and ladders are stored inside. One of the best means of protection is to bolt (not screw) a heavy-duty padlocked bar to the door, to be used with a closed shackle.

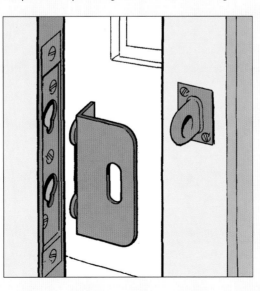

Padlock bars (1)

Sheds, garages and outbuildings need to be protected, especially if they are some way from the house. As well as fitting a mortise lock, it is advisable to fit a padlock bar. This angled bar can be detached when not in use. The fixed plate is fitted to the door edge.

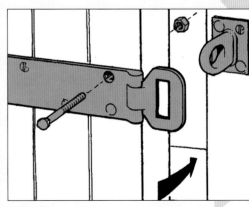

Padlock bars (2)

Make sure that the doors of outbuildings are properly maintained and that the hinges are strong enough. This padlock bar is bolted to the door and the short staple bolted to the frame.

Plumbing

If you have a garden, no matter how small, an exterior tap is not just a luxury but an essential. It makes life so much easier, for example for watering plants by hose or spray, for replenishing a pool or pond, or for washing a car. An outside supply can be use to provide water to a tap in a garage, an outhouse, a greenhouse, a shed or an extension. The simplest form of water supply is by a bib tap fixed to an exterior wall. It will be connected to a rising main just inside the wall. This will probably be the main supply in a kitchen near to where the main stopcock is situated. A typical garden tap is one that tilts down slightly with a capstan head and a threaded outlet to take a hose connector. The bib tap will have to be protected from the weather probably by means of a simple box insulated against freezing conditions.

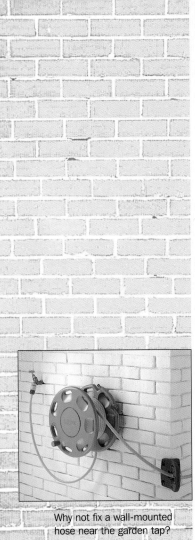

Why not fix a wall-mounted hose near the garden tap? They go together – with a detachable coupling, you've got water for all those gardening jobs, without carrying buckets!

There is one very important factor to take into account when the garden tap or water supply is run to the outside from the main supply inside. To protect you and your family from water contamination, regulations state that a non-return valve or double seal check valve must be installed between the tap and the connector at the mains junction. This is a fundamental part of a new plumbing installation and will be the means of preventing foul water being sucked back into the mains water system. Without a check valve, if a hose end is resting inside a pond or pool, pressure inside the plumbing system can draw the pond water back into the mains piping system. The simple means of solving the problem of providing an extra tap outside is to make the run of pipework as short as possible. Drill an 16mm (⅝in) hole with a masonry bit at a convenient position having checked that you can make all the connections easily accessible and join a 15mm (½in) copper pipe to a T-joint fitted to the rising main. Near this fit a stopcock which will give control of the new tap. Next to that, fit the check valve and an in-line drain-off valve (draincock). The instructions will tell you which way round to fit the valves (arrows indicate the direction of flow). All of this is inside the house. Then go through the wall with a length of copper to be picked up with an elbow which connects to a short length of pipe and the bib tap. The back plate of the tap is screwed to the wall.

There are also by-laws covering the installation and supply of water to swimming pools so if you're not clear about any supply contact your local Water Authority who may request that you have a water meter fitted. No planning permission is normally required for installation except if a permanent roof is erected.

Winter checks It is best to check all the plumbing runs and fittings that are installed around the outside of your house long before winter comes to make sure that you have protected pipes from freezing in the frost. Check your defences early in autumn so that you don't have to repair split pipes in the middle of winter. Once the temperature outside has dropped to zero, you'll be pleased to have carried out a complete insulation job earlier on. One thing to remember: don't lag pipes with material that holds water as this only adds to any freezing problems. Use one of the proprietary brands of pipe lagging sold in all DIY outlets. Solving the problem of a split pipe on an exterior run is not difficult. You can use either a resin repair kit or make a connection by cutting out the split piece to replace it with a short length of copper and two compression joints. Repairing copper splits has been dealt with elsewhere in the book but it is worth repeating. A handy repair application comes as a stick. This can solve hundreds of DIY problems, not least sealing a leak, as it hardens in just five minutes. Not only will it repair leaking pipes but you can use it on leaking hoses, gutters, fish tanks and connectors. If you have a split in a copper pipe caused by an ice plug, it is better to turn off the water supply at the stopcock. Once the ice plug has melted, gently tap the split together without distorting the copper. Cut off a small piece of the sealant stick and knead it until the two colours blend and you have one consistent biscuit colour. Only then is the sealant ready to repair the leak.

This illustration shows a cross section of a cavity wall with the component parts (fitted together) of a garden tap installation. Shut off the water supply to fit a tee joint in the rising main, next to which fit an isolating stopcock. Note the arrow in the direction of the flow of water. Then comes a non-return valve – to comply with the by-law – to prevent contaminated water being drawn back to pollute the system. Fit a draincock to which a hosepipe can be attached for draining down. Through an inch hole a length of pipe will join the inside fittings to the bib-tap. A sleeve of plastic pipe is run through the hole and the 15mm ($\frac{1}{2}$in) pipe housed in it. Screw the bib-tap to its backplate which is fixed to the wall. Fill the holes that are left exposed with expanding foam and insulate the tap and exterior pipe against frost.

If you prefer to make a repair by inserting a new piece of copper, simply make two good straight cuts either side of the split, having first turned off the water at the stopcock. Make certain that any distorted pipe is removed because it will prevent the compression joint from sealing with the copper olive ring inside the screw nut. Plumbers merchants and DIY outlets stock the parts and the only tools you need are a junior hacksaw and a wrench or spanner. Don't forget to renew any insulation that might have been disturbed.

If you decide to box in pipe runs in the garden, use timber that has been pressure treated against rot and water penetration. If it hasn't, there are many 'brush-on' treatments that effectively seal the surface of timber without changing its colour or texture. Consider re-running in plastic to solve the problem of exterior pipes freezing every winter. Medium-density polyethylene pipe has been used for some time by plumbers running pipework underground for domestic use. This is easily run in narrow trenches and comes in long lengths to make installation easy. The great thing is that once back-filled and laid to a depth of, say, 300 mm (12 in) there is no risk of corrosion and they are resistant to pressure. Other plastic pipes are ABS, CPVC, PVC and PB. Leaflets at the plumbing counter of your local merchant will give specifications of each and guide you to solve your particular problem. PB, for example, comes in a continuous coil, is used for hot and cold supplies and if an ice-plug forms in a PB pipe it will not cause the pipe to split and burst. If you often experience burst pipes, solve the problem by asking at your local merchant for a brochure on this type of coiled pipe.

Trees and plants

Quite rightly, we are hearing more and more about the need for tree preservation, not only in the rain forests of South America but also very close to home, in our streets and in our back gardens. Known in suburbia as soft land-scaping, lawns and trees are essential to create a more gentle environment in towns and inner cities. Trees particularly soften the harsh lines of architecturally unattractive buildings. They have always complemented the beauty of classical buildings.

Test for cables and pipes before drilling into a solid wall to install an outside tap. Use a hammer action drill and a masonry drill bit just larger than the pipe diameter. Seal around the pipe with expanded foam after installing the tap.

A tree that has been in our garden or close by in the street has unwittingly become part of our lives. We see the changes every season. We curse the blockages caused by leaves, but we love the evening sun behind the foliage! However, we need to understand the annual changes and the growth patterns of trees around our homes to be able to combat what can be serious problems and damage caused by maturing trees. Trees on our property or in the street adjacent to our property can be troublesome.

The structure of a house can be seriously damaged by a growing tree reaching maturity that is too close to a building. If you plan to plant a tree close to your house think carefully about the species and its proximity to your property. Get advice from the Local Council which will have a tree expert on its staff to oversee pruning of street trees within their jurisdiction. The safest distance to plant any tree from your property and to offset potential tree root problems is at least half the mature height of the tree. A tree that is going to grow to 18 m (60 ft) should not be planted closer

than 10 m (30 ft) from your house. Some trees spread their roots as far as or further than their height, so check with a nursery gardener first.

Did you know that you are not allowed to cut down a tree on your property without planning permission if you live in a conservation area or if a tree on your property is registered as Protected. Many trees are in fact registered as Protected without us even knowing. You will have to check with your Local Council. Even if a tree is causing problems, like roots disturbing the drainage system, you could be prosecuted for cutting it down without first getting permission from your Local Authority. However, it is possible to lop and prune branches, even to cut some roots to prevent further damage, but you must seek advice. I am sure there will be a friendly, knowledgeable tree surgeon or nursery garden adviser in your area who will give you proper information and instruction, but I think it is wise to make your first approach to the Local Council. Even on a mature tree, it is possible to trim the roots without affecting its growth, so that the

Problems with trees

A tree that is too close to a house can have serious consequences. The soil can dry out and the roots spread, searching for moisture from under the foundations. This can cause the earth to collapse and the foundations to slip. Cracks will appear from window corners.

Problem trees

Tress that cause the most problems to buildings are 1) Ash 2) Oak 3) Weeping willow 4) Plane and 5) Elm. Slightly less serious are 6) Silver birch 7) Maple 8) Beech and 9) Lawson cypress.

Tree roots can break pipes, disturb foundations and move walls!

troublesome spread of certain roots can be controlled. A tree surgeon must be consulted in this instance.

Drains   Roots grow and spread seeking water and food and respect no obstacle like drains! The drainage system around your home can be damaged over a long period if you don't monitor what is going on. This can result in a totally blocked system. Manholes, drain runs and collared joints can be affected by the strength of a root seeking moisture. Large roots become exceptionally strong and literally break open rigid earthenware drainage pipes. The breakdown of a drainage system is serious enough but not as serious as the potential damage to a property's foundations and, as a consequence, the structure of the house.

In order to prevent this problem happening, make a full check of your drainage system by rodding all the drains with a set of hired drain rods. Check on the structure of gullies and manholes. Sometimes cracks in the parging (the cement render) will indicate movement

inside an inspection chamber. When you lift the inspection cover, there should not be a nasty odour if the system is being flushed properly each day by ordinary domestic use. If there is a blockage causing a back-up of waste, then it could be caused by tiny roots growing in through joints to spread and grow inside the pipework. Go to the next interceptor and if it's dry this indicates that you have to rod a blockage between the two.

Subsidence   The first part of any house to be built is the foundation. This is built on to a compacted or solid soil base. The whole structure and fabric of the building is then keyed together and stabilised. The base could be stone, brick or concrete, or a part of each, but in any event it is built as one compact unit. Any weakening of the subsoil supporting the structure will cause movement, creating structural faults and cracks above ground. Trees can do this in two ways. A mature tree is a thirsty tree and will search for moisture by spreading its roots. When the roots mature and send out extra roots, more moisture is taken from under the foundations and the earth could collapse, just a little to start which might not be noticed. It takes time for the already compacted and stabilised subsoil to become unstable resulting

This enormous tree is growing too close to the house. The results are always the same – foundations affected by the roots and subsidence cracks in walls.

in subsidence. When you begin to see cracks in the corner of a building, or to and from a window or door opening, where the structure is weakest, you can suspect that movement under the foundations is occurring.

Underpinning

Your Local Council Building Control Officer, who will visit by appointment, will advise if a building needs underpinning. If the foundations have been affected by subsidence caused by tree roots, it is possible that the officer will recommend that you to talk to a specialist builder. The process involves excavating below the original foundations in the problem area, then shoring up the walls in order to pour in concrete to provide extra strength and stability to the house.

Heave

Trees can cause structural cracks in another way. Damage can be caused to a property when a mature tree is cut down. The damage is then caused by 'heave' as opposed to subsidence. Over the years soil and subsoil become extremely hard and stable. Roots seeking moisture actually help to stabilise the surrounding ground. However, when that tree is cut down the ground is suddenly left with a great deal of moisture and actually swells because the tree is no longer taking water away. This causes upward movement of the ground, which is so powerful that even the corner of a building can become distorted, causing cracks in exterior walls and displacement inside. Cracks in plaster are the first indications, then cracks following stepped mortar courses in exterior brickwork. The problem of heave can be solved by laying land drains. The excess water has to be moved from the area causing damage. Again your Local Authority will advise on the procedure. The local Building Control Officer will advise on laying land drains, the depth, the fall and the direction. Channels will then have to be dug running to a soakaway. Pea gravel is used to surround the drainage pipes. The soakaway is a square hole filled with rubble. The depth of the drains and size of soakaway depend entirely on local conditions and you must get advice on this from the Officer.

Leaves

We've all had experience of troublesome leaves in autumn when gutter, gullies and drains become blocked, but it's only by constantly clearing out the leaves and debris that potential problems are averted. The outlets in all gutters leading to downpipes should have a wire balloon inserted. This simple device has prongs that fit inside the top of the rain water pipe and a small gauge web of crossed wires form the balloon to prevent leaves blocking the pipe. A simple gutter clearing tool can be made with a rod screwed to a half circular piece of ply to fit the profile of the gutter.

Plants

Check that any climbing plants like clematis, honeysuckle and ivy are not causing problems to tiles and slates. Strong ivy growth can actually move slates, causing water to penetrate the inside of the house. The plants do not necessarily affect or damage the walls of a house, as is commonly believed. They send out suckers only to hold the plant in place, although tiny roots might seek moisture from an existing crack in perished mortar. It is best to position climbers where they cannot do any damage to the pipes and drainage system surrounding the house. Careful pruning and training of the shoots can prevent problems occurring.

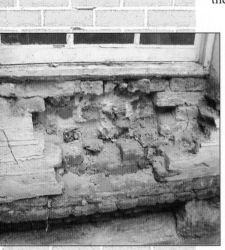

This gives an idea of the amount of damage a tree can do! The roots feed on the moisture under the foundations and weaken them causing cracks in the fabric of the house. It will be necessary to dig out and underpin with concrete.

Garden bonfires must be kept small – make sure they are completely out before leaving.

The desire to pile up earth to plant more flowers outside our houses can be disastrous! The damp-proof course gets covered so that wet earth feeds moisture above it into the walls to rot plaster and spoil decorations.

Ponds

Installing DIY ponds and fountains is easy, but only with approved kits.

The sound of tinkling water on a summer's evening can add charm and enchantment to a garden setting. A small pond with a fountain or cascade is one of the simplest of DIY jobs for the enthusiast. Bearing in mind 'SAFETY FIRST, DIY SECOND' the only proviso to the preceding statement is that instructions for running a power supply to the pump are followed step by step. Only then is it easy and safe.

Always remember to be vigilant when children are around the pond!

Siting Think first of where to site the pond, which can be as small as a square metre. A popular misconception is that a water pipe has to be run to it and that the pond requires a constant supply. A pond simply continually recycles just a small amount of water by the action of the pump. Leaves can clog a pump and putrefy in the water, so try to site it away from overhanging trees. Birds love moving water so place it where you can also enjoy watching them. For proper protection, you will also have to consider where to run the electric cable and to safely locate an exterior socket. All of this will be contained in the instructions supplied with

Pond fountain
Follow the instructions to install a plastic preformed pond liner. Always remember SAFETY FIRST, DIY SECOND when working with water and electricity.

the pump and fountain. As the pond and fountain provide an attractive focal point in your garden, a dramatic addition could be some pond lighting. When I designed a garden makeover for the actress Liz Carling, she actually asked for a small pond and fountain and knew

The same safety rules apply to a wall mounted water feature with a pump as to any other. Read the instructions and stick to them.

Once the plastic preformed pond and the pump has been positioned and connected, choose a conventional fountain or be adventurous with a cascade falling over a stainless steel ball!

exactly what the lighting arrangement should be. She had researched garden design and wanted the fountain to play on a circular mound of beach pebbles contained in the rigid pond liner – this made my job easier. This gives the clue to good garden layout – check as much as possible, research books and ask questions of the experts. Inexpensive pumps are available that are small but powerful enough to give a cascade type of fountain.

Wiring a fountain
I always recommend installing an extra low-voltage submersible pump to operate your pond fountain. Larger pumps for large ponds with waterfalls and cascades can be operated by mains electricity but it means contracting a qualified electrician who is a member of the NICEIC. A low-voltage pump, however, operates from a transformer – which conforms to my catchphrase SAFETY FIRST, DIY SECOND, because the transformer knocks down the voltage to a very safe level.

Once you have filled your pond, lower the pump on to a level base, a flat slab will help, and get the height of the fountain head correct as directed in the instructions. The cable, which is sealed to the pump, can then be run to a waterproof connector, which in turn runs to the safely protected transformer. If the fountain water falls to one side, simply ease and support it to a vertical position. The plastic fountain head tube needs to be in the vertical position. There will be an easily accessible filter in the pump which needs to be cleaned from time to time. Servicing the pump and the pond will be covered in the instructions, so don't lose the leaflet – keep it safe for future reference. It will also be a reminder to annually check the installation!

Installation
Whether your choice is a small 1 m (3 ft) diameter pond or a majestic 2.7 m × 1.8 m (9 ft × 6 ft) pool, there are pumps and accessories to cater for all tastes and pockets. Visit a garden centre that has installations to view and discuss your requirements with the knowledgeable staff.

Pool liners can be rigid or of the flexible type. The flexible types mean you can design your own shape to suit your garden layout. One of the best types of liners is made from butyl which has a long life, but the great advantage is that it will drape tightly to practically any pond shape that you dig. Once again only tackle this relatively easy but laborious digging and fitting job after you have fully read and understood the instructions. Obviously, the main consideration is sharp stones or roots being left to cause a leak, but a layer of sand over the smoothed soil base will solve that problem. One trick used by all professional pool installers is to use a garden hose to create a smooth curve on the ground. Dig out to the required depth, smoothing and sloping the sides as you go.

Garden pond
Decide on the best location for the pond, remembering to keep it close to an RCD-protected power point if you want to include a fountain. Ensure that the contours of the hole and shelf match those of the liner after sand has been added. Use a spirit level to get all the surfaces horizontal. Use boards to protect edges and grass as you dig.

You'll probably choose to dig to a shelf level first for water plants like lilies and rushes. Find room also for oxygenating plants which help to keep the water fresh. It is best to plant them in containers. A second lower level will accommodate the submersible pump. If the ground is not completely level, it will be necessary to level the stone slabs that form the edge of the pond by using a long straight plank and a spirit level. Cut away the turf, if it exists, around the pond edges then drape the overlap of the butyl liner over the trimmed edge and check that the stone slabs will be level and about an inch below the surrounding ground level. The liner will be trimmed later.

Hold the liner in place with a few slabs while filling with water from a hose. As it fills you'll find the liner being pulled and pushed and creased against your smoothly dug sides of the pond. When the pond is almost three-quarters full stop filling, because you now need to trim the edges of the liner. It needs to reach about half way under the slabs, but fix the trimmed liner in position with 100 mm (4 in) wire nails so that it doesn't move when laying blobs of mortar and the slabs.

Edging   Your chosen large slabs will now have an overhang of about 50 mm (2 in) over the water. It helps to hide the liner and it casts an interesting shadow. Now comes the not unpleasant task of shaping the slabs to fit the pool top. Use an angle grinder but at a distance away from the water and, of course, use personal protection like goggles, mask and gloves. At the stage of laying the slabs keep all debris away and make certain that no mortar falls into the pond when you slide the slabs into place. Mix sufficient mortar to complete the job. The mix will be one part of cement to four parts of sand. Make it a fairly stiff mix so you need only a little water to stop the mortar becoming sloppy. If you're unused to a pointing trowel, use an old tablespoon to feed the mortar into the joints as you go. This will ensure that you can guide it where it is wanted – the mortar can easily slide off a trowel into the water. Any cement in water will contaminate it.

Rigid ponds   When you visit your local garden centre to view small rigid fibreglass ponds, ask for an illustrated brochure of the product. Look particularly at the installation instructions before you decide finally on the shape and size to buy. This will also give you all the answers to the pertinent questions about digging for an electric cable, siting of the pond, how many gallons of water are needed for a particular size pond, maintaining it in winter and keeping the water pure.

Preparation is essential to keep your pond in good order, so carefully dig a properly shaped hole to comfortably fit the shaped rigid liner with a tolerance space all round of about 100 mm (4 in). Place the liner into the hole on to a bed of sand, checking it's level at the base and across the top edges. Put distance pieces of timber between the liner and the sloping sides of the earth to hold the liner in place. Then start filling with water and at the same time fill in the space around the liner with sieved soil to ensure that it fills all gaps and no stones can distort the shape. Push in the soil, which can be mixed with sand to make the job easier. Fill up to 5 cm (2 in) from the top. Pack around the top and lay on flat slabs as with the butyl liner. Alternatively, if the pond is surrounded by turf, complete the edging in turf too.

Polluted water   Most pollution problems in ponds are caused by debris, particularly by rotting leaves fallen from nearby trees. Just scooping out the rotted material from the bottom of a pond will indicate how severe the problem is. The decaying matter needs to be completely removed, the plants lifted out in their baskets and the liner cleaned. Don't use chemicals as these will leave a residue which will react with fresh water. Take care to switch off the pump and isolate the electric supply before cleaning out a pond. Refill the pond with a proprietary brand of water purifier which is harmless to fish and to plant life. It is important to follow instructions for the correct amount of purifier related to the number of gallons of water in the pond.

Introduction

Myths have grown up surrounding the techniques of painting and decorating, both of which are really fairly easy to master. So I want to give you heart and convince you that with all the new wonderful materials and innovative tools available, and with application and determination, you have all that you need to begin. Do you realise that you have completed at least 50 per cent of the work of redecorating a room when the preparation work is completed? It might be a bit of hard physical work, but it's not beyond an enthusiastic DIYer's ability. The apparent tedium of preparation (or preparing the substrate as the professionals call it) is not to be exaggerated, but there is no short cut to the success of this most rewarding of DIY jobs.

I have often said that the most satisfying DIY jobs are those where material costs are low but labour charges could be very high. Decorating is a fine example of one of these jobs. To convince you to make a start, think of this: of the total cost of redecorating a room, only 20 per cent of the total cost is chargeable to materials. The rest is attributable to labour charges. For example, redecorating a small bedroom at, say, a total cost of £400 means 20 per cent for the materials, or £80. You'll save £320 by doing it yourself. Decorating is therefore a DIY task in which you can save a lot of money. It is also very satisfying. Mind, it will take longer than a professional, but then we DIYers have time on our side!

Painting

80 per cent of a painting job is labour, so buy the best and do-it-yourself!

Preparation

Planning   Pay particular attention to the planning and preparation stages. Before rushing out to buy a pot of paint, relax, sit down with a pen and paper and begin to note all the preliminaries. You might feel that you don't know enough to even begin, but read on. You're about to begin the first and very important part of the job. Do it properly and in the end you'll have a finished decorating job that you'll be proud of.

A few notes and queries for you to jot down at this point are as follows:
Surfaces must be clean and dry (this can mean and lot scraping and sanding). Household dirt is mostly silica and carbon found as a coat of grease. Often it is indiscernible but it prevents paint adhering properly! All you need to do to get rid of the grease is to prepare the surface by thoroughly cleaning it with an ordinary household cleaning agent.

If there is a chimney, maybe have it swept before you start?

Is there ingress of rainwater anywhere, maybe from a cracked windowsill or from a gap between the window frame and the brick window reveal? Is putty cracked on the lower edge of a window allowing water to seep in?

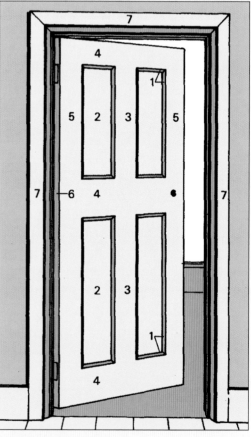

Painting a panelled door
After the preparation, allow plenty of time to paint a panelled door. Allow plenty of time for the edges to dry properly before shutting a door. Paint the beads and panels first, then follow the order as shown so that the natural joins will be invisible. Leave the handle edge to last so it is easier to open and close the door while you are working on it.

Pigment and medium separate in paints, so stir gently to blend them.

Different methods of stripping paint depend on area, flat or moulded, vertical or horizontal. A new paste stripper takes off seven coats in one go and leaves the wood almost as new – as this door testifies!

Paint skin in old paint will never mix in – strain the left-over paint through old tights.

Painting old wooden windows

These need a lot of careful preparation. If the original paint is sound there is no need to strip it, but you do need to 'key' it by gently sanding with a fine gauge paper. Replace perished putty and take off the stay and handle. It is easier to paint a small casement window when it has been unscrewed. Check for open joints and rotted end grain. Use a wood-hardener if necessary. Paint in the order indicated in the drawing.

It is worth stripping all self-adhesive foam insulation from doors and windows. It attracts dirt and grime.

Wipe off the tops of doors and window frames where a layer of dirt can hide, otherwise you could find grey streaks of dirt in your bright new paint.

Vacuum dust out from keyholes and around window latches (another source of grey streaks in paint). Dust of course, is the enemy of the painter, not only does it leave grey streaks but a gritty surface too. Another enemy is damp. Never ever paint a damp surface or wood that has a high moisture content.

If you can possibly lift out any window, sliding sash or casement, you'll find painting it much easier, especially if it is not on a ground floor.

If you have been told to strip all paint from a surface before redecorating (or just think that you have to), then you could be wasting a lot of time. Yes, you do have to make sure that the surface is properly prepared, but if the paint is sound, tough and smooth (with no flaking or cracking) then all you need is a piece of sandpaper. What you have to do is to 'key' the surface. A build up of paint layers on the edge of a door or window can often cause it to stick. This occurs usually on the hinge edge of the door when the brush has been overloaded and wiped down the face of the door to leave a build up on the edge of the stile.

A useful tip, before you start painting, is to make certain that you can get a coin into the gap between the door and the frame. If you can't, use a paint scraper to remove the build up of paint. Then you'll have to start as if for new wood. If paint is chipped, flaking or cracked, remove it and any loose surrounding paint.

When only a thin film of paint has to be removed, one easy and effective method to solve the problem is to use an orbital sander with a fine grit paper. Wear a mask and goggles for this dusty job, even if the machine might have a vacuum dust extractor. Always use a rag dipped in white spirit to remove residual dust before applying paint.

Chemical paint strippers   Liquid paint strippers are difficult to apply to a vertical surface and will sometimes run down forming rivers which could show through the repainted surface. A thick jelly type stripper is best for vertical surfaces. Use it only where necessary and take careful note of the instructions. Use gloves and protect your eyes and nose. Don't forget to protect the floor: old newspapers are best as they are easily disposed of. When you see the paint shrivelling after applying the liquid paint stripper, remove it with a flat steel painter's scraper. A filling knife looks similar but is too flexible for this job. You'll soon get the hang of it, but do allow the stripper time to work. Get rid of the debris by folding it into the newspapers. Tie them up and then dispose of them in a plastic bag.

Sugar soap removes grime and grease from painted surfaces.

Finish off, after again checking the instructions and the expected result, by rubbing over the surface with medium steel wool. The wood will suck the liquid stripper beneath the surface, so you'll need to neutralise it before applying paint. The instructions on the tin will tell you which solvent to use otherwise use white spirit on a clean lint-free rag to rub over the entire surface. When stripping paint from door mouldings, you'll need to use a shave-hook. These are inexpensive flat pieces of metal with a wooden handle. A heart-shaped scraper will deal with all the mouldings on doors, but apply two or three layers of stripper, then the wood will be revealed more easily. Use a metal container, pouring in a little of the stripper. Brush it on liberally. It will shrivel quite quickly, then apply another coat. Protect your hands and eyes and provide added ventilation if working inside. A test on a small area will tell you how much you need to apply, how long it needs to react with the paint and whether you need to use the scraper between successive coats of the stripper.

Heat gun

A heat gun is a marvellous tool for removing large flat areas of paint. Buy one with a reputable brand name because a power tool needs to have a guarantee. Obviously where the heat is the source of energy you'll need to take a certain amount of care, but, as with many power tools, these are easier to use than most people think. Around the area where you intend to work, remove curtains and inflammable materials even though there is no actual flame round the gun. There are usually two levels of heat controlled with a rotor switch. Keep the trailing flex safely to one side and, if you stop, switch off the power. Try it out in a hidden area or on a scrap of painted wood to get used to handling the gun and the scraper. Don't scrape up into the hot loosened paint, it could fall on to your hands. You'll actually be amazed how easy it is to loosen the paint and to see it melt, but keep moving the gun so as not to scorch any wood surfaces that have been bared.
Some guns come with a built-in scraper and other accessories. You'll be told in the instructions to hold the scraper at an angle so that the hot paint falls to the floor. Make sure not to use

newspapers on the floor! Use a sheet of non-combustible board instead. You must have protection from the fumes which will be generated and open a window to get plenty of ventilation. Eyes and skin too can be vulnerable, so again, please wear protection!

Abrasive papers

One of the irritating aspects of burning-off paint is clogging. To solve this problem, apply a solution of garden-lime and water to the painted area some time before using the heat gun. To complete the stripping process, use, as the instructions indicate, different grades of glasspaper, wire wool or wet-and-dry paper (silicone carbide paper: wetted as you might use it on cars). You should be able to judge just how much 'smoothing' the stripped surface needs by rubbing the palm of your hand over it. If any of the grain (wood fibre) has lifted, it will be necessary to use a medium glasspaper first to get a smooth surface before finally smoothing it like glass with a finer paper. The best results on large areas are obtained by rubbing with a strip of abrasive paper wrapped over a block of wood or a specially formed cork block (available at all DIY stores). Usually, glasspaper comes in three types – coarse, medium and fine – but in the trade code numbers are used to order intermediate types. The lower numbers show coarser grades (or grits) than the higher numbers. Yellow glasspaper is the most common type and has different 'grits', either closely packed to produce a fine finish or widely spaced to do two things – reduce clogging and to take off more surface. If you are working on oak or other hardwoods, you'll need to order garnet abrasive paper. This deals with hardwoods quite easily because it does not shed its grits as quickly as glasspaper and only comes in the finer grades. However, silicone carbide wet-and-dry paper gives the smoothest of all finishes, especially on oak, beech, birch and other hardwoods.

Most chemical paint strippers need to be neutralised after use – check on the label.

Paint stripping
Use a cordless hot air gun to strip large areas of paint. Scrape with a stripping knife, not with a filling knife. Wear gloves.

New wood

Try this as an experiment. Wet your finger and touch some new wood. You'll find that the moisture is readily absorbed into the wood so sealing is the first step in the preparation work. A priming coat of paint provides this essential seal base, so that the undercoat (and gloss or top coat) is not sucked into the wood. The primer must be worked well into the grainy surface and the wood totally covered in an evenly applied coat. The priming coat also acts as an inhibitor to damp and moisture. This is why it is important to paint the back and front of wood to be newly fixed, like skirting boards and architraves. Don't be tempted under any circumstances to use the lazy person's method of priming, that is, with emulsion paint. It is water-based and therefore dries quickly but is not compatible with oil-based paints and does not offer the protection of a priming coat.

Use floor and furniture coverings and dust sheets to protect the surrounding area. It's good practice to transfer paint from the tin into a smaller paint 'kettle'. Tie a piece of string across the paint kettle from handle to handle, and wipe off any excess paint from the brush. Another tip – dip only a third of the length of the bristles into the paint, any deeper and you'll find it running back down the handle as you paint.

Follow instructions when painting new wood. Preparation, properly carried out, ensures success. Don't skimp on materials and always use good brushes. Sand the surface between coats and allow plenty of drying time. Cover a third of the bristles and brush from dry to wet when 'laying off'.

Application

When you think about it, what we're really doing when we are painting is providing an enhanced, overall surface effect on wood and protecting its surface at the same time. We are forming a continuous surface film on the wood. Only by following correct procedures is it possible to build up a good, hard wearing and easy-to-clean surface. After the priming coat is dry and hard, sand it to obtain a smooth surface. Wipe off residual dust with a cloth dipped in white spirit. The next layer of a conventional painting job on new wood is the undercoat, sometimes called the obliterating coat. This is because it gives a good 'cover'. This coat has 'body' and helps build up the paint film. When you take a brush loaded with paint to the wood, it has to end up evenly spread with no runs and no apparent joins. To achieve this, spread the paint in the direction of the grain and then lightly across it at right angles. Finally, working from the adjacent (unpainted) area, stroke back into the painted area very lightly, lifting the brush off after each even stroke. This is called 'laying off' and is the solution to irritating blobs, thinly spread paint and runs. Never put the brush into the wet area to draw it along to the area where fresh paint is to be next applied. Let the undercoat dry thoroughly.

Get help with the next stage, which can be very satisfying but laborious! Ask anybody, with the energy to spare, to lightly sand over the whole painted area. To get an even surface use someone with a gentle touch so that the same pressure is applied. Avoid too much exertion. A fine abrasive paper is all that is necessary, but to get the top coat with a mirror finish that looks professional, it is essential to get the undercoat beautifully smooth. I cannot overemphasise the importance of this stage. A final smoothing with wet-and-dry paper will get the desired finish. The paper should be kept just damp and use a cork sanding block. A fine residue is always produced but is easily washed off. Remember, use a dampened cloth with white spirit to give a pleasing undercoat job.

The top coat of paint must be applied in the same way as the undercoat, always working in the direction of the grain to start with. After the final brush strokes have laid off the finished coat, make sure that there are no residual brush marks. Slight variations in the paint application should flow out as the paint dries. Don't ever be tempted to go back on to the work after it has become tacky, you'll end up with an awful mess. But don't despair, if you're not too happy with your first results you can always go back when it is dry. If that's the case give it a good rub down and start again. Of course, this time you won't need to apply a priming coat, just another coat of gloss, but do make absolutely sure that you've smoothed the surface properly before any application of paint.

Sometimes new wood will have been prepared with a preservative before reaching the merchant. If you know, or suspect, this is the case and you want to paint it, the solution is aluminium wood primer. There are some 'don'ts' though. For example, never use it on hardwood such as teak, which has a greasy surface. You'll need to degrease this with white spirit first. Allow it to dry thoroughly.

Manufacturers' instructions on paint tins are the result of their own research and must be followed. Different paint brands are not necessarily compatible and the unsuited chemical constituents might give a lot of problems if you try to mix them, so stick to the same brand of primer, undercoat and top coat. Adhesion may be compromised, as may be the flexing and contraction properties of each coat under different weather conditions. This could result in flaking, blistering and cracking. Check with your paint supplier, who will tell you about the new paints on the market. For example, if you're not interested in a conventional approach to painting, there are paints that have two coats in one. This is obviously a quicker method of painting, but because of the texture of the paint it is sometimes more difficult to obtain an absolutely mirror-like finish. Other paints like acrylic resin-based paints are very flexible and will move with the expansion and contraction of wood. This will prevent the problems of cracking and peeling if the paint is exposed to the weather. Two other positive factors are that they are very easy to apply and you simply wash out brushes (and your hands) under the tap.

Paint a front door only after removing the handle, knocker, letterbox, etc.

Before opening a can of paint, wipe the lid to stop dirt falling inside.

Problems

Runs and rivers   It is not always possible to see runs and rivers forming on a vertical surface when painting in bad light. Even if you've correctly applied the paint with not too much on the brush, unless it is evenly distributed runs can occur and it's only when the paint is dry that these runs and rivers show up badly especially in a side light. They can also occur if the brush is unwittingly overloaded or if not enough time is taken to 'lay off' the paint by drawing the brush back into the wet paint from the last application or the 'dry' area. Patience is a virtue in relation to painting finishing techniques. You should only try to remove unsightly runs when they are dry. If they are showing up heavily, use a jelly paint stripper and start again as from new wood. Fine runs can be gently removed with a medium to fine glasspaper. Try to 'feather edge' the runs into the surrounding paint until you are unable to feel any ridges with your finger, then you'll only need a top coat to complete the task.

Blisters   There are a number of reasons why blisters appear on a painted surface, depending on the substrate (what's underneath) or the type of paint used. Emulsion paint, for example, used on an oil-based painted wall which was not properly prepared for emulsion paint, results in blisters appearing. These can also result by painting on a damp wall. A wall has to be thoroughly dry to prevent them. If necessary, hire a dehumidifier, especially if a room has been replastered. A wall has to be firm, flat and degreased. A stabilising primer should be used to bind powdery or flaking plaster wall surfaces.

Blisters on a painted wooden surface can be caused by painting on to damp wood or by knots that do not have a shellac coating to prevent the resin pushing up the layer of paint. Use an aluminium primer before painting. Resin can break out in new wood anywhere along the grain, so check thoroughly before applying any primer. When carrying out the initial sanding, a sticky patch will certainly indicate resin escaping and will need sealing.

Dimpled paint Condensation or any dampness in the air when painting can cause this irritating problem, so make sure the room is well ventilated whilst you are painting. If condensation forms as the paint dries – most often this can be seen on oil-based paints – it may be that warm moist air from a boiling kettle or from cooking has come into contact with the colder surface that you are painting.

Another reason for dimpled paint is that the surface being painted has not been prepared properly. All surfaces must be firm with no friable, powdery surfaces and absolutely clean and degreased, and keyed ready to receive the paint.

Pitting There are rules that have to be followed when painting any surface with any paint. Nothing can be left to chance. Recommended procedures are important to avoid common problems. A common mistake is trying to paint when rain is imminent. The tiniest raindrops on fresh paint will result in a surface pitted with unsightly marks. This also happens if damp air indoors becomes atomised from a steaming kettle or something similar. If it has occurred and you have the problem, let it dry completely before rubbing down with fine glasspaper until you have an absolutely smooth surface, one where you cannot feel anything but a mirror-like finish beneath the tips of your fingers. Clean off the residue with a rag and white spirit, allow to dry thoroughly and then apply a new top coat under proper painting conditions.

Flaking Moisture will cause lack of adhesion, resulting in the paint lifting off and flaking. This can occur after painting if moisture has been allowed to continue its migration to the wall surface. Other reasons for flaking paint are (a) painting on to a damp or contaminated surface, (b) applying emulsion over a glossed painted wall and (c) painting on to a powdery surface. If flaking has occurred, strip off all loose and flaking paint and thoroughly sand the wall back to a stable substrate. Clean off, allow the wall to dry and apply a coat of primer sealer, obtainable from all suppliers.

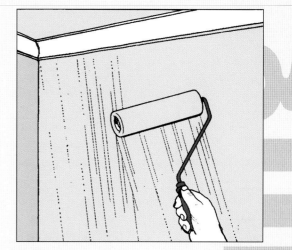

Flaking interior paint
If the paint on an interior surface has 'flaked' or blistered, remove all signs of the loose material. Fill, level and allow to dry. Then apply a coat of stabilising liquid or diluted PVA adhesive with a roller to give a base for the final finish.

Exterior painted wood with a flaking surface is unsightly and the direct result of poor preparation. If the timber has not been allowed to dry out before being painted, the moisture will try to escape when the summer sun warms up the wood. Sometimes shoddily prepared timber will have been given a coat of emulsion before a top coat of gloss. This will not last a season and flaking is bound to occur. Remove all traces of unsound paint and allow the wood to dry thoroughly. Only when the wood is absolutely dry can you start the preparation work for recoating. Use a medium grit sandpaper to feather edge the edges of the solid paint that is left, then proceed with a primer, undercoat and top coat. I am sure that you are now fully aware of how important it is to observe the drying time, the sanding and the cleaning for each successive coat.

Crazing A painted surface appears to have been done professionally with no apparent blemishes or faults, but if a top coat of an oil-based paint has been applied to an undercoat that was not completely dry and hard, crazing will result (we are not talking here of crazing intentionally carried out on, for example, antique furniture or reproduction furniture). You can also find it happening on surfaces that had not been properly rinsed of any chemical cleaning material. To solve the problem there's

105

no alternative but to rub down with wet-and-dry paper when the paint is dry in preparation for an application of fresh paint. However, if the crazing is deep and you don't want to remove the paint or varnish over a large area, there is an alternative. Simply use a proprietary brand of filler, smoothed over the entire surface with a hard plastic spatula or float. Once it is dry, use the finest grit glasspaper to get a mirror-like finish. Then go through the painting processes as before.

Efflorescence   This is a white deposit of salts found on surfaces of plaster, concrete, brick or stone. It is caused by alkaline salts, naturally found in the building materials, being brought to the surface in the drying out process. It is often seen on the brickwork of new houses, where in time it disappears when all the salts have migrated to the surface. Never be tempted to wash off the salts with a liquid cleaner or with vinegar – a Victorian idea! This will only compound the problem and not solve it. Simply rub off the white deposit with sacking, and keep doing it until no more appears – it's got to end some time! If it occurs on an indoor wall, hire a dehumidifier to help the drying out process. This will help speed up the 'bringing-to-the-surface' of the salts. Once the wall has dried out, clean off completely and, if you want to decorate, apply an alkali-resistant primer first. Follow the manufacturer's instructions exactly and then redecorate as you had planned.

Walls

Even newly built or newly surfaced walls will need a certain amount of preparation before paint can be applied. Older walls and those that are uneven or cracked will need even more! However, whatever preparation work has to be done, safety and a proper foundation for your choice of wall finish are the most important considerations at this stage. If ladders or stepladders are to be used, get to know how to handle and stabilise them. Stepladders should always have the feet against the skirting board. If you place them parallel to the wall any slight pressure on a drill or even a scraper can tilt the ladder away from the wall and cause a fall. Ladders should be erected at the correct angle, that is for every 1200 mm (4 ft) up the wall the feet should be 300 mm (1 ft) out from the wall. Stepladders are best with good wide flat rungs, so one doesn't get too tired standing on one for long periods. A clip-on tray or a fixed, folding platform to hold paint kettles and tools is a bonus.

Cracks   A crack in a plastered wall will need to be raked out and given a key shape by widening the crack at its deepest point, so that when filler is forced into the crack, it becomes its own anchor when dry by forming a wedge shape. Filler can be mixed with emulsion paint if that is to be the wall coating. In this way, the crack repair will absorb the emulsion paint at

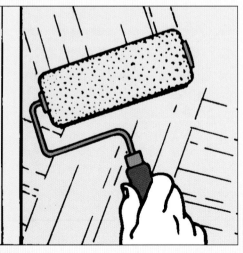

Painting walls
'Cross' paint walls with emulsion paint two or three times. This spreads the paint evenly. Do the same with stabilising solution, which is best applied with a roller.

Painting window frames
Use masking tape to prevent paint from spreading onto glass, but leave 2 mm (1/16 in) so that the paint can make a seal between it and the wooden window frame.

the same rate as the surrounding wall and not show up as a dried repair. When the repair is drying, smooth and feather edge it with a dampened paintbrush. When completely dry use a block with wet-and-dry glasspaper wrapped around it to get an invisible repair. If the crack is deep and wide you'll need to reinforce the repair with a fine net tape but back-fill the crack first before bedding the tape into the filler and use a wide plastic float to get an even finish with a feather edge. If the crack is worryingly deep, check that the wall is not a 23 cm (9 in) wall with a corresponding crack on the outside of the brickwork. If this is the case, you'll need to get professional advice. It could be that this has been caused by subsidence underneath the foundations. Please refer to the sections on 'Subsidence' and 'Heave'.

Uneven surfaces

If a plastered wall is to be redecorated but has an uneven surface, solve the problem by smoothing out the bumps and filling in the hollows. Alternatively re-surface the whole wall with plasterboard – this is termed dry-lining. To carry out the former, a tub of one-coat plaster is best for the hollows, but first of all hold a long straight-edged batten horizontally and vertically against the wall at different levels, so that you can mark the hollows and the bumps. Use a scraper to get rid of the biggest bumps, finishing off with a sanding machine. Wear protective clothing and personal protection against the dust. Also, either keep windows open or, if the room is empty, seal around the door with masking tape to stop dust getting through the door cracks. Once you've got rid of any bumps, the rest is relatively easy. The premixed plaster is easily spread and levelled with a small straight batten before smoothing it with your plastic float. Before applying the plaster in small lumps with a filling knife, dampen the whole area. Finish off each repair very gently smoothing the plaster with a wet paintbrush. You might need a second coat, when the first is dry, to fill any misses. Finally, a coat of plasticiser or diluted PVA will give you a great levelled wall ready for decorating.

Dry-lining

If you decide that the wall needs a completely new surface and you have room to lose 50 mm (2 in) off the length of the room, dry-lining is the solution. This is simply battening out the wall to receive plasterboards or a decorative panelled wall finish like tongue and grooved boards, or even laminated boards of simulated wood grain pattern (see the section on 'Panelling'). You have to take into account windows and doors to get good corner joints, also electric power points and switches have to be brought forward for safe fixing to the new wall surface. Another method of fixing the plasterboards to the wall is by using blobs of plaster. You have to decide whether or not you are going to remove the skirting boards and replace them on top of the new plasterboard surface. If not, cut the plasterboard to fit tightly against one of the side walls. If coving exists, the plasterboard will fit tightly to it and discrepancies can be filled with plaster later. With blobs about every 450 mm (18 in) apart, press the board firmly into the blobs of plaster and support it until it is dry. Turn off the supply to any circuit that supplies a socket or a switch which you intend to bring forward. You should find plenty of slack in the wiring to be able to bring the switch forward by 25 mm (1 in). Accurately cut the squared holes in the plasterboard and by using longer holding screws through the switch plate, you should be able to safely tighten up the switch plate to the new plasterboard surface. Switch back on at the mains to check. Joints around the plasterboards and the butted vertical joints can be filled with plaster and smoothed ready for decorating. A coat of plasticiser or diluted PVA is a good idea to help seal the new plaster wall and prepare it for decorating.

Stabilising

There are various methods of treating walls before beginning the redecorating stage. It depends on the substrate (what the wall is under the finish), what condition the surface is in and what the wall has been coated with previously. Brickwork that has been stripped of plaster to reveal the original bonding and mortar courses will need to be sealed to bind the border to prevent it becoming powdery. At the same time, the bricks will benefit from a coating of stabilising primer. If an attractive brick wall has been exposed for aesthetic reasons and you've decided to leave it as part of

Cover cracks between walls and ceilings with easily fixed coving.

A wall with blemishes needs a matt finish, gloss will highlight the high spots.

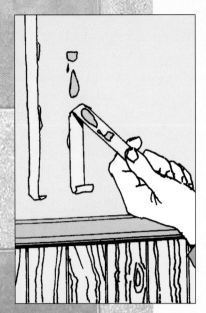

the decor with a coat of paint, prime it with a stabilising primer as the base coat. A general purpose stabilising solution can be made by diluting a PVA bonding agent with water, but do not confuse it with stabilising primer which is specially formulated for powdery surfaces only. It will bond flaky wall surfaces but it is advisable to scrape off as much loose material as possible without disturbing the stable surrounding area. Fill the small indentations with a proprietary plaster filler, which should be a quick drying one, so you'll not be held up on the preparatory part of the work.

You can get information leaflets from your DIY store or a builders merchant on all the available primers and sealers. Find one that is going to suit your particular repair job. A general purpose primer will give you sufficient sealing properties for porous walls and if you have an area on a wall that has lost its protective coating and is now patchy, it will provide the base for your chosen finish. It is suitable for solid walls and chipboard, hardboard and plywood walls. An alkali-resistant primer can be used very effectively on walls of brick, plaster, stone, concrete, render and absorbent fibre boards. This type of primer will give protection to oil-based paints, should any of the above have an alkali content, which could have an adverse effect the paint if it were not protected.

Finishes

Think of paint as a film covering a hard surface, which will provide protection as well as a decorative finish to suit your personal taste. The film of paint covering a wall provides protection against general wear and tear and should be durable enough to last years, or until your creativity demands a different colour. Painting and decorating is a rewarding experience so don't be afraid to express your own taste in your own home because that is what it's all about!

Choosing paint for interior walls is fairly easy, usually we choose emulsion for ceilings and

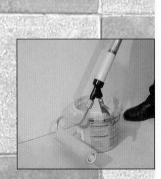

Using the incredible paint stick, it is possible to paint 6 sq m (64 sq ft) of wall space in under 5 minutes. The transparent hollow handle has a suction action to hold the paint, and comes with an adaptor to fit any container.

walls and gloss paint for woodwork. Emulsion paint is water-based, so thin it with water if you need and wash brushes and your hands in water too. Emulsion paint does have a constituent, a vinyl or acrylic, which makes it tougher when dry. The choice of finish is personal too, be it matt (a dull finish with no sheen), eggshell, silk, satin or whole gloss.

Follow the manufacturer's instructions carefully, especially if you choose a thixotropic (jelly-like) or a microscopic (moisture permeable for new plaster) paint. What they don't tell you anywhere on the label is how to paint over old distemper (the old-fashioned whitewash used up until the 1950s). It was not a good covering because it came off on your hands when the wall became wet. The mix was simply powdered chalk, glue and water, so no wonder it had no lasting quality. If you do have to solve that problem on a wall, scrape off flakes, brush off loose material and apply a specially formulated stabilising primer which comes in clear or white. Then you can safely paint the wall with no trace of the original covering.

Victorian decoration in a hall often included a dado rail (chair back protection) and a heavily embossed wallpaper between it and the high skirting board. This attractive feature is being restored in many houses of that age by DIYers to give an authentic feel to period property. The embossed wallpapers were often painted with oil paint, which gave a lovely gloss finish and extra protection at the same time. However, the surface of your wall must be very flat before you attempt to give it a coat of gloss paint. Any cracks, not properly levelled, and uneven surfaces will show up. Working by artificial light is much more difficult, so if you're planning to redecorate a room, schedule it for the weekend, so that you get as much daylight as possible. Buy the best tools and materials that you can afford.

Emulsion paint

Painting walls with emulsion paint is easier and quicker with a roller or a pad. Kits are available for both. Paint rollers come in different forms and paint sticks hold sufficient paint in the long hollow handle to paint 6 sq m (64 sq ft). It takes only 5 minutes to

Paint pads and rollers are quicker to use than emulsion brushes.

comfortably cover that area – a great innovative idea. Other rollers in kit form have the paint actually poured into the roller itself, so there is no stopping to climb down a stepladder to dip into a paint tray.

Paint pads in kit form are now as popular as rollers were when they were first introduced to DIYers years ago. A large pad, about 200 mm × 75 mm (8 in × 3 in) covers evenly with none of the effort needed to wield an emulsion brush. Smaller pads are used for cutting in to frames and around switches. There are even triangular shaped pads to ensure that walls meeting at a corner are not left with misses. The pad kit comes with a narrow deep tray with a built-in roller that dispenses the paint evenly on to the pad. Other innovative ideas are the extension handle for getting to the tops of high walls without having to use a stepladder and curved pads to fit cornices and coving.

To paint narrow walls without getting joins and misses, start at the corner with a neat line up to the adjacent wall. Continue the line for about a metre (a yard) along the ceiling and the skirting board. Fill in that strip. Filling in is the fun part because you get immediate results. Now work in metre length strips along the wall vertically. Unless you have a cove or cornice between the wall and the ceiling, you'll find that most plastered walls at the ceiling joint are not exactly straight. It may only be a slight indent or just a bit uneven, but your job is to make it look straight. The best way, to avoid emphasising an uneven join, is to keep the wall colour at the lowest part of the join and in a straight line. Never let the wall colour creep on to the ceiling and never paint a straight line actually in the whole of the join even though you think it's absolutely straight. It really will show up badly after the paint has dried. For a wider room, work right round the walls in horizontal bands. Standard emulsion paints will need two coats. However, there are one-coat emulsion paints on the market that are more opaque than the standard type. This high-opacity emulsion paint must not be spread too thinly, otherwise you'll defeat the purpose of using it, that is to save time and to get density in one coat.

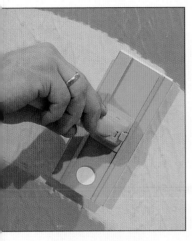

Paint pads can be used successfully on all surfaces, inside and out. Here a stippled exterior wall is being painted with just one application.

Ceilings

Always paint ceilings first if you are decorating a room completely. If you decide to use a roller, you will still have to use a small brush to paint round the edges first. However, pads have a plastic edge which gives a straight tight finish around the edge of the ceiling. There is no strong argument for using a roller or a pad because both can come with extended handles that can be used without the need to climb a stepladder. Safety must be a prime consideration when painting a ceiling. If you work from a plank or platform make certain it's safe and stable, and place it so that you don't have to change its position too often. Wear protective clothing because rollers can spatter paint even when you take great care. Don't worry about the ceiling looking patchy as you roll as long as you roll back and forth and criss-cross to even up the paint. You might be alarmed at how the paint is drying but within a short time the painted ceiling will look flat and even. Emulsion paint has that quality. Remember whether you've chosen a paint that is meant for two coats or a more opaque one coat paint. Follow the manufacturer's instructions.

Mentally divide a ceiling into square metre (square yard) areas for painting. Paint in 'bands' across the areas so that joins are not visible.

You can start painting the ceiling in a corner but you have to work out the direction of the first 600 mm (2 ft) band by deciding which way the light from the window falls. You should work away from the light. Try to blend in all joins and meeting areas so that there are no misses. The only fitting to paint around will be a light rose. These are usually the type that have a cover to unscrew to get to the terminal block and wiring. It is easily accessible but the first thing to do is to switch off at the mains and tape over the switch or, if the circuit has a removable fuse, take it out and keep it in your pocket until the job is finished. This, of course, means that you have to work in daylight, so start the job early on in the day. After unscrewing the ceiling rose let it slip down the light cable to rest against the bulb holder (after removal of the light shade). When the cover is rescrewed it will cover any blemishes and have a professional clean finish. Once the base coat is completed, you can use any paint technique covered in this section to give a special effect.

Furniture

A great deal of furniture is purchased in kit form for you to assemble. It is usually unpainted but has been sealed with a primer. If you choose to paint it, assemble it first with the screws and bolts fairly loose. Leave it for a while to acclimatise to the ambient temperature of the house. This is for a good reason. Primer or a first spray coat seal is not good enough to protect the furniture from moisture. As a consequence it will have been subjected to moisture at the factory, at the store and in transit. This causes the individual parts of the wood to swell. If different woods have been used they will react

A new elite system for decorating ceilings has been developed based on a coating, which is then cleverly patterned with an incised roller. The edging also has a matching coving, easily cut and applied with fibrous plaster adhesive.

High ceilings give some DIY decorators excuses to skip the preparation work. Cleaning and applying stabilising solution or rolling emulsion is easy with a long-handled roller!

differently, so it is important to allow the furniture to shrink as the warm atmosphere dries it out. In a centrally heated home, timber normally has a moisture content of between 12–20 per cent. Some timbers in transit have up to 35 per cent. When your assembled piece of furniture has been in your home for a couple of days, tighten up all the fixings and you're ready to decorate.

Gently rub down the surface with glasspaper in the direction of the grain. Dampen it very slightly only to raise the grain, but not to add to the moisture content. Then use a sanding block with fine glasspaper to get a mirror-like finish

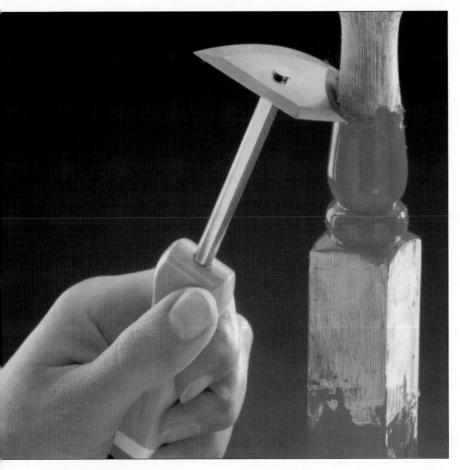

For hundreds of years the classic-shaped 'shavehook' has been used to remove paint from flat areas and particularly curved surfaces such as spindles and chair legs.

to take your primer which will be compatible with the top coat. Patience is certainly a virtue when applied to decorating furniture. It cannot be rushed. Whether you are painting a kitchen chair, a chest of drawers or a wardrobe, there has to be a step-by-step procedure to follow. So think carefully. The techniques that can be applied after you've painted a finished top coat will be covered next in this section.

Both solvent-based and water-based paints are suitable for decorating furniture, but it does depend on what piece of furniture is to be painted. For example, a linen cupboard which isn't used daily like, say, a kitchen cupboard, can have a less tough finish. A piece of furniture that has a lot of wear needs far more protection and therefore more coats of paint. The bare timber needs to be sanded thoroughly, then all knots must be sealed with knotting or shellac. When dry, rub down again and remove dust with a rag dipped in white spirit. Apply the primer, let it dry, sand and remove dust. It is best to apply two coats of undercoat, with each drying completely, then sand and remove any dust again. Too often this stage is neglected resulting in a pitted surface. One top coat should give a professional finish. Some tips to remember are:

• Sliding parts like drawer runners must not be painted. Paint only the first inch of the sides of the drawers. Varnish the insides of drawers.

• Set a kitchen chair upside down on a bench to paint its legs and cross-members first. Pop a small wire nail into each foot, so that you can stand it up on the nail heads to complete the painting.

• Use a 15 mm (½ in) brush for mouldings, rails and legs. Take care with these details. For this part of the job it is better to thin the paint a little and using it sparingly. Apply two coats rather than risk – running and curtaining – when too much is applied to, say, turned spindles. The instructions on each can of paint will tell you how to use a particular product. One-coat acrylic paints need to go on quickly and liberally. Solvent-based paints dry less quickly and will need more time to complete a job. Some one-coat paints don't need brushing out and laying off. Acrylic paints are non-flammable, dry more quickly but can leave brush marks. Also they suffer from being affected adversely if applied when any moisture is present in the air. It is important to check very carefully on the specification, content and details of how to apply your chosen paint.

With a steady hand and a long-haired dragging brush, interesting and professional effects are possible on any surface. You get finely-muted vertical stripes by gently dragging the dry brush flat against the wet second coat.

After applying a base coat and letting it dry, paint on a second decorative top coat to be grained with a special graining tool. Pull and rock through the wet paint to get interesting grain patterns to transform bedroom furniture in hours.

Dragging To totally change the look of a piece of furniture that is a plain colour and to add an interesting decorative striped pattern, you'll need a long-haired 'dragging' brush and a fairly steady hand! This technique has been used for many years on doors and surrounds. It also creates fine muted patterned stripes on furniture by keeping the brush marks vertical. A dragging brush is specially designed to give a soft, regular effect. Lay the dry brush almost flat against the wet paint and gently drag it down to make your decorative stripes. Apply a special 'paint effect' colour wash (available at DIY stores) on to a dry base colour of oil paint, working in areas about a square metre (square yard). Work with the dry dragging brush immediately. As you go to the next area work back into the preceding striped pattern so that no apparent join is seen. This 'laying off' can be mastered very easily, and remember, as it's wet paint you can always go back over it!

Graining I must say that I like the beauty inherent in the natural grain of wood, but sometimes we have furniture that is plain or painted. Now, however, it is possible to simulate natural grain to give a most attractive grain finish to plain furniture. If the piece has an oil paint finish, just give it a key with fine wire wool, then apply a coat of the new special melamine primer (available at paint stores), followed by your choice of a base colour in matt or soft sheen. A graining 'rocker' tool kit is available at DIY stores. This easy to use tool has a 50 mm (2 in) half circular rubber end incised with a grain pattern. When pulled and rocked along the wet top coat in a straight line, amazingly you'll see what looks like open grained wood. A quicker rocking motion even produces knots in the wood. There is also a 'graining comb' in the kit which produces a straighter and closer grain effect and for a really tight grain, angle the comb at 45° so that the teeth marks of the comb on the wood are tighter together. Combine and stagger the two techniques together to add a truly convincing wood look to what was an ordinary piece of furniture.

Techniques

Victorian decorators developed extraordinary techniques to give an individual look to the porches of middle-class houses. Using only feathers, rags and sponges, and cutting their own patterns for stencilling attractive decorative features, their skill and expertise has been handed down over the years. My own grandfather was a great exponent of paint techniques. Born in the middle of the Victorian era and apprenticed at a young age, he was soon in great demand in South Wales for his painting skills. I learned a great deal from him in the mid-1940s. Much of this information has been superseded by modern techniques, like cutting stencils by machine, but skilled painters are still in demand not only for their colour sense but also for the brilliant effects that they achieve. Today, statistics show that ladies generally are best at colour coordination and painting techniques. Trompe l'œil is the ultimate in paint technique decorating. Imagine a plain, dull wall at the end of a passageway being totally transformed into a scene that actually looks real, for example, like looking out through a window on to an Italianate balcony overlooking a sunlit bay with scuttling clouds and bobbing boats – that is how good it can get!

Stippling There are three stippling effects described here for you to get pleasure from. Transform a room that has been painted with a base colour into a professionally looking decorated room using a paint technique that is applied with a brush, sponge or rag. The great thing about this simple technique is that you can always have a second go if you're unhappy with your first attempt or if your choice of colour combination is not really to your liking once applied. After a base coat has been applied and has dried to a pleasant even colour, you're ready to apply the stipple effect. At this stage you should experiment. On a board which has been painted with the same base colour, try to get an effect that pleases you. First, apply a two tone effect of the same colour, then try a two colour effect. Often a two tone scheme has a calming feeling, whereas a two colour textured wall can be more exciting. Using a primary

Crackle glazing
We are familiar with criss-cross crackle lines in old oil paintings. Achieve the same mature look on furniture by painting two coats of special crackle glazes. Worn linen chests and picture frames will be much admired after being ëmellowedí with crackle glaze.

Sponge stippling is soft and gentle, whereas rag stippling is vivid and bold. Wear gloves to wet a rag in the paint, randomly stipple, and turn the rag to change patterns. A clean rag dipped in the base colour will blot out mistakes.

colour, say a deep red as a base coat, sponge your stipple effect with a pale peach colour or your own favourite combination of colours. Warm colours always give a cosy feel to a room, whereas blues and greens, the cool colours, give a more restful feeling. Get to know how colours work together in harmony or how they behave when applied as contrasting colours. Before you buy your paint supply, take home some tiny pots of paint that are available at the stores, just for experimenting.

We all know the three primary colours – red, blue and yellow – and that mixed together in equal amounts you get the secondary colours. Red and yellow in equal proportions give you a bright orange, red with blue gives violet, and blue and yellow make green. Change the amounts of each and you'll change the density and tone of the resultant secondary colour. Warm colours are reds and yellows and combinations of them. Use a more intense red and you get a more vibrant feel. Cool colours, blues and greens, make us think of the country, fields and sky, a more relaxed and calmer feel. Only by experimenting can you begin to get a feel for colour and a background knowledge of how colours work for you personally. Interestingly, some artists actually use a stipple brush to get an effect usually gained by mixing colours together. For example, some French Impressionists stippled dabs of yellow against dabs of green to give the impression of a tree in full leaf. Colour experimentation is important, as is the surface on which you apply the colour. A heavily textured wallpaper will look totally different to a smoother lining paper of the same colour scheme. The textured wall will be more interesting to look at but that's not to say it is more attractive to you personally.

Brush stippling   Try out a stipple brush, available at DIY stores, on one part of the board. Pour a small amount of paint into a shallow container, and with only a little paint on the brush, delicately dab at the board to make an attractive pattern. The closer together the 'dabs', the denser the effect, but a random circular movement or an overlapping square pattern might be your choice. You have to

choose which is going to be the dominant colour by a light touch or by a dense brush application. In any case, once you've experimented on your board, you'll know exactly what you are aiming for. Remember that whatever you do to start, it is not there for good, so you can always use the base colour to cover mistakes such as if you concentrated too much stippling in a patch.

An alternative is to use more than one colour to stipple. Very interesting effects are possible with two or three colours applied in succession after each coat has dried. The first stippling coat can be applied sparingly and the second even more so, then the base coat is still the dominant colour of the scheme.

Stippling
Stippling is something that most children learn at school. Variations are numerous – try a few. Turning a brush gives a random square effect, swirling it gives irregular curves.

Rag stippling   Another stippling technique is to use a wad of rag soaked in the paint. Wearing rubber gloves, squeeze the excess paint out and apply, again experimenting on a piece of stiff card or a board painted with your base colour. The more you experiment the better effect you'll get and the bolder you'll become. In fact, it becomes a joy when you're aware that you are getting effects similar to some that you've appreciated in the rooms of a country house or a municipal building. You really do see that luck and a bold approach can get some amazing results. Vary the pattern by unrolling the rag and creasing it into a tighter ball. Never use the rag without first squeezing the residual paint back into the container and never push the rag hard to the wall.

When the paint is dry, with a clean rag dipped into the base colour, get a constant pattern across the wall by obliterating the stippling just in parts where you consider the colour is too dense.

Sponge stippling

A more sensitive touch is necessary when applying the stipple effect with a sponge because slightly too much pressure will result in a solid patch. Always use a natural sponge but before starting leave it in a bowl of water to expand. Get rid of the residual water by squeezing it until almost dry. Then, with only a small amount of paint in a bowl or tray, dip the sponge just to touch the surface of the paint so as not to saturate it. Have a piece of cardboard handy for testing the desired stipple effect before application. Press the loaded sponge on to the board to remove the excess paint and check the finished effect. Immediately start your sponge stippling on the wall but go gently. It is best to spread the stipple impressions wide apart to start with, remember it is always easier to fill in rather than have to use the base colour to separate the impressions. Some rather interesting all-over effects are possible when you use two or three subsequent sponged coatings.

Rag rolling

The one big difference with this particular technique is that you should do it with a helper. The reason is that instead of getting the effect by adding paint, as in stippling, this technique involves removing wet paint. As one person rolls on paint, the second removes it by literally rolling a rag up the wall. Leave a pale base colour of a satin solvent paint to dry, then have your helper apply a diluted darker satin paint coat. Dilute by just a half but be careful to check the label for the correct solvent to use. Your rag should be about 200 mm (8 in) long when twisted into a roll of about 50 mm (2 in) diameter. The resulting effect is quite wonderful as you roll the rag up the wall in bands and, when dry, it will look like a piece of Chinese silk. You've now mastered the ancient painting technique of 'scumbling'.

Marbling (or feathering)

Once again, leave a base coat of oil-based eggshell paint to dry. An oatmeal or pale grey will give a grey-veined marble finish. Experiment with pink marble (base coat) with grey streaks, or, on a base of off-white, try a warm peach streaked on with the tip of a turkey or goose wing feather. However, for a realistic finish this effect should only be used on surfaces that could actually be marble.

The background colour is known as a glaze and can be a mix of two parts of eggshell finish, one part of scumble glaze and one part of white spirit. I always add artist colours to tint the glaze – inexpensive tubes are easily available from any art store. Pour one tablespoon of white spirit and one of scumble glaze into a non-plastic container, then add the mix to the eggshell paint. You can control the tone and depth of colour by the amount of artists' oil colour that you use. Some painters use a rag to distribute the base glaze coat and then, with the same rag dipped in white spirit, gently change the density of the colour in some areas to give interest to the background colour. You can even add a blend of a subtly matching colour, based on the look of real marble, but merge the colours so that no hard edges are seen. A very soft brush gently stroked over the merging colours will create the background ready for the veins to be added. To add the veins, dip the feather into your chosen colour, cleverly twitching it with small hand movements to create a marbled vein effect running diagonally across the background. Mix the colour washes with artists' oil paint thinned with white spirit and glaze. Check pictures of real marble and note the variation in background colour and in the veining. A natural colour base mixed with either black or white will alter tones, but your imagination will be rewarded with a surprising result if you are patient and persistent. If you

If you can achieve a sensitive touch with a natural sponge dipped in paint, your wall will look great with its subtle tones and shades. Stipple gently and wide apart to start, you can fill in as you go along. Add subsequent colours to create even more interesting effects.

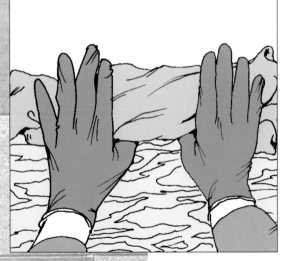

Rag rolling
Allow a base coat to dry thoroughly. Apply a second coat and immediately start rolling a rag over it. The paint is removed in part to reveal the base coat in an interesting pattern.

prefer a heavier or thicker vein effect, use an artist's or signwriter's brush, say a No. 3. Remember that marble is a randomly patterned stone with no parallel lines but plenty of wandering vein lines. By keeping the paint workable and moistened with white spirit, you can then soften the whole effect with a wall-paper smoothing brush. Professionals use a long, flat, soft bristled brush called a 'flogger' for the final softening effect.

Once the marbling is completed to your satis-faction, there is one more task to do and that is to protect the surface. You can do this in one of two ways. One is to paint on, with a soft paint-brush, a coat of semi-gloss polyurethane varnish. Alternatively, mix a little of the base coat and white spirit with the varnish to give a more delicate look to the marbling and to make the veins appear less bold.

Stencilling
As children, many of us were given cut-out designs of cartoon characters, or of rabbits and ducks, and shown how to make repeating patterns on, say, a border around the classroom. The chubby stencil brush was a great tool for little fingers, because the effects were immediate and generally foolproof! Nowadays, great strides have been made in this technique. Buy almost any design that you fancy from art shops or as kits from large DIY outlets. Alternatively, design your own or repeat a pattern already on something in the room. If curtains have a large rose pattern, it is very easy to copy it, simplified, on to a stencil sheet or on to a thin board made non-porous with a couple of coats of lacquer. Cut out the shape with a sharp trimming knife, always working away from your fingers. Hold the stencil in position either with a 'low-tack' spray adhesive or with masking tape. Dab the brush on to the design using only a small amount of paint. Work inwards from all the edges, so as not to allow the paint to creep under the card or stencil. Apply,

Cutting and using a stencil of one's own design and pattern is quite exciting because the results are immediate and simple to achieve! This circular motif was designed by my wife and used on a hall cupboard at home.

on to a dry base coat of universal primer, a top coat of eggshell with a brush or mini-roller, and leave to dry. The stencilling can be done with another colour of eggshell. Small sample pots of paint are available in vinyl matt emulsion if you only have a small amount of stencilling to do. If you are repeating the pattern around a room, use a spirit level to make sure that the top of the stencil or card is always horizontal. Mark each successive stencil position exactly with a pencil mark on the wall that can be matched against a registration mark on the stencil.

Liming
Time after time, on visiting some great buildings in France, I came across old furniture, doors and woodwork that had a very special, appealing look. As a young architectural student I was intrigued by the English transla-tion which I was told was 'limed-oak', but nobody could tell me how the emphasising of the grain by making it a lighter colour than the rest of the wood, was attained. Back in Wales, my grandfather once again came to my aid. It really is a simple but effective technique involving only white paint and white spirit. The technique was simply to paint on and wipe off with just enough pressure to leave the grain filled with the paint.

This adds charm and a patina of age to charac-terless softwoods, and is perfect for kitchen cupboards, doors and furniture. However, if you want to retain the natural grain of the wood but also to colour it, there are antique pine or light oak wood stains available. Dark blue, ebony or black base colours add drama. Modern wood stains can leave a light or dense colour and do not obscure the grain of the wood. An alterna-tive method is to use a clear matt polyurethane varnish thinned with white spirit to seal the surface before applying the lime wash. One part white spirit to one part white paint will give a consistency that will spread evenly over the surface but when wiped off the residue will remain in the undulations of the grain. Use a dry sponge across the grain to remove the excess paint. Some specialist painters actually use an undercoat mixed with white spirit as the lime wash. You can choose eggshell, satin finish or non-drip gloss.

Coatings

Wall coatings are different from any other paint effect because, once mixed, they are of a stiffer consistency and applied to a thickness of 3 mm (⅛ in) before texturing. There are two good reasons for using a wall and ceiling coating. One is to produce an unusual textured finish and the other to successfully hide cracks and gaps in walls, concealing defects like bumps and undulations. DIY coatings come in ready-mix tubs and in bags of powder to be mixed with water. Some are available in colours but all can be decorated with emulsion paint to fit in with your decor. If you have irregularities in a wall or ceiling surface, they can easily be hidden by applying a textured finish coating. You can sculpt almost any pattern into the coating because of its stiff consistency, and it remains workable for some time (check the instructions on the pack) so you have time to perfect your chosen swirl, comb or tree bark effect.

Paul O'Grady (alias Lily Savage) was absolutely intrigued to find that it was so easy to produce a series of swirls just with a screwed up plastic bag into which I popped a pair of my socks! Wear plastic gloves to protect your hands and screw the bag into a tight ball, press it into the wet coating and twist without sliding to get a very decorative swirl. Repeat it at random, overlapping each swirl all over the wall and you'll be as thrilled with the final result as Paul was!

Textured All textured coatings can only be applied to a wall or ceiling that has been properly prepared. This means total degreasing and then the usual stages of filling, smoothing and stabilising. After masking switches, sockets and edges, use an old emulsion brush to apply the coating to the wall or ceiling. A roller can be used but the coating will become thinner as it spreads more. Experiment with different rollers to produce different textures. I've tried elastic bands around an old hardened roller and found it gave a most interesting bark effect. Another experiment I tried for rolling a sand colour on to a deep green base colour was to haphazardly wind elastic bands around a long-haired lambswool roller. The startling result was a deep underwater shimmering effect. Before you begin, have all materials and tools together, working from a complete tools and materials list. Remove as much furniture from the room as possible, lay floor coverings and have a safe stepladder to hand. As you are going to cover only 2–3 sq m (2–3 sq yd) at a time, there is no need for a plank between two stepladders. A DIY 'hop-up' is ideal for getting to the tops of walls. Remember that the coating will cover and conceal many of the irritating blemishes that you may discover when working close to the wall. You do not have to be so fussy as you do when preparing your wall for wallpapering or painting. If you find any mould lurking from past condensation, treat it with a proprietary fungicide. Once all the areas adjacent to the

A good quality wide 'float' or scraper with a sensible handle is a boon for applying wall and ceiling coatings. It is also used for creating patterns and to smooth points on a textured surface that can occur if the consistency is too thick. Experiment on a spare board with the toothed scraper. You'll find that the recognisable comb 'shell' effect is easily achieved. Spread the coating evenly with the 'float'. Press on one point and sweep an arc!

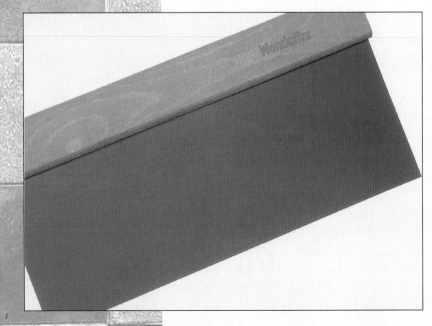

Textured wall coatings
Apply with a large brush, 'crossing' a couple of times to get an even finish before texturing.

walls, like architraves, window sills, switches, sockets and skirtings are masked, you should be ready to start.

Inexpensive, special rollers are available that are specially designed for patterning wall and ceiling coatings. Use one, for example, with a single diagonal groove to produce an oak tree bark effect. Another has crossing diagonal grooves to get an all over diamond pattern, but this is better in a large room. One interesting one that I found has open grooves running around it which produced a knotted bark effect. Another has concentric indents and makes a small circular interlocking pattern which looks very professional. It is easy to join each part of the pattern because the circles intertwine and are not complete circles. It looks very 'art deco'.

Swirls The best and easiest swirls can be produced with a square stipple brush. Apply the coating liberally but don't spread it 'out', spread it 'in' instead. In other words, don't tease it out to cover more wall space, just eke it out by brushing only on the area covered by one application. You can start anywhere in the 2 sq m (2 sq yd) area and work out in any direction. The swirls are going to overlap randomly. Press the brush into the coating and immediately give one complete twist of the wrist maintaining an even pressure. The trick is not to move the brush sideways. Lift off cleanly

to leave a positive swirl. This really is easy and the effects are stunning. Don't leave any spaces between the swirls and you'll be amazed at how quickly a wall can be covered. Go as close to the ceiling as possible and the edge of a border is no problem because with a small brush drawn around the wall and tight to the ceiling you can professionally define the border by flattening the coating.

A sponge will also give a very satisfactory swirl effect. If you start at one side and work towards the centre you'll get a pleasing layered effect but take care to repeat each twist of the wrist with the same amount of overlap of the preceding swirl. A stipple brush lifts off very little of the coating, but a sponge, because of its nature, will need to be cleaned by dipping into a bucket of water and squeezing dry, probably after each swirl.

Combed Once all the preparation work is completed and the first small area coated properly, run a roller over it to get a slightly thinner and more even surface. This is because a combed effect does not need to be raised too much. Use the special toothed spatula that comes with a wall coating kit. Try first to hold the comb (spatula) as if offering a dinner plate, then turn your hand upside down and apply one corner tightly to the wall so that it becomes the fulcrum or turning point. Now, gently press the comb to the wall but maintain pressure on

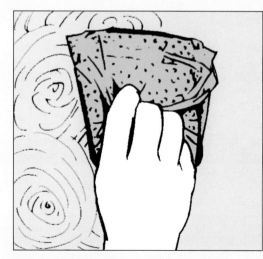

Textured wall coatings – swirls
Wrap a sponge in a polythene bag to get a variety of patterns. A swirl is obtained by simply twisting the sponge.

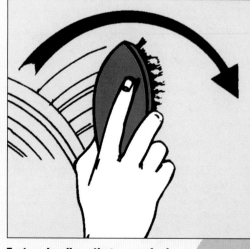

Textured wall coatings – combed
An ordinary scrubbing brush will give an interesting shell pattern.

Wall coatings are probably the easiest of all finishes to apply, because some licence in the application adds interest. An even coat is not essential, the stipple brush will give the whole area cohesion! Dab the brush gently; overlap each time in another direction.

A popular choice of texture is the clever 'combed' effect. Mix Wondertex to a firm consistency by slowly adding to hot, warm or cold water. Apply it with a brush or roller in one metre strips, then texture a metre at a time from top to bottom.

You can pick a pattern to apply to a ceiling, or invent your own. Try a sponge inside a plastic bag. Just press it, scrunched up, and twist it without sliding. Overlap each stroke and you can accomplish some fascinating effects.

that one corner. Sweep the comb around in a 180° arc to create your combed pattern. Try not to let it slip – if it does you can always start again – and keep working at it until it's second nature, then you're ready to cover the wall with wonderfully combed patterns or scrolls. Overlap only in one direction so that you get a professional looking regular pattern.

Geometric

There are rollers available that create many geometric patterns such as diamond, squares and circles. One type produces a small squared pattern with lines running alternately horizontally and vertically in adjacent squares. This basket-weave pattern can also be produced on a larger scale by cutting notches into the edge of the lid of a square plastic container. To increase your knowledge of what is available, ask at your local DIY store for brochures on rollers, spatulas and rubber serrated tools. These will give different geometric effects. For example, with a tile cement-spreader that has large teeth, you can create a herringbone pattern or a chequerboard effect, or with the rounded end of a triangular spatula, draw it vertically and horizontally at regular intervals to make a geometric harlequin design. Once the pattern has been finished, if too much coating has been raised in patches, it will harden into sharp edges. To solve this problem, hold a large plastic spatula at a low

angle and draw it very lightly over the whole of the pattern.

Stipple

There are two main methods of producing a stipple effect on wall coatings. Both methods can be used to create similar effects but with slight variations.

Use a wet sponge to pat the coating to give a pitted effect. Take care not to apply too much pressure as this will bring up the coating into tiny spikes. These sharp edges play havoc with woollen garments that can snag on the tiny points (sleeves are particularly vulnerable). You'll need to rinse the sponge each time that you move to the new area. At the same time as sponging the coating, stroke the finished stippled 2 sq m (2 sq yd) area of the wall with the flat straight edge of a plastic spatula to lay down the sharp points.

Alternatively, use a stipple brush – an essential part of a wall coating kit. This rubber bristled brush is perfect for getting a regular effect over the whole of a wall or ceiling surface. Just pat the wet coating with random light strokes, moving the brush to different angles so that there is no square edge left in the coating. The resultant effect is less sharp than with a coarse sponge, but it might still be necessary to stroke down some of the pitting.

A lath and plaster ceiling will probably be quite old and sagging in places. Providing it is sound, give it a new lease of life with a textured coating and a bold pattern.

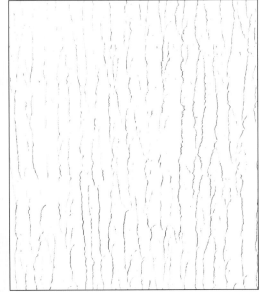

High ceilings with cosmetic cracks are sometimes difficult to maintain. Solve the problem by applying, a textured coating with a long-handled roller.

Painting tools

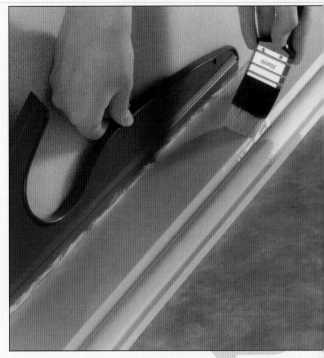

The paint guard is a recent painting innovation. It prevents paint creeping where it is not wanted.

More and more DIYers are finding out how painting pads can transform their concept of painting large areas, with no fatigue or aching arms! This small kit is sufficient to do most painting jobs inside and out, oil- or water-based on wood, metal and masonry!

Wrap rollers, pads and brushes in cling film to keep them fresh for a long time.

Brushes Conventional painting brushes have for a long time been made with animal hair or bristles. Usually, these are hog (pig), ox or horse, each used for specific purposes. The best has always been hog hair, the most versatile material for painting. Bristles should be tapered at the tip so that you can smooth the surface to a very fine finish ('laying off'). For painting on to timber surfaces, you'll need a range of widths, 75 mm (3 in), 50 mm (2 in), 25 mm (1 in) and 12 mm (½ in). A 'devilled sash tool' is a cutting-in brush with an angled tip, useful for painting right into corners of a sash, along the sash bars on a window frame and to get a straight line against the glass. A radiator brush has a long wire handle, so named to paint behind radiators without having to remove them. There are stencil brushes and grainers for creating wood effects (these have been super-seded by the new graining tool).

Recently, paintbrushes have been developed that do not shed their bristles. These are a boon to the professional and DIYer alike. They come in all the regular sizes and look like conven-tional brushes. The bristles are man-made and when you see the gleaming side of one of these new brushes you can understand why it is claimed that it will glide over the paintwork with no 'pull'.

Take time when choosing brushes, especially large ones. Wielding a 100 mm (4 in) emulsion brush for a weekend can be extremely tiring. Find the best that suits you, taking into account how much experience you've had decorating and painting. Most brushes are designed for general use on wood and metal, but wall brushes can be heavy when fully loaded. An extra wide brush might cover more area, but you must have the strength to wield it! Try holding a wall paintbrush by the stock (the part between the bristles and the handle). You will experience less strain in your wrist and forearm – it is the way a professional decorator has been taught to hold it. A narrow brush is easier to handle – hold it as you do a pencil. The bristles are called the 'filling' and are usually set in resin or rubber and securely held by a metal 'ferrule', tightly fixed to the wooden or plastic handle. Good quality bristles, when flexed and released, should spring back into shape. The tips of each bristle on a hog's hair brush will taper and the ends of each bristle are split into fine 'fila-ments', giving a soft feel to the end of the brush. Because of the density of the tip of a good brush, paint is held well and very evenly distributed.

When painting, the accepted rule is to dip the brush into the paint until the bristles are almost half covered. This will obviously vary depending on the size of the brush and the viscosity of the paint. You cannot, for example, load as much thinned paint on to a brush as you can with a more viscous paint. Use a paint kettle. They are cheap and very useful. Dispense just enough paint from the tin into your kettle for ease and comfort. Always dab the brush on the side of the container to remove excess paint. If you draw the brush across the top of the paint tin, you'll fill the rim and it will drip down the outside to obliterate important instructions. A filled rim will dry hard with the result that you'll need a hammer to force the lid on to the tin with awful results.

When you've finished using water-based paints, clean the brushes thoroughly in warm soapy

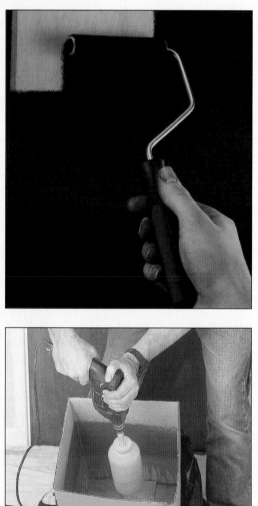

water to get all the residual paint from deep within the bristles. Rinse in clean water, dry on a towel, pop on an elastic band loosely around the tip of the bristles until they are dry. This will help the bristles to retain their original shape.

For solvent-based paints, cleaning is similar but more laborious. Lay the brush on newspaper and push a small batten from the stock to the tip to squeeze out residual paint. Do both sides. Check the instructions for the type of solvent to use. Get rid of excess paint by immersing the brush in the proper solvent (usually white spirit), agitate the brush, squeeze out as much of the solvent as possible, then wash with detergent in hot water. Dry it flat on towelling before wrapping an elastic band loosely around the tip of the bristles.

There is now available an award-winning brush and roller cleaner that supersedes these old established cleaning methods. This product can totally clean a brush, even one that has been used for red paint, in less than a minute, and have it ready to use immediately in white paint! How is this done? Well, the simple answer is by centrifugal force. The brush is clasped in a holder, which is held in the chuck of your drill. By spinning for only seven seconds, inside a plastic bin, most of the paint is thrown off. Agitate the brush for five seconds in a solvent and after spinning again for seven seconds you have a dry, perfectly clean brush.

Rollers Rollers came into their own when it was realised that enthusiastic DIYers really wanted to redecorate rooms with paint rather than wallpaper. This useful device has since developed from the simple foam or lambswool sleeve roller to more sophisticated rollers with built-in paint holders. Originally developed for painting walls and ceilings more quickly, more easily and with less fatigue, rollers come with outer coverings of foam, sheepskin or synthetic fibre. These are interchangeable on a sprung wire cage linked to a shaped, cranked handle. Rollers come in standard lengths of 225 mm (9 in) and 175 mm (7 in), but smaller rollers are available too for wood and special paint techniques. Others are shaped for corners of rooms

Rollers come in many types and sizes from 10 cm to 30 cm (4 in to 12 in). Roller sleeves can be made of foam, synthetic fibres or lambswool, and come in different lengths for different paints and surfaces. Use a long pile on masonry, medium pile for emulsion or oil on smooth walls and short pile for gloss on wood.

A 10 cm (4 in) mini roller is the ideal painting tool for small areas of emulsion. It is easy to handle and even the inexperienced DIYer will get surprisingly good results.

One of the most successful inventions to benefit decorators is the brush and roller cleaner that literally spins off the paint. Based on the centrifugal principle, the roller is spun in a drill and is ready for a different colour in less than a minute.

and there is even a small two-wheel roller for pipes. Outside, use a long sleeve pile for emulsion paint, which can also be used with masonry paint on rendered walls. Gloss paints call for a short pile sleeve or a mini dense foam roller. Check at your DIY store, where a comprehensive guide is available, covering all types of rollers and their uses. They will also advise on a powered roller with a battery driven motor if you are contemplating painting the whole house! This gives five hours of continuous use and the paint is delivered from a portable reservoir to the roller via a long flexible hose. It is estimated that you can cover a wall measuring 4500 mm × 2400 mm (15 ft × 8 ft) in less than 10 minutes.

Before using a roller on a wall, get a clean edge all round with a brush.

As with brushes, there are now available new and innovative designs of rollers. One of these has a solid central cylinder to hold the paint. A small funnel allows the paint to be fed from the tin into the cylindrical container (the roller) around which the removable sleeve is fitted. After inserting the stopper the paint is totally enclosed in the cleverly perforated core of the roller body. The simple action of rolling on the wall brings the paint to the surface of the roller to give an even coat over the whole wall without any splatter whatsoever. The great thing is that the roller can hold sufficient paint to cover an average sized ceiling or wall without having to be refilled. After you've finished, any residual paint can be poured back into the container. The kit comes with its own jug together with a clip-on base which also acts as a lid for the jug. Washing the sleeve is very simple because it literally slips off from the solid core of the roller. Rinse it under a tap with warm soapy water as you would a flannel. The kit also contains a mini roller with a flip-over guide which allows you to paint close to a light switch, for example, without getting paint on to the sides of the cover plate. A truly innovative idea being used by professionals and DIYers alike.

There is yet another development of a roller with an attachment that holds paint – this time in the hollow handle. Surprisingly, sufficient emulsion paint can be drawn into the cylinder by the piston type plunger to cover 6 sq m (64 sq ft) of wall surface. Without stopping you can cover 2400 mm × 2400 mm (8 ft × 8 ft) in less than two minutes. At the base of the cylinder is a clip to hold the filling tube firmly in the paint. The cranked roller handle keeps the roller clear of the tin of paint but is still attached to the handle. When you pull on the handle the rubber disc at the end of the piston forms a vacuum which draws the emulsion paint into the space. You do not have to wipe any parts because the whole operation is carried out easily by pushing a spigot into a tight fitting rubber ring on the clipped hose. Kits come with all parts ready assembled and with full instructions. Any paint left in the translucent cylinder handle is cleanly and efficiently returned to the paint tin by pushing the plunger. This means that there are very few parts to clean. However, every part is detachable and simply cleaned in warm soapy water.

Filling knives and scrapers These two helpful tools are used to prepare surfaces before redecorating. They are very much the 'tool for the job in hand'. I've often been asked to advise on how to solve the problem of damaged plaster when stripping wallpaper. Invariably, the DIYer has used the filling tool and not the correct tool, the scraper. These two steel tools might look alike but must only be used for the designated purpose. A filling knife is the more flexible and could easily bend if pushed on a wall to remove wallpaper. The result is that a lump of plaster can be easily hooked out. For filling gaps and cracks in plaster walls and ceilings a high-quality steel blade held securely with rivets to a hardwood handle, is best.

Use a filler knife to easily smooth plaster filler into cracks and gaps in plasterwork, but first it is best to widen the inside of a crack and to remove all debris. Cover the crack with a coating of dilute PVA then force in the filler. The flexibility of the pliable blade helps to get a feather edge either side of the repair. Always wash the knife after use and wipe the metal with an oily cloth to keep it pristine. Before using it next time wipe off the surplus oil, so that it does not contaminate the next plaster repair.

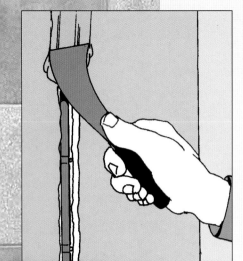

Filling knife
Cracks in plaster and in cable and pipe channels should be filled with cellulose filler applied with a flexible filling knife to ensure smooth filling.

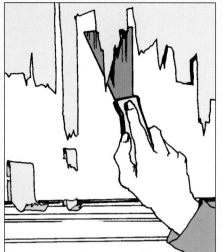

Scraper
A scraper has the required rigidity to run behind softened wallpaper. Never use a filling knife which could hook out chunks of plaster. The scraper can also be used to scrape wood to smooth it.

Shave hooks
Use shave hooks to get paint off difficult mouldings. The Victorians were adept in their use because picture rails, dado rails and architraves were more intricately shaped than today. However, now we want to restore more old features in our houses, it is time to learn how to use these tools once again to solve tricky stripping problems.

Painting tools
Never use a screwdriver to open a tin of paint as it will distort the lid preventing a good seal. Buy an inexpensive can opener, but use it upside down (the point upwards). Place it on the edge of the tin and gently lever.

Never use paint straight from the tin but pour 5–8 cm (2–3 in) into a plastic paint kettle, which is easy to clean.

Scrapers are similar in size and shape to filling knives but are thicker and have little flexibility. Used in conjunction with a wallpaper steam stripper, a good quality 75 mm (3 in) steel scraper will perform well without damaging the substrate or plaster. After removing all the wallpaper, the scraper can also be used for removing dry hard nibs and blemishes, as well as scraping off small bumps.

Paint kettles   In Victorian times, paint was often mixed by the decorator who always decanted a small amount into a separate tin or 'kettle'. This made the job easier and safer. It meant that a large tin did not have to be carried to the work site or held by hand or hook on a ladder. Nowadays, paint kettles are inexpensive, literally a fraction of the cost of a 5 litre (1 gallon) can of paint, so it makes sense to use one every time you reach for the paint and the brush. It also makes it easy to add a solvent or thinners, something almost impossible with a full tin of paint. All paint kettles were previously made from galvanised metal, which made them much heavier than the present day light plastic kettles that are easy to lift, safe to handle and easily cleaned.

If the instructions from the paint you are using says stir the paint before use, always do this before decanting even the smallest amount into your kettle, then you'll be certain that all the constituents in the paint are properly mixed. This also ensures that you never ever get a build up of residue in the bottom of the tin. Return any paint that is left over to the tin and clean the kettle with the proper solvent. If, by chance, you let some paint dry hard in the kettle, it is easily removed by flexing the plastic sides.

For a small paint job, fit a plastic bag inside a saucepan to hold the paint.

Paint kettles
Always decant paint into a paint kettle. A piece of string tied across the kettle serves as a brush rest and is useful to remove excess paint from the brush. Clean brushes with a spinning device and put an elastic band around the bristles afterwards to maintain their shape.

Materials

Solvents Solvents are liquids capable of dissolving another substance. They also act as thinners, making a particular substance, like paint, less viscous to make it flow more freely. When used in large quantities, as in a factory, precautions have to be taken under the Health and Safety Executive's Regulations, to make a safe working environment. Even in the home it is wise to ensure that you have plenty of ventilation when using solvents and thinners to dilute paints and varnishes, and it is unwise to smoke when using white spirit or any other recommended thinners for an oil-based paint. Keep all solvents and thinners in childproof containers or, better still, in a locked cupboard. It's common sense really!

Solvents are not good for the skin, even though they are sometimes used by DIYers for cleaning paint from hands! I use a proprietary barrier cream when tackling a painting job that involves white spirits for oil-based paints or thinners for cellulose. Water is the solvent for emulsion paint and is used for thinning and cleaning. If you use a masonry paint on the exterior of your house, it is usually water-based. It is good practice always to thin the emulsion paints and masonry paints for the first coat. Thinning also means better penetration of the water-based paints so the substrate absorbs the coating to form a seal. Water-based acrylic paints used for a finish coat on wood give a tough sheen finish even though the solvent used is water. The vinyl, synthetic resin in emulsion paint produces a hard, washable finish, despite being water soluble in the tin.

Oil paints Choose decorative oil paints to get an attractive, durable and hygienic finish. The base, or medium, for oil paints depends on a manufacturer's choice of the proportion of oil to resin. In the past, natural resin was chosen, but it was so slow drying that a synthetic resin was produced to supply the demand for a faster drying paint. Strong and subtle colours are available depending on the pigment used and the amount of pigment related to the amount of resin used in the manufacture of oil paint.

Imagine being able to paint radiators at the same time as the walls, with the same water-based paint. Radiator Clearcoat gives any standard emulsion the heat-resistant, wipe-clean properties of traditional radiator paint.

This also makes the difference between gloss and satin. Nowadays, oil paints are available that are called 'low odour'. These paints have very little smell and no problematic fumes to irritate those DIYers with breathing problems. Doors and windows painted with oil-based paints should only require a wipe down with warm soapy water where dirt and dust has settled.

When repainting a surface that is sound, with no flaking or blemishes, you will only need to 'key' it with fine wire wool before applying one coat of paint. Alternatively, you can use a 'one-coat' gloss which is also formulated for use without an undercoat. Use an oil-based one-coat paint, which obliterates and glosses in one, on primed, new wood. It has a higher pigment content and is thicker in consistency, but flows easily without having to brush it out too much. A great development for professionals and DIYers.

Painting wood
When applying oil-based paint to wood, always paint in the direction of the grain and never put the wet brush into an area that has already been painted. 'Lay-off' from dry wood into the wet paint.

Water-based paints One of the most interesting developments in the manufacture of paints has been that of water-based paints like acrylics. Technological advances in the formulation of these paints mean that we now have a water-based paint that gives a tough finish on wood inside or outside the home. Advantages are that it is non-flammable, it dries quickly, has little smell and offers less risk to one's health than solvent-based products. Some manufacturers recommend using a synthetic bristle

brush with their acrylic products. Another advantage is that, because one has to work more quickly, there is then less chance of leaving brush marks. One disadvantage is that you will not get a high-gloss finish on wood.

Other water-based paints are emulsions and masonry paints (ask for one with a mould inhibitor). These are covered elsewhere in this section. All water-based paints are obviously more environment-friendly than solvent-based paints, but be careful when disposing of all tins and residual paint deposits (particularly of solvents). Contact your Local Council (Environmental Department) for advice.

Coatings   Interior coatings

Interior wall coatings are very different from exterior coatings like rendering (which is a mix of sand and cement). The former are used for two main reasons: to cover blemishes and imperfections in a wall or ceiling without the need for repairing cosmetic cracks and to produce a textured surface using one of the many incised or patterned rollers, combs and spatulas designed for this purpose. The art of texturing, that is imaginatively creating a unique patterned, all-over, raised design, is covered in the section on techniques. Artex has come into our language when referring to wall coatings in the same way as Hoover did for vacuum cleaners, but coatings or textured coatings which are thicker than paint, come in various forms for different purposes. A ready-mix coating in tub form is a one coat application requiring no undercoat. Some ready-mix coatings can fill cracks to a depth of an inch without sagging. Other coatings come in powder form for mixing with water. In these cases, follow the instructions very carefully to prevent lumps forming. Use a 'paddle' mixer fixed to your drill to get a truly professional

mix – all decorators do this as they usually work with large amounts. Always sprinkle the powder on to the water and not the other way round or you will get lumps!

Coatings are best applied with an old emulsion brush, but if a light coating is wanted use a roller to spread it over a wall or ceiling. After the surface has been properly prepared and is smooth, flat and even, apply a coat of diluted PVA to act as a seal and a stabiliser. This provides a good key for the coating material so that it becomes bonded to the substrate.

Exterior coatings   Exterior coatings are usually a mix of cement, sand and lime. This mortar mix must not be stronger than the wall to which it is going to bond. For example, a higher proportion of sand to cement, about 1 to 6, is needed when applying the render to, say, a garage wall of block work or a house wall of soft bricks, whereas a mix of one part cement to four parts sand would be suitable for solid concrete or hand-fired bricks. Carry out all repairs to perished pointing, friable surfaces, old flaking paint and then stabilise the area using diluted PVA. Add either an inhibitor to the mortar or when the coating has completely dried use a proprietary surface sealer applied by either spray, brush or roller, to prevent the future problem of water penetration through an exterior render coating. Fix temporary wooden battens to contain the render within a particular area on an outside wall. It is a fallacy to believe that mortar sets or cures by drying out. The longer it is kept damp the stronger the finish coating will be. Hydration takes place as soon as water is added to the mix to create a chemical reaction for the 'curing' to begin. Types of finishes for exterior rendering are covered separately in this book.

Wallpapering

Types of covering

Wallpaper Nobody need feel that there isn't a colour or pattern of a wallpaper to suit their taste! Machine-printed wallpapers are relatively inexpensive and produced for the mass market in a myriad of colours, designs and patterns – we've all experienced the frustration of trying to make a choice from the innumerable pattern books available in a store. The secret is to make a few notes before visiting the shop. Stick to a basic combination of colours and think in terms of large or small repeating patterns or vertical lines or even classical patterns. Think also of how much you want to spend. Last of all, do you want a vinyl, flock, grass cloth, paper-backed cotton, linen or silk (beautiful, but costly), or perhaps a coarse hessian? With your notes to hand the sales person should show you the pattern books limited to your choices.

Embossed The use of wallpaper as a decorative wall finish was established in the UK in the sixteenth-century. However, the greatest expansion of papers available and of the firms producing them, happened in the nineteenth century when mechanised printing came into its own. Victorians demanded what we would call 'fussy' effects to be painted or varnished after being applied to the wall. So Anaglypta® was born. This dense paper, into which the pattern was embossed during manufacture by the use of metal dies, gave a richer effect than that of simple printed papers. The pattern remained prominent even after painting or varnishing. At this time 'flock' wallpapers, which incorporate a shallow velvet pile, producing a similar effect, were also developed. However, flock could not be over-painted when the original surface became discoloured. At the same time other wallpaper manufacturers competed by producing Lincrusta®, a rival to Anaglypta®.

Thousands of elaborate wallpaper patterns were designed to meet the Victorian demand. Some of these are still available today. However, modern day wallpaper designers have produced Victorian patterns and colours on a wide range of contemporary papers, but you will pay more for these than the standard vinyl wall coverings.

Woodchip Wallpaper is available in a wide range, from the popular woodchip to the more exotic paper-backed fabrics. Woodchip is used a great deal by developers because it is inexpensive and it easily covers some imperfections. Small particles of chipped wood are layered between two papers giving a raised relief covering. When such a pronounced textured paper is lit by a side light, the overall look can be stronger than any blemishes, such as where two adjacent sections of a wall are not in line. Woodchip is tougher than most papers so a good sharp knife and a straight edge is best for initial cutting. Use one of the new, angled aluminium trimming guides or long sharp scissors to trim woodchip.

Linings

Lining paper Never leave to chance that a wall covering will cover all blemishes. It is true to say that 'it is all down to preparation'! The wall has to be as flat and even as possible before hanging wallpaper. It is mistakenly believed that wallpaper will contract on drying out to cover a crack or a nib that has inadvertently been left. It is true that wallpaper will contract but only to compound the problem. The crack or the nib will show up even worse. Even heavily embossed paper needs a perfectly flat wall to get a professional finish. Lining paper will help with minor blemishes but hang it horizontally. If you are right-handed work from the right of the wall holding the concertinaed paper in your left hand and smoothing with the brush held in your right hand. (Lining paper hung in preparation for a painting technique application should be hung vertically.)

Polystyrene One of the most common problems related to wallpapering is mould, usually caused by condensation. This is often found when a free-standing wardrobe is moved from a corner of a bedroom being prepared for decorating. Spores feed on the damp wall surface leaving a black mould. Condensation is easily explained. When you breathe warm moist air on to a cold window we all know that we get rivulets running down the pane of glass. Wherever warm moist air is in contact with a cold wall you run the risk of condensation, so this can happen inside wardrobes fixed to outside walls. Mildew on leather shoes is a good indicator of this type of condensation. One method of solving the problem is to hang sheets of expanded polystyrene on the wall before hanging the wallpaper. Clean off the mould with a fungicidal solution before stripping the old wallpaper, then compress the pieces into a dustbin liner ready for disposal. It needs to be contained, so as not to allow the contaminated paper to spread the spores. The polystyrene comes in rolls and can be hung by pasting it as you would ordinary paper. You'll find that the material is easily dented so take care handling and hanging.

Polystyrene feels warm when you lay your hand on it and this is a clue to what is happening when you hang polystyrene sheets on a wall to be covered with wallpaper. The polystyrene will retain its warmth and prevent the cold from the exterior wall travelling through to the inside wall, so condensation cannot happen. Sometimes, if the problem is bad you might need sheets up to 25 mm (1 in) thick fixed to the wall with special adhesive and faced with a laminated sheet.

Stripping

The easiest and most effective way to strip any wallpaper is by using steam stripper. If you don't own one, it is cheap to hire one for a weekend. Follow the instructions carefully and you will quickly learn how to use it. It really is amazing how swiftly one wall can be stripped with just this tool.

Scoring   In the past, paper was stripped by soaking it with a sponge after having scored it with a wire brush, a knife or a 'hedgehog' (a small spiked wheel on the end of a wooden handle). These made perforations in the paper

so that the warm water could penetrate to soften the old paste. In effect what one has to do is to lessen the paste adhesion so that the paper comes away easily without leaving strands. Requiring many buckets of soapy, warm water, it proved to be a laborious operation. Meanwhile, designers and manufacturers were putting time and money into the design and development of a machine that was safe and efficient to make the job of stripping wallpaper a more enjoyable operation – the steam stripper.

Steaming   Steam strippers run off the mains so follow the instructions that come with your steam stripper and you'll have no problem using one. A floor-standing water container has a heating element to produce steam which passes through a long hose to the steam plate. The flat, tough plastic plate is not distorted by the steam so that the steam is delivered exactly where you want it and does not escape through

Stripping wallpaper
Hire a steam stripper to remove the old wallpaper safely, quickly and efficiently. Make sure you read the instructions carefully. They're important for your safety and to professionally prepare a wall for repapering.

Put stripped wallpaper in plastic bags.

Hire a steam stripper to remove wallpaper. An industrial machine is quickest.

Before steam-stripping paper use a 'hedgehog' – a roller with spikes.

the sides. Take all the usual precautions like protecting sockets and switches to prevent water rivulets entering the boxes to cause problems. Use coverings to protect the floor and plastic bags for disposing of the stripped paper.

Once the steam is generated, hold the steam plate at your starting point. Lift the saturated paper off with a scraper whilst holding the plate at your second position. You'll make it a continuous action with no stopping – a very satisfying task, which gets immediate results.

Wallpapers that have had a coat of paint are more difficult to remove by traditional methods, but by using a steam stripper you should have no problems.

Certain types of vinyl wallpaper are easy to strip because they come as two layers, a top patterned plastic film and a lining paper. Sometimes you can get a sharp tool or even your fingernail behind a corner of the top layer to peel it off in one long length. You are then left with the lining paper. Some decorators leave this in place if it is still sound.

Anaglypta®

Anaglypta®, and similar embossed wallpapers, are still used today especially for authentic restoration projects. These were usually manufactured as two layers with a raised pattern. If you have to remove them, you'll probably find it a bit brittle, in which case more steam treatment will be necessary. The top layer will come off separately after steaming but you'll also have to remove the backing paper because it too will have the raised pattern on it.

Stripping wallpaper
Always use a stripping knife to strip paper. Never use a filling knife which looks similar but is flexible. The filling knife will snag and flick out the plaster.

Scraping When removing wallpaper, the one problem that many people face is damage, however small, to the plaster wall. Once the paper is properly soaked, use your scraper (not a filling knife) at the correct low angle to be able to remove the paper in one long piece. Remember that your stepladder must be placed with the feet against the skirting board for your own safety. Once the first piece of wallpaper has been soaked across its width, only 520 mm (21 in), and loosened at the top with your scraper, its weight will cause it to flop down if you're working from above. However, wherever you start, check that the water caused by the steam condensing and running down the wall is not seeping behind sockets, behind the skirting board or through any protective floor covering. Use a sponge to continually mop up the rivulets. Scrapers come in various widths and, as with all steel tools, you get what you pay for. Buy the best you can afford. A 100 mm (4 in) wide scraper is ideal for wallpaper stripping. Get one that has a long wooden handle riveted to the steel, which should be in one piece through to the tip of the handle. A longer handle allows you to get lower angles preventing it from digging into the plaster.

Disposal Stripping wallpaper can be a messy job but need not give problems if you are properly organised. We all know that getting rid of the floppy, wet lumps of paper and picking bits off the floor and from our footwear is the irritating part of the preparation! Solving these problems is simple. Start by using plenty of floor covering and have two large plastic sacks open near you. A professional decorator always rolls down the bag to half way so that the tight roll provides a firm edge that is not going to collapse and the folded pieces of wet paper can go straight into the bag. You'll never again carry around bits stuck to your shoes. Always first fold the pieces paste side in and then fold it as many times as you can before it goes into the bag. Screwed up paper takes up much more room, and of course your hands could get covered with paste.

Hanging

Position a stepladder safely, feet against skirting board.

Only stand stepladders parallel to a wall when using two to support a plank.

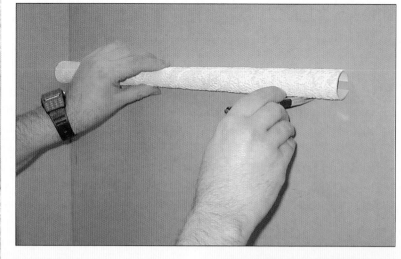

For the first 'drop' (the piece to be hung) at a corner, mark 12 mm (½ in) in for the plumb-bob line. Mark the position, holding a roll into the corner.

1

3

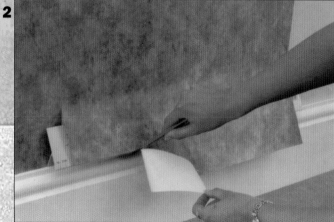

2

4

Hanging wallpaper:
(1) cutting guide in position;
(2) hang the 'drop' as usual with about 10 cm (4 in) of overhang for trimming; slip the cutting guide under the paper, tight to the wall; (3) brush the wet paper tight to the guide and cut along the front edge;
(4) remove the guide and brush the paper down to a perfect line with the skirting.

Measuring Wallpaper rolls are not necessarily of a standard width and length, however most machine-printed wallpapers in the midprice range are 10 m (33 ft) long and 520 mm (21 in) wide. When you contemplate a DIY wallpapering job calculate how many rolls you'll comfortably need for a particular room. Once you have made the calculation, write that number on top of the room door and it's there for good!

First measure the length, width and height of the room. For a standard roll, divide the roll length by the height figure, say 2.4 m (8 ft), giving approximately four strips (or 'drops') from each roll. There are other considerations

After papering rooms, write the number of rolls used on top of each door, for next time!

but we'll get to them later. Add two room lengths and two room widths together to get the measurement right round the room. For example, a room of length 4.2 m (14 ft) and width 3 m (10 ft) gives 14.4 m (48 ft). The number of rolls needed to paper this room, 12, is found by dividing the total distance round the room by the number of pieces from one roll (48 ÷ 4). The doors and windows have been included to allow for wastage. Now, if the paper has a large repeating pattern, you'll have to line up the pattern when hanging it thereby having a certain amount of wastage at the top of each drop. Check by how much when you're looking through the pattern book and take into account the following – 12 rolls will cover the walls without a drop repeat. So, 12 rolls at four pieces to a roll makes 48 pieces to hang. If a repeat pattern wastes, say, 300 mm (12 in) at the top of each piece, you'll need another 48 × 300 mm, which is 14.4 m (48 ft) – an extra two rolls. In this case, you'll have to order 14 rolls for the drop-patterned paper whereas for a non-repeating pattern paper you'll need only 12 rolls.

Cutting   The old way of trimming wallpaper was to crease the paper before cutting it with scissors. However, at the ceiling and at the skirting this calls for a certain amount of skill when following the crease line, so with the pasted paper tucked into the ceiling angle and with about 100 mm (4 in) spare, run the tip of the scissors along the crease line and peel the pasted paper away just sufficiently to cut along that crease line without stretching the paper. Use a hanging brush to force the paper back into place. Always work at the ceiling first, then do the same at the skirting angle. Slide up each subsequent piece of paper to butt against the last one. Repeat the action of creasing and trimming. Do the same around architraves, window frames and electrical fittings.

A powered wallpaper trimmer is foolproof and will give professional straight cuts. The long guide that fits into the joint, at say a skirting board or an architrave, ensures that the cut is true.

Manufacturers are continuously striving to make the DIYer's life easier and their products more economical, and to help us get a professional finish. Nowadays, scissors and wallpaper knives are no longer necessary because an award-winning proprietary electric cutter is available which cuts the paper directly on the wall. There is no need to even lift the pasted paper. This ingenious tool is foolproof and there are absolutely no problems at ceiling angles or at corners. Cutting around a door frame is simplicity itself. It even cuts through overlaps to give a perfect butt join. Electrical fittings do not have to be unscrewed because the blade point cuts tight to the cover plate. This precision cutter is battery powered and cuts standard, heavy duty and textile wall coverings. As a bonus it can also be used for cutting cloth patterns for tailoring. You have full control by means of a simple pressure switch. Insert the blade-point, like very tiny scissors, at an angle underneath the wallpaper, ease the runner into the crease which then positions the machine for cutting by pulling the tool backwards. This tools is indispensable for perfect wallpapering.

Pasting   The days of flour and water paste have long gone but the technique of pasting paper is the same as the Victorians practised. Nowadays, pastes are manufactured for special purposes, so choose exactly the paste that is recommended for your particular wallpaper. When you begin to unroll wallpaper, tucked inside will be a specification and instruction leaflet. These instructions are the result of much research and must be followed to get perfect results. The type of paste, the soaking time for each piece of paper and the method of hanging are all important. For example, if you soak one piece of paper for two minutes and the very next one inadvertently for four minutes, the second piece will stretch and become longer than the first, so patterns aren't going to match and the subsequent contraction of each as they dry out will be different.

Different pastes are available for different papers: standard paste for lightweight papers; heavy duty paste for embossed and heavier

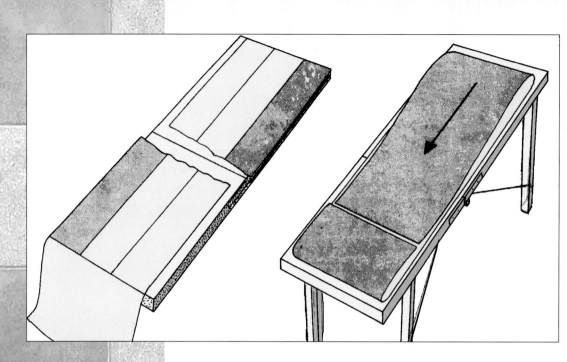

Pasting wallpaper on a pasting table
Make sure the wallpaper overlaps the edge of the table to prevent the paste getting onto the face of the paper. Slide the paper to each edge in turn.

After applying the paste, fold the paper as shown and allow it to soak for the recommended time. Lay the long end of the paper to the top of the wall.

In some situations, like around radiators, you can paste the wall and not the paper.

If you choose cotton-backed vinyl wallpaper, paste the wall not the paper.

DIY beginners can use a roller and paste to get an even covering on wallpaper.

wallpapers; ready-mixed paste formulated for paper-backed fabrics; and border paste in tubes for solving the problem of open joints and borders which are notoriously difficult when sticking on to vinyl wallpaper. Spores and mould are more commonly found under vinyl wallpapers, so check on the instruction leaflet and get a special paste that has a fungicidal additive.

Cut the first piece of paper about 150 mm (6 in) longer than you need. On the back of the paper, with a pencil, write a capital T for the top and the number 1, indicating the hanging sequence. When you begin pasting, put part of the roll on a

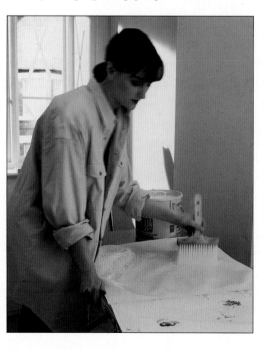

Paste standard wallpapers evenly down the centre, brushing out in turn to each edge that overlaps the pasting table. Fold over one end and leave to soak for the recommended time.

clean covering on the floor. Brush a long strip of paste about 200 mm (8 in) wide along the centre of the paper. Slide the paper to the far edge of your pasting table to overlap about 3 mm (⅛ in) and then paste the far strip. The overhang prevents paste seeping under the edge of the paper on to its face. Slide the paper towards you, making the front edge overhang the pasting table and paste this nearest strip. Work out from the centre in a herringbone fashion ensuring that there is an even covering of paste. Work fairly quickly so that the whole length of the paper is covered in seconds and the soaking time of the first and last pastings are as similar as possible. After pasting about 1500 mm (5 ft) make one fold in the paper, paste to paste, lining up the edges. Slide the rest of the paper on to the board and repeat the process. Fold longer pieces of paper into a concertina, always paste to paste.

Thin papers can go straight on to the wall without soaking, but standard and thicker papers must be soaked for exactly the recommended time. However, the recommendation for certain wallpapers might be to paste the wall rather than the paper. These wallpapers are usually hand-printed or of a more delicate type. Paste a vertical band about 600 mm (2 ft) wide, which means that for the next piece, the problem of pasting on to the face of the paper is overcome. If you find a large pasting brush tiring, try using a short pile roller.

Ready-pasted wallpaper, usually vinyl, is also available. The paste is wetted by immersing each roll separately in a trough of water on the floor under the hanging position. Again, it's important to soak for exactly the prescribed time. Lift the top end slowly, bring it up to its hanging position, letting the residual water run back into the plastic trough. Follow the instructions for unrolling and hanging. For example, they might suggest you use a sponge for smoothing the wet paper.

It's not a good idea to paper over existing wallpaper – you'll get bubbles.

Disconnect electricity when wallpapering – start early morning to get daylight!

Hanging   Only hang wallpaper when the ceiling has been redecorated and the woodwork painted – you can allow paint to creep on to the walls when covering architraves and skirting boards. This really is good practice because it ensures that if the paint line is not absolutely straight, the paper will give a straight edge along the whole length. If you are hanging a very bold patterned paper, start at the centre of a chimney breast and work your way around the room to the door frame. Then work your way around the room from the other side of the chimney breast to stop at the door. If there are two windows on one wall opposite the door, mark a centre line between them and start hanging from there, working out either side.

First you need to mark a vertical line on the wall, against which your first piece of paper (the drop) will be positioned. This is because the walls and corners of a room are usually out of square. The best way to obtain a vertical line is the struck chalk mark. Don't use a pen or pencil, it's possible that the marks can creep through to the surface of the paper. Chalk the string of a plumb bob, pin it at the top, hold your foot against the weight at the bottom and strike the chalk string against the wall. The position of the plumb (vertical) line will govern the position of the first piece of paper. If it's in a corner of the room, mark its position by holding a roll of paper against the corner but deduct 10 mm (⅜ in) from its length. The reason for this is that the 10 mm of the first piece to be hung will be actually pasted on to the adjacent wall and the other edge of the piece will be tight to the plumb line. When working on the adjacent wall the first piece of the second run will be plumbed from another line but just to cover that 10 mm of paper, ensuring complete cover of a corner joint.

Then, unfold the top half of the pasted paper and slide it against the plumb line. Allow a couple of inches at the top for trimming. Using a hanging brush, gently smooth down the centre of the paper and out to the edges so that no air

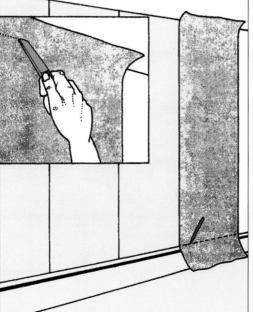

Trimming wallpaper
Use a pair of scissors to trim a 'drop' of wallpaper. Hold the wet paper tightly to the ceiling joint (or skirting board) and 'crease' it without tearing. Pull back the paper and trim it before brushing it into position.

Hanging wallpaper
Start the papering in a corner with the paper overlapping the adjacent wall by about 12 mm (½ in).

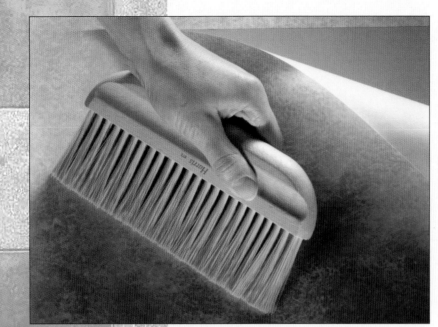

anywhere on the surface of the wallpaper, wipe it off quickly, but gently, with a clean, damp sponge using a lifting, not rubbing, motion.

Start hanging paper with a large pattern central to a fireplace or focal point.

Chimney breasts   The external corners of chimney breasts are rarely truly vertical, so wallpaper will not look vertical after it has turned the corner. Also, if about half the width of the roll has to be pasted to the side of the chimney breast, often it ends up in folds. The trick to solve the problem is to cut the length of paper so that it only overlaps 12 mm (½ in) on to the side wall after having pasted it to the front. Then use the next piece of paper to cover the overlap by 10 mm (⅜ in). Scissors are rarely successful for cutting lengths of paper so use a sharp trimming knife and a steel straight edge. However, a proprietary electric cutter makes a perfect butt joint where the two pieces overlap.

When wallpapering on a chimney breast, crease and cut the paper along the mantle shelf first. The paper will fall down either side after cutting diagonals each end. Then trim and brush the paper under the shelf as far as the upright of the surround. Take the weight of the pasted paper, otherwise it will tear. Never ever tug at wet wall-paper. Little nicks in the paper will help you turn it around small mouldings.

Doorways   When wallpapering around a doorway, be prepared to wipe off paste from the door frame as you go! Using the frame as a guide, cut a diagonal up into the mitred corner of the architrave and crease the paper into the upright at the side and into the horizontal above the door. Trim the paper as already described. Electric cutters give a straight, clean cut the whole height of an architrave making it look very professional. Repeat on the other side of the door frame to leave a small gap above the door which is easily filled with a cut-to-size piece of paper. One important point to remember, if you're using a patterned paper, the pattern on all three pieces must be matched.

One of the sure signs of a caring DIYer is the condition of the tools he or she uses. But quality is also important! Buy the best that you can afford. A classic paper-hanging brush with soft springy tufts (with no parts to rust) is best to smooth out wrinkles and bubbles.

Hang each piece against the last piece to be hung, carefully butting the edges with no overlaps. Immediately wipe off any excess paste on the surface with a clean damp sponge.

When papering a ceiling, it's easier with two people, two stepladders and two planks.

bubbles are left. Don't press too hard otherwise you'll get paste oozing out at the sides. Gently unfold the bottom half and repeat the action, again using the hanging brush to press the paper against the skirting board. Each subsequent piece of paper will be slid to butt against the last one. Wipe surplus paste off skirting boards as you proceed – never let it harden, you'll forget it's there until it dries dull. A seam-roller is useful to flatten down the edges of each butted piece of paper at the seams, but don't use it on embossed paper. If any surplus paste appears

Wallpapering around doors

Papering around a door frame is not difficult if you follow these instructions but be ready to wipe off a lot of residual paste from the frame! Butt the piece of paper that hangs against the architrave to the last piece and allow it to overlap the door. Cut off the surplus paper and cut a diagonal into the paper following the mitre of the frame. Use a proprietary cutter to get perfectly straight cuts at the side and top of the frame or crease the paper and cut it carefully with a pair of scissors (or a trimming knife and straightedge).

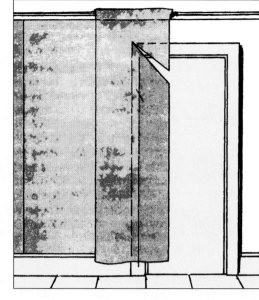

Wallpapering around windows (1)
When papering around a window opening, always paper the 'reveals' and the 'soffit' first. These are the recessed parts of the wall nearest and adjacent to the window frame. Start at the centre above the window and continue to the frame.

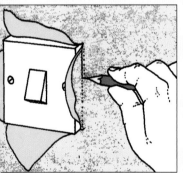

Wallpapering around light switches
Older round switches will not unscrew so trim the wallpaper close to the switch base.

You can unscrew and remove square switches and sockets (after turning off the power at the mains switch box!) Trim the paper so that 3 mm (¹/₈ in) goes under the switch cover.

Electrics

Depending on the age of your house you'll either have round switches or square ones. The round ones are usually fixed. The square ones you can unscrew and lift off. You'll obviously get a much neater job if you can tuck the cut ends of the paper underneath the switch so you must turn off the electricity on that circuit. Turn on the light and switch off the circuit at the consumer unit. Either tape the switch in that position or, if it's a removable fuse, take it out and put it in your pocket. Turn off the light switch and lift the switch plate a little by undoing the screws. You will have to make straight cuts around the switch plate so that at least 12 mm (½ in) of paper tucks underneath the switch plate before screwing it back into position. Hang the paper down over the switch and cut out from the centre to the corners or edges before trimming and brushing the paper back into place. The same applies to a socket outlet but make certain that the circuit is switched off by plugging a light into the socket. Then repeat the process at the consumer unit as described above.

Window openings

The easiest method to paper around windows is to paper the 'reveals' and the 'soffit' first. These are the recessed parts of the wall nearest and adjacent to the window frame. Paper these, overlapping the main wall by about 12 mm (½ in). Continue to paper the main walls covering that small overlap. The alternative, and more professional

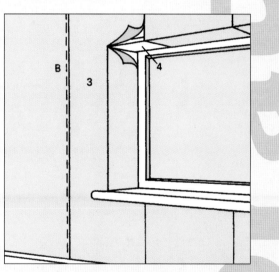

Wallpapering around windows (2)
Cut and fold the ceiling-to-floor lengths of wallpaper either side of the window. Cut at the top of the opening and at the windowsill so that you have a sort of hinge. Tightly brush this to the frame and trim. The short pieces under the window are the easiest!

way, is to paper the wall and reveals in one, in which case start above the window at the centre. Paper right into the window frame from the ceiling and continue either side until you come to the top corners of the window frame. When you hang ceiling-to-floor lengths either side of the window, cut the paper at the top of the opening and at the window sill with straight cuts so that you'll have a hinge. You then brush it on to the reveal. Crease and cut against the window frame in the usual way. The short bits that are left to be hung underneath the window sill should come as light relief – they will be easier and quicker!

Don't use scissors to tuck trimmed paper behind loosened switch plates!

Some tips

After a wall has been stripped, filled, levelled and sanded it is good practice to 'size' (seal) the entire wall. Propriety sizes are available but diluted PVA is better although, perhaps, a little more expensive. Some decorators size with a diluted mixture of the same paste used for the particular wallpaper. Obviously the compatibility factor will make the adhesion even stronger.

A conventional radiator need not be removed from the wall to paper behind it. Transfer the positions of the bracket to a piece of wallpaper and make two slits from the bottom to the top mark of each bracket. Allow 100 mm (4 in) extra on the length of wallpaper at the skirting board position. Gently drop the pasted paper so that the slits coincide with the positions of the brackets. A long handled roller is best to roll it to the wall. Finish by carefully trimming at the skirting board.

Never attempt to paper a stairwell on your own. Hang the longest drop first. Your helper will need to take the paper's weight whilst you start hanging at the ceiling. To work at height, use a scaffolding board supported by a stepladder on the landing and a ladder against the head wall. Position the scaffolding board so that you can reach the ceiling comfortably. In your calculations, allow for extra paper where it meets the angled stringer at the side of the stairs.

Flock paper is attractive to many people but it can prove difficult to hang. Instructions for pasting come with each roll, but sometimes you'll find that the edges are not perfectly straight. To get a professional finish to the butted joints, make an overlap and then cut through both thicknesses and remove both spare strips. Gently press back the edges and you'll get a perfect joint. Again an electric cutter will make a clean, neat joint. Never use a hard seam roller, it will mark the flock. When using the hanging brush, it's also a good idea to protect the flock with a piece of standard wallpaper.

It's easier when two people are working together to wallpaper a ceiling. Even though the pieces of paper are longer, the concertinaed strip end can be held by your assistant whilst you hang the remainder from the starting point. Methods and techniques are basically similar to papering a wall. Erect a platform of scaffolding boards from which to work and work backwards from your starting point, positioning the first piece against a side wall. Remember the rules for working around electric fittings. Switch off, check for power, remove shades, make star slits in the correct position to feed through the bulb holder and cable, then trim around the rose as for a light switch.

To clean marks off wallpaper, try the backs of crusts of white bread!

Use a dry paint roller to smooth expanded polystyrene onto a pasted wall.

Tiling

Mosaic tiles come already stuck to a backing sheet. They are ideal for curved walls. After grouting in the usual way, leave the residual grout powder to dry – you can use it as a polish.

Vinyl floor tiles, properly glued with tight joints, provide a waterproof surface.

Cork tiles are warm – and attractive on walls too.

Stick mirror tiles, with sticky pads, only on absolutely flat walls.

Untreated cork floor tiles need three coats of polyurethane varnish to seal them.

Tiling changed from being strictly a professional's job to a DIY enthusiast's project with the introduction of new technology in tile manufacture, tiling tools and adhesives. It is now possible for anyone to create a beautiful, tough and hygienic wall finish. A new range of tiling tools helps to make any tiling job easy, speedy and enjoyable. Tile adhesive and grout are now combined in one tub for easy application. They give a smooth finish to the joints between tiles and contain anti-mould ingredients.

Removing tiles

Because of the lasting qualities of Victorian and Edwardian tiles, still admired in many homes, we might still be confronted with problems when we are planning to renovate. Quarry floor tiles, for example, were a favourite floor covering for kitchens, passage ways and downstairs WCs. These tiles are never laid on a suspended wooden floor but always on a concrete solid floor and so are sometimes very difficult to remove. The fired clay tiles were manufactured mainly in Staffordshire but the famous brand of Heather Brown quarry tiles came from Ruabon in North Wales. The

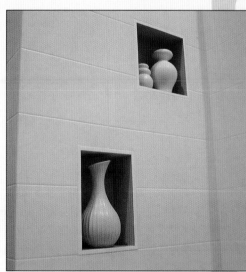

Don't be afraid to be ambitious with tiles. Plastic edge strips give a clean crisp edge to corners, sills and open shelf spaces. Tiles provide a hygienic and decorative surface, but they don't have to be dull!

distinctive blue, red and buff colours of these unglazed tiles with their silky surface finish are still being produced today.

You must loosen the adhesion of the screed into which the quarry tiles were buried to remove them. You might find a loose or rocking tile, in which case simply put your bolster chisel

You can't save tiles that have been cemented in place for years. To remove them from a brick wall, tap or drill each to make a crack. It makes it easier to lever them off in pieces.

It's always easier to carry out a job with tools specifically designed for a particular task. This long-handled tile remover is one such tool. You get incredible leverage and the steel blade slips under tiles with ease. The sharp blade also deals with residual cement.

at a low angle underneath an adjacent tile and strike with a club hammer. Otherwise a series of holes drilled along the edge of a tile with a masonry bit will give gap for the bolster chisel. Once you've removed all the tiles, clean off the residual nibs to leave a flat clean surface. Any undulations can be filled with a 'self-levelling' cement available at DIY stores.

If you have a large area of floor or wall tiles to remove, a compressor with a small spade chisel (similar to a Kango) will do the job in no time and with less energy expended! Some of these work with a hammer-like action that you can easily control. You can ease the chisel under the edge of the first tile and proceed with ease along a whole row of tiles. Obviously this would be too heavy for thin ceramic wall tiles, say on a stud partition plasterboard wall in a bathroom.

Removing ceramic tiles is much easier than taking off quarry tiles. They are usually bedded in a plaster-like tile cement and once the first tile has been broken up and removed, the rest should come off easily by prising with a bolster chisel or similar. Because a broken tile edge can be sharp, obviously take precautions – wear gloves and safety goggles. Use floor coverings and have a bucket to hand for dropping broken tiles into immediately they are removed. Remember that slithers of tile can damage a floor when inadvertently walked on. When working around fittings like taps and showers, take extra care.

There is always a tedious second stage to removing wall tiles. Small patches of tile cement will invariably be left and these will need cleaning off. A power tool with a disc can be used but, of course, it produces dust, so

If a concrete floor is uneven, use a self-levelling compound before tiling.

you'll have to protect yourself with tight fitting goggles and a mask that has a special filter for fine dust. If you consider the dust is too much of a problem in that particular room, there's no alternative but to chisel or scrape. In order to get a professional flat finish to the new tiling job, it is essential that the wall is flat and clean before sealing the plaster with a coating of diluted PVA to make a sound base.

It is prudent to check levels once the tiles have been removed from the wall or floor in readiness for new ones and before you seal the surface. If you suspect that the wall is not properly vertical or that the floor slopes, now is the time to check with a long batten straight-edge and spirit level. Remove any bumps and fill hollows with a one-coat plaster. If two walls are adjacent at the lowest part of the sloping floor, take off the skirting boards, and if a door opening is involved, you might have to shorten the door by planing the bottom. Be sure to take into account the threshold and the adjacent floor. With all this in mind, use a self-levelling compound or mix sand and cement in the proportions of 1 to 4 to level the floor. Brush on a PVA seal before the mortar. Use a long batten with your spirit level laid on top to ensure that the repair is level ready to take your new tiling.

Use a builder's square to get a perfect right angle when laying floor tiles.

Tiling – setting out
To help set out the walls correctly for tiling, use three battens: one marked out as a gauge-stick and the other two nailed to the wall at right angles to each other to support the tiles. The gauge-stick must be marked accurately by laying tiles and spacers on the floor against the stick. Mark the centre of a plain wall for the first tiles. Arrange the tiles centrally to a window.

Plot positions of tiles on a wall with a 1m (3 ft) gauge-stick, with marks of tiles marked on it.

Battens

A simple aid to help plot the exact position of the tiles on a wall is a DIY batten gauge-stick. Lay a piece of straight batten with a 25mm × 12mm (1in × ½in) cross-section on the floor and lay tiles along it in a straight line. Leave the appropriate spaces for grout. Mark carefully on the batten the position of each tile and space or joint. If the tiles you are using have spacing lugs, the spaces will be uniform and pre-set, otherwise use plastic spacers to give the correct positioning. Make a second batten gauge-stick if your tiles are not square. The gauge-stick can now be held against the wall, but use a spirit level to ensure verticals and horizontals are correct and the exact position of tiles is marked on the wall.

To help set out a wall correctly for tiling, two battens can be nailed in temporary positions predetermined by the starting point. For example, if you are going to be tiling around a window in a bathroom, full tiles should start underneath the window. Check with your gauge-stick how many tiles are needed from the window sill to the skirting board or to the floor. If, say, it is three and a half, your first nailed horizontal supporting batten must be fixed underneath the third tile down. Start laying on this batten, working upwards so that the whole section is supported on the batten until the cement has gone off. The same applies with a vertical batten against a side wall. You can actually mark the position of the tiles accurately on these supporting battens by laying your gauge-stick alongside. With the use of your spirit level the battens should be fixed at right angles to each other ensuring a perfect finish.

Special dado tiles are available if you're tiling only half way up a wall. These tiles are matched to your full tiles and give a very professional finish to the job. They come in plain, rope design, classical designs and other patterns. If you are tiling a bathroom to a half way mark, don't be tempted to work from the floor. It is better to have full tiles around the edge of the bath, then work up from a temporary batten fixed to support the lowest row of full tiles.

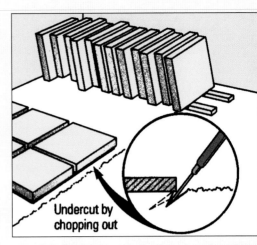

Undercut by chopping out

You will have to relay quarry tiles if they have been laid on a bad screed (too much sand). Use a 24 oz hammer and a bolster chisel to left them. Chip off surplus cement after soaking them in a cement cleaner – follow the manufacturer's instructions. Lay a new screed with a damp-proof membrane beneath.

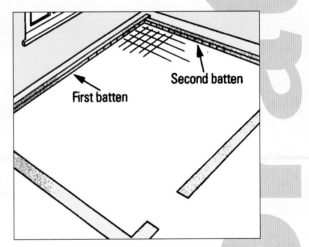

Second batten
First batten

A common method of laying floor tiles is the 'square'. Fix temporary battens at exactly 90° (use your builders square) to give you a starting point opposite the door. Use a spirit level to get the tiles flat. Work back to the door, checking constantly with your 'square'.

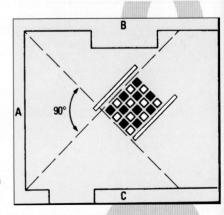

Another common pattern for laying floor tiles is the 'diagonal' or 'diamond' pattern. Transfer the length of the shortest wall (A) to the adjacent walls (B and C) to get a square. Draw diagonals as shown in the drawing and use your builders square to check for a right angle. Use two temporary battens to guide the tiles as you lay them. Hire a special tile cutter with a diamond wheel to cut the tiles near the walls.

Tile in small areas at a time. Apply the cement with a filling knife, then use a serrated spreader to form undulations which are essential for the adhesion process.

With your level guide batten temporarily in place, start spreading the tile cement. Lift it with a separate tool so that the back of the serrated spreader is kept clean. Keep the cement lines even and horizontal. As you tile, twist each one to get good adhesion.

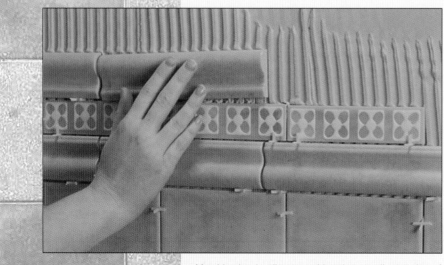

Matching border tiles can add to the overall attraction of a well-tiled bathroom, but make sure that the tiles are designed to match your chosen pattern. Border tiles are applied in the same way, but they must be properly spaced and level!

Cementing

Once you've planned where to start tiling a room, on which wall and against which focal point, fix your supporting battens in preparation for spreading the tile adhesive. Lift out the adhesive from the tub using a separate scraper tool (a very useful tool for carrying adhesive to the wall) not a serrated spreader (this is for levelling the tile cement) which could get the adhesive over the handle. Often tile adhesives come with a special spreader with teeth of a particular size suitable for that adhesive. Using the scraper tool, spread the adhesive over an area of about a square metre (square yard) and use the toothed spreader to form ridges by dragging it horizontally through the adhesive. Wipe any excess adhesive from the spreader with your scraper tool and put it back into the tub. Never allow the scraper to dry without cleaning it first. Dry it with a towel and apply a thin film of oil to protect the steel. Lay the first tile at the corner angle made by the guide batten. Suction is improved by making horizontal ridges with the spreader such that the tiles are less likely to slip.

There are many types of tile cement on the market for the DIYer. Some come as powder to be mixed with water. These will have explicit instructions which must be followed. It is essential that the powdered tile adhesive is sprinkled on to water and not the other way round as this will produce lumps. Ready-mixed adhesives come in tubs and have a circular protective plastic covering to prevent drying out. If there is adhesive left in the tub after finishing a job, scrape it from the sides and level it out, then push the protective plastic cover on to the tub top so that it will not lose any moisture content and be dried out the next time you want to use it. Make sure that the lid is securely fixed. There are tile adhesives available with additives which prevent against mould and against water penetration (they are waterproof). Some types are heat proof, others are blended to be used as tile cement and as a grout. If the tiled area is to be subjected to water, for example, in a shower cubicle, use waterproof tile cement. Anywhere else a standard tile adhesive is suitable.

Positioning

The easiest wall to tile is a plain flat one with no door or windows. Always plan to finish with full tiles at the top of the wall. Use a gauge-stick to mark the positions of the tiles from the ceiling to the skirting, where a cut tile will probably be needed. Nail a temporary long batten to support the lowest row of whole tiles. Use a spirit level before the final fixing. Find the centre of the wall and, with the aid of a gauge-stick, mark the positions of tiles and spacings as far as the corner. Setting out tiles is very easy if you work carefully. If you've positioned your centre line correctly you'll have equal cut tiles either side of the room. When tiling around a window, as well as centring the tiles, plan to position a row of full tiles below the window sill as described previously. Your gauge-stick is an invaluable tool in the preparation, arrangement and positioning of the starting point. The top of a handbasin is generally about 250mm (10in) above that of the bath. You might be tempted to start your tiling with whole tiles above the basin but then you'll probably find that you'll have a row of cut tiles along the top of the bath – not a good idea! Start with full tiles along the top of the bath so that you'll only have a short row of cut tiles over the top of the hand basin.

For awkward corners, a template allows angles to be easily measured and cut.

Tiling – window sills
Decide whether you want a tile or a joint to be at the centre of the sill. Arrange a row of full tiles under the sill. Use matching edging strip to cover the cut edges of the tiles to make an attractive finish for the external corner. Use a flexible mastic sealant where the tiles butt against a wooden window frame.

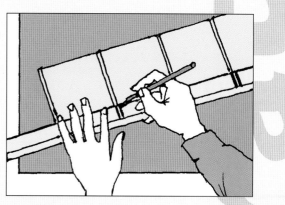

Wall tiling – gauge stick
Lay the tiles on the floor at the correct spacing. Mark a straight edge to coincide with the tile size and the grout joint.

Fix a temporary batten as a starting point for laying the first row of tiles. The batten can be removed after the tile adhesive, supporting rows of tiles, has hardened. Apply the tile adhesive from the tub with a scraper, not the spreader. Then use the spreader to obtain a uniform layer of the combed ribbing, ready for laying the tiles. Work on an area of about a square metre (square yard) at a time. As you lay a tile, twist it a little to ensure that it's firmly bedded. Place plastic spacers between the tiles to get an even grout line. Use a proprietary grouting tool to apply and work in the grout. A wooden handled 'squeegee' type is best with a neoprene blade (it is gentle on the tiles and gets the grout into the joints. Grout residue on the tiles acts as a wonderful polish!

Mark lines at right angles and work on one quarter of the floor at a time. Lay the first tile carefully against the crossed lines, twisting it slightly to get good contact.

Without letting it slip, very gently lift the tile with a trowel to check that it is completely covered with adhesive.

Bacteria grow in cavities under tiles, especially in a kitchens where hygiene is most important.

There is no set pattern to laying out floor tiles. One way is to set out tiles from the centre of the room so that you have an even border all round the edge. To find the centre, with a helper, stretch a chalked string from the halfway point on two pairs of opposite walls. Having marked the halfway point on the walls ensure that the string crosses at right angles then fix each of the four ends to the floor near the skirting board. Carefully pluck the string to leave strong chalked positioning marks on the floor. Always 'dry' lay tiles in one area from the centre to the wall to check what space is left at the skirting. If one particular wall is more exposed and more in your eye line, it's easy to adjust the centre position as you wish.

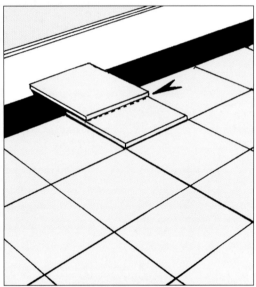

Floor tiling – cutting edge tiles
Place a tile on top of the last full tile. Use a low-tack pad to hold it in place. Place another tile on top of it touching the wall or edge. Score along the first tile. When cut, the part showing will fit the gap exactly.

Having laid tiles with an attractive border almost to the wall, measure carefully the distance required for a cut tile (allowing for grout lines). The cut edge goes against the wall!

Grouting

Use waterproof grout for showers and baths, but epoxy-based grout for work-tops.

Dried residual grout powder makes a great tile polish when the grout is totally dry.

Floor tiles should be left for at least 12 hours before grouting. Nobody must walk on them during this time because the slightest movement of one tile will affect the bonding process. Some spacers can be left in to be grouted over, but if you've used DIY spacers you can remove them after about 24 hours. Manufacturers recommend a wait of anything between 36 and 48 hours before cleaning off the floor ready for grouting. Many tile manufacturers advise which grout to use whether it's a premix, which comes in a tub, or a powder grout which has to be mixed with water to a creamy consistency. Add the powder to the water and mix only enough to last for about half an hour because after that time it could become unworkable. Cover only a small area at a time and work the grout into the joints with a sponge or a wooden batten that fits comfortably between the tiles. If you use a sponge, make it a close textured man-made one rather than an open textured natural sponge. Have a bucket of water to hand so that you can keep the sponge clean but squeeze it almost dry before spreading the grout. The grout should be lifted from the container with a straight-edged spatula, but the manufacturer's instructions might ask you to pour it on to a small area so that it flows into the grout joints. Leave the grout to harden in the joints for the recommended time before gently wiping off the surplus with a damp sponge. Rinse frequently with clean water until only a thin film is left over the tiles. This film will dry as powder which can be polished off with a dry cloth. To avoid any chance of softening the grout, avoid washing the floor for at least a week. Grouting a ceramic-tiled wall is a pleasurable DIY job because it is easy and satisfying. A white grout on coloured tiles or coloured grout used cleverly can lift a tiled wall to a new dimension. Amazingly a tiled wall, before it is grouted, can look disjointed. Minor variations in the positioning of tiles can easily lead one to believe that one has not been too careful. However, once the grout has been applied, hardened and the tiles polished, the result is always surprising! Instructions come on every pack or tub of grout and they are there to be followed. Do it and you'll be assured of a professional finish.

Floor grout is mixed to specific proportions and viscosity. A special spreader helps it to flow into the joints to completely fill them, but it must not be too sloppy or it will not set. Once it begins to cure, use a damp sponge to create a smooth surface.

Wear gloves when grouting the joints. Knee pads prevent future 'ache' problems and a grouting tool with a neoprene blade makes the job quick and easy!

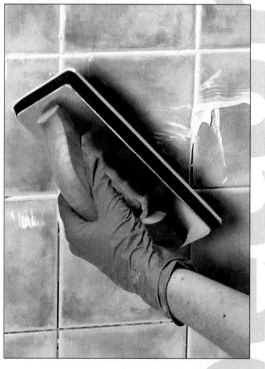

Manufacturers produce excellent tubs of water-resistant cement that also acts as a grout. Use a grout spreader to cover a square metre (square yard) at a time, working the grout deep into the joints. Use a little at a time to prevent bubbles in the joints.

To replace a
ceramic tile,
drill centre
holes, hack out
and scrape
adjoining
grout.

Replacing

Ceramic wall tiling is chosen not only for its aesthetic qualities but because it is hard wearing, hygienic and made to last a long time. However, you might at some time discover a cracked tile that needs replacing. This can happen either by accident or by movement in the fabric of the building. I always recommend that when ordering tiles, order more than you immediately need not only to cover any wastage such as accidentally breaking tiles when scoring, but also for emergency purposes like replacement. To replace a damaged ceramic wall tile, you'll first need to remove as much grout as possible from around it. There are grout remover tools available but be certain to get one that is slightly narrower than the grout space. These are short-handled tools with a hardened metal, fine-toothed scraping end. Take great care to keep the tool in line with the edge of the tile. The slightest side movement will damage the glazed edge of an adjacent tile that is good. If possible, remove the grout as far as the tile cement base. With a masonry bit drill a series of holes to weaken the centre of the tile, then, using a small cold chisel or a bolster, chip out the rest of the tile which should now come out quite cleanly. Remove as much of the residual tile cement so that you can bed in the new tile level with the surrounding tiles. Cleaning the space for the new tile is a delicate job requiring sensitivity and care. The reason for this is that when bedding the new tile any slight pressure on a raised point left behind will crack the new tile. Any tools used (a trimming knife is best) to scrape away residual tile cement or grout left on the sides of the four adjacent tiles must be carefully used. A small scraper or a flat putty knife is good for gently smoothing the background area which can be dampened to prevent dust flying around. Before finally cementing a square tile into place have a trial run with the tile in different orientations so that you get the best fit – mark the tile with a non-permanent felt pen so that it goes in the correct way.

Regrout between tiles if the surface has suffered the effects of cooking around the stove in a kitchen, or where tiles have not been dried after a shower has been used (if the shower doors are kept closed spores can breed very easily producing a black mould). I've already described the small regrouting tool used for raking out old or perished grout. Another powered tool, used by professional tilers and DIYers alike, is a smaller version of a cordless screwdriver but with a tiny circular saw blade that cuts easily through any grout. Once you've taken the grout from the area that is to be regrouted, brush the whole area with an anti-fungal solution. In areas of about a square metre (square yard) liberally spread the grout and press to fill every gap and crevice in the grout joint – excess grout can go back into the container. Clean up the surface with a damp close textured sponge.

Another solution to this problem is to simply enhance the grout lines. Providing that the original grout is firm and only discoloured, use a proprietary brand of a tile renovator that comes with a sponge applicator to totally revive the grout line. Follow the instructions to get the best professional results. The process is so easy that a whole wall can be done in minutes. Simply paint on the 'grout-revive', allow to dry and then wash off. The solution is absorbed by the grout to bond with it but does not stick to glazed ceramic surfaces. An alternative is to use an applicator where a small wheel delivers the solution to the grout line.

Replacing a cracked tile
The only way to successfully remove a damaged tile is to loosen it in parts, sufficiently enough for small sections to be taken out. So that surrounding tiles are not chipped, remove the centre of the damage tile first by drilling a number of marked holes.

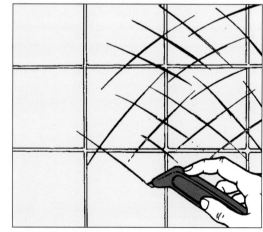

Tiling over existing tiles
If the old tiles are firmly fixed, it is possible to tile over them, providing you 'key' their surface by scoring first Remember to clean off all grease and mould. Remove silicone sealant.

Cutting and marking

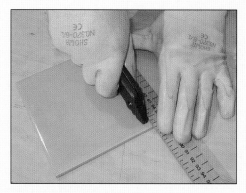

You must obey certain rules to ensure that you do not break a tile when scoring and snapping it. Lay the tile on a flat, clean, resilient surface. Carefully mark the exact line of the score. Use a thin straightedge (so that you can see the mark) but allow for the thickness of the end of the scoring tool. Position a piece of cable or a matchstick under the end of the scored line. Simply press on the tile to snap it.

The gap between a skirting board and the floor can widen over time. This will allow air to bring dust into a room. Use a silicone matching sealant to seal the gap and create a more attractive finish.

Break a quarry floor tile with a club hammer for renewing, but wear goggles.

By following simple guidelines and using inexpensive tiling tools it is possible for any DIY enthusiast to carry out any of the tiling jobs previously done by a professional. There are always tiles to be shaped, but before cutting any, you first need to accurately mark them. Curved cuts at the edge of a handbasin can be carried out using a template. Fix the full tiles first of all, leaving one space for the curved cut tile. Now cut a piece of card to the exact size of the tile that is to be cut and fixed against the basin. Sometimes the card can be slid behind the basin and fitted into the space so that you can then draw an exact profile of the curve on to the card. Cut the curve on the card and transfer that to the new tile to be cut. If you can't do it this way, measure the short top line and the bottom longer line of the space and transfer those measurements to the card then cut between the two in a straight line. Force the card into the space against the vertical straight edge and crease the sloping side against the curved edge of the basin. Cut at the crease and transfer that curved cut to the new tile.

To fit tiles around a socket outlet, you should cut them so that at least 3 mm (⅛ in) slips behind the loosened plate so that it can be tightened up to the tile surface. Again, all whole tiles must be laid and the cut tile spacers left until the last. To cut the corner out of a tile hold it in the horizontal space first and mark where the corner of the switch plate touches the tile. Do the same for the vertical adjacent side. Measure how much the tile has to slip in both ways so that you have a matching grout line horizontally and vertically. Make these marks on the tile ready for cutting.

Fitting tiles against sloping ceilings is easier! One mark, one scribe, one cut. Hold the tile against the sloping ceiling but in line with the vertical grout lines of the already laid full tiles. Use a short wide batten as a guide. Hold the

Use contrasting tiles to make an attractive chequered floor pattern but run the tiles to the wall before the skirting is fixed. Then apply silicone sealant along the skirting to prevent water seeping under the floor.

Cut curves in heavy duty floor tiles to fit around the pedestal handbasin and WC. Use either a comb profiler or cut a cardboard template to transfer the shape to the tile.

Cutting heavy-duty floor tiles is not a difficult task with the right tools! Always measure the exact space to fill, then deduct the same amount each time for the grout joint.

batten against the slope of the ceiling and up against the tile to be cut. This will give you the exact angle for cutting. Measure either side of the space, transfer it to the tile and make a straight angled cut.

Tiling – curves
To cut a curve so that a tile fits accurately around a handbasin, make a cardboard template of the exact space to be filled and transfer the shape to the tile. A tile saw has a long-life, tungsten-coated carbide blade making it easy to cut curves. Use it to cut tiles up to 10mm (⅜in) thick.

Snapping tiles
Use a proprietary tool that measures, scores and snaps. This ensures that a number of tiles can be cut consistently and precisely.

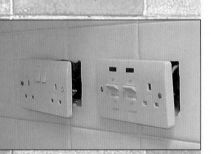

Square ceramic tiles are cut so that the edges are covered by socket faceplates. The power must be switched off when working near to sockets and switches. Only restore the power when you have screwed the faceplates back into position.

Curved cuts In the past, cutting curves in tiles was a tedious business. As much as possible of the waste tile was cut off after scoring straight lines, then the tiler worked up to the curved line with a nibbler or a pair of pincers. Tiny pieces were nicked out as far as the line and then a file was used to obtain a smooth curve. As more and more DIY enthusiasts began to do their own tiling, there was more demand for tools and equipment to make things easier, speedier and more economical – and so the DIY tile saw was born. This saw, similar to a junior hacksaw but slightly larger, has a long-life tungsten-coated carbide blade of circular cross-section so it cuts all around it. This makes it very easy to cut curves. The saw can even cut curves in tiles up to 10mm (⅜in) thick. Support the tile on the edge of a bench and cut around the curve with the tile saw. Alternatively, clamp the tile, protected with thick cardboard either side, in a vice and then carefully make the cut remembering that the saw is cutting on both the pull and the push action. Because the kerf (the slot left by the blade) is only the width of the blade, you cannot afford to tilt the blade either way. One slight movement to the left or to the right will put pressure on the brittle tile and probably break it, so take care.

Sometimes water pipes shoot out from a wall in the most inconvenient position! To cut around a pipe accurately and neatly need not be a problem. If the pipe is positioned at the edge of the tile, simply draw lines from the pipe's outer edges on to the tile with the corresponding curve in the right position. Support the tile on the edge of a bench and cut around the curve with the tile saw. If, as is more likely, the pipe position is somewhere in the centre of the tile, solve the problem by scoring the tile and snap-ping it at the position of the pipe centre. Draw parallel lines with the outer edges of the pipe on to both halves of the cut tile and draw corresponding curves to match the shape of the pipe. Cut both halves. When stuck in position you'll see little or no join.

An alternative method to making a cardboard template to transfer a shape to a tile is to use a 'profiler'. This brilliant device looks like a fine-toothed comb with long teeth. The polished steel teeth are held in grooves in a central bar. Each tooth slides in and out independently of the others. If you push the profiler against, for example, an architrave, the exact shape of the architrave is reproduced along the edge of the profiler. It's then a simpler matter to transfer this shape to any tile, whether it's a wall tile or a floor tile. Practically any shape can be reproduced using this ingenious device and it is an essential part of the DIYer's tiling tool box.

Straight cuts It has long been the practice to make straight cuts on tiles by first scoring along a marked line, placing two matchsticks under the tile (one either end under the scored line), and then pressing down either side to snap the tile. Larger tiles, floor tiles and frost resistant tiles need to have something larger than a matchstick, and professional tilers often use two pieces of electrical cable, but a tile jig or a 'snapper' is best when many repeat straight cuts are needed as it makes accurate and clean cuts every time. This is because you can actually see the line and the wheel that does the scoring. The hardest part of this process is the accurate marking of the tile after measuring the space, taking into account grout lines either side of the cut tile. Place the tile on the platform underneath the scoring wheel, lower the handle and pull it so that the scoring wheel is in contact with the whole length of the tile. You can be sure that you can solve the problem of scoring exactly on the line by taking into account thickness of the tool at the point where the spindle holds the scoring wheel. Lift the tile into the jaws of the 'snapper', press down on the handle and you get a straight accurate cut. Always smooth the sharp edge of any cut tile with sandpaper or even with a nail file.

Take a corner out of a tile by scoring. Cut the short side with a tile saw, then snap.

Use safety goggles when snapping or 'nibbling' shaped tiles.

If you have a gentle curve to snap, say, up to 25mm (1in) out of a true straight line, you can still do this by putting matchsticks under each end of the scored line and gently pressing down either side. This will snap the tile exactly where you want but only if you continue the scored line to either side of the tile.

To successfully snap quarry tiles, the scored line must be strong and continuous from the one edge to the opposite edge. With a lightweight hammer tap the back of the tile along the line of the score until you get a clean break. Contemporary quarry tiles are 150mm (6in) square and so they can be comfortably held in the left hand whilst tapping its back until it snaps. Obviously wear gloves to protect your hands. The secret to a clean cut, especially on a floor tile, is to have a scoring tool with a high quality wheel. Tools are available that have the capacity to successfully score ceramic wall tiles, quarry tiles, frostproof floor tiles, laminates, glass and mirrors. It is recommended that every time you use these tools that you add a little oil to the wheel. This not only stops the wheel jamming but also aids the scoring process.

Holes   Often it is necessary to drill into a wall tile or a floor tile either before or after fixing. For example, you might need to run a cable under a conservatory floor that you're going to tile. If you then go to screw a fitting to the tiled floor, say a lampholder, a water feature or a fish tank, you'll need to drill into the last tile where the cable appears. A variable speed drill is best with a tile spade bit running at a slow speed. Drill, again at slow speed, a pilot hole with a small diameter masonry bit then go to the size of bit that is required for the plug and the screw to hold the fitting. There are special bits available for drilling holes into frostproof tiles. These will literally drill into any building material, heavy gauge metal and even glass bottles!

Use masking tape at the drill bit position to drill into a tile without skidding.

Before you drill holes in ceramic wall tiles for hanging mirrors, wall cupboards or pictures, be certain that you know what the wall material is and then for your own safety, check with a cable and pipe detector that where you're drilling is safe. These are inexpensive and can save you a great deal of time and money. Remember – SAFETY FIRST, DIY SECOND. You might drill into a water pipe which will obviously cause a great deal of hassle and damage. This actually happened to former tennis star Annabel Croft. As a keen DIYer she was helping in the preparatory work for a 'make-over' in one of the rooms at her home. She knew the procedure for drilling through tiles, but not for checking for pipes and cables before drilling. She drilled into a water pipe with dire consequences which could have been worse had she not known where the stopcock was.

Cutting a wall tile to fit around a socket or switch (1)
Hold the tile against the socket and mark the cuts allowing 3mm (⅛in) to go under the faceplate. Make the shortest cut with a tile saw.

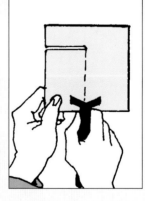

Cutting a wall tile to fit around a socket or switch (2)
Score the tile along the longest cut mark. Use a simple tile snapper to remove the corner piece. Switch off the mains, loosen the cover plate and slip the cut tile under the edge. Gently bed it into the tile cement.

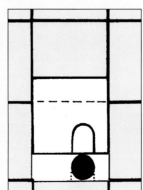

Cutting a wall tile to fit around a pipe
Hold the tile in line with the fixed tiles. Mark the outer edges and cut with a tile saw to the marked depth and to the circular shape.

Floors

Interior carpentry

This sectional drawing clearly shows the areas where interior carpentry can be carried out as a DIY task and where constructional work must be left to a professional.

Roof trusses must never be disturbed without expert knowledge, so an attic conversion needs Building Regulation approval (and possibly planning permission).

Staircase treads sit on risers which are housed in notches under the treads. A 'closed' string holds the risers and treads in grooves cut into the sides.

Stud partition walls need horizontal timbers (noggins) at regular intervals to support plasterboards. Shelving supports should ideally be screwed to the studs and noggins.

A loft hatch should be insulated (but prop the flap open if you go away in winter as warm air from below will help prevent freezing).

'Tongue and groove' ceiling boards can be fixed directly to the joists. Alternatively, fix battens to the joists first. Switch off at the mains to fix pendant lights.

Never remove a supporting wall or make an opening without first consulting your local building control officer.

Link smoke alarms to all areas except the kitchen and bathroom.

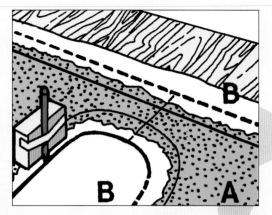

Laying floor coverings around obstacles

To replace a floor covering, such as vinyl or carpet, first make a template. Use felt paper which comes in long rolls from DIY and carpet stores.

Cover and temporarily fix a sheet of felt paper (A) over the whole of the floor area but cut it short of the walls and any other obstacles. Mark an outline of the obstacle onto the paper by running a block and felt-tipped pen held against the obstacle. Keep the wood block at exactly 90° to each surface so that you get an replica of the room but reduced in size by the width of the block.

Lay the floor covering in a larger room and place the felt paper template onto it (B). Now with the wood block and pen held against the drawn outline reverse the drawing order to make an exact copy of the shape of your room. Cut the floor covering with a sharp trimming knife. (Don't forget that you will need to cut a slit to fit the covering around the back of an obstacle such as a lavatory.)

Suspended timber floor

A typical construction of a suspended timber floor showing the damp-proof course (A) 15 cm (6 in) above ground level and extending on to the sleeper wall which supports the joists (B) on a timber wall plate. Lay 15 cm (6 in) of concrete on a bed of compacted hardcore (C).

Bouncing

From about 1870, depending on local building by-laws, a damp proof course (DPC) had to be inserted into the walls of new houses to prevent rising damp. Prior to this ruling, the saturation of stone and brick by moisture from the ground often resulted in deterioration of internal decorations and rot in joists let into the walls. In Victorian and Edwardian houses ground floors were almost invariably of timber boards laid on timber joists (suspended ground floor construction). The joists themselves were let into openings in the brickwork or supported by 'sleeper' walls. It is the unprotected, untreated ends of joists that are vulnerable to damp, resulting in rot. The ends of the joists become spongy and the floor will then suffer from 'bounce'. The joist ends have to be replaced as a matter of urgency.

Around the walls of a house that has suspended wooden flooring on the ground floor you will find air vents about 230 cm (9 in) above the outside ground level. This is just above the level of the DPC. If earth is allowed to pile up over the air vents or they become blocked in any way, the space beneath the floor becomes damp and a stagnant atmosphere congenial to dry rot forms. It is essential that the space is well ventilated so any earth, weeds or climbers blocking the air vent need to be shovelled away. Clear the vent holes with a rod.

Millions of Victorian and Edwardian houses have been renovated in the UK over the last 50 years. Many homeowners have found to their cost that the nineteenth-century building construction was not what it could have been. Builders found difficulty in damp-proofing floors next to the ground. The approved method was to lay a 150 mm (6 in) thick layer of concrete at least 300 mm (12 in) below the ground-level floor joists. The large section wooden joists which supported the floorboards were usually resting on a wooden wall plate running right round the room sitting on an inner ledge of the external wall. In many houses it has been found that the concrete ground-layer has been left out and the centre part of the joist, where sag could occur, is supported by a sleeper wall. Obviously the sleeper wall, resting on brick rubble, has caused subsequent problems. Consequently, the two areas to look at in order to solve the problem of a bouncing floor are at the joist ends, where they may be rotting, and the centre, where sleeper walls are no longer giving support. You also need to discover if any of the joists have twisted. It is good

You can buy a claw hammer to suit your own strength – from 16 oz to 24 oz.

Use a block under a hammer head for extra leverage to extract a long nail.

building practice to insert herringbone strutting between joists to make sure that damp from the air space or heat from central heating does not distorted the joists in any way. You will have to check whether herringbone strutting exists. Sometimes, as an alternative, solid joist sections called 'noggins' were nailed between the joists.

Lifting boards   The next detail to check is whether the boards are butt-jointed or are of 'tongue and groove' construction. If you can't get a knife through the gap between two boards then it's very likely that you have a 'tongue and groove' boarded floor. If you have to lift a board in a certain area, choose the shortest possible. Shorter boards were often used to facilitate the work of plumbers and electricians. To lift a 'tongue and groove' floorboard at the side of a room is fairly simple. These boards will have had the underside of the groove removed in order to lay it as a last board. Prise up the board either with a bolster chisel or with a small hooked nail removing bar and then remove all the nails. If you have to remove a more centrally placed 'tongue and groove' board you will need to saw either side of the board in order to cut through both tongues. If a number have to be removed, start at the skirting board, lift the easy one, then the rest can be easily prised away from each joist. You'll now discover whether the floorboards were fixed with floor brads 15 mm (½ in) from each edge into each joist, or 'secret nailed' through the tongue. Take care when lifting not to damage any part of the board.

Butt-jointed square-edged floorboards are easier to lift. To remove a board in the middle of the room, you'll need to prise up the centre

of the board to bow it. With a bolster chisel under one edge and a claw hammer under the other, start prising in both directions towards each joint. Another method is to ease a tube or rod into the gap underneath the bowed board and having freed the one end press on it with your foot. Continue to roll the rod along under the board as the nails are lifted. Where the cut end of a floorboard is near the wall (it should not actually be touching the wall) prise up the board to, say, 45°. The end of the board should then slip out from underneath the skirting. For safety's sake always remove nails from boards and joists immediately they are exposed.

You might find that floorboards are in a continuous run underneath a partition wall and are trapped by whatever is supporting the wall. Make a cut close to the wall to free a board. A simple method is to drill a hole into the board so that you can insert a narrow pad saw, then saw through close to the partition wall. Carpenters and floor layers usually have in their tool kit a curved floor saw, but these can be hired. This clever cutting device will cut across the board very easily. Alternatively, by removing the skirting board, a powered jigsaw can be used at a slight angle and makes life easier still. When the board is replaced and the skirting board refixed you'll won't see any joint.

Checking joists   The cut ends of joists are the most vulnerable to wet rot. Once you've exposed the ends, check the amount of moisture in the joists by using an inexpensive DIY moisture detector. If the end of the joist is spongy, then it has to be replaced. Cut away the soft section plus at least 600 mm (2 ft) and treat the cut end and the surrounding timber with a wood preservative. If the bounce is in the centre of the room, it's likely that sleeper walls are no longer supporting them. As is often the case, sleeper walls over the years have settled. The solution to this is easy if you've got an old piece of slate. Cut it into pieces and place them in the gap between the top of the sleeper wall and the underside of the joist. It is prudent and good building practice to insert a piece of DPC felt between the slate and the underside of the joist.

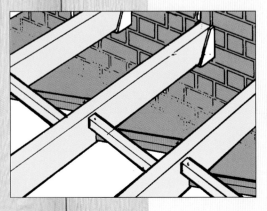

Floor joists
Joists can be supported in a number of ways. They are traditionally built in to the brickwork, but extra building work or renovation work involving joists is easier with metal joist hangers as shown.

Herringbone struts (a series of battens cut at angles and crossed like braces) keep the joists rigid.

If one joist has twisted, warped or bowed, this can also give a gap between the floorboard and the joist. You'll now need to do two things. Tension the affected joist between the joists either side by inserting herringbone struts or noggins, then nail a tapered batten to fit into the gap between the joist and the floorboard.

Replacing joists
A joist that is suspect throughout its length needs to be removed completely and replaced with a pretreated one of exactly the same section. If the joist is resting on a ledge on which the wooden wall plate is sited, make sure that there is damp proof felt underneath that section of wall plate. If half a joist has been removed and has to be replaced, replace a new joist long enough to rest on a sleeper wall and on to the wall plate. Where it overlaps the old joist, bolt the two together. After having drilled the holes for the bolts treat that raw timber with preservative. Joist ends were sometimes housed in pockets, that is a brick left out of the wall into which the end of the joist rested. It is a good idea to wrap the end of the joist in a sort of envelope of bitumen felt. Make sure that none of the timber is in contact with any of the brickwork and fasten the folded ends with large headed clout nails.

Ventilation
If a path at the side of a house has been raised in order to make a base for the slabs, it is possible that air vents will have been covered. Even if they are only partially covered, this will be sufficient to prevent the passage of air which ventilates the space under the suspended ground floor.

In the first decades of the twentieth century, air vents disappeared from small terraced houses and cottages. Architects thought they could build more cheaply by building directly on to a concrete base slab, so, suspended ground-floor construction with its ventilated void beneath it was superseded by this new approach. Asphalt, 25 mm (1 in) thick, was laid directly on to the concrete in order to waterproof it, then either a sand and cement screed was laid as a subfloor or joists of a small section were positioned to support timber boards. You can assume then that there is no void beneath your floor if you cannot find air vents around the outside of the building. This is presuming of course that all the air vents have not been covered over!

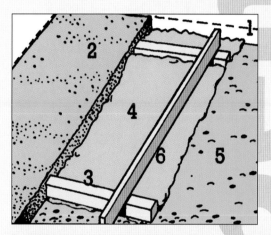

Replacing a wooden ground floor with a concrete floor

The dotted line (1) is the finished level of the top of the screed (2) which has been already laid in the first bay. Lay battens (3), of the same thickness as the screed, in mortar. Lay a cement grout (4) between the battens on the concrete floor (5). The screed is laid between and on both sides of the battens and levelled with a tamping batten (6). Lift out the battens and fill in with screed material.

Problems with a rotten suspended wooden floor can be solved by removing the entire underfloor construction and laying a concrete floor according to these strict guidelines.

Use a sheet of 1200 gauge polythene membrane to link up with and overlap the damp-proof course in the walls.

Excavate so that you can lay 10 cm (4 in) of hardcore (and sand to blend it in). Lay the membrane into the sand. Fill in with 8 cm (3 in) of concrete to bring the level up to a horizontal line drawn around the walls for the screed. Mark this line 8 cm (3 in) below the finished floor level. The screed takes up approximately 5 cm (2 in).

There is no twisting or warping of these joists because the original builders fixed herringbone struts between them. The lath and plaster ceiling has been removed to install sound insulation. All the nails need to be removed before installing the insulating material which will be covered with new plasterboards.

Concrete floor
A typical solid concrete floor construction showing the damp-proof membrane (A) continuing up the wall to overlap the damp-proof course laid 15 cm (6 in) above the outside ground level. Under the 10 cm (4 in) of concrete is a similar amount of compacted hardcore on to which is spread sand before the membrane is laid. 5 cm (2 in) of mortar screed supports the finished floor above the concrete.

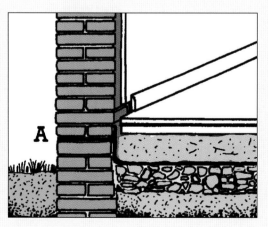

After every job with a hammer, rub the head on emery paper on a board.

Hold a claw hammer at the end of the handle, but a club hammer in the middle.

To lift a 'tongue and groove' floorboard, borrow an electrician's 'skate' to cut the tongue.

Lifting floorboards
Lift a flat-edged floorboard by using a steel pipe rolled under it after it has been raised sufficiently with a bolster chisel and claw hammer. The illustration also shows a rounded-end floor saw.

Creaking

In general, floors are made up of two elements, the structural (or supporting) part and the flooring (the boarding or covering laid on to the structural base). The structural element can either be timber floor joists or a concrete slab. In an ordinary house the ground floor is solid or suspended, whilst the upper floors are constructed of heavy timber joists supported either end in the wall. By the late 1920s to early 1930s solid concrete floor construction had generally superseded the timber ground floor in houses in this country. Where extra rigidity was needed to stabilise joists proprietary metal herringbone strutting was inserted. Without bracing or strutting, an integral part of upper floor construction, joists can warp and twist and this is often the cause of cracks in ceilings as well as movement in flooring. Any movement between boards or between boards and joists will eventually give rise to creaking sounds. The nail holes enlarge, the floor nails lose their hold and the floorboards rock and creak.

Floor nails or brads can lose their hold for other reasons. Rot or woodworm will cause the timber to crumble. Shrinkage in the actual floorboards can cause movement and creaks. Warping and bowing can be caused by central heating pipes being too hot or too close to the floorboards. Floorboards not properly fixed or rocking on bent or rusted floor brads will also cause a squeaky noise.

Lifting boards   When faced with the problem of creaking floorboards always observe the golden rule – SAFETY FIRST, DIY SECOND – and never try to nail a board back

before checking for pipes and cables. Electric, television or telephone cables and domestic water, central heating and gas pipes can be found running through slots cut into the joists just beneath the boards. If any of these services run parallel to the joists it is easy to isolate them from floor fixing nails or screws, but if they run at right angles to the joists they were probably directed through the centres of the joists by cutting slots into the top edge. These are obviously vulnerable to floor fixings – this is bad building practice and is not allowed today. Ordinary floorboards are fixed by nailing or screwing near the edges of each board into each joist, so you can see how important it is to know exactly where these services are when refixing boards.

Incidentally, if you see the tell-tale flight-holes of woodworm, treat the joists and the surrounding timbers with a proprietary prevention fluid. If necessary strengthen the floor joists by bolting a piece of timber alongside it. Rotted or broken floorboards must of course be replaced.

It could be that you have a problem with floorboards that are 1800 mm × 600 mm (6 ft × 2 ft) made of flooring quality chipboard. One long edge will have a tongue and the other a groove. These large boards are usually fixed by screwing with 'superscrews' into each joist and not by using secret nails through the tongue. If you encounter a problem here, use a cordless screwdriver with the appropriate bit, usually a Philips, to simply remove the screws. You will still have to saw down each side of the board to remove the tongue when you want to remove a board in the centre of the room.

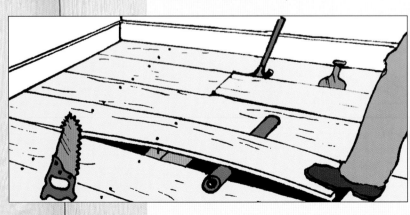

Cutting a floorboard
A pad saw will cut through a board at an angle close to a joist. Nail a batten to the side of the joist to support the cut board.

150

If large boards have been fixed with flooring brad nails, this is slightly more of a problem. You still have to saw down either side of the board before prising the board with the tools you have available, probably a bolster chisel, a wood chisel, a claw hammer and a wrecking bar. Timber joists are tougher than chipboard, so it's very probable that you'll find that the flooring brad nails might pull through and be left in the joists. It is good practice to fill those holes immediately with wood filler. For your own safety, remove the brads from the joist as soon as you lift it off the board.

You'll need to remove the skirting boards if you have to lift the whole of the floor in any one room. Use a trimming knife or a small bolster to produce a straight cut between the plaster and the top of the skirting board. Skirting boards that are mitred each end into the corners of the room will either have to be bowed and sprung from the centre or cut. Drive a bolster or a wrecking bar into the skirting to get the first purchase. Drive in two wedges either side of the bar. With the skirting away from the wall you can now get a saw in between the wedges to cut the board at an angle. When replacing the boards this will make hiding the angled cut easier. Skirting boards are usually nailed to 'grounds'. These pieces of wood are firmly fixed to the wall before the wall is plastered. A cut clasp-nail is hammered into the skirting to hold it securely in place. Often when prising the skirting free the clasp-nail is held in the wooden grounds and the head pulled through the back of the skirting board. However, because the head of the nail is usually driven deep into the skirting board and then back-filled, you might be lucky enough to find the surface of the skirting board still in one piece.

If an ordinary floorboard is badly split or part of it needs to be replaced, cut out the part to be replaced centrally over joists.

Packing joists
If the replacement board is of a different thickness you can do one of two things. If the only new board available is thinner, use packing pieces of hardboard or ply nailed to the joists. If the new board is slightly thicker than the others, you can cut grooves in the underside surface to coincide with the position of the joists. When either packing joists with pieces of plywood or chopping out grooves in the underside of thicker floorboards, it is essential to treat all freshly exposed timber with a wood preservative. At the same time as treating the packing take the opportunity to treat the joists as far as you can go.

Safety
My maxim SAFETY FIRST, DIY SECOND is just as applicable when working on floors, exposing joists and the voids between floorboards and the ceiling underneath. Holes can still trip you if you're working on the ground floor. The main consideration when working in close proximity to pipes and cables is obviously not to disturb or pierce any of them, so a DIY pipe and cable detector is a must. This will tell you where all runs of pipes and cables are lurking dangerously beneath the floorboards. If the floor is to be covered by a carpet, take the time to do the following. Trace the runs of pipes and live cables separately and with different coloured felt pens mark them on the boards. It is safer to drive in screws rather than nails along the edges of boards where no pipes or cables should have been laid, so with everything marked and with screws holding down the new boards, any problems to solve in the future are going to take less time and you'll know you can work safely. When using wood preserver, always keep a window open to ensure good ventilation. Another good safety point is never allow anybody else in the room whilst you're working. If floorboards have been lifted and not repositioned by the end of the day, lock the door to the room so that nobody can enter the room in your absence. Keep the key in your pocket. Heavy tools and equipment should never be left close to a floor opening. A slight slip, a heel against a club hammer or a power tool, and you could end up with a hole through the plaster ceiling!

Refixing boards
If there is woodworm infestation, lift the board that is worst affected. The back of the board might show even more holes, which will mean that there's a honeycomb of larva tunnels inside the wood. Examine

Tongue and groove

Traditional square-edged floorboards have a number of drawbacks. Gaps are left when the boards shrink causing curling and nails to become loose. 'Tongue and groove' (T and G) boards have a tongue running centrally along one edge and a matching groove along the other. This makes a strong joint. The boards are fixed into the joist with 'secret nailing' through the tongue. At the skirting, cut the board to width and cut off the lower section of the groove.

Replacing floorboards

When part of a floorboard needs replacing cut half-way over a joist (1). Mark the new board (2) if it is too thick, ready for chiselling as at (3) and (4).

Replacing with a thicker board

If a replacement board is slightly thicker than the existing board, cut parallel lines, with a tenon saw, slightly wider than the width of the joist. Use a bevel-edged chisel to remove the waste wood (4) so that the thickness of the remaining board will bring the floorboard level to that of the existing board. Turn the board (2) over and fix it as for normal boards.

To stop wood splitting when nailing near ends, tap the nail point to 'chisel' it.

Glue laths into large gaps between floorboards, leave proud, then sand flat.

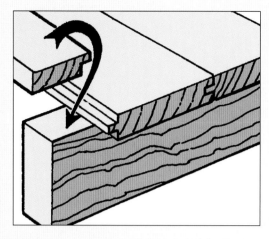

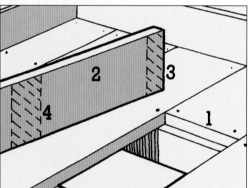

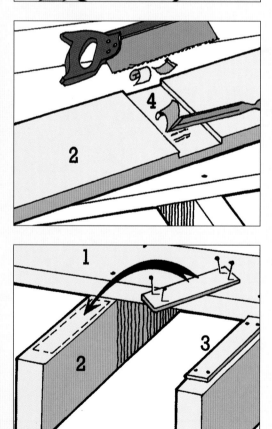

Replacing with a thinner board

If the replacement board is only slightly thinner than the existing boards simply cut and fix packing pieces of hardboard or plywood (3). Glue the pieces in place and use 25 mm (1 in) panel pins for fixing to the joists.

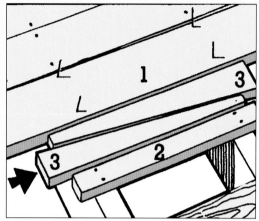

Fixing floorboards

If you do not have a floor clamp, make your own! Each board must be wedged tightly into position before fixing. The next floorboard to be fixed (1) can be forced into position to make a tight fit by using folding wedges (3). First nail a batten (2) to the joists as a temporary support for the wedges. Slide the wedges (cut diagonally from a spare board) into position. Hammer the wedges as indicated by the arrow to get a tight fit before securing the floorboard with nails into each joist.

the adjacent boards and burn those that have more than just a few holes. Treat all the surrounding timber before laying the new matching floorboard.

For a professional finish to your floor there should be no gaps. It is not too difficult to lift boards and to relay them tightly butted together. The last gap left next to the skirting board must be filled with a new board. Relaying the floor provides a good opportunity to thermally insulate it too. See the sections on sound and thermal insulation. Every nail holding down a board must be punched at least 3 mm (⅛ in) below the surface. Screws must be driven in to the same depth.

Always use screws to refix boards in problem areas. The advantages are that you'll get a firmer and longer hold. They are easy to remove at problem times and quicker to fix with a cordless screwdriver.

If you are refixing a number of floorboards use a flooring-cramp to push each successive board against the last. If you are reusing lifted boards, these will be well seasoned and therefore less likely to cause any problems in the future. The flooring-cramp has jaws that grip the joist and the turning handle puts pressure on to the bar

Skirting boards

The gap between floorboards and a skirting board can be filled with cork strip. However, it is better to glue and pin (with a tacker gun) a scotia moulding (or quadrant moulding). Do not glue to the floor as any movement will scratch the skirting.

Stop a brass screw breaking off in oak by screwing in a steel one first.

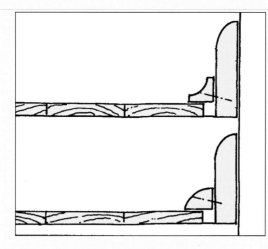

that pushes one board against another. Nail or screw in position before moving the clamp back one width of a board.

If a flooring-cramp is not available and a number of boards have to be replaced, use folding-wedges – a DIY method of tightening the boards to each other. Folding-wedges are made from a spare piece of square-edged board about 600 mm (2 ft) long. Cut the board diagonally lengthways. Lay the wedges in position against the last loose board, then slide them apart about 200 mm (8 in). Nail a temporary batten support against the folding-wedges. By hammering the wedges together you get an extremely tight fit between the floorboards. Always brush the undersides of the boards and the tops of joists before fixing to ensure that there is no debris to cause creaking problems in the future.

The ends of each laminate board need to be tapped into position using a specially designed short block with a metal handle. There's no need for sanding or sealing! No glue is used, so a damaged board can easily be replaced, or an entire floor can be taken away when you move!

Laminate floors

Laminate flooring is real wood faced so that you can enjoy the beauty inherent in the grain. There are many types and methods of laying the laminates. I have installed several proprietary laminate floors for various media personalities, such as for a kitchen I designed for hypnotist Paul McKenna. All makes are as good as each other, but my first piece of advice is to get the comprehensive brochures on as many makes as you can from your local stockists. Check the installation procedure for concrete floors and for suspended wooden floors. Make sure that you have sufficient clearance on the bottom of doors. Take account that you may need to remove skirting boards and check the method of cutting and

Levelling for laminate flooring

A concrete base must be perfectly level for laminate flooring. Fill holes or uneven patches with a quick-cure self-levelling compound.

Spreading levelling compound for laminate flooring

Use a float. Work across the floor in strips, feathering the edges to meet the high spots. The compound sets to a very smooth finish ready for the laminate flooring.

This attractive laminated flooring looks like a full board, but closer inspection will show that it is made up of three boards. The boards are interlocked to give a perfectly flat finish. The boards are not fixed down but 'float' so it's easy to lift them to take with you when you move house!

If problems with old flooring calls for a changes, solid planks of walnut or laminated floorboards are a fairly simple DIY solution. Most problems can be solved by laying the boards over the old ones or by removing the old boards and replacing with tongue and groove. Use the 'secret nail' method of fixing so that nothing is seen on the beautifully polished surface. Wall panelling is similarly fixed to battens.

The comb-like profiler is a simple device that takes the guesswork out of trimming any material around a moulded shape. When pushed against the moulding, the slim teeth slide separately out to follow the outline, which can then be transferred to the flooring, tiles, etc., that are to be cut.

fixing around a hearth. Even though the laminate boards are only 7 mm (¼ in) thick, you have to consider all these constraints.

Patching Most laminated floors these days have a hidden locking device to hold the smaller sections of boards tightly together in their 'tongue and groove' joints. A laminate floor 'floats' on an existing floor and is not screwed or fixed to it. A membrane is supplied to lay on the floor first. The planks, usually about 230 mm (9 in) wide, slot into each other and are then clipped together. Often the manufacturers suggest using wood glue at the top and bottom edges of the planks.

It is not difficult to patch a worn part of a laminated floor but you'll have to find a board that exactly matches the existing piece in thickness and other details. Each long length piece can be three strips bonded together, but think of it as just a single plank of wood. In order to remove the worn plank you'll need to set a circular saw to cut just through the thickness of the board. This is in case there are cables or pipes below. Now carefully cut out a squared piece, about 25 mm (1 in) in from each of the two lengths and the two ends. Lift out the piece. You're now left with long strips either side of the hole. One will have a tongue and the other a groove still in place attached to the adjacent boards. Carefully saw and chisel out the thin strips that are left and remove residual glue, particularly at the ends.

Now deal with the replacement board. Cut off the undersides of one length and one end of the groove. Use a strong bonding adhesive to glue the tops of the two cut grooves to the corresponding tongue. The other two tongues will have been eased into their grooves first, of course. Use weights to hold the new board in position. You might need a screw or two, but cover the heads with matching wood filler. Wait

for the glue to completely cure before either staining or polishing the patch the match the rest of the floor. Any slight gaps between the boards can be filled with wax polish.

Relaying You might choose to relay a different laminated floor to the one that was originally there. If you are relaying on a concrete subfloor, check that a thermal insulation polystyrene board is under the screed. All concrete floors have, by regulation, a damp-proof membrane so you should have no problem with rising damp.

Having lifted the old boards, you will probably find the once resilient underlay is no longer doing its job. If there is condensation between the original floor and the old laminate, allow a couple of days for the subfloor to acclimatise, especially if the house is centrally heated. Mark each board as you lift it so that it goes back in the same position but don't forget to allow for a 10 mm (½ in) gap around the edges of the room for expansion. Every floor that is sold comes with a DIY laying set which includes wedges to maintain that gap. The old cork strip filler that fills that gap has probably deteriorated. Replacement cork is easily available. If you haven't kept the detailed instruction booklet, these are also available.

Cutting profiles All flooring, at one place or another, needs to have a shaped profile cut into an edge. For example, at a door opening where the post has a moulded architrave fixed to it around which the flooring has to be cut as accurately as possible. Before the advent of steel or plastic comb profile kits, you would have to cut a piece of card or ply as close as possible to the moulding. Push the sliding steel teeth of a comb profile against any shape that is to be reproduced. The teeth slide in a central bar and are held there whilst the shape is reproduced on the piece to be cut. Even central heating pipes that may be 5 cm (2 in) from the skirting and run up to the radiator can be perfectly reproduced in shape, size and distance. We now no longer have to bear the tedium and guesswork of folding and cutting card to get a good reproduction of a shape.

Nails must be punched in, extracted or cut off, before sanding floors to prevent the floor sanding sheets being torn.

Preparation
Before using the sanding machine check the entire floor for signs of worm holes and treat as necessary. The raised head of a floor brad (nail) will rip the abrasive paper of the sander so make sure that every nail is driven below the wood surface with a nail punch. A proprietary wood filler can be used to fill the nail holes – use one that matches the floor colour.

Sanding

Technical developments in the building industry have contributed to the need for less maintenance in our homes. UPVC windows, for example, once installed, are maintenance-free for life. Roof, ceiling, wall and floor coverings are all available in durable man-made materials and over the past decade there has been an upsurge in the interest and use of them. However, there are still people for whom there is no substitute for natural materials. The 'disenchanted' are joining the 'traditionalists' in their great love of the beauty, texture and warmth of natural materials in the home. There is no substitute for a smooth, highly-polished oak, beech or pine floor with a sparkling finish highlighting the beauty of the grain. Obtaining this high-quality floor finish is no longer a job for professionals as the necessary tools, such as a sanding machine, can now be hired. All you need is the patience to see the job through. It is a time-consuming one and sanding machines make a lot of noise and dust. However, a vacuum bag is incorporated in a drum sander, but you still need to use protective clothing, a face mask (with very fine removable filters so that you can renew them when necessary) and even goggles.

A note on hiring tools. It is very important for your own safety and the protection of others who might be using the tools that you check:

- that the hire shop is a member of the Hire Association Europe (HAE);
- that a list of charges is displayed;
- that customer service is guaranteed;
- that expert advice is given;
- that the operation of the tool is taught:
- that all safety factors are conveyed and that you understand them.

It is also worth asking if the plugs have the right fuse rating, if continuity testing has been carried out since it was last used and if they give

you a fully illustrated instruction booklet to accompany the power tool. If you have a friend who is a satisfied customer of a hire shop, then you're off to a good start!

There has been a tremendous growth in the DIY hire business and it costs relatively little to hire an expensive piece of equipment or tool for a weekend's DIY job. By hiring an industrial sanding machine, a rotary sander and a hook scraper for a couple of days, it is possible to change a scratched, discoloured and neglected floor into a smooth, flat sanded one that you're going to be proud of.

Preparation, as in all DIY jobs, is very important. After the room has been emptied of furniture and floor coverings, thoroughly vacuum the floor so that all blemishes and any wormholes are exposed. Deal with these as discussed earlier in the section. Every nail holding down a board must be punched at least 3 mm (⅛ in) below the surface so that the abrasive paper attached to the spinning sanding drum will not be torn to shreds! Check very carefully loose boards, especially where a cut board has been relaid over a joist. Plane a piece of lath to fit tightly into any odd gap between boards.

Apply wood adhesive and hammer it home. Use a smoothing plane to level it, and stain it if necessary.

Most old floors, especially those made of standard pine boards, are likely to have uneven surfaces across the width of some of the boards.

Edge preparation
There are areas of the floor that cannot be reached by the sander. Use a hook scraper in these places. This is a long-handled, simple-to-use tool that cuts as it is pulled backwards. The blades can be changed so you can get into tight corners.

Floor sanding

Very few floors are absolutely flat. To solve this problem, sand diagonally one way and then the other way. Then sand parallel to the boards with a medium grade sanding paper to give a smooth finish and to sand out any scratches.

Taping up the doors
Sanding floors can be very messy, especially if the boards are 'cupped' and need a lot of wearing down. Tape up gaps around doors, but keep open a window. Wear protective clothing, especially a mask (change its lint pad frequently).

An inward curve, called cupping, is the most common and obvious. Before even thinking about the final smooth finish, it is necessary to level the floor. Full instructions come with the hired machine so read and reread them in order to make no mistakes! Only fit a new sheet of abrasive paper after unplugging the lead from the electric socket. Make sure that the sanding sheet is wrapped tightly around the drum and aligned properly. The information leaflet will also suggest sealing door and window openings with masking tape as fine dust is drawn very easily through any gaps. One window, however, can be left open to provide fresh air. Now make sure that the machine is switched off before plugging back into the mains.

Often it is very useful to know the professional's method of carrying out a job! No one serves an apprenticeship in floor sanding, but a carpenter knows that planing or sanding diagonally across a piece of wood will level it. That is why the professional sander sands diagonally over the whole area of the floor one way and then diagonally the other way. Do this and you'll end up with a perfectly level floor, with no cupping across any of the floorboards. Use a rotary edging sander to work close to skirting boards. A small orbital sander or a hook scraper will clean up the corners. Three or four grades of abrasive paper are normally used, working progressively from the coarse grade to a fine grade to obtain the smoothest possible finish. Remember always to unplug from the socket before making any change or adjustment to an electrically operated machine.

An upright drum sander is quite heavy and very powerful. It can exert a strong pull, so take care not to let it run away. With the cable over your shoulder, hold the sander very securely, tilt it back and switch it on. When it's up to speed, lower the drum gently to the floor and allow it to move forward. Try not to be hesitant, walk slowly and steadily as it moves forward under its own power. Only hold the machine to control its pace forward and never ever leave it stationary – holding a rotating drum in the same spot for even a moment will cause gouging! When you reach the end of one line, push the handle down to lift the drum off the floor. Switch off and wait for the drum to stop revolving before starting the reverse line. Use a vacuum cleaner as often as is necessary to remove the dust.

Soft knee pads are required for the next part of the operation as kneeling is the best position for using the edging sander! It's not a difficult machine to use because it generates its own gliding action and has back castor wheels to lift the disc off the floor. Make sure that the electric cable is over your shoulder before switching on and lowering the machine. Again it is essential to keep the machine moving but no pressure must be exerted. Always tilt the machine back on its castors before switching off. Each time you change the abrasive disc, remember to first pull the plug from the socket.

After levelling the floor with a coarse grade paper, change to a medium grade to sand in the same direction as the boards. Never ever sand at right angles to the boards. Overlap each line so that there are no misses. Don't forget to use the same grade of abrasive paper each time on the rotary sander too. Continue to use the vacuum cleaner to remove spillage and excess dust and to prevent too much dust rising into the room. After using the finest of the abrasive sheets you'll be satisfied that you've obtained a smooth satin finish. Vacuum the floor then use a clean cloth and white spirit to remove all traces of dust. Every trace of dust must be removed, including from the tops of skirting boards, before the sealing treatment is started. Now go outside and shake out all your working clothes – you'll be surprised at the amount of dust stuck in clumps to the bottom of your shoes!

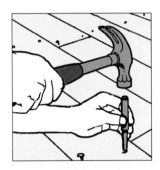

Sealing floors
First remove or knock in any protruding screws or nails. Then sand and seal with three coats of a proprietary sealant or varnish.

Who would have thought that this amazing replacement floor, with its extremely hard-wearing, sealed-in gloss finish, could be laid by an enthusiastic DIYer? With a basic tool kit, common sense and limited expertise, this laminate flooring is a DIYer's dream come true.

Sealants and coatings

If you leave the floor untreated after sanding, it will quickly pick up dirt and become stained and less resistant to wear. This makes it harder to clean so sealing a sanded wooden floor must be tackled as quickly as possible after cleaning. A clear finish sealing treatment not only makes the floor more attractive, but it is necessary to preserve, seal and protect it. The principle of a satisfactory seal is that it should completely coat the surface and penetrate a little below it.

All the major paint and coatings manufacturers have their own brand of liquid sealer. Stains, polishes and varnishes can also be used to good effect on floors to give colour to the wood without losing the natural beauty of the grain, whereas transparent finishes are a good alternative which seal and maintain the natural colour of the wood flooring. Floors undergo more wear than any other wooden component in the house so manufacturers have formulated preservatives, coloured stains, hard-wearing protective coatings and varnishes suitable for this purpose. Solvent-based and water-based products are available for you to choose from. Polyurethane

varnishes and wax polishes are alternatives. Some people find solvent-based finishes inappropriate because of the smell. In this case, try the more modern water-based varnishes, which are very quick drying (touch-dry in 20 minutes) and hard enough to be recoated after two hours.

Measure the floor area and, in the DIY store, check the recommended coverage per coat, so that you buy enough for the job. The instructions will also help you to decide whether you should brush on the base coat or you should use a closely textured foam roller. A foam roller is great for the base coat because it always applies the sealant very quickly to the untreated wood, and, therefore, thinly. Read the label carefully because you need to know whether the sealant is solvent based or water based. Kneeling pads are essential for this task! Remember to start on the floor at the opposite corner to the door you want to leave by!

Apply two or three coats of sealant, the last of which needs to be hard wearing, attractive-looking, easily maintained and readily renewed in the course of time. Many modern sealing products meet these criteria and whichever you use, always follow the manufacturer's instructions for recommended times between coats. Between coats, always lightly rub down with a very fine glasspaper, making sure that the seal is hard and dry first, and remove any dust with a clean cloth and white spirit.

Once the first coat has dried completely, the wood will be sealed and cannot soak in the solution so easily. The second coat will glide over the surface. If you choose to varnish the floor to enhance the natural colour, you'll need a further two coats of clear varnish on top of the base coat. If you want to change the colour of the timber floor using a coloured gloss or satin varnish, use a roller to apply as many coats as are required to reach the desired shade – two are usually sufficient. Finish with a protective top coat of clear varnish in a gloss or satin finish, but do remember to check the instructions regarding the time before subsequent coats can be applied. By using a 100mm (4in) brush it is easy to change the colour of a floor using a wood dye. This is much better for large areas and looks great when finished. You just need one coat, brushed in the direction of the grain, then finish with three coats of clear varnish. Brushes are better here because a roller, when loaded with a dye, could leave a distinctive mark across the grain at its first point of application.

Now that you've seen the extraordinary difference in the new finish to your old floor, you might now consider going for an extra fine finish. The last but one coat of varnish needs to be very lightly and carefully sanded, the dust vacuumed up and the residue washed off with white spirit. Leave to dry before brushing on the final coat. Remove all existing coatings before smoothing with steel wool or fine grade sandpaper to produce a smooth finish. Then use white spirit on a lint-free cloth to remove dust. To get a successful finish to your new coating there must be absolutely no sign of oil or wax left on the floor.

Floor insulation
Drape garden netting over the joists. Use sufficient to hold the insulation material. Use a staple gun to hold the netting in place. Note the ventilating air-brick to give a through-draught.

Noise

When a family house has been converted into one for multiple occupation, one of the greatest sources of unneighbourliness is noise through ceilings and floors. When a conversion of this nature is carried out it should be the responsibility of the builder to isolate one unit from the other. A dense material absorbs sound well and the Victorians knew the value of lead in this regard. It was found to be effective against the two main sources of noise through walls and floors, namely airborne noise and impact noise. Today, one manufacturer has produced rolls of very thin gauged sheet lead which are laid flat, overlapping and tight to the wall on a prepared floor. The floor covering is then laid over the sheet of lead. Researchers into noise problems in houses reported that the tiniest crack in an otherwise heavily insulated floor will allow sound waves to travel through.

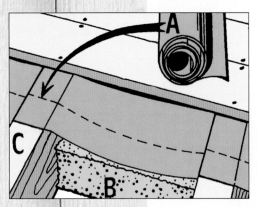

Lead sound insulation
Sandwich a layer of 100 mm (4 in) Gyplas® (B) between the joists (C). Then lay specially made, thinly rolled, lead-based sound insulation (A) directly on the joists. Fix the floorboards in the usual way, ensuring that they are firmly tightened to each other using a clamp or wedges. Overlap the lead sheeting by at least 75 mm (3 in) and use a flexible mastic sealant on the lap.

Floor insulation Any solid, compacted or dense material either on a floor, between the floor joists or beneath the ceiling underneath the floor (the person living beneath the noise problem can install a false ceiling) is going to help solve the problem caused by bad building practices.

One manufacturer has successfully designed and manufactured a totally effective system to overcome the problem of noise between existing timber joisted floors, but it does involve lifting the floorboards first. This system effectively improves the internal environment by reducing sound transmission through the upper floor. As a DIY application for the enthusiast, it provides a sound absorbent material fitted between the joists supported by metal channel sections which are fitted over the top of the floor joists and located on metal clips. A Gyproc® plank is cut and fitted between the joists resting on metal flanges. To complete the work, relay the old floor, heightened only the thickness of the thin metal strips resting on the top edges of the joists. The components come in kit form and do not require professional specialist skills. Other advantages are that the system is simple and economic to install and has good standards of airborne and impact sound insulation. It has minimum increase in floor depth and the added bonus of being fire resistant for one hour. There are no added problems reaching pipes or cables because after lifting a floorboard the Gyproc® plank is simply lifted out too.

Another technique, simpler but just as effective, involves laying a new floor on top of the existing floor. The new floor has two layers. The first is a roll of insulating foam, the second a thin protective layer of plywood. Both are glued in position so it makes sense to check all the underfloor plumbing and electrical installations before laying the new floor. If access traps are necessary, now is the time to cut them. This new and simpler system, designed for DIY installation, raises the floor by 8 mm ($5/16$ in), so it does mean that doors opening into the room will have to have the bottoms planed. Fully illustrated instructions come with the insulating kit. The bright yellow insulating material

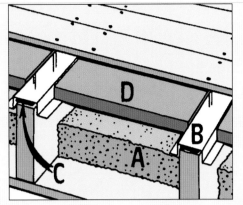

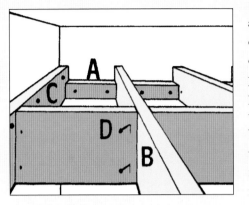

Sound insulation between floors – First method

Lay 100 mm (4 in) of glass wool mat (Gyplas®) (A) between the joists making sure that there are no gaps. Lay metal channel sections (B) on the joists with resilient strips (C) located between the metal channel and the joists. Cut 19 mm (³⁄₄ in) Gyproc® plank to fit and rest on the metal flanges (D). Complete the floor by screwing the floorboards through the plank in to the metal flanges.

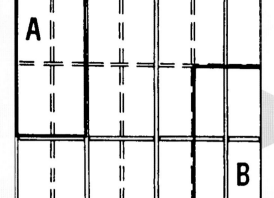

Sound insulation between floors

The diagram shows a typical layout of timbers for a 4.25 m × 3.6 m (14 ft × 12 ft) bedroom ceiling. The solid lines indicate the supporting timbers for the first layer of plasterboards. Fix plasterboard A first. The dotted lines show the fixing positions for the second layer of plasterboards, ensuring that no joints coincide. Fix plasterboard B as the first one of the second layer. Fix each layer into all intermediate timbers too.

When the ceiling is finished, fit coving to make sure that no sound can escape around the ceiling–wall joint.

Sound insulation between floors – Second method

If only the underside of a separating floor is accessible, construct an independent ceiling. Drill, plug and screw 50 mm × 50 mm (2 in × 2 in) battens (A) at least 150 mm (6 in) below the existing ceiling on the end walls making sure they are level. These will support notched joists (B) that are skew-nailed to the battens. Fix the side joists (C) to the walls with plugs and screws. Skew-nail intermediate noggins (D) to support the ends of the plasterboards. The lower edges of all the joists, battens and noggins must be level to take the plasterboards. Lay mineral fibre insulation between the timbers before fixing the plasterboards.

at the heart of the system comes in rolls which are easily cut with a trimming knife. The principle of this floor sound-proofing system is to separate the new floor surface from both the skirting boards and the original floor by a sound-insulating barrier, in this case a roll of foam insulating material. It has to be turned up at the skirting board so that when the new plywood floor is glued to the foam with the ready-mix adhesive there is a tight join. The foam is then trimmed level with the plywood. There is now no physical link between the plywood and the original floor or skirting

board, so no sound will pass through. Lay a carpet on top of the plywood to increase the insulation density. Where floor levels change, for example at a doorway, screw a standard threshold strip in place to cover the difference between the floor levels inside and outside the room.

Thermal and sound insulation between floors (1)

Gyproc® provides good thermal and sound insulation as well as providing some fire protection. Rest a metal 'top hat' section strip on foam inlay on the top edge of each joist. Lay Gyproc® planks on the flanges of the metal strip. Tightly wedge mineral wool between the joists. Tightly screw the floorboards to the metal strips, through the Gyproc® plank and into the lower flange.

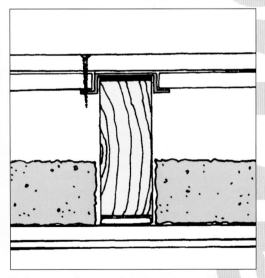

Thermal and sound insulation between floors (2)

Section of a Gyproc® insulation system. Gyproc® planks can also be fixed to the underside of the joists. Ceiling boards are then fixed to them.

Legal solutions Unless you are very lucky, everybody hears some noise from their neighbours, such as raised voices, laughter and occasional loud music. Your neighbours may hear similar noise from you! However, if you think that your neighbours behave in a reasonable way but you're frequently disturbed by their noise, it may be that the sound insulation between your homes is below average. New houses and flats have to meet the requirements of the Building Regulations. These say that certain walls and floors must be constructed in such a way that they have reasonable resistance to the passage of sound. These regulations are enforced by your Local Authority. You can get a copy of an approved document called 'Resistance to the Passage of Sound' from the Stationery Office. Some Local Authorities include a requirement in any planning application so that you can check to see if it has been complied with when there's been a conversion in your property.

If your neighbours make excessive noise (particularly at unreasonable hours such as late at night), they may be causing a statutory nuisance. If speaking to them doesn't result in an improvement, then the Environmental Department of your Local Authority may be able to help. If they agree that your complaint is justified, they can take action under the 1996 Noise Act by issuing a notice. If this is ignored it could result in court action.

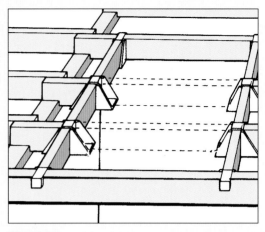

Floor joists
When a staircase has to be removed, replace the floor joists with metal joist hangers or double hangers for running joists in line passed an intermediate joist at right angles.

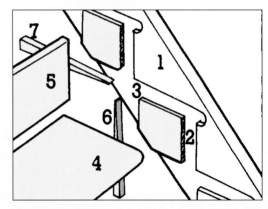

Creaking stairs
This illustrates the components of a 'closed' string stair. Knowing how it is constructed will help you understand how to solve any problems such as loose treads, creaks and missing glue-blocks.

The two side supports, the 'strings' (1), have grooves cut into them. The vertical grooves (2) take the 'risers' (5) and the horizontal ones (3) hold the 'tread' (4). The grooves are tapered so that wedges (6 and 7) can be hammered in behind the risers and underneath the tread to ensure a tight fit that will not creak.

Stairs Creaks

A creak in a stair becomes what I call a 'familiarity syndrome'. It registers only momentarily and these unwanted sounds around our homes become part of our lives. Subconsciously they become familiar and we accept them until the inevitable happens and the creaking stair become a noticeable bounce. We can be far more comfortable and worry less in our homes by having a positive attitude to what appears to be an irritating but significant repair job. It's so easy to say 'I'll do it later!' The inconvenience, coupled with the fear of the unknown, tends to put us off the minor jobs, especially when you

peep underneath the stairs and see what appears to be a complex carpentry construction. However, you don't need a professional joiner or carpenter to solve this problem. When confronted with a creaking stair, it is often a very simple matter indeed to put things right.

A good staircase is the result of the carpenter's skill at measuring, cutting and fitting together component parts with great precision. Stairs are formed from three basic elements – treads, risers and stringers – which suffer from constant wear. It is helpful to know how they are constructed, so that repairs can be carried out whenever creaks and gaps begin to appear.

Stairs have two main side supports called stringers or strings. The top edge of a closed string is parallel to the lower edge, but an open string staircase has the string cut to the shape of the steps. Each step of an ordinary straight flight is made from two boards, the horizontal tread and the vertical riser which forms the front of the step. The riser is fixed underneath the nosing of front edge of one tread and the back edge of another. The strings have a matching series of vertical and horizontal grooves cut into them. The risers and treads are glued into these tapered grooves and held in position with long thin wedges of hard-wood. The wedges are driven in to ensure a tight fit with no creaks.

Joints between treads and risers can be made in a number of ways and small triangular glue blocks are fixed into the joint underneath the stairs. Check the illustrations to see exactly how the component parts are assembled. With this information it is now easy to appreciate that creaks in stairs begin only when joints become loose and start rubbing. Shrinking timber can also contribute to the slight gaps that allow movement and creaks. Solving these problems is simply a matter of refitting, gluing and screwing.

If the underside of the stairs is boarded, tackle the problem from above, but the best and easiest repair is to be made if the exact location of the creak is obvious and the underside of the stairs is accessible and not boarded over. You will need help to locate the problem from below. A child will do, but preferably a big one! Their simple contribution is to walk up and down the stairs a couple of times while you locate the exact position of gaps and creaks from underneath. Mark each tread and riser showing where the creaks occur.

If you don't have access below the stairs you will have to work from above but you have the

carpet to contend with first. A professional fitter will have used spiked gripper strips and have started at the bottom of the staircase. Gripper strip is fixed to the back of the tread and bottom of the riser. The carpet is pushed into this joint with a tool similar to a bolster chisel and held securely. Simply jerk it free to remove it. On winding stairs the excess from the tread is tucked behind the carpet covering the riser. At the top of the stairs the carpet is nailed against the riser on the last tread and the landing carpet brought over the top step to meet it. By reversing the process you can then unroll the carpet down the stairs as far as you need to carry out your creaking stair repair. Now identify the area of the problem by shifting your weight back and forth on any part of the stair that is moving and creaking. If the creaking joint is underneath the nosing of the tread you just need to use screws to pull the joint together. Notice that the nosing actually overhangs the riser by about 25 mm (1 in), which makes accurate measuring essential so that the screw from above centres on the riser itself. After having drilled countersunk pilot holes, inject wood glue into them so it is spread into the wooden joint around the screw.

If the stairs are uncovered polished wood, there is a DIY method for covering the screw heads and producing a professional finish. Change the bit in your power drill to a plug cutter bit and use matching timber. The plug cutter will be the same diameter as the countersunk hole which of course must be drilled slightly deeper. Making plugs is very satisfying because instead of drilling holes, the bit actually drills and brings out perfect small plugs. Ten can be produced in as many seconds! These plugs are then glued into the countersunk screw holes to cover the screw heads. Use a fine grade sanding block to obtain a smooth finish.

If the problem is looseness at the point where the tread or riser meets the string, it is possible to drive screws in at an angle. The bit making your pilot hole should emerge at the bottom edge of the tread. Use a 50 mm (2 in) No. 8 countersink screw.

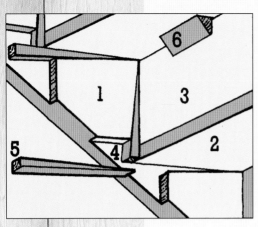

Wedges

General wear and tear of stairs, the much abused functional link between one floor and another, contributes to the problem of loose or missing glue blocks. Normally two blocks are fixed to each joint between riser and tread. A loose or missing block is likely to be one of the locations for a creak. It is also possible for glue to fail on just one place and the block to remain in position giving rise to a creak. Original blocks fixed by the joiner are never nailed so it should not split when you carefully prise it off. The smallest nib of old wood glue left on the block will prevent flush contact when it is replaced. Use a medium glasspaper to thoroughly clean all surfaces.

If the end of a tread or a riser is loose in its groove, you'll find that the wedge will need refitting. Carefully prise out the original wedge and clean it up with medium grade glasspaper. If the wedge is missing or damaged it's a very simple job to make a new one. Usually the wedge to the riser is put in first, sawn off flush with the underside of the tread, and then a longer wedge is driven in underneath the tread. If you have to remove or replace a wedge to a riser, you might have to loosen or lift out the longer wedge first. Very little skill is needed to apply wood glue and to rewedge the joint. Use a claw hammer and a spare piece of timber to protect the end grain of the wedge. Don't be tempted to use nails as the wedges will easily split, especially if they are hardwood. Your assistant can now do the bounce test by shifting weight to and fro above the replaced wedge for you to listen if the staircase is cured of creaks.

Here's a DIY tip to ensure a better result! With a long screwdriver, gently prise open the joint between the tread and riser and apply the wood adhesive there. Drill a pilot hole at an angle so you can pull the joint together with a screw.

Use a 38 mm (1½ in) countersink screw and make sure the head is set below the surface of the riser. After applying glue to both surfaces of the block, slide it back and forth three or four times whilst pushing it home. This will get rid of bubbles and ensure perfect contact and adhesion. Small panel pins can be used whilst the adhesive sets but they will need to be removed. Leave a note on the stair above the repair to tell users not to use that tread until the wood glue has had time to set properly!

If you cannot find the missing blocks underneath the stairs, new ones can easily be cut from 50 mm × 50 mm (2 in × 2 in) softwood. Four 75 mm (3 in) blocks can be made by setting a piece of timber upright in a vice and sawing down diagonally about 150 mm (6 in). Reposition the timber horizontally, cut accurately across the grain and there you have your new glue blocks.

Treads

Loose treads On a conventional staircase, the back of each tread, the part on which your foot goes, has a groove running the length of it into which a tongue on the underside of the riser fits. This 'housing' joint is very vulnerable to heavy pounding on the staircase. It is not possible to use a screw to pull the two parts together if the tread is loose. If you can only work from above you will have to glue and pin a small triangular section of timber the whole width of the stair.

The joint at the back of the tread is the final one to be tackled. If the staircase is carpeted lift it to glue and pin a long length of triangular moulding between the horizontal and vertical gripper strips. Try also to prise open the joint to inject wood glue as deeply as possible. Of necessity, the moulding will have to be a small section otherwise the gripper will not get adequate hold. If, on the other hand, the staircase is uncarpeted, a larger section of matching wood can be glued and screwed in the joint between the riser and tread. Make sure that nobody uses the stairs until the glue has set hard. A matching wood filler will

Creaking stairs
This illustrates the component parts of the stairs as seen from below with the string (1), tread (2) and riser (3) in position. The vertical wedge (4) is trimmed so that the horizontal wedge (5) can be hammered into place. Two glue-blocks (6) are fixed into the angle between the tread and riser. Creaks will occur if any are missing. Cut 150 mm (6 in) blocks from 50 mm × 50 mm (2 in × 2 in) softwood.

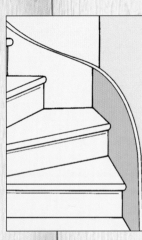

Staircases
The 'wind' is joined to a straight flight and is the part of a staircase most vulnerable to creaks.

Screws and metal brackets can help overcome creaks by stopping the tread from sagging.

Long screws in pre-drilled holes will hold treads and risers together. Glue and pin quadrant beading into joints into the joints if the problem is not severe.

This shows how badly a staircase suffers when untreated wood has been used in a house built about a hundred years ago. The undersides of the treads and risers have dried out and are splitting. The wedges have shrunk and are loose in their grooves giving rise to creaks. The wood glue-blocks have lost their adhesion, also causing creaks.

cover the countersunk screw heads. The construction of staircases is subject to stringent Building Regulation Specifications. The only one that is of any concern here is remember to leave 220 mm (8¾ in) measured back from the nosing of the tread to a mark vertically below the nosing of the next highest tread.

Nosing On an uncarpeted stair, most wear will occur in the centre of the rounded nosing of the tread. This is where friction occurs from the soles of shoes. You only have to replace this centrally located worn part. Set your circular saw so that the depth of cut is the same as the thickness of the wooden tread. You'll need to make a cut parallel to the front of the tread to be able to take out the worn part. By temporarily screwing down a batten, again parallel to the front edge, you can use it as a guide for the saw's sole plate. Once you've done that, unscrew the batten and make two saw cuts either end of the worn part to be able to lift it out. A simple trick to ease its removal and to help locate the new nosing is to cut at an angle. Angle out the blade of a tenon saw at the top so either end will make a V-joint. Now use a bevelled-edge chisel to tidy up the repair. Cut and fit the new piece of timber and don't forget the groove into which the riser fits. Glue and screw it into position, countersink the screws and use matching filler or plugs to cover the screw heads. Stain, varnish or paint to match when the sanded repair is totally dry.

Balusters

Fixing Balusters give essential protection at the side of a staircase and are fixed to the underside of the handrail and to the outer string. They come in many forms, but I think a square section is the most popular. However, most Victorian and Edwardian houses have turned balusters or spindles. The balustrade, which is the whole framework, is formed from the newel post at the bottom of a staircase, the handrail and the string. Balusters are held in position on a 'closed-string' staircase in a number of ways. A groove usually runs under the handrail into which the top of the angled cut of the baluster is fixed. It can be simply nailed in position, fixed by a tenon cut on top of the angled baluster or it can be housed where the whole of the top of the angled cut goes into a housing joint. The same applies on the top edge of the closed string. Consequently, refixing a loose baluster is simply a matter of squeezing in glue between the joint and drilling a countersunk pilot hole through the baluster, either top or bottom, so that a long No. 6 screw can hold the loose baluster in place. Use filler or a wooden plug to cover the head of the screw.

A square section baluster is the easiest to replace because it is cut at a matching angle top and bottom and simply 'tosh-nailed' into the top of the string and under the handrail. Measure vertically between the string and the handrail, the marks left by the old baluster will help. Saw at the same angle, glue and pin.

Open stairs have the side 'stringers' cut to the shape of the treads and risers. This makes it easy to replace balusters because usually a nose-moulding is nailed to the stringer after the square baluster has been glued into a notched housing.

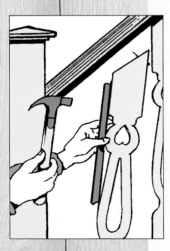

Once a repair has been carried out to replace a square section baluster, glue and pin the top and bottom. Drive in the pin with a nail punch. Use filler and paint over.

section or a spindle (turned) baluster that has square sections top and bottom.

While at your DIY store, check out the many proprietary brands of staircase components to suit any location. By reading the illustrated brochures, you'll get a full understanding of each and every component of any staircase. This will help and guide you in solving any problems related to staircases and their maintenance and repair. With this information to hand, if you need to consult a carpenter on a major structural alteration, at least you'll be able to speak the same language. If you are inspired by all this information about staircases, it is important to know the Building Regulations related to the stairway design in a domestic building. The regulations are there to ensure our comfort and safety and are covered in the Building Regulations Part 8, Groups 1 and 3. John Stephenson's book 'The Building Regulations Explained' is the definitive layman's guide to the regulations and is a must for all DIY enthusiasts.

Spiral staircases are being installed more and more where space is at a premium. There are specialist firms who manufacture wrought-iron spiral staircases with either wooden treads or steel ones. These can come in kit form, so those of you who were good at Meccano® should be handy at the assembly and installation. However, the manufacturers are an important and integral part of the installation team. They will advise on the cutting and trimming of the floor above. This is all subject to Building Regulations.

Replacing   In my experience, most damage to balusters is the result of moving heavy furniture up or downstairs! Square section and spindles balusters can be purchased at DIY stores where kits of staircase parts are sold. Of course you will need to take a template. It is relatively easy for the DIYer to copy an Edwardian patterned baluster. Hold a stiff card behind it and outline the whole of the baluster including curved or linear cuts inside. Transfer this to a matching piece of square-edged timber. With the timber firmly clamped it is now quite easy to follow the curves with a jigsaw. Clean up the edges of the cuts with sandpaper, smooth all the cuts to a fine finish before decorating to match.

If the balusters are fixed to an open-string stair, you'll have to prise off the nosed cover moulding that covers the bottom of the joint. You'll find recesses cut into the tread of the stair into which the baluster fits. This applies whether it's a wide section baluster, a square

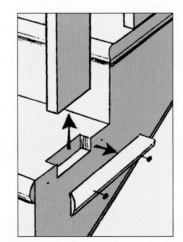

Removing balusters
To remove balusters (spindles) of any shape, first tap them out from under the handrail. Check for the groove. Use a scrap of timber to protect the baluster.

Replacing balusters
To replace balusters, take off the 'nosing' nailed to the side of the 'open' string at the end of the tread. Replace with a new baluster of the same size and design. Replace the cover 'nosing' bead.

Windows Sliding sash

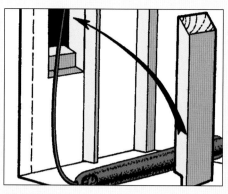

Sliding sash

Remove the pocket piece after lifting out the parting bead from its groove. This gives you access to the weight. Some pocket pieces are screwed into place so take care not to split the wood if paint or filler has been used to hide the screw head. Lift out each pocket piece marking it Left or Right. Sometimes the weights differ for outer and inner sashes, so mark these accordingly.

Replacing cords

Sash windows are less common these days but those remaining still need maintenance, mainly in the form of a sash cord replacement. Never just replace the cord that is broken, it's always worth doing both. The box frame which houses the sliding sashes is not the mysterious assembly of pulleys, ropes, pocket pieces and hidden weights that it seems. Once you've taken one apart you'll find it simple to understand and easy to repair. The staff beads prise off very easily. As they are mitred at the top and bottom, you'll first need to spring them out from the centre. Normally it is only necessary to release one staff bead to ease the sash out. The cord is secured in a groove by clout nails which are easily pulled out. Gently ease out the pocket piece to get at the weight and the rest of the cord. Work from the bottom, because the top of it is chamfered (sloped) to wedge it into position. Try threading a new cord over the pulley at the top and down the box to the pocket opening. If it is difficult, drop down a 'mouse' (any small weight) on the end of a piece of string tied to the cord. The string can be used to pull through the cord. This deals with the upper window.

If the cord is broken on the lower sash you'll have to remove the parting bead which separates the two sashes. Both sashes will have to come out in this instance, but then proceed as before.

Replacement sash cords are available from all DIY stores for repairs to double-hung sash windows. However, it could be that the sash weight is missing or needs to be replaced. In this case it is essential that the combined weight of the replacement weights for an upper sash are at least half a pound heavier than the window, whilst for the lower sash the weights must be at least half a pound lighter. This weight difference helps to keep the sashes close together and tight against the window head and sill when closed. If a cord is broken the weight will have become separated and so you'll have to remove the pocket to be able to lift the weight out. After rehanging the lower sash, use oval nails to refit the stop beads. Make certain that the pocket is tightly secured so that it does not obstruct the lower sash when it slides up and down.

Sashes sometimes work inefficiently because the pulley wheels, being exposed to the air, become rusty. The exposed face plate of the pulley is usually brass so care is needed to avoid damaging it when removing it for cleaning. Two screws usually hold the sash pulley. Take care when prising out the body of the pulley because the brass finish to the face plate is often only a thin face riveted on to the cast-iron case. This simple axle pulley was improved in more recent windows by adopting a grease-packed race of ball-bearings allowing the concave section pulley wheel to revolve freely within the pulley case. It is essential that these moving parts are maintained in good order for smooth operation. Use a proprietary brand of rust remover and grease the moving parts before refitting.

To remove a sliding sash for a cord replacement, slide out the sash by prising the stop beads away from the frame. If a sash rattles, take off the beads and fix them closer to the sliding sashes.

Rattles Stop rattles by releasing and refixing the stop beads closer to the sliding sashes. This is covered in general terms in the section on Exterior Windows but sometimes it is necessary to replace the beads because of excessive wear. These are readily available at timber merchants and the timber departments of larger DIY stores. The beads are still the same shape as they were in Victorian days. Over many years of wear sash cords have obviously been replaced many times. Every time this happens, it means that the stop beads have to be removed. For years nails have been driven in through the same holes enlarging them each time so the loose beads will allow the windows to rattle.

Excessive wear also takes place at the centre chamfered rails. The central fastener should bring the two meeting rails together horizontally and push them in opposite directions vertically. This should hold the sashes fast to prevent rattling. If there is a problem of wear, one of the rails will need to be built up. Open and close the fastener by the amount of wear, and the resulting gap will determine the thickness of the piece of timber that has to be glued and pinned to the worst worn of the rails.

Loose joints Before you tackle the problem of loose sash joints you first have to determine what has caused them. It could simply be that the glue holding together the mortise and tenon joint has perished over the years. It might be that there is rot in the joint or perhaps some dowels have worked loose. The worst of these to solve is obviously the rot. If you are a skilled carpenter you won't find the problem too difficult to solve: just copy the construction as it exists. Start in the morning on a sunny summer's day and you might get it finished by sunset! Otherwise, it will be necessary to call in a professional. The other two problems are easily solved with the aid of a sash clamp.

Ease out the window and remove it from the sash cords. Make a knot in each of the sash cords so that they don't disappear over the pulleys. Clean out as much of the joint as you can, inject as much wood glue as possible into all the openings around the joint, and clamp it tightly together. It doesn't finish there. Drill two holes diagonally across from each other, whilst the sash is clamped together, and insert tight dowels with a liberal coating of glue. Make sure the dowels are slightly too long in order that you can plane them down to the level of the face of the sash frame. A sash frame and its glazing can be quite heavy, so for safety's sake, when removing the sash and replacing it, take extra care.

Over the years the sliding of the sashes against the central parting bead can wear it considerably. It could be that after so much wear, the stop beads have been closed up so many times that the sliding sashes are binding on the parting beads. The only solution to this problem is to renew the parting beads. These also come as standard and are simply pushed into the central groove to make a tight fit. Never be tempted to paint the edges of the parting bead, the sliding parts of the sashes or the inside of the stop beads. If there is still a problem in sliding, even after another adjustment, just rub a candle along the wooden sliding parts.

Casement

Rot Because windows and their frames are exposed to the air, any rot found is usually minimal and easily treated. As a proud homeowner you should be constantly monitoring the outside of your home to preserve your possession, so it's unlikely that you will find extensive rot. If the rot was really bad, the casements or glazing would have fallen out long ago! When repainting casements and their frames, during the preparation period, check with a penknife for any soft or spongy timber. If the timber is sound you won't mark it by doing this.

When wet rot in timber dries out, it becomes brittle. However, it is dark in colour and spongy when it is still damp. Remove all the softer wood until you get back to a hard base and

Window stays hold a casement firm in a chosen position and should be lockable. A worn stay allows the wind to cause movement, friction and wear. Joints open, frames are rubbed and screws loosen. As soon as wear is detected, fit a new stay, after repairing the corner joints.

Remove a broken pane and stop glass flying by criss-crossing with sticky-tape.

then, with a proprietary brand of a wood repair system, you can effect a good repair. The first part of these systems is a wood hardener liquid. The second part, a resin and hardener mixed together. Mix sufficient for the gap that is left so that the repair is proud of the surrounding timber. This is so that you can plane or file it down to get an absolutely flat finish.

Reglazing   Interestingly, it was only in recent years that glass was sold for domestic glazing by its thickness measurement. Before that glass was sold according to its weight per square foot. The glass was available in weights of 15 lb to 36 lb. Domestic glazing was at one time carried out in 26 lb glass which is less than 3 mm (⅛ in) thick. Now, however, 4 mm (⅙ in) and 5 mm (³⁄₁₆ in) is the accepted norm.

Many DIYers these days think nothing of reglazing with a double-glazed unit. Slightly thicker and a little heavier than a pane of ordinary float glass, a double-glazed unit is simply two sheets of glass totally sealed together round the edges to create a vacuum between. Most rebates in casements are large enough to take the extra thickness. Reglazing is described in the section on Exterior Windows and the same techniques apply to double-glazed units.

If a small vulnerable rear toilet window, for example, has to be reglazed think seriously about a piece of laminated glass. This is virtually burglar-proof, shatter-proof and there is no

difference in the reglazing process. A sheet of laminated glass can be ordered from your local glazier and costs less than double the price of an ordinary piece of float glass.

You might have a window at the side of a front door giving light to the hall. Think about putting stained glass in here. Leaded lights are easily obtainable to fit most standard casement sashes. They provide a focal point from the outside and give added interest from the interior. Putty them in as a normal window but obviously they need extra protection. Cut a piece of laminated glass to fit the inside of the frame. Fix it about an inch away from the stained glass window held securely in the frame with quadrant mouldings either side of it.

Binding   Wooden casement windows are constructed so as not to let in rainwater. When first installed, sufficient gap was allowed between the opening window and the frame for a build up of two or three layers of paint. Whilst carrying out a redecorating job, it is so easy to miss the top edges of a casement window, and this is where problems start. The two stiles that make up the side pieces of the framework have end grain which, if not protected, will suck in moisture like a sponge. The wood then swells and causes binding when the window is being closed. The problem is solved only by allowing the wood to dry completely so that it contracts sufficiently to stop the binding. To ensure that the problem doesn't happen again, plane the sides and the top so that there is a gap of about 3 mm (⅛ in) and allow for at least three coats of paint.

When planing the top edge of the frame always plane in from the outside to the centre. This ensures that the top corner does not split. It is always better to remove a casement window to work on it, especially if it's an upstairs window. If you see there is plenty of gap around the whole of the window and yet it is still binding, check that the hinges are not too deep in their recesses. If they are, this is going to cause binding at the hinge edge. The solution is to remove the sash by unscrewing at the frame. Cut pieces of a tough card to fit the recesses so that the sash is now going to close without binding. These 'shims' are protected by the hinge and will last for years.

Old putty   Let me warn you against being tempted to just paint over what looks like faint hair cracks across putty. Also, don't be tempted to just fill in a little gap in the putty on the lower ledge of a casement window. These cracks and gaps point to the need to hack out and remove all the old perished putty. At the first sign of the minutest crack, get rid of the lot.

Putty is soaked in linseed oil to keep it pliable and to retain its bond. Once it has dried out through lack of care and protection, it has lost its essential properties. If, from the inside through the glass, you see any signs of staining below the top level of the putty, you can be sure that you have some problems. Now you have to hack out and reputty as described in the section on Glazing.

Hinges   It is always best to use brass hinges and compatible brass screws where they are subject to weathering. If the frame is hardwood, then it is sometimes very difficult to get in brass screws because they are a softer metal than steel. Steel hinges rust and so do steel screws. However, one can help the other. Drill a pilot hole, then put in a steel screw to make the space for a brass screw of the same size. The constant opening and closing of casement windows puts a great strain on the knuckle of a hinge. This movement also tests the holding capacity of the screws in the wooden frame. Any moisture in the timber will cause the timber around the screws to weaken, often seen as a darkening of the timber around the screws. There's only one thing for it and that is to replace the screws and plug the holes. After wooden plugs have been tightly forced into the glued screw hole and allowed to dry, pare off the ends of the plugs level with the recess to give the plugs a square end. This is will allow you to more easily drill a pilot hole into the wooden plugs.

If you find that the original hinge has become distorted in any way or there is any opening of the metal at the knuckle, there is no choice but to replace the hinge. Never ever replace just one hinge. Take the original hinge with you so that you can get an exact copy of the original. This is important because hinges, or 'butts' as they are commonly called, come in a wide variety of shapes, sizes and metals.

Sills   Condensation is the prime cause of rotting wooden sills. The wood sucks in moisture and retains it for long periods, often holding it there when painted over. Rot is then inevitable. It is fairly easy to remove the old sill if you know how the sill was fixed in the first place. They were usually nailed into timber pieces set into the wall below the sill and then plastered to the reveals to cover and secure the ends of the sill. The reveals are the side vertical parts of the wall at right angles to the window. Now, all you do is to reverse the process. Hack off a little of the plaster from either end of the sill and then lever it up to release the nails. Never bang, always lever or prise! Make the job easier by first cutting the nosing or front edge of the sill with a panel saw to remove it. Clean out the space for the new sill, which must fit snugly against the window frame. Prime and treat the hidden parts of the new sill before securing it, but also nail through the back edge of the sill into the window frame.

The construction of a window frame is actually very simple and similar to that of a door frame. In both, the wooden sill is an integral part of the framework. The interior window sill or window board, as it's commonly called, is sometimes let into a slot in the back of the main sill. In older houses the front part of the internal sill underneath the nosing often had an attractive moulding to support the overhanging board. None of these presents a problem because they can all be prised off quite easily.

Repairing an inside windowsill (1)

Condensation is the prime cause of rotting sills. Moisture is often painted over making rot inevitable. To remove a sill, first saw off the nosing. Then hack away a little of the plaster at both ends. Lever out the sill.

Repairing an inside windowsill (2)
Remove all the fixings. Clean out both slots in readiness for the new sill. Fill any holes and create a firm, flat base. Prime with a stabilising liquid.

Repairing an inside windowsill (3)
Cut the new sill to fit. Locate the fixing points – usually these are blocks let into the under-sill. Treat all the exposed timber and the back of the new sill with preservative. Countersink and fill the screw head holes. Sand and paint to match.

Doors

All rooms have a couple of holes in the walls, purposefully made for windows and doors. We know that timber in any part of house construction can move, warp, contract or expand, so lets look at doors and their problems. Doors are subjected to a great deal of wear and tear, from daily use, from moisture and the wear on handles, hinges and locking mechanisms.

Doors shrink in dry weather causing rattles and expand when it's damp causing the door to bind. Overheating can cause a door to dry out, so that the glue in the mortise joints no longer holds and the door begins to sag. Loose hinges can result from any of these problems and so too can warping when the door twists. This leads to further problems such as having to relocate the latch, handle and lock.

A door that binds has probably swollen with moisture. This has usually penetrated through the end grain at the top and bottom of the long side timbers (stiles). Let the door dry out, unscrew it if it's an internal door and lay it flat. Check if paint, another potential cause of binding, has built up on the edges. A power plane simplifies the job of smoothing the wood to a professional finish. If the height needs reducing, this tricky job is made easier by planing in from each corner. The power plane takes off only the amount you want and gives a smooth, flat finish without exertion! Ensure that the timber is absolutely dry before repainting. Paint the top and bottom of every door, taking particular care to completely seal the vulnerable end grain of the stiles.

Another method of adjusting a badly fitting door, which is too loose or too tight at one side, is to slightly move the position of the hinge. Bring it in by deeping the hinge recess with a bevel-edged chisel or push it away from the hinge edge by packing the recess with cardboard 'shims'. Check also that the existing screws, which should be countersunk and brass, are not left proud of the hinge leaf. Screws that don't 'hold' should be replaced with larger

relieve door here

Hanging an interior door

If the door stop is not rebated into the frame (that is, if it is not part of the same piece of wood as the frame) and is nailed on, take off the doorstop and fix the door in position first. Then put back the doorstop against the closed door. If rising butts are used to clear a carpet, it may be necessary to taper the corner of the door as illustrated.

Door problems

Rubbing and binding along the locking edge of a door can be overcome by a slight 'cut' The lower hinge needs to be let deeper into the recess, so just chisel it so that the 'cut' allows the door to settle closer to the hinge jamb.

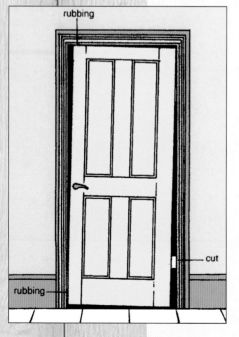

rubbing

cut

rubbing

ones. Alternatively, glue in a dowel to fill the screw hole and make a new pilot hole.

If a door has warped, it'll be touching the frame at one point. Natural wood doors will warp under too damp or too dry conditions. A glazed door should be taken off its hinges to remedy this. Remove the glazing. Refix the door and check where it touches the frame. If the door touches at the top, pop in a wedge there and then force the door back to the frame at the bottom. Inducing a twist with blocks of wood in strategic positions. Reglaze the door or, if you are worried about security, replace the glass with marine ply.

I came across a bad case of sagging doors when I designed a kitchen for actor Neil Morrissey at his North London home. As an enthusiastic DIYer he was thrilled to discover a rather simple solution to the problem of the front edge of a door marking the floor. With his feet on a sheet of sandpaper placed under the door, he shuffled the door back and forth, thus abrading the bottom of it. Another door, however, was more serious. This had loose joints at the corners. So we laid the door flat, forced the door back into shape and drilled through the mortise joints to glue in dowels. While the door is unhinged, also force glue into the joints.

If a front door rattles, try sticking draught excluders on the doorstops. Unlike interior door stops, exterior door stops are an integral part of the frame and cannot be prised off. It's an easy job to fix excluders against the closed door to seal gaps. An alternative solution to a front door rattle is to move the keeper on the frame. The recess must be recut nearer to the stop, so that the door closes

tighter to the stop. Chisel out the slot and glue in a piece of packing. Fill the original screw holes then screw in position.

You might encounter a problem of refixing an existing door over a newly laid carpet. The solution is to fit new hinges called 'rising butts'. These lift a door as it opens. The leaf with the fixed pin is screwed to the frame, whilst the corresponding knuckle goes onto the door. Get it right because a door that is left-hand opening has the pin on the right side of the hinge-leaf and vice versa. In order to clear the frame as the door rises on opening, plane a shallow bevel off the top corner on the hinge side. It will be hidden when the door is closed.

A good idea for solving a loose frame problem is to use a couple of Fischer frame fixings. A special long drill bit goes through both the frame and into the masonry. This is compatible with the long plug and equally long screw. The plug is contained in the frame and the wall. As the screw is driven home, the part of the plug in the wall expands to give a rigid hold.

Problem hinges can be removed if the paint is first scraped out of the screw slots. Then, whilst turning the screwdriver back and forth, strike it a couple of times to loosen the screw.

BS: 3621 will mean a lot to anybody conscious of door security at home. If you need to change or fit a new door lock, insist on this British Standard. This job used to be one for a specialist, but no longer! Previously it was a long-drawn-out job of drilling a series of holes to form the slot for the lock, followed by a careful bevel-edged chiselling job. It was mostly trial and error for the DIYer. But not any more. Now it's possible to form the slotted hole in less than a minute using a new three-dimensional bit. This innovative bit can drill conventionally, but amazingly it can cut sideways too. Without a mallet and chisels, a slot can be cut to the required width and depth, with straight sides, ready to take your new mortise in seconds. After marking the position for the lock, follow the instructions given with the bit to form the slot. A series of holes are drilled, overlapping

Fitting a hinge (1)
Lay the door on its locking edge. Hold the hinge in position and mark around it. Mark its thickness on the door's side.

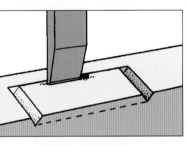

Fitting a hinge (2)
Tap a chisel into the mark with its bevel edge towards the waste wood.

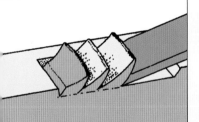

Fitting a hinge (3)
Make several cuts across the width of the recess to the depth of the thickness of the hinge leaf.

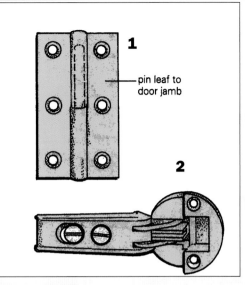

Useful hinges (1)
(1) Lift-off hinge; (2) Concealed hinge.

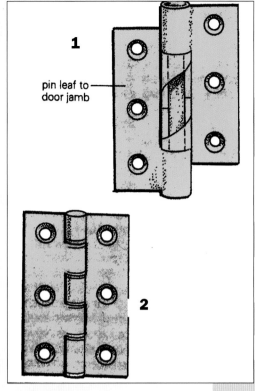

Useful hinges (2)
(1) Rising butt; (2) Brass butt.

each other, then the bit is moved side to side to cut the straight true sides of the slot. Mark the positions for the keyhole and the spindle and use the correct size bits to drill the holes for the face plate and for the striking plate on the door frame.

A door viewer is an added security feature which is easy to fit with the three-dimensional bit. The peephole enables you to see who is at the door before opening it. Use a 12 mm (½ in) bit but drill from the front until the tip is seen at the back. Then drill from the back to prevent splitting. Pop the body of the viewer in from the outside, then screw the eyepiece into place from the inside.

Rack bolts are tough, secure and easy to fit. They are simply inserted into a hole drilled into the edge of a door (or window) and a smaller hole is drilled from the front for the key. Mark the positions of the keyhole plate and the face plate, then screw in place. The racked key drives the bolt into a recess drilled into the frame.

Similarly, hinge bolts on front and rear doors can give extra security and are easy to fit with a three-dimensional bit. Position them near the hinges so that the bolt, screwed into the door edge, slips into the metal locking plate in the door frame when the door is closed.

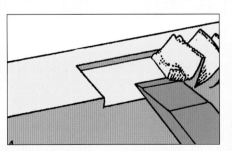

Fitting a hinge (4)
Tap out the 'feather' cuts with the bevel side of the chisel upwards. Try the hinge in the prepared recess but err on the side of caution before finally making the wood smooth.

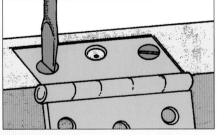

Fitting a hinge (5)
Screw the hinge into position. If you are using brass hinges on a hardwood door, drill a pilot hole and drive in a steel screw first.

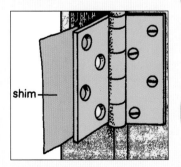

Fitting a hinge (6)
If a recess is too deep, bring the hinge out by inserting a cardboard 'shim' behind it before replacing the screws.

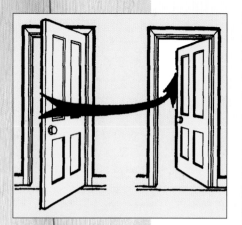

Rehanging a door for more space
Rehang a door to free up more space against a wall. Cut new hinge recesses and move the door stops. Fill in the unwanted recesses. Cut a new keeper recess and switch the latch.

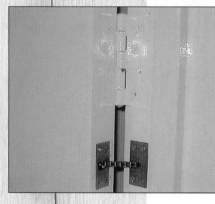

A central hinge for a heavy door, finely recessed flush with door edge and frame. Automatic door closure devices come with full instructions.

If a door is binding on its lower leading edge, it would usually need to be unscrewed to plane it. However, to solve this problem you can now purchase a plane with a blade that is flush with the front of the soleplate. This planes to the bottom of the door without it having to be removed!

If you choose to fit a rim lock, make it a deadlocking cylinder lock. This ensures that it locks automatically when the door is closed, but, better still, it cannot be forced back without a key. Again, by turning the key one complete revolution, it cannot be operated even from the inside without a key. Full instructions come with all locks purchased.

Loose door joints
These will cause a door to bind and can occur at any corner. Correct this by drilling or banging in wedges and forcing the joints back with sash clamps (or take the door off its hinges, set it on edge on the floor, and bang the joints together remembering to use a protective piece of wood). Either using dowels as shown or glue in small wedges into the loose joint. A combination of the two might be necessary.

Correcting a warped door
If a warped door touches the frame at the bottom only, pop a wedge into where it touches then force the door back to touch at the top. Hold it there overnight with a batten and off-cut piece of wood. Swap positions for a door that touches at the top.

When hanging a door, put one screw first in each hinge, to get it right.

Loose door frames
A proprietary long plug and screw can be driven to solve a problem of a loose door frame.

Walls Panelling

Attractive 'tongue and groove' V-jointed wall boards look even better when mature! Fix battens at regular intervals. Check for pipes and cables before drilling. Use the secure nailing method to fix the boards with a nail gun.

Timber cladding, with its beauty in the natural pattern of the grain, creates a warm atmosphere, attractive to most people. Scandinavian countries and Canada have enjoyed the beauty of wood cladding inside and outside their homes for centuries. Timber-framed houses are traditional in some parts of the world, but the interest in wood and wood panelling is spreading. No wonder so many DIY enthusiasts are wanting guidance on the principles involved in its application. Natural timber appeals to all the senses and, of course, offers so many possibilities for different designs in the home.

It is not difficult to improve and change the look of a room using natural timber on some walls. It adds insulation and enhances the appearance and atmosphere of any room. There are other advantages too. Uneven walls become straight and even, panelled walls need not be plastered and unsightly pipes and cables can be attractively covered. Wall-cladding offers many imaginative and useful ideas. It is possible to carry out the transformation of your chosen area, to your own unique design, with only a basic tool kit.

The easiest area to clad is probably an alcove the surrounding walls frame your chosen cladding. Attractive finishes are achieved by using one of the proprietary brands of clear wood-finishes or coloured stains.

Steel screws in oak make a blue stain, so use only brass screws.

Before you start there are three rules to be observed. These are:

1 if the walls show any signs of damp, trace the source, cure it and let it dry out thoroughly;

2 store the timber cladding in the room where it is going to be used for a couple of days, so that the wood adjusts to the temperature and atmosphere;

3 if you have to move or bring forward a switch or socket, turn off that circuit, seal the miniature circuit-breaker with coloured tape, or take out the removable fuse and put it in your pocket – don't try to work late in the day when it is getting dark!

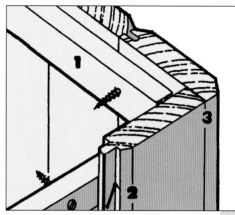

Interior wall vertical cladding
Fix battens horizontally (1) for vertical cladding. Fix 'tongue and groove', V-jointed (TGV) boards with the groove sliding on to the tongue of the last fixed board. Nail through the inside corner of the tongue at an angle (2). Use a nail punch to hide the nail head below the wood surface. Remove the tongue and grooves from adjacent corner panels (3).

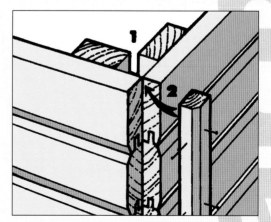

Interior wall horizontal cladding
Fix battens vertically (1) for horizontal cladding. Form an attractive and protective corner by gluing and pinning a moulded prepared batten (2) to the end grain of the panels. Fix horizontal cladding with the tongue uppermost. Slide the groove of the next board on to it after nailing and punching through the inner corner of the tongue so that no nails show.

Illustrated instruction pamphlets are always included with the packs of panelling. The packs are made up of individual boards so that each pack has its own grain pattern. Boards come in different lengths with, usually, ten boards to a pack. You might choose to use tongue and groove separate boards and I'll deal with these later in the section.

Measuring Accurately measure the area to be covered so that you can assess the amount to buy, allowing at least 10 per cent for waste. The cladding or panelling will cost more than conventional wall coverings but has the distinct advantage of many years of wear. It also has good acoustic as well as thermal qualities. Stop all panelling short of a heating appliance, boiler or open fire. A non-combustible material must always be used in such situations. Metal guards or trim should be installed to protect boards near any source of heat.

Make a small scale drawing of the area to be covered, using the measurements already taken. This is the basis on which you can design your own pattern and draw in the fixing battens. Fix battens horizontally for vertical cladding and vertically for horizontal ones. Depending on the width and thickness of your particular boards, use the appropriate size of batten always recommended by the manufacturer. Remember that the actual width of a board is wider than the 'finished' width because of the tongue and groove. Thinner boards need battens closer together, but the instructions will say how far apart to space them.

Hollows in walls can be packed out and ridges removed with a chisel and hammer (or plane the back of the batten). What you are effectively doing is designing a framework on to which the cladding will be fixed. Buy treated softwood for the framework. An external wall will need a vapour barrier or polythene sheeting stapled or pinned to it. If you are cladding or panelling a full wall you will need to remove the skirting boards. Check for pipes and cables using a DIY metal detector (cable and pipe finder) and arrange your battens to miss them.

Fixing to a stud partition wall is relatively easy because the battens can be nailed or screwed to the studs and noggins. A stud sensor is inexpensive and useful in this instance. It's like the metal detector but can only be used to find the wooden frame behind plasterboard.

Fixing to a solid wall usually means drilling, plugging and screwing. New plugs are available which dispense with the need for screws. They come with a compatible masonry bit and full instructions. You simply drill through the batten and into the wall in one go and then hammer in the plug, which has a unique device to hold it in the hole. The arrangement of battening is important because you don't want to end up with a wall that 'gives' or with split ends to the cladding boards. Battens must not be positioned close to ceilings or corners, otherwise fixing nails will split the boards.

Setting out You will need to place the battens 510 mm (20 in) apart if you are panelling a wall with 12 mm (½ in) thick cladding boards. If the boards are less thick, then fix the battens 400 mm (16 in) apart. Use a spirit level at all times. The ideal cross-section of the battens should be 38 mm × 25 mm (1½ in × 1 in). However, work out by trial and error the position of battens on your particular wall. Keep them fairly close to the switches and sockets but do be careful and take into account the live cables feeding those switches and sockets. A plastic switch box held to a stud partition wall by two 'flick over' arms is simplicity itself to bring forward on to your cladding, but check that there is sufficient cable first. If you need to bring the mounting box forward, remove the two fixing screws and refix it flush with the cladding, using battens on to which you can fix metal box mounting flanges. Alternatively, you can purchase special mounting boxes for use on boarded walls.

Fixing Timber wall cladding offers many possibilities for different designs, features and variations in appearance. For example, two recesses either side of a chimney breast could have a diagonal design in sloping opposite directions. In this case, ensure that the edges are all

You owe it to yourself and your family to have a means of testing for buried cables and pipes in walls before drilling is done. An easy-to-use cable and pipe tester operates by battery power. Glide it over the area where you need to drill and it gives an audible bleeping sound when it encounters hidden cables and pipes.

cut at exactly the same angle, use a sliding bevel tool which can be adjusted and locked off at the angle that you require. Always mark and cut on the face of each board. Keep the sawn ends clean by sanding the back edge of the cut only. Use a fine tenon saw (one with brass stiffening along its top edge) for best results.

Remove architraves around doors and windows, nail the planed battens in position, fix the cladding to coincide with the edge of the batten and refix architraves. Depending on the finish, you might need a strip to cover the planed edge of the cladding. External corners can be butt jointed, where two pieces of timber are held together, not with a traditional joint but with glue, nails or screws, and should have a cover strip of thin batten to hide and protect a gap between the two meeting pieces of wood. If you are fixing vertical cladding, chamfer each edge at 45° and glue the two edges so as not to show the joint and to give a professional finish. Sometimes an attractive finish can be achieved by leaving a gap at the ceiling or skirting board. Use a narrow, straight batten as a temporary spacer to ensure a straight and even gap.

Fixing techniques are fairly easy to understand. Make certain that your battens are fixed firmly to the wall and that hollows are taken up with small packing pieces of ply. Make certain that the screw has at least 25 mm (1 in) of hold in the wall and not just in the plaster coating! Fixing to a stud partition wall is, of course, easier, but the same principle applies. The head of the screw needs to be countersunk beneath the surface of the batten. The best method of fixing the panelling boards to the battens is to 'secret nail' them. Nail through the tongue of the board using a thin moulding pin at an angle. Use a nail punch to get the head just below the surface of the wood, then the pin is covered by the groove of the next board. An alternative and cost effective way of fixing the boards to the battens is to use a nail gun. Remember my catchphrase when using a power tool – SAFETY FIRST, DIY SECOND – so never ever load or change the pins whilst the gun is plugged in. Using a powered nail gun will effectively cut down the fixing time to a quarter of that by the conventional method.

When the self-adhesive dust-bubble is in position, the drill bit is encapsulated by the bubble so that no dust will escape when drilling.

Using a powered nail gun to fix vertical boards to form panelling between a dado rail and the skirting board. Each board is ësecret nailedí, allowing the groove to slip onto the tongue.

Finishes   Now you'll have to consider what finish you want to achieve. Manufacturers have been made aware of the increased interest in natural wood finishes in the DIY market and a number of excellent products have appeared on the shelves at the DIY stores as a result! There are attractive coloured stains which the wood absorbs, allowing the natural grain to still be appreciated. Seals, varnishes and clear wood finishes are all available with full instructions.

Noise

We live in a noisy world. More often than not the sound levels are not ours to control. In the workplace, in parks, whilst on holiday and travelling, we often have to suffer unnecessary noise. It should be different in our homes where we need to relax and be quiet. That should be our right, but unfortunately, it isn't always so.

In theory, thoughtfully designed buildings, whether for single or multiple occupation, should have no acoustic problems. Building regulations ensure that adequate density insulation is provided in the structure to prevent the risk of sound transmission through walls and floors. However, we often suffer the results of cheapness and poor workmanship in blocks of flats and hotels!

The consequences of low standards of conversions of large houses in this country are being suffered by millions of people. Where the houses have been subdivided horizontally or vertically into separate dwellings, very little thought has been given to insulating walls and floors against the transmission of noise. Developers often overlook or disregard the need to achieve a prescribed level of sound insulation during conversion work. Three different forms of noise transmission have to be prevented: impact (for example, footsteps and hammering on a wall, etc.), airborne (for example, voices, television, etc.) and flanking noise (which is any sound travelling along an adjacent wall or window to bypass the party wall between buildings). During building work it is quite easy the install materials of high density to create a noise

Sound insulation in walls (1)

Remove the skirting board (to be reused). Cut away the plasterboard and lift the floorboards. Lay Gypglas® insulating material between the joists filling every gap. Seek professional advice if electrical or plumbing services need to be moved. Fix timbers to the ceiling and floor joists and to a vertical line on each wall for an outer frame of the new stud wall.

Sound insulation in walls (2)

Multi-purpose slabs of mineral wool are ideal sound insulation when used as infill between studs. If the studs and noggins are fixed directly to a solid wall simply cut the slabs to size and press them against the brickwork. Otherwise use a plastic mesh stapled to the back of the timbers to prevent the slabs from falling into the void. Use gloves and protective clothing. Finish by fixing two layers of plasterboard with staggered joints.

Sound insulation in walls (3)

For best results on a solid concrete floor, construct a wall of acoustic building blocks (A). Metal crocodile stainless steel wall plates (B) make it easy to fix the new wall to the solid side walls. Fit slabs of mineral wool (C) between the existing wall and the new one making sure they are packed tightly together and into the ceiling void. Fill every cavity as far as possible. Build the blockwork wall tightly to the new header timber (D) fixed to the underside of the joists.

barrier, but, of course, it costs the developer time and money. It is easier and cheaper to disregard the problem because the skimped work is hidden.

Manufacturers are aware of this basic need for peace and quiet in our homes, and products have been designed to help the DIY enthusiast. The best sound insulators are dense materials. Victorian builders used sheet lead, one of the best sound insulators known, on the floors of bathrooms and toilets located over sitting rooms – nobody ever complained of noise!

Concrete is another good insulator. The floors of larger properties converted into flats are usually constructed of timber joists to which floorboards are nailed above and plasterboards are fixed to the ceiling below. The material between neighbouring flats or between your sitting room and your bedroom might only be 18 mm (¾ in) of floorboard and 16 mm (⅝ in) of ceiling board or lath and plaster. Rating sound insulation from one to ten, this type of construction rates only four. Any gaps in the floorboards lower the rating even more.

Air leaks, gaps around windows and door frames and between skirting boards and floors, and air-bricks are a common source of sound transmission. Direct air gaps provide paths to let even more sound through. Porous, unplastered building blocks used in the construction of the wall can also give rise to the problem. Sound can pass up through the ceiling of one room along the void and down through the ceiling of an adjacent room. Even poor mortar joints between mortar blocks or where the ends of joists have not been carefully backfilled both leave gaps along which sound can travel. It is important to understand and believe that the tiniest hairline crack between a wall and ceiling, in an otherwise high density material, will allow you to hear whispering in an adjacent room. It is a fairly easy job to install insulation to overcome a noise problem, but it is imperative that no gaps or cracks are overlooked and neglected.

The local Environmental Department can deal with noise caused by unreasonable behaviour in a next door dwelling. If you're woken late at night by noise, report it as a statutory nuisance and action can be taken. If the noise from an adjacent room or building goes on for too long it may even be causing a health problem. Your neighbours will then be served a notice ordering them to keep the noise down, and failure to comply will result in a fine. The Environmental Health Department can measure the intensity of the nuisance sound.

You may discover that the party wall between your house and next door is one that is poorly constructed and that you are being disturbed by noise that is normal in everyday activity. The first point to establish is just how the sound is being transmitted from the adjacent room. There is a means to prevent noise coming through a wall but first you need to establish whether it is airborne, impact or flanking noise.

Reverberation is another problem. When sound waves hit stiff, thin barriers these reverberate and can increase the intensity of the sound on the other side of the barrier. This will occur where there are lightweight stud partitions.

Dry-lining One of the easiest and quickest way to improve the sound insulation of a stud partition wall is to increase its density by adding an extra two layers of plasterboard. Tapered-edge board is best for this job as the joints can be easily hidden and the surface decorated without the need to plaster. There are two ways of fixing the plasterboards to the stud partition wall. One is to nail directly into the studs and noggins (noggins are the horizontal timbers between the upright studs). The second is to use blobs of plaster every 45 cm (18 in) on the wall against which the board is pressed. You might find it easier to strip any wallpaper that might lessen the adhesion properties of the plaster. You will need to bring forward switches and sockets. Remember – SAFETY FIRST, DIY SECOND – so switch off at the mains or take out the fuse or fuses of the relevant circuit and pop them into your pocket, or tape over the switches and mark them. Socket tops and switch plates usually have sufficient cable to be able to bring them forward. You might need to use longer screws to hold the plates in position against the new plasterboard surface. A DIY stud detector will indicate precisely where the studs and noggins are located which makes it easier to transfer the centre lines on to the new plasterboard surface. If you decide to nail, use only galvanised plasterboard nails for fixing. Remember to stagger the joints of the second layer of plasterboard and to fill every gap.

A more effective method of soundproofing is to construct a separate stud partition wall leaving a small air gap between the two. However you can only do this if you have room to reduce the floor area because the new wall must be isolated from the original. Use 100 mm × 50 mm (4 in × 2 in) sawn timbers, fix a sole plate to the floor and a header to the ceiling vertically above it. At 400 mm (16 in) intervals fix upright studs. In between the upright studs fix short pieces of 100 mm × 50 mm (4 in × 2 in) timbers (noggins) to stabilise the structure and to support the edges of the plasterboard. Staple plastic netting to the back edges of the struc-

Obtain a smooth and professional finish on an uneven wall simply by 'sticking' plasterboard to the wall. With blobs of plaster on the wall, press the measured board hard up against the adjacent board.

Dry-lining walls (1)
After battening the wall use either batts of insulation material or specially manufactured 'sandwich boards' of compressed material wedged between the timbers.

Dry-lining walls (2)
When all the boards are fixed, fill and smooth the joints. Use 'joint tape' or simply fill with a proprietary plaster filler. The tape is bedded into a layer of joint plaster and is so thin that it is almost indiscernible.

Dry-lining walls (3)
When you have applied the covering of jointing plaster dampen it with a clean brush and smooth it with a steel float or a caulking tool (a flat plastic float). Feather edge at the outsides ready for decorating.

ture to support a semi-rigid mineral fibre insulation board. This is easily cut and must be a tight fit on all four sides. You might be tempted to use polystyrene panels but these are not much good as soundproofing material. Another effective material is Gypglas® 1000. When you are at your local builder's merchant or DIY store, get as many pamphlets as you can on the materials available. You might use higher density board in place of your second plasterboard. This special purpose insulating board has remarkable sound insulating properties. It's a sandwich made up of dense plasterboard and a highly compressed material. It is easily sawn and light to handle. Blobs of plaster or special adhesive can be used to fix it to your first layer of plasterboard and, something that is specially good for DIYs, is that the decorative side will take any wall covering or paint!

Before wallpapering or painting to match the existing decor, take a second look at all the joints on the wall and surround. Make absolutely certain that you have deep-filled any gaps or cracks. Skirting boards and coving that might have been removed will now have to be put back. Tools are available to help you cut precise and exact mitred angles with a professional finish. Once the boards have been properly jointed and flush finished, seal the whole surface with a coat of stabilising solution or diluted PVA. This will give good adhesion to the wallpaper or to your choice of paint decoration.

Cupboards

Wall cupboards Wall cupboards, whether they are self-assembly or pre-assembled, are designed to carry a certain weight, but this depends on you being certain that the system is securely fixed to the wall. This means you must use the correct fixings for the type of wall. Make sure that you drive screws directly into the upright timbers (studs) and into the horizontal timbers (noggins) for a stud wall partition with a plasterboard face. Never use cavity wall fixings, like toggle bolts – your

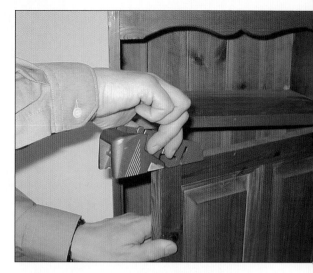

Repairing doors, small or large, involves the same principles. One of the most important is to avoid splitting the corners when planing to make a door fit. When planing the top or bottom, always plane inwards from any corner, otherwise the end grain of the stiles (the long side timbers forming the frame) will easily split.

When building a flatpack, first check that you have all the parts in the kit, then read and understand the instructions! Follow them step-by-step. For example, ensure that hinge holes meet so that doors line up!

hopes of these holding a wall cupboard could be shattered along with the contents! Use your DIY stud sensor to find the timber frame which will properly support any wall hangings.

Flat-pack wall cupboards will come with full assembly and hanging instructions. There are usually screw fixings inside at the two top corners allowing screws to go through into the studs of a partition wall or into pre-drilled holes and plugs in a solid wall. Use a spirit level to

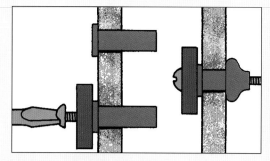

Wall fixings for plasterboards
Rubber-sleeved toggle

Push the rubber fixing into the drilled hole with the screw attached and holding the fitting. A couple of turns of the screwdriver and the fixing will fill the hole, opening up to wedge closely to the back of the plasterboard.

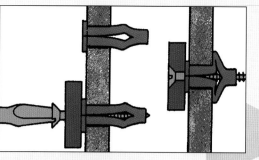

Wall fixings for plasterboard
Nylon collapsible anchor

Use a screw that is longer than the length of the anchor. Push the anchor into the drill hole with the screw half in the anchor. As you drive in the screw the fixing is pulled to the wall.

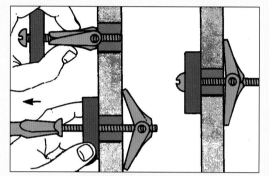

Wall fixings for plasterboard
Spring toggle (retrievable)

These can support heavier items as the load is spread over a greater area. Push the fixing through a drilled hole. The springs will pull the wings apart. Unscrew to collapse the wings and retrieve the fixing.

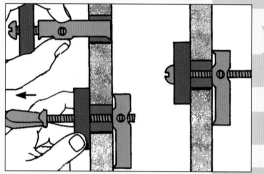
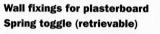

Wall fixings for plasterboard
Spring gravity toggle

This fixing can also be retrieved but the back of it will fall into the gap behind the board! Once the fixing has been pushed into a drilled hole, it opens by gravity. As you screw it in place the toggle is pulled to the back of the plasterboard.

ensure that the cupboard is both level and vertical before you attach it and ask a helper to hold the cupboard in position whilst it is fixed. A good tip is to use a small moulded batten, maybe to match the panelled door moulding, underneath the cupboard to support its back edge. This will help to take the loaded weight of the cupboard, whilst the holding screws will keep it firmly to the wall.

Old solid walls sometimes have a bulge which will prevent the back of the cupboard touching the wall with all the four back edges. If you are going to redecorate the wall anyway it's an easy job to remove the plaster high spot. Otherwise match the bump with an appropriate slither of timber fixed to the wall or to the back of the cupboard.

An acknowledged method of solving the problem of hanging wall cupboards on a stud partition wall where there is no solid fixing is as follows. All stud partition walls should have vertical studs approximately 450mm (18in) apart. Locate the two nearest to where you wish to hang the cupboard. Mark a horizontal line with a spirit level at the position of the top of the cupboard between the upright timbers. What you're effectively going to do is insert a horizontal timber of the same section as the stud, which will be fixed firmly either side. With a trimming knife or a pad saw cut out a piece of the plasterboard sufficiently for the noggin to slide in between the studs to make a very tight fit. If you cut the plasterboard about an inch longer either side of the slot then you've got a fixing not only to the noggin but to the studs

Free-standing cupboard (1)

Parts of a free-standing cupboard. (1) Sides (two pieces); (2) doors (two pieces); (3) top and bottom (two pieces); (4) back (two pieces); and (5) pelmet (one piece).

Only hang wall cupboards to a stud partition wall by fixing to the studs.

either side. With glue on the back of the noggin and on either end, force it into position. Then drill pilot holes 4 cm (1½ in) from either end of the noggin at an angle of 45° into the noggin and through to the studs. Countersink both holes. Use 10 cm (4 in) No. 8 screws to hold the noggin firmly in position. Re-cover with the plasterboard strip and make good. When the glue is dry you have a very sound hanging base for your cupboard.

Built-in cupboards Usually, when extra storage space is needed, one of the best ways is to use the existing space either side of a

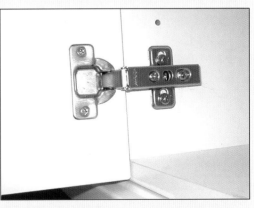

This shows a typical kitchen cupboard hinge that allows the door to open to about 100°. The boss fits into a circular hole in the door and the base plate is screwed to the unit. The hinge arm slides on the base plate and has screws for adjustment.

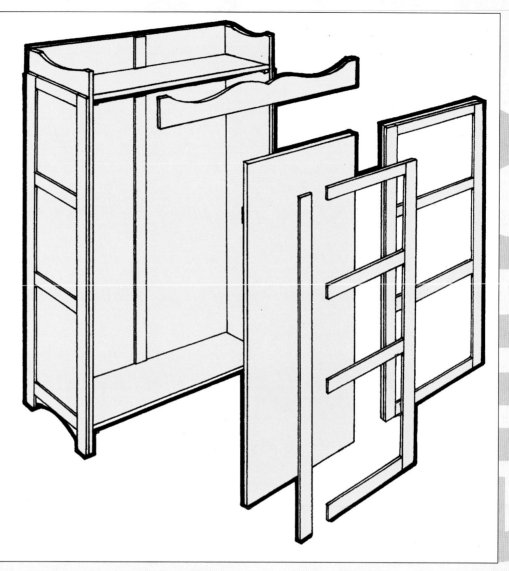

I made this free-standing cupboard which fits perfectly into our hall and was decorated with a hand-cut stencil by my wife.

Free-standing cupboard (2)
Exploded view of a cupboard showing the individual pieces and method of construction.

chimney breast. A great advantage of a self-designed cupboard or wardrobe that fits into a known space is that every square centimetre of space is exploited. Shelves can be placed where you want them and doors can be hinged on either side. You can even fit sliding doors if space is at a premium in front of the unit. You can choose the finishing touches like handles and mirrors to suit your taste. The visible front of the cupboard or wardrobe can be built to be level and vertical even though the back in the recess may not be. The carcass or framework of a built-in cupboard is often very basic, made up of a framework of 50 mm × 50 mm (2 in × 2 in) timber, slightly wider than the gap, so that it can be built at least 250 mm (10 in) in front of the chimney breast. This allows for a similar framework to be built at right angles to it to meet at the corner of the chimney breast. Another framework is fixed to the ceiling, or lower, to suit the height of the front of the wardrobe. Side cladding and doors form the aesthetic part of the design. Use coving and skirting boards to match the existing ones in the room.

If you need to fix a cupboard with a loose front frame, check that it is simply the front frame, holding the doors, and not the entire back framework that is loose. After removing the entire contents, make a thorough check. It's a simple matter to add 'knock-down' fixings to bring two parts of the front construction together and to hold them firmly. Alternatively, use L-shaped steel brackets, discreetly placed, to bring the two loose parts together. If you need to fix the back frame, check with a pipe and cable detector that there are no hazards before drilling and adding holding screws.

Often, after a period of time, built-in wardrobe doors, especially if they have mirrors attached, will prove too heavy for the hinges. If the doors are binding at the front lower edge, check that the hinges have not pulled apart at the knuckle. If this is the case there is only one remedy and that is to replace the hinges. When you take the hinge off take it with you to the store so you'll be able to get an exact replacement. You might have to use larger gauge screws or glue in a wooden plug which, when dry, will give you a new start for a pilot hole.

Floor-to-ceiling built-in cupboards or wardrobes can, after a time, give rise to problems. Timber joists in floors and ceilings, in all houses, move, sometimes indiscernibly, but often enough to cause binding problems. If the height of a wardrobe stops at the level of, say, a picture rail, then this problem will not occur. Binding problems mean that all the doors will need to be reduced in height so that they will be able to open and close properly. If this is the case, take off all the doors and mark them on the back edge and on the facing post with the amount to plane off from the bottom of the doors. Remember to plane in from each edge to

the centre. If the doors are softwood, it is important to seal the newly exposed timber.

Most built-in wardrobes and cupboards come in a kit form which contains panels and doors of standard sizes. Replacements can be bought at DIY stores. 'Knock-down' fittings, such as plastic joint blocks, are often supplied with these kits, so if any of the panels are loose and the fixings at the back have pulled out, then it is easy to replace them. If any of the panels, especially the end panels, have disintegrated where the screws have been working loose for some time, replace them with a matching one.

The hinges of built-in wardrobes and cupboards are subject to a lot of harsh treatment because the doors are usually quite tall and often heavy. If the unit originally came as a flat-pack, then suitable hinges would have been provided. However, if the cupboard was a self-build project, then you'd better check the hinges and fixings for wear.

Hinges are fitted in one of three ways depending on the type of door and hinge: recessing, housing and surface-fixing. There are basic rules which apply to the fitting of all hinges. Hold the hinge in the finished position and trace with a pencil around the outline of each hinge leaf on to the door and the frame. If three hinges are required on a door the centre one should be equally spaced between the top and the bottom hinges. All hinges should be positioned absolutely vertically above one another with the knuckles of the pivots in a straight line and, of course, held with countersunk screws (preferably brass for brass hinges) or with fixings recommended by the manufacturer. The screw gauge specified for the hinge is also important. Check whether you have a lay-on door, a flush door or an inset door. The hinge side of a lay-on door covers the frame, whereas a flush door sits inside the frame which is in the same plane as the front of the door. An inset door is similar to a flush door except that it is slightly recessed with the frame just proud of the face of the door. The most common type of hinge, certainly on kitchen cabinets and more often than not on cupboards and wardrobes, is the 'concealed' hinge. There are two types, one with a circular boss which is pushed into a circular hole drilled into the back of the door and the other is 'lay-on' concealed hinge. One version has a spring closing system that opens to about 100°. The hinge arm which is slid on to the base plate has adjusting screws which might need checking to solve any problems.

Stud partitions

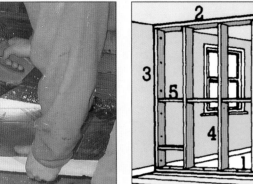

Sawing compressed insulation material with reflective backing to prevent condensation and to provide thermal and sound insulation in a stud partition wall. Cut and fit tight to all studs and horizontal timbers (noggins).

Stud partition walls

The component parts of a stud partition wall are: (1) sole plate fixed to the floor; (2) header fixed to the ceiling; (3) vertical wall studs; (4) studs; (5) horizontal noggins (where horizontal joints occur in the plasterboard); and (6) door framing.

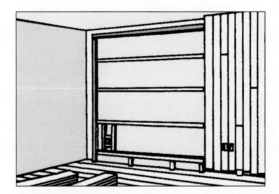

Insulating a wall

Before fixing treated battens to the inside of an exterior wall, tack on a sheet of polythene to prevent condensation. Remove the skirting boards, picture rails and coving, and be prepared to bring forward switch and socket covers. Construct a framework of battens to which the cut ends around the sockets are fixed. To prevent splitting the ends of the panelling boards, keep the wall battens in from the corners and ceiling. Fix short 'grounds' for refixing the skirting boards. Always switch off at the mains or remove the fuse before unscrewing socket or switch covers.

Another solution to insulating a wall is to dry-line an exterior wall with a barrier. Place sheets of plasterboard (foil-backed is best) or polystyrene between the battens to give good insulation.

Dividing a room   Recently, there has been a trend to remove a dividing wall and convert two rooms into one, but as a family expands or the need to work at home demands extra space, a large front bedroom with two windows can be converted into two rooms. Providing that you have adequate space and that the room has two windows then it is not too difficult to convert the large room into two rooms by building a stud partition wall. It may seem like a formidable task, but you really don't need to be a carpenter. Once in place, insulated, boarded and decorated, it will look like a professionally built solid wall. You can also achieve good thermal and sound insulation properties by using a proprietary insulating material.

Before you start planning and buying materials, make a phone call to your Local Authority Building Control Officer who will make an appointment to come to your house and advise you. Regulations exist to ensure that safety and design standards regarding fire spread, durability and suitability are adhered to. The officer will advise you on the regulations with reference to ventilation and natural light in each room. If you plan to divide a room for a kitchen, bathroom or WC, then you must consult the Environmental Health Officer.

There are a number of stipulations that you need to consider before deciding to construct the stud partition wall. The Building Control Officer will check the size of opening windows in each room, which must be related to the floor area of the new room. Consider, too, access to the second room. If privacy is required in the first room, a corridor will have to be constructed by building an extra stud partition wall to make the rooms self-contained. The next consideration is the position of the new stud partition wall in relation to the floor and ceiling joists. Obviously extra weight on a bedroom floor will require adequate support underneath the wall. Ideally the new partition wall will run at right angles to the floor and ceiling joists so that all joists will share the extra load. You will not be bound to locate the wall at a specific point, however you cannot build a new wall directly on to floorboards at a point between

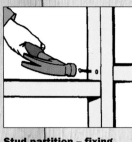

Stud partition – fixing noggins

Stagger noggins so that they can be fixed with 10 cm (4 in) wire nails straight through the studs into the end grain of each noggin. Two nails should support each end. Make sure not to nail too close to an edge which could split and weaken the timber.

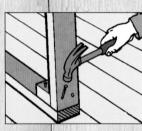

Stud partition – fixing studs

To prevent a door post (end) stud moving as it is nailed to the sole-plate, fix an off-cut of timber at the top and bottom of the stud. Drill pilot holes at an angle so that the nails go where you want them to go!

Stud partition – cutting plasterboard

To accurately cut plasterboard, cut to half-depth on the face-side with a sharp (retractable) blade and straight edge. Snap the board on a length of timber. Cut through the paper to separate the two pieces.

the joists when the new wall will run parallel with the joists. Instead, locate directly over a particular joist. When the Building Control Officer visits you, ask him whether you will need to reinforce that particular joist (by bolting extra timbers either side of it). While you have the floorboards lifted, check and mark electric cables and pipe runs. Check the walls either side of the new wall for possible pipes or cables buried in the plaster by using a metal detector or a cable and pipe finder.

Cutting and fixing

A stud partition wall is constructed from pretreated 100 mm × 50 mm (4 in × 2 in) sawn softwood. A timber frame is made up of tight fitting uprights with shorter pieces nailed firmly between them to stabilise the whole frame. This framework is firmly fixed between a 'soleplate' on the floor and a 'header' fixed to the ceiling. Allow a gap in the soleplate for the doorway. The door frame will not be built in until the stud partition wall has been erected and made firm.

Measure and calculate the number of timbers to buy and have them delivered a week before you intend to build so that they stay in the room to acclimatise to the drier and warmer conditions than those in which they were stored. Look at the illustration and use it as a guide to make a scale drawing of your own layout. There are simple basic construction principles you must be aware of which will help you overcome problems during construction. The head or top timber is screwed through the

Stud partition – fixing plasterboard

To help lift plasterboard off the floor, use a DIY triangular lifter. Cut the corners off a piece of wood 50 mm × 75 mm by 225 mm (2 in x 3 in x 9 in).

ceiling plaster into the joists above because nailing is too harsh for a ceiling. The end wall studs must be drilled, plugged and screwed firmly to the supporting walls at both ends of the stud partition. All studs must be cut slightly overlong, so that they can be tightly wedged in place before securing.

Lay the bottom timber, or soleplate, on the floor in position, parallel to the facing wall at right angles to its adjacent wall. Draw guide lines either side of the flat 100 mm (4 in) timber. Use a spirit level or a plumb bob to continue the 100 mm width up each wall to the ceiling. The lines across the ceiling should now be vertically above the floor timbers – use the spirit level to check with a timber held between them. A stud sensor will make the job very easy, otherwise use a nail to tap through the plasterboard until you find the centre of each joist (the nail holes can be filled and will be covered by the construction). Again, check your drawing to familiarise yourself with the fixing of the timbers either side of the door opening.

Screw the floor timbers into position first, either side of the measured door opening. Starting from the door opening, mark the positions of the studs so that their centres are 400 mm (16 in) apart. These measurements are to support 1200 mm (4 ft) wide plasterboards nailed upright. Lay the ceiling timber on the floor beside the floor timber and transfer the marks of the studs on to it. Now prop it in position and screw (through predrilled holes) into the ceiling joists. Cut the two side studs to a tight fit and drill, plug and screw them to the wall. Next, the studs either side of the door have to be fixed but not before a horizontal timber is housed in joints just above the door position. After the studs either side of the door have been cut and wedged into position, measure and mark, on one stud, a combined height of the door, the thickness of the door lining, a 6 mm (¼ in) gap at the top of the door, an allowance for floor coverings and another 6 mm. Use a spirit level to transfer this mark to the other stud. Remove both studs and lay them on the floor face up. Mark and cut a simple housing recess to take the 50 mm (2 in) head timber.

Wedge each stud back into position and fix by skew nailing (at an angle) having checked with a spirit level that they are vertical. Slot the horizontal door-head into housing joints and nail from either side of the studs. Cut and fix two short stud pieces between the door-head and the ceiling timber. Cut and tightly fit the rest of the upright studs. If plasterboards are to be joined at their ends, cut and fix noggins to secure those ends. Two rows of noggins are sufficient between the top and bottom of the plasterboard, but for hanging cupboards or any other fixings insert extra noggins at this stage. At the door opening, fix a second stud to the original studs between the floor and the door-head. Once the door lining is fixed the door should have a gap of approximately 3 mm (⅛ in) at each side.

Boards   Plasterboard has a decorative side, which is ivory coloured and does not need to be skimmed with plaster, and a plaster side, which is grey. Use a fine-toothed handsaw to cut plasterboard or do it the professional way with a trimming knife and a straight edge. Cut on the face side, not right through. With the edge of the board on the floor, fold the board back at the cut and run the trimming knife carefully down the back of the cut. Plasterboard nail indentations and gaps are easily covered with a plaster filler. Feather the edges while the filler is still firm to give a professional finish.

The first plasterboard is fixed flush to the inner stud of the door opening. Use galvanised plasterboard nails 150 mm (6 in) apart but not too near the edge of the board or it will crumble. Alternatively, it is quicker and easier to use a staple gun with staples specially designed for plasterboard. Above the doorway, cut the plasterboard vertically to the centre of the main stud. The smaller piece of plasterboard above the door opening will share the stud for its fixing. Fit and fix all the boards on the one side first.

At this stage it is best to insulate all the walls. Slabs of fibreglass or mineral wool can be cut and fitted tightly to the studs and noggins. The insulation will be ineffective if a gap is left anywhere between the insulating material and the timber. Instructions for cutting and fitting come with the material. All the plasterboard edges must line up with the centre of the studs and fit tightly to the floor and ceiling.

If a screw is loose, glue two matchsticks in the hole – let it set, then re-screw.

Finishing   The ivory-coloured decorative side of a plasterboard is very simple to finish and does not need a plaster skim. If the boards are bevel-edged, buy a taping kit from your local DIY store to seal and cover the joints. Minimum skill is required to apply the filler and to fix the covering tape with the plastic applicator. The edges are feathered off with a special sponge to give a perfectly flat surface. Once the whole wall is dry, apply a coat of sealer ready for painting or wallpapering.

Door linings can be bought as a kit. Nail the linings to the studs finishing flush with the outer surface of both plasterboards and covering the vulnerable edges. Fix the two side pieces first and then wedge the header in between them and fix with lost head nails. Moulded architraves give a professional finish to the door opening and cover the gap between the door lining and the plasterboard. Fix the architrave with oval nails at least 12 mm (½ in) away from the edge of the door lining. Having mitred the top corners, now mitre the top horizontal architrave to give an exact fit. Kits are available to make this an easy task. Wedge the door in the open position with the necessary gap at the bottom edge and 3 mm (⅛ in) at the top. Hold the hinge in position and mark on the door top and bottom. Cut the recesses as described in the section on Doors and fit the appropriate leaf of the hinge to the door. Again wedge the door in position and with the leaf of the hinge against the door post, mark it, remove the door and cut the recess. Finally, after fitting the handle and lock, nail the door stops tightly to the closed door.

Ceilings

Cracks

It's not only great fun to renovate an old house, but it is economically sound and the simplest jobs can make a significant difference to its appearance. Repairing cracks is one of these satisfying tasks.

When, for example, central heating is installed into a house previously heated by an open fire, the materials will be exposed to new levels of humidity. Timber, especially flooring joists, suffers movement under these new conditions causing cracks to appear in ceilings. Open cracks between the wall and ceiling are often filled with a proprietary brand filler, but will then open up again at different times of the year as the temperature and humidity vary. That is why these cracks appear with startling regularity!

Owners of newly built flats and houses also face problems. Kiln-dried new timber cannot possibly retain the ideal 12–15 per cent level of moisture content in a centrally heated home. Estate agents and developers traditionally treat complaints about cracks appearing in plaster-work very lightly. Unfortunately, it is one of the hazards of current speculative building. If you complain, you'll be told, 'Of course you'll get cracks, it's natural, it's just settlement!' You need to know a little about floor construction to identify what has gone wrong (see the section on Floors).

It is unlikely that a mainly steel and concrete construction will suffer cracks in the plaster skim. If any do appear they are likely to be superficial. These hairline cracks should be raked out with a sharp knife and cut in an inverted V-shape. This makes the crack widest at its deepest point. By pushing filler hard into the crack it will form a key similar to a dovetail joint. This will stop the filler, which should be mixed with emulsion paint, from falling out when it dries. You should be able to obtain a very smooth finish by correctly using a flexible filling knife. When it's almost dry, slightly dampen the surface to get a polished finish with the steel blade of the filling knife.

Bulges and cracks will continue to occur in old lath-and-plaster ceilings, mainly because of age. Plasterboards superseded the old method many years ago, but many still remain. Soot, dust and debris collects to settle on top of old ceilings. It is better to screw new boards onto the old ceiling.

Coving Obviously, changes that are constantly taking place due to temperature and humidity variations in an older property need to be tackled in a different way to those occurring in a more stable structure. A crack between wall and ceiling is more noticeable because the eye is drawn to the light and shade where the two surfaces meet. Something more is needed than normal plaster filler.

Manufacturers have produced the ideal DIY solution to hide visible cracks in both new and older properties – coving (or cornice). Fixing attractive coving is not only a practical solution, it is also aesthetically pleasing and enhances the look of a room. Coving comes with a comprehensively illustrated leaflet, fully describing how to fix it.

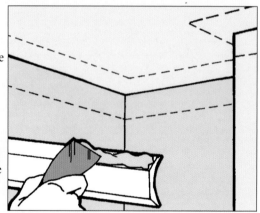

Fitting coving (1)
Draw guidelines along walls and ceilings 67 mm for 100 mm girth cove (83 mm for 127 mm cove) from their angle of intersection. Scratch the areas to be in contact with the cove to provide a key for the adhesive. Use a mitre block or the special template provided to cut the cove. Apply the adhesive about 3 mm thick to the two surfaces along the whole length of the cove.

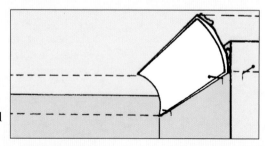

Fitting coving (2)
Gently position the cut cove between the guidelines (you will need help if the cove is longer than 2 m (6 ft 6 in). Remove any excess adhesive with a scraper and use it to make good the joints and mitres. Draw a moistened brush along the joints. Use small nails below the cove to support it while the adhesive dries. Use excess adhesive to fill the holes later.

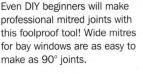

Even DIY beginners will make professional mitred joints with this foolproof tool! Wide mitres for bay windows are as easy to make as 90° joints.

Measure right round the room and include the chimney breast recesses. Make a rough sketch with the measurements and take it with you to your DIY store when you choose the coving for your room. There is a wide choice so take particular care to balance the coving size with the room dimensions. Use your sketch to work out all the lengths needed and cut the coving – it is quicker and easier to cut all the mitred angles before fixing any.

What might appear to be a complicated part of the job, that is, accurately cutting internal and external mitred corners, is actually very simple thanks to proprietary kits. These allow you to cut professional looking mitred joints, and not just on coving. In fact, they're so good that you will never need to backfill them with plaster. Sometimes, a pivoted angle finder is provided, which you hold against the corner whether it's internal or external. This gives the actual and exact angle of the wall, which you transfer to the two locking arms on the mitre box. What you've effectively done is to transfer the angle of the wall to the adjustable mitre box. The two pieces of coving are separately cut, guided by

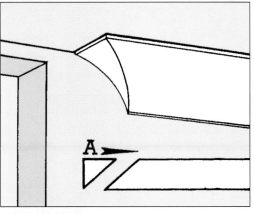

Fitting coving (3)
Where a window or door extends to ceiling height, cut stop-end or wedge-shaped end pieces to terminate the cove. Cut the external mitre, then cut it off square to fit the prepared end.

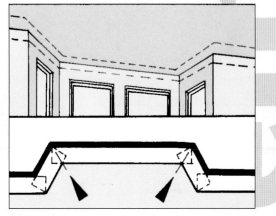

Coving corners
The illustration shows a bay with lengths of cove in position before the mitres are cut. The angles of the cuts are indicated by the arrows. Use a proprietary tool to cut the mitre angles with complete accuracy.

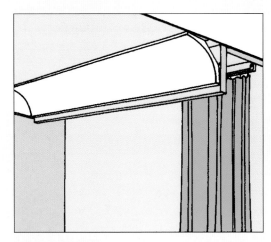

Fitting coving (4)
A pelmet is made from two timbers fixed to the ceiling joists. Curtain rails are hidden behind. Coving is attached to the pelmet and ceiling.

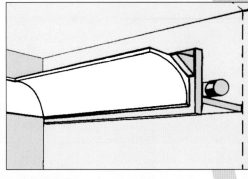

Coving lighting
Dramatic effects can be achieved with the subtle use of an inverted pelmet construction with coving fixed to the front. Fix a length of prepared timber between the side walls. Screw a vertical piece of timber to it to give a minimum of 50 mm (2 in) to the ceiling. Fix a triangular fillet in position so the cove can be fixed to it. Tube lighting can then be hidden in the box.

this angle. That's why I say it is foolproof, because the two pieces can only fit together at the prescribed angle of that particular corner.

Number each piece as you cut, mark it on the back and on the appropriate position on the wall so that you don't get them muddled and fit a length in the wrong place! Draw pencil guidelines on the wall and ceiling just inside the area of the coving. A spirit level will help make the task easier. Provide a key for the adhesive by gently scratching inside the pencil marks. Brush away all loose particles and dust. I advise that you ask for help when you are fixing lengths of more than 2 m (7 ft), but you can tack 25 mm (1 in) panel pins, about 450 mm (18 in) apart, along the line on the wall to use as a support whilst pressing the coving into the adhesive. The nail holes will be filled later with the adhesive. Use galvanised plasterboard nails or alloy screws if you need any extra fixing, for example, where the wall might be uneven. Tap the nail heads to just below the coving surface, but don't puncture the paper. Fill with the coving adhesive which must be mixed with water to the consistency recommended on the packet. If the plaster to which the coving is to be fixed is very dry, dampen it with water just before offering up the coving. Mix sufficient adhesive for about half an hour's work because it stays workable for about that time. Once in position, it will set hard in about an hour. The adhesive must be applied, approximately 3 mm (⅛ in) thick, to the two surfaces that will be in contact with the wall and ceiling. Excess adhesive can be wiped off, but at the same time fill in any gaps and joints. Before the adhesive begins to set, draw a wet paintbrush along the horizontal joints to give a clean, smooth finish.

Occasionally, it is necessary to terminate the end of the coving at a stairwell or where a doorway extends to full ceiling height. Do this by cutting a stop end. Cut a mitre at the end of an offcut, which is then cut off square. This piece will fit the end of the long length of coving to give a very professional finish.

If the coving has to run around the interior of a bay window wall, first cut squared-off lengths to fit each wall with a bit extra. Pencil marks drawn around each piece on the ceiling will intersect. This is the line of the mitre.

Gyproc® coving has an ivory-coloured surface similar to the decorative side of plasterboard but the material is not suitable for skimming with plaster. It has an excellent surface which should be primed with a PVA-based primer to seal the surface ready for your chosen finish.

Covering cracks is not the only reason for using coving. It can hide electrical circuits and pipes, and interior designers and decorators use curved plaster coving as a decorative feature. The clever use of battens and tube lighting, covered at the front by the matching coving, gives a very attractive diffused lighting effect.

Positioning a pelmet to hide a curtain rail fixed close to the ceiling joint presents no problems at all if you use coving. Use a very simple arrangement with two long battens and fix the coving to the vertical one to make a very attractive pelmet. This can be mitred at both ends to join the side walls as a continuous run.

Some rooms lend themselves to a more decorative form of moulding. A range of coving accessories is available for use with the standard plaster coving. For example, the addition of a central, moulded ceiling rose could totally transform the look of a room. This decorative plaster moulding or 'ceiling centrepiece' usually has a pendant light fitting hanging from it. In an Edwardian house, for example, why not install a reproduction moulding made from fibrous plaster?

Suspended

There can sometimes be noise problems through floors in flats and in large houses that have been converted into self-contained flats. Noise from upstairs neighbours can be a constant source of stress and annoyance. Many people have discovered that, after purchasing a flat in a house conversion, noise transmission issues were not addressed and that an insulation

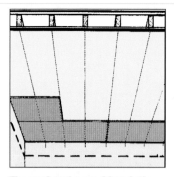

Thermal and sound insulation between floors (1)

A secondary suspended ceiling will help cut out noise from above and will have good thermal properties. Mark the joists and measure for plasterboards. Mark a line for the new ceiling.

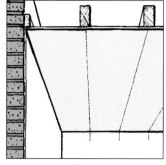

Thermal and sound insulation between floors (2)

Fix battens around the walls to support the edges of the board following the level line. Fix intermediate joists to the wall timbers notching the joists to sit on the battens. Fix short timber noggins between the joists to support the ends of the boards.

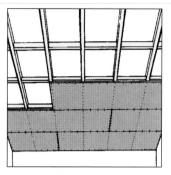

Thermal and sound insulation between floors (3)

Stagger the positions of the plasterboards so that joints in one row do not run into joints of the next row.

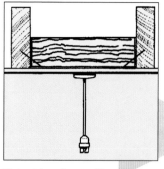

Thermal and sound insulation between floors (4)

Tightly fix a supporting timber between the joists to support a light fitting.

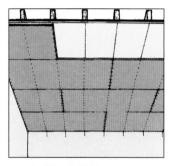

Thermal and sound insulation between floors (5)

A staple gun that fires special plasterboard staples is so much easier than hammering in single nails. Use self-adhesive tape over the joints, finish with joint filler. Feather the edges with a damp sponge.

Thermal and sound insulation between floors (6)

Before decorating, fix a decorative cove to seal any cracks or gaps that could let in sound.

Accurately cut sound and thermal insulation material to make a tight fit between joists and noggins. It is essential that no air gaps are left on any side of the material.

barrier was not installed. It's often the case that one's own lifestyle and, in particular, hours of sleeping, differ considerably from that of one's close neighbours. Often, the only place where owners or tenants can tackle a noise problem is on their own floors. This is dealt with in detail in the section on Floors and Noise Insulation. Noise coming from upstairs is solved by insulating the ceiling or by building a false ceiling. In your own house you have the choice of tackling it from the bedroom floor area or by fixing a suspended ceiling below.

The floor construction of large old properties converted in flats is usually timber joists with floorboards nailed above and a lath and plaster

ceiling below. The material between two neighbouring flats might be only 25 mm (1 in) of floorboard and even less ceiling board or lath and plaster. Unless something has been done to increase the amount of insulation material, sound will be transmitted in both directions.

The first thing to do is to identify the sound problem and list the areas from where it comes. Noise can be airborne (passing traffic, barking dogs, transistor radios and televisions) or impact (caused when somebody walks across an uncarpeted floor above or when a neighbour bangs on the wall). Direct air paths such as ill-fitting skirting boards, loose floorboards and even power sockets can allow a great deal of sound through, while thin barriers of building materials can actually amplify the sound on the other side.

If you are troubled by noise coming from upstairs, the best and simplest DIY method is to erect a new and totally independent ceiling below the existing ceiling. It is important that a gap of at least 150mm (6in) is left between the two ceilings. Remember that a new ceiling will change the room's proportions and hide the original ceiling's features. You must also make sure that the walls can bear the load of the new ceiling structure. One other important factor is that there is at least 25cm (10in) between the ceiling and top of the highest window.

You will need to build a framework structure to hold the new plasterboards. This will consist of timber joists spanning the width of the room with intermediate joists to stabilise the whole structure. The joist positions must coincide with the edges of the plasterboard for fixing. Begin by fixing a 50mm × 50mm (2in × 2in) timber batten to the wall, with its bottom edge on a horizontal line drawn on the wall about 175mm (7in) below the ceiling. Hold the batten to the wall at its central point with a frame-fixing plug and use a spirit level to make sure it is horizontal before drilling the other fixing holes. Fix a similar batten to the opposite wall, at the same level. The two battens support the new ceiling joists. Complete the outer framework by springing the two remaining joists tightly to those already fixed. Secure with plugs and screws.

Having checked for pipes and cables right round the room you're now ready to add the fixings every 600mm (2ft). For a room up to 2.8m square (9ft) square, the inner framework joists can be cut from 150mm × 50mm (6in × 2in) timber. First of all, cut the joists to span from one wall to the other at a minimum of 450mm (18in) centres. Then notch the joists at each end to rest snugly on the battens with the lower edges of the joists and battens at the same level. Use an offcut of a batten to mark the joist ends and saw out the notches on the waste side of the lines.

The notched joists need then to be skew-nailed to the battens. All the edges of the plasterboards have to be supported, so saw offcuts of the joists to fit tightly between the joists, then skew-nailed in position. The whole framework is braced with intermediate noggins (shorter pieces fixed to the long joists). You'll need help to put up the plasterboards. Used galvanised plasterboard nails every 150mm (6in). Lay rows of mineral fibre insulation over the noggins between the new joists, leaving no gaps, to improve the sound insulation qualities of the new ceiling. Use a broom handle to make sure that the insulating material is properly laid over the last noggins and tight to the joists. Screw, don't hammer, the plasterboard. Lay your insulating boards on top of and tight to the framework. Continue across the room making sure that the last board is a half board. Stick the insulating material to the last board using the appropriate adhesive, before fixing it in place to the framework. With a one-coat plaster and tape, seal around all the edges and the plasterboard joints. When it is dry, use a heavy duty textured coating to completely cover your new false ceiling.

A second layer of plasterboard will ensure more noise protection. It is important that the joints of the second layer do not coincide with the joints of the first.

There are two things to bear in mind. First, fix a noggin directly underneath the central light fitting if one exists. Drill a hole through it to coincide with the position of the rose above. The second point is it is better to use non-rust screws rather than plasterboard nails. Banging in the nails could disturb the insulating material thereby lessening the effectiveness of the barrier.

It is relatively simple to change over the existing cable from the light fitting but if you don't understand electrics then, for your own safety, get professional advice and help. Take out the mains fuse for this particular circuit or switch off the trip and seal it with tape. Remove the ceiling rose to expose the terminals. Cut a new longer length of cable, remove the outer insulation and core wire insulation. Remove the existing cable, noting which colour of wire went into which terminal, and replace it with the new cable making sure the wire of the correct colour connects to the correct terminal. Check that the screws are sufficiently tight to hold the core wire and that no uninsulated copper filaments are left straggling. Transfer the bulb holder to the new hanging cable, pop the bulb in and check that the circuit is complete. Replace the rose to protect the original fitting. A new rose can be fixed in position on the new plasterboard ceiling.

The second layer of plasterboard is fixed with its grey side up. A jointing kit is available which includes filler, tape and tools to give a smooth flush finish to the joints. Make sure that all wall-to-ceiling joints are completely filled, with no air gaps to spoil the insulation treatment. When the ceiling is finished, coving could be fitted to make sure no sound can penetrate round the edges. After testing the improved ceiling for a few days, I am sure that the noise level will be lower. The independent ceiling will effectively reduce the noise from the room above.

If the ceiling can be installed with at least a 15 cm (6 in) gap between it and the existing ceiling, the void can be filled with batts of rock-wool or dense polystyrene sheets. Even 15 cm (6 in) of fibreglass insulating material can be used.

Lath and plaster

Repairing   Many ceilings in Victorian and Edwardian homes, and in those built before, are still sound. However, if rain water or a leaking tank has been allowed to saturate the ceiling in one spot, the plaster will have softened resulting in a loss of adhesion and a bulge. The construction of a lath and plaster ceiling is simplicity itself. A series of thin laths are nailed to the ceiling joists with enough space between each one to allow the plaster to be squeezed through and bulge over the sides and tops of the laths. This provided a very effective key to hold the plaster in position. It is unusual to find that the laths have actually parted company from the underside of the joists.

You will have to remove and replace the plaster where water has damaged this type of ceiling. Use a trimming knife to incise a line right round the bulge. Get as deep as you comfortably can so that you can cut away the damage. If the bulge sounds hollow yet is still solid, drill a few holes in the centre of the bulge so that you can get the claw end of a hammer into it to prise away pieces. Once you've cleared the damaged plaster right back to the sound parts, apply water to the laths to dampen them before an applying metal lathing

Lath and plaster walls and ceilings have not been built for decades. Those that remain must be checked for perished plaster and corroded nails. When renovating, replace them with plasterboard.

plaster. This is the first coat of the treatment. When it is almost set, scratch the surface to form a key for the second coat. Repeat the process before the applying a top coat of gypsum plaster. When the plaster has almost set use a steel float to 'polish' the patch repair. A soft decorator's brush dripped in water will feather-edge the patch to the surrounding area so that no join is seen. Stabilise the patch before redecorating the whole ceiling.

If there is a noticeable dip in the ceiling but there are no hollow sounds indicating loss of adhesion, use a decorative treatment to hold the ceiling more firmly.

Decorative battens   Period properties often had plain but panelled ceilings which were divided into squares about 600 mm × 600 mm (2 ft × 2 ft), each subdivided by flat moulded battens about 75 mm (3 in) across. The nails on the floorboards above will tell you exactly the position of every joist, which you can then transfer to the ceiling below. Otherwise use a stud sensor to detect the positions from below and mark them on the ceiling so that you can make your fixings through the battens into the joists. Use a cartridge gun and a builder's mastic adhesive run along the backs of the battens to help secure the battens. Never be tempted to bang nails into an existing ceiling, you can cause cracks or even disturb the plaster adhesion. Use countersink non-rust screw fixings which can be covered over.

TGV boards

Depending on the size of the room and its decor, a 'tongue and groove' V-jointed boarded ceiling can be an added attraction. It really is a worthwhile project, even though it might be tedious looking up and fixing from below for a day!

First decide on how you are going to place the boards, whether diagonally or across the length or the width of the ceiling. Order sufficient boards to cover the ceiling area with some to spare for waste. Attach the firrings (the battens that are screwed to the joists and to which the separate boards are fixed) at right angles to the ceiling joists and at 450 mm (18 in) centres. Kits of pre-packed boards are available and come with special metal clips which locate in the groove of the board leaving a small lug extended with a hole to take the fixing nail. The first board to be fixed against the wall must have the tongue showing and held with panel pins through the face of the board to hold it in position – a powered nail gun is useful for this. The rest of the boards will slide one after the other, the tongue fitting into the groove of the board before it. The clips are hidden by the next board to be fixed. Boards are joined end to end to coincide with one of the firring strips. The last board to be fixed will also have to be profiled to the wall and cut very carefully. It will also have to be fixed through its surface with nails punched below the surface and filled.

Traditionally normal fixings for tongue and groove are by nails through the tongues at an angle so that the next board covers the nail and the tongue. With this type of fixing it is necessary to fix the first board with the grooved edge to the wall. This means the first one will be held by surface fixings. Subsequent boards are all nailed through the tongue using 25 mm (1 in) panel pins. Each board will need a slight tap with a hammer but use a protective piece of timber to prevent damage to the tongue. Again to join pieces at the ends, cut the two lengths to join over a firring strip.

A light fitting cable can be dropped through a decorative wooden rose which has been glued to the boards to cover the existing one. Switch off at the mains before altering the cabling – remember to turn it on again after refixing the light holder and shade. Decorative wooden mouldings or wooden cornices are available to fix at the wall-to-ceiling joints. Two applications of a matt, water-based sealant will give a truly professional finish. Sand lightly between each coat to remove nibs and to key for the second coat.

Cladding a ceiling
Use 'tongue and groove' cladding to simply and effectively board a ceiling as an alternative to straight butted boarding. Draw diagonals from the corners and fix battens both sides of the lines, around the edges and at 1 m (1 yd) intervals. Secure nail with a nail gun. Cut the boards to within 12 mm (½ in) of the walls and fix scotia moulding with a glue gun.

Shelving Hanging

The supports of a 'cliffhanger' shelf system are hidden. It is simple to fit. The triangular, slotted metal support is screwed to the wall and the shelf firmly fixes into the slot. An end cover-piece completes the fitting.

Make sure the drill bit, the plug and the screw are all compatible for wall fixings.

Fixing Before you decide how to fix shelves to the wall, you have to know what kind of wall you're fixing them to! Fixing to a solid wall is relatively simple. The standard method is to use a wall plug and screw, which should be long enough to go through the plaster and at least 18 mm (¾ in) into the solid wall behind. Hollow walls present a trickier problem, but inexpensive purposely designed fixings make the job a lot easier. Get it wrong and the shelf will collapse. The most secure fixing is made by screwing into one of the vertical timber wall studs hidden behind the plaster. You can often locate the wall studs by tapping along the wall and listening for the sound to change as you tap over a stud. Alternatively, you can use a stud detector with a safety device to avoid driving screws into pipes or cables hidden in the wall.

You can fix light shelving directly on to the plasterboards by using a cavity fixing. These have been available for years, but the addition of a nylon toggle is an interesting development. To use it, you drill a hole of the right diameter (marked on the pack) through the plasterboard. Then squeeze the toggle into the hole, tap it flush and screw up your bracket. As you screw, the 'wings' of the toggle flatten against the back

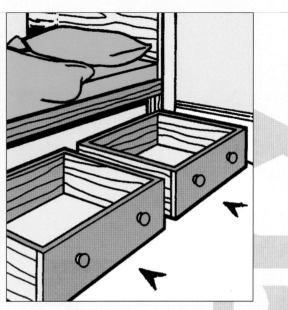

Storage space (1)
High beds have an enormous area underneath that can be used for storage. A shelf can be fitted to support self-assembly drawers.

Storage space (2)
Open up the panelling under a flight of stairs, but leave the supporting posts (newels). Fit shelves in the space for storage.

of the plasterboard, holding the screw firmly in place. Another type of cavity fixing uses a rubber material. When the screw is tightened inside it, the fixing swells allowing it to take quite a heavy load. These fixings also come in a metal variety which folds back on to the reverse side of the plasterboard when the screw is tightened. All these devices are readily available in DIY shops and with their help you should soon 'get the hang' of it!

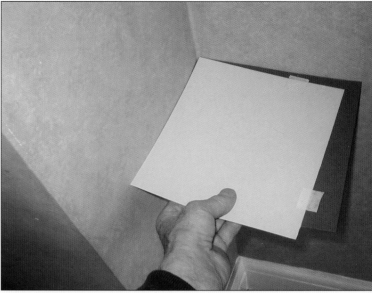

(1) Often the walls of a recess are not a true right angle, but it is easy to cut a shelf to fit any angle perfectly. It's not important to know the exact angle, simply make a template!

(2) Hold two pieces of card against each wall to fit the existing angle and tape them together. Transfer this to the end of the shelf to be cut.

In the past, fixing a doorpost to brickwork meant an HSS bit for the wood, a masonry bit for the brick, and a prayer that the holes lined up for some tough screwdriving! Now, drill through both together and hammer in a tough plug with a screw-nail inside it!

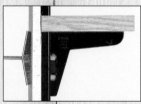

Metal toggle fixings are not only good for fixing light shelves to stud walls but can be used on wall boards too. Drill a hole as recommended and close the wings. They will then spring back when inserted to give a tight hold. Toggle fixings come in different materials and sizes. Choose from a catalogue the type to suit the job in hand.

For conventional fixings in a masonry wall, it is essential that the masonry drill bit, the plug and the screw are all compatible to prevent the fixing being too loose or too tight. If, inadvertently, you drill a hole that is too large, there is an extremely effective method of taking up the space between the plug and the enlarged hole – use a product that comprises a disc of webbing, about 6 cm (2½ in) in diameter, impregnated with plaster. Take one from the box, immerse it in water and with the plug end at its centre, wrap the now malleable disc around the plug and press it into the hole so that the plug end is level with the surface of the wall. In a short while the plaster hardens so effectively that once the screw is driven into the plug it cannot be shifted!

There are many types of fixings for plasterboard, but you can check out what is available and most suitable by a visit to your DIY store and reading the instructions on each pack. Most DIY stores stock the many variations of fixings including a nylon anchor, a metal collapsible anchor, a plastic collapsible anchor, a toggle cavity anchor and a rubber-sleeve anchor.

Light aggregate   In many houses, the inner leaf or skin of a cavity wall is built of a light aggregate block. The outer skin of brick and the inner skin of larger blocks are tied together to stabilised the entire wall with galvanised metal butterflies ties. The blocks are not only strong enough to support weights (for example, the roof) but can also be drilled and plugged to support weights on brackets attached to the block wall. But again, check at the DIY store that you buy the correct fixing for whatever you want to support. Threaded plugs, for example, are good for use in aerated concrete blocks. These are lighter in weight and less dense than a full concrete block. The plugs actually have a thread on the outside to be able to screw it into the block to provide a holding for screws. Another innovation is a locking pin which one type of plastic plug has for extra security and holding, but the latest innovation for fixing supports to block walls, and in fact to any solid walls, is the Hercules plug. A demonstration of its powers amazed me and I'm sure, when you first use one, you'll pleasantly surprised too. A masonry drill comes with the pack. To use this type of plug, drill through a board and into the wall at the same time and then drive the plug through the board into the wall with a hammer. Amazingly there are no screws because the plug is manufactured from a particularly strong and steel-like material that can take incredible loads.

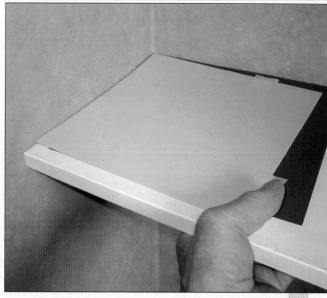

(3) Tape the cards to the shelf in position so that the exact line of cut can be transferred to the board ready for the saw cut.

(4) With the end of the shelf sawn at the correct angle, it fits exactly into the corner.

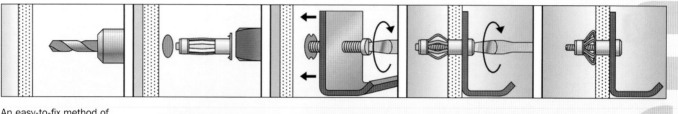

An easy-to-fix method of holding brackets or lightweight timber battens to plasterboard is by compressing the back plate when the screw is tightened. Back plates can be metal, hard rubber or plastic.

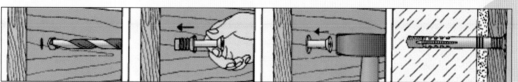

This combination of secured plug and screw is suitable for both solid masonry walls and block walls. Use the recommended size drill bit, drill to the correct depth through the work piece and the substrate (wall). Drive in the screw-nail and plug to grip like a vice inside the wall.

Only cut MDF board outside – use a mask with a filter.

Levelling You might have a problem getting long shelves horizontal, but a very simple home-made 'water level' will help. To make one, take a length of clear plastic tubing, which you can buy in a DIY store or motor accessory shop. The tube needs to be as long as your shelf. Almost fill it with water (which is easier to see if you add coloured ink). Put the tube against the wall with the water in one end of the tube level with your shelf mark. You then take the other end of the tube up to the wall where the other end of the shelf is to be and simply mark the water level again. As water always finds its own level, your marks are bound to give you a truly horizontal shelf. This method of finding levels is really indispensable when, for any reason, you have to find a level around a corner on an adjacent wall.

Shelf materials Laminated, man-made boards with a core of chipboard, blockboard or plywood are available in a range of standard shelf sizes much wider than natural wood sold in timber merchants. Melamine®-surfaced chipboard is inexpensive and very suitable for shelving. Look at the rows of laminated, simulated wood grain effects available in DIY stores and it's quite surprising how difficult it is to tell the difference from real wood! If you find the cost of natural timber, hardwood or softwood, prohibitive for your simple shelf arrangement, you have many other choices available!

Recessed

The space beside a chimney breast, the recess, is ideal for installing simple shelving. It is very unlikely that both internal corners will be a right angle. Start by deciding how many shelves you wish to install and their separation. Now decide whether you want to support the shelves directly on the wall or on wooden side panels. Choose your shelving keeping its intended use and weight load in mind. Generally, the thicker the material the stronger it will be. For heavy loads like books, go for a material that is at least 18mm (¾in) and preferably 25mm (1in) thick. Solid wood is traditionally used for shelves, but this can be an expensive option and other materials may be a better choice, particularly where practical concerns outweigh aesthetic ones. Shelves and shelving systems can be purchased at most DIY outlets and come in styles from the traditional to the highly contemporary. A good compromise between strength, appearance and economic considerations, is a wood veneer shelving system. Melamine®-coated chipboard provides a hard-wearing, hygienic surface that is ideal for kitchen shelves, bookshelves and storage shelves.

Recesses can be anything between 200mm (8in) and 300mm (12in) deep. If you opt to cut and fit side panels, making it look more like a fitted unit, then these should be the same depth as the shelves. Cut side panels of equal length and make sure that the tops and bottoms are square. Having decided on the number of shelves and their relative positions, fix the two side panels to the wall with plugs and countersink screws; position these at the shelf ends so that they are covered. If you are going to place a panel across the top of the unit make sure that it is longer than the shelves by twice the thickness of a side panels.

It is important to get the exact angle at which to cut each end of the shelves. Take two pieces of card, about 200mm × 150mm (8in × 6in) and hold them into the recess corner so they overlap. Tape them together so that you get the exact angle. Do the same at the other corner. Cut the shelf board to the greatest recess width. Mark on the wall the position of a shelf and label it underneath. Hold the card angle template on the shelf, mark the angle, score it and cut.

There are a number of options available for hanging shelves The simplest method is to buy a pack of plastic shelf supports. Some are like dowels that you simply push into holes drilled just underneath the shelves. Others are screwed in position and have a flat top for the shelf to rest on. Alternatively, you can cut small matching battens and screw them either to the wall or to the side panels to support the shelf along its depth. Make sure you cut the batten at least 12mm (½in) shorter than the depth of the shelf and angle it back so that it is virtually hidden.

The back edge of a long shelf can be supported with similar wooden battens. If, however, for aesthetic reasons you don't want a batten, you might need to increase the thickness of the shelf itself. There are recommended maximum distances between supports depending on the material that you use. For example, 12mm (½in) thick blockboard should be supported every 450mm (18in) and 25mm (1in) thick chipboard can span 750mm (30in) between supports. Ordinary timber, on the other hand, such as 25mm (1in) thick pine, can span as much as 1m (39in).

Remembering my catchphrase – SAFETY FIRST, DIY SECOND – always check for cables and pipes before drilling into any wall. Cables to power points normally run up from the floor, while those on a lighting circuit to light switches normally run down from the ceiling. So never drill holes either vertically above or below those fittings.

You can dispense with visible supports and brackets by drilling holes on the back of the shelf and firmly pushing it on to projecting steel rods. This makes an incredibly strong and attractive shelf which can now support quite heavy loads.

Supports

Brackets Angle metal strips are available which do the same job as wooden battens. Screw holes are predrilled so you just need to mark the position of the screws on the wall or your side panels. Use a spirit level to mark the position of the first strip. Screw them in place as for battens making sure you use a screw size to match the predrilled holes and that at least 38 mm (1½ in) of the screw is in the wall plug or that the screw is long enough to go right through the wooden side panel. You can, if you want, cut a recess in the edge of the shelf so that the metal strip will be invisible when the shelf is in position. Place a bracket on the shelf side edge and draw round it with a pencil to mark the cutting line. With an electric router, cut the recess but stop just before the front edge of the shelf so that the bracket will be concealed. With both ends cut fit the angled strips to the side walls of the alcove and slide the shelf on to them.

Decorative L-shaped metal angle brackets are also available in various forms and materials. Most brackets have one arm longer than the other, so you must fix the longer arm to the wall. Mark, using a spirit level, the top edge of the supporting brackets in the required position, with the end ones a short distance in from the ends of the shelf.

After fixing the first bracket hold a long spirit level on top of it to level and position the furthest bracket away from it. You have to fix the two end brackets in place first. With all the brackets in place, lay the shelf in position and mark the screw hole positions through the brackets on to the underside of the shelf. Drill pilot holes to take the screws, replace the shelf on the brackets and screw in place.

A shelf slot for board shelves is an extremely strong extruded profile of aluminium, powder coated in white, black, cream or matt silver. Boards come in a variety of colours and moulded front edges. Even though the slotted shelf supports come in standard lengths they can easily be cut to exact sizes to suit your requirements. End cover pieces give a professional finish to the shelf supports. In this system there are shelf slot supports designed also for glass shelves of between 6 mm (¼ in) and 10 mm (⅜ in) thick. For 15 cm (6 in) deep glass shelves there are also shelf grip brackets. These come in pairs so have to be accurately levelled before fixing so that the shelf is perfectly horizontal. Surprisingly two screws hold each bracket.

This particular system of shelf slot supports is probably one of the simplest. It is simply a matter of accurately lining up the one edge of the board against the outer edge of the long bracket, easing the board into the slot and

Cliffhanger shelving designed specially for corner fixings. Attractive chrome slotted brackets are positioned using a spirit level and the toughened glass shelves forced into the cushioned slots.

The traditional steel shelf-bracket is a good strong support for holding heavy weights but make sure not to position them too far apart!

These shelves appear to have no visible means of support! Although some might prefer a well-designed shelf support, this kit gives a modern look to a recess! A metal bar has two welded rods, which slip into predrilled holes in the back of the shelf.

gently tapping with a protective piece of timber against the front edge. Board shelves will take some gentle persuasion because the bracket will close very tightly around the back edge of the shelf. Make sure that the whole of the back edge of the shelf is in contact with the back of the slot. Glass shelves on the other hand are eased in gently with no upward or downward pressure and are held rigidly once fully home.

Rails Vertical rails come with adjustable shelving systems but are available in different materials and finishes so that you can find one which will fit in with your chosen decor. A silver satin finish or a matt anodised finish in gold/silver on black in hardened aluminium is often used for uprights and brackets. Sometimes they come with matching shelves too. However, you are not limited in choice because you can also get a wood unit, for example, teak uprights with brackets with matching teak finished shelves.

There are different types of rails, some with slots into which the brackets are fitted and others with a continuous channel into which the shelves are slid, clicked or locked into place at a particular position. Brackets of the slotted type can be moved at 25 mm (1 in) intervals. The sliding type is easier to adjust, but take care in lining up the brackets to ensure that the shelves are level! Always ensure that the rails are absolutely vertical and the slots or holes in each rail coincide with its partner. There is even a system which has an integral adjustable light which can be fitted anywhere on the upright. Electric cables for lights or hi-fi equipment can be run inside the uprights and hidden with a cover strip. Another innovation that is available is a switch which can be fitted on an upright for connection to a lamp or other appliance.

Brackets are specifically designed for a particular type of rail and come in different sizes to fit standard shelf depths – from 150 mm (6 in) to 600 mm (24 in). Allow the shelf to overlap the bracket slightly unless the bracket has a lipped edge, in which case the shelf will fit exactly. Some wood brackets or supports have rubber grip pads to hold the shelving, while other types have a hooked edge which fits into a groove into the shelf. Other systems have special supports to hold glass shelves. All manufacturers supply instructions and recommendations, so please follow them. The instructions will tell you the exact spacing between supports, which will be dictated by the load the shelves will carry. You will also be told the size of screws required if they are not supplied with the kit.

An English designer decided that he wanted something less obtrusive than a normal shelf bracket, so he set about designing one. The result is a shelf that appears to literally hang from the wall. This is probably the neatest way to support a shelf that I've seen. These unobtrusive and quite delicate long slotted supports made of light alloy are almost indiscernible when the shelf is slotted into the tightly fitting long continuous groove. Within the groove are predrilled holes to hold the shelf support to the wall. After checking for pipes and cables in the wall, offer up the support in your chosen position and use a spirit level to get it absolutely horizontal. Drill and plug one hole first and drive in the one screw but loosely. You can then check the level again before drilling the far end screw hole. Loosely fix that end too before marking the intermediate screw hole positions. Take out the one screw and let the shelf support flop, before drilling the rest of the holes. Make absolutely sure that the masonry drill bit, the plugs and the screws are compatible if you've not been supplied with these in the kit. Sagging cannot be a problem in this system because the horizontal slot supports the entire length of the shelf.

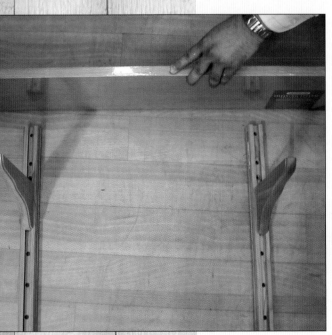

One of the easiest shelf systems to install is the 'rail' system. Use a laser line generator to obtain true verticals and horizontals so that the shelves are level and in line. The easiest fixing, which also dispenses with the need for screws, is to attach the rails to a solid wall with Hercules plugs.

General Repairs

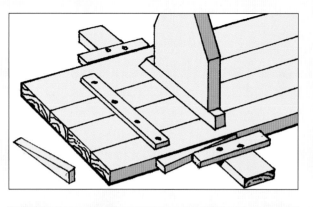

Repairing furniture (1)
Any table top, bench seat or desk top made from a number of planks will sometimes open up at the joints. A simple wedge arrangement will solve the problem by allowing you to glue the planks to one another. A batten screwed in an unobtrusive position will help to hold the pieces together.

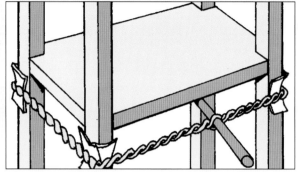

Repairing furniture (2)
Legs of chairs, tables and desks that have sprung apart can easily be glued back together. While the glue sets, hold the assembly with a length of string twisted with a rod as illustrated.

Joists The importance of joists in the construction of a house can never be overemphasised. Any joist anywhere in the house that has split, rotted or broken must, as a matter of priority, be reinstated. Not to do so is to compromise the stability and safety of that part of the building. Joists that separate the attic from bedrooms not only provide support for a plasterboard ceiling and for the floor in the attic, they also tie together rafter ends opposite each other. The rafters are tied at the ridge to form a number of triangles making a stable roof construction. Together with purlins and tie-ins (and other posts if it's a large roof construction) the structure is capable of supporting tons of roofing material (and snow!). Sometimes you'll find that a joist that has been installed for a number of years might have a longitudinal split that is not an immediate problem but could be in the future. Joists are supported at both ends by either a metal galvanised joist hanger, which is fixed to the wall plate or to the wall, or by sitting on a damp proof course (DPC) pad on a brick shelf in a space in the brickwork. It can be notched to sit inside a slot cut into a wooden wall plate.

To reinforce a split joist you'll need two supporting timbers of the same section bolted either side of the split and projecting passt it. Find the best places to ensure the full support along the length of the split. If the split is along the centre of the joist drill below with a cranked-drive drill. Transfer the three, four or five positions of the drill holes to the supporting timbers, but you have to be very accurate here. One way is to clamp each timber separately and drill in through the holes in the existing joist so that the new holes match properly. Then you will need to bolt the three together but, in between each of the timbers, use a spiked timber connector. Don't forget the steel washers! When working on any constructional timbers, especially joists, treat all sawn ends with wood preservative and extend the treatment as far as possible. If you have a problem with the end of a joist, the 'bower beam' could be useful. This is a galvanised metal channel which replaces the decayed end of a joist. After the decayed end of the timber has been removed and the remaining wood sprayed with insecticide/fungicide, the bower beam is bolted in place allowing the sound part of the post to be retained. The bower beam becomes an extension of the joist to whatever length you want, but this method depends largely on the construction of your house.

Skirtings

Daily vacuuming, heavy furniture and clumsy feet, among other things, can cause havoc with skirting boards. Splits in skirting boards can be caused by hot central-heating pipes. Leaking radiators, condensation, and earth that has been allowed to pile up over the DPC will, if not spotted, cause the back of the skirting board to rot. Check around floorboards for the exit holes of woodworm. If you see any, the skirting is certain to be affected. The problems are adding up!

Skirtings come in all sizes and types of moulding, complex and simple, from the 300 mm (12 in) high Edwardian skirting board with 100 mm (4 in) of top moulding, down to the very simple 100 mm (4 in) chamfered modern day version. If you have to replace a high skirting board, remember that three quarters of it is a straight plank, so it is possible to replace that part separately and get a length of moulding to fix to the top.

Skirting boards have to be prised from the centre of the run. Either use a block of wood behind a bolster chisel or a claw hammer, but, best of all, use two wooden wedges about 300 mm (12 in) apart knocked down behind the skirting to release it and then use a small crowbar to gently ease it away from the wall. If one end of the skirting board has an exterior joint, this makes the replacement much easier. Each end is mitred at a corner for gluing and pinning together. It is simple to obtain a professional finish using a mitring kit. At an internal corner gently ease the length of skirting away to leave the adjacent piece still firmly fixed.

Sometimes you will find that replastering has been allowed to encroach on the top surface of the skirting board. In this case it is better to separate the top of the board and the plaster by skilfully using a trimming knife. This will ensure that when you prise away the skirting the plaster will not be disturbed.

Now check the fixings. Ordinarily skirting boards were fixed with long cut nails hammered through the skirting board and into blocks of wood which had been previously fixed to the wall. These blocks of wood are called 'grounds'. However, you might find that dowels have been used for the fixings.

In older properties, where a skirting might be loose at one particular part, it could be that the grounds have perished. If that particular run of skirting board finishes at an architrave, this is an easy area at which to start prising. The reason is that the end of the skirting board is cut flat and straight to the architrave and therefore will be released quite easily. To replace the skirting board you have to replace the grounds first. This is simply a matter of cutting a piece of timber, dunking it with preservative and refixing with plugs and non-rust screws. Never attempt to pull the long nail through from the back and uncertainly do not drive it through to the front. You won't have noticed the nail head from the front because the surface will have been made smooth. To solve the problem simply cut off the nail flush with the back of the skirting board then you'll have to refix as close to the original as possible without disturbing it.

If you have a bad dent or a piece of spongy wood that needs replacing, the solution to the problem is to use a two-part wood filler. A bad dent needs to have a little more of the timber removed so that you undercut the edges to key in the filler. A small area of rot, only on the face of the skirting board, is unlikely to be dry rot and therefore the spongy material can be removed back to a hard edge. Treat the area with a hardener which is part of the wood repair kit. Mix the two component parts, the hardener and the resin, and work it well into the hole. Very slightly overfill so that when the repair is cured you can sand it flat. The filler material can be stained or painted to match the existing colour.

If the number of woodworm holes is small, they can be treated with a water-based eradicator which is safe to use in the house. If you see any fine dust, known as 'frass', this is a sign of activity in the woodworm fraternity! Obviously if the infestation is serious you can get advice either from your Local Council or from a specialist firm. DIY woodworm eradicators are available in all DIY stores. A tiny nozzle at the end of the applicator is inserted into the holes and the liquid injected to do its job!

Dado rails Apart from being a decorative feature around a room, a dado rail has two other functions: to prevent chair backs damaging decorations and as capping along the top of tongue and grooved panelling. Dado rails come in softwood and hardwood, simple and intricate mouldings. They were once fixed by drilling, plugging and screwing to the wall. Countersunk screws were either covered with a wooden plug or with proprietary wood filler, so it is often difficult to find exactly where a fixing is. Today a new system of fixing has been introduced using metal clips.

When a dado rail has come away from a plaster wall or needs replacing, solve the problem by fitting a new one. Fill the holes, sand smooth any ridges of old plaster and redecorate. Draw a level line to fit the replacement with secret nailing.

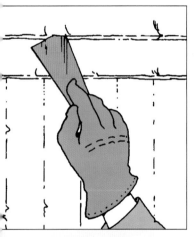

Repairing a dado rail
Prise off the old rail (never use a hammer and chisel!). Remove lines of old plaster with a scraper (not with a filling knife as this will hack out more plaster). Use plaster filler to finish the surface, smoothing it with a filling knife. Sand with a block. Stabilise with diluted PVA.

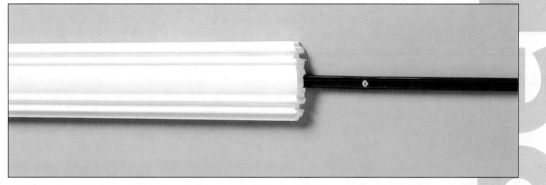

(1) Dado rails come in sections which are easily offered up to the rail and fixed in position. This is a simple DIY answer to the problem of attaching long wooden rails, whether they are dado or picture rails.

(2) The expertly machined rail is completely aligned to the preceding butt end as it is slid into position. The joint is indiscernible and remains so when the corner is fixed.

Take great care when prising a dado rail away from the wall. Use a block behind whatever tool you use so that you don't damage the plaster or decoration.

If for any reason you have to insert a new piece into an existing dado rail, there is a simple way of cutting out the damaged piece. Prise the piece away from the wall so that you can get two wooden wedges either side. Then cut out the damaged piece but cut at an angle of 45° with the slope in towards the back. This means that you can accurately cut a replacement part in a mitre box, or other mitring tool, to give an accurate fit. Before you take the wedges out clean out any loose plaster and dust so that you can apply an adhesive to reinstate the two cut pieces. Apply a wood adhesive to the chamfered ends but on the flat back of the replacement piece use a builder's adhesive from a cartridge gun. These new adhesives hold to most building materials. Now somehow you have to wedge a heavy weight against the repair, wedge a prop in between it and a solid surface. Drill or plug and screw into the centre of the repair to hold it firmly into position. Countersink the head of the screw and cover it with filler. You'll probably have to do a bit of sanding to remove the surplus glue and to get a neat finish. Repaint or stain to match the existing.

Loft hatches Joists, and especially those in attics, were covered in the opening para-graphs of this section. It is inadvisable to cut any joist without first consulting with an expert and getting sound advice. The reason is that you don't want to compromise the integrity of the structure of the roof. However, openings formed in the original structure to allow access to an attic void were designed to be structurally sound. You'll find that one joist has had a piece cut out, probably over a landing, about 750 mm (30 in) in length. The cut ends were then 'trimmed' to the joists either side. This simply means that timbers of the same section as the joists were cut to a tight fit and fixed to the ends of the cut joists and into the sides of the adjoining joists. The opening was usually formed of sawn timber, however the linings which were slightly deeper than the joists were fixed to the four sides and stops similar to door stops were fixed around about half way up. A hinged lid rested on these stops. Original flap doors are probably made from a quite heavy material.

Interestingly Victorian carpenters constructed special ladders with treads wider than an ordinary ladder to make it easier for walking up to the attic. Never ever try to balance on the top of a stepladder that is not long enough to make access easy and safe. Also, ordinary ladders have rungs that are not meant for indoor shoes adding to the difficulty of climbing up to the attic. To solve the problem it is worthwhile investigating the possibility of a collapsible loft

Form a new hatch opening by cutting a piece out of the joist, but compensate with 'trimmers' fixed to the cut ends and to the adjacent joists.

ladder. There are many manufacturers who make them to different specifications. Most are telescopic and can be housed out of sight in the attic above the hatch opening. They are sprung balanced so a gentle pull with the hook pole provided will extend it and you have easy access to a space that you can now exploit for storage. If you want to use the loft space for anything other than this you must tell the Planning Department of your Local Council about your proposal.

Most attics are thermally insulated with material between the joists but most hinged hatch doors are not. This means that a large amount of heat will be lost through the door. The hinged door does not have to be of a heavy material. It can be a single sheet of 12 mm (½ in) ply, which is not going to buckle. You can then glue to the back of it one solid piece of 5 cm (2 in) polystyrene insulating material which you can buy as a sandwich. The polystyrene needs to be tight to the lining so you can dispense with the hinges. A lightweight door can be easily pushed up and slid on to the floor. Before removing any hinges, mark the flap in position so that it goes into the same position minus the hinges.

Cutting mitres

There is only one neat way of joining two pieces of wood to form a right angle without seeing a joint on the sides of the timber and that is by mitring. Mitring means that you make a cut at 45° on both pieces of timber so that they form an exact square or right-angled corner. The corners of a picture frame are perfect examples of mitre jointing. From early days carpenters made their own mitre boxes with three pieces of timber fixed together to make a U-shape. Then they accurately cut straight across the two uprights at right angles, almost to the base timber. With the piece of timber to be cut held tightly against the base and the saw in the slots, it was then easy to cut at 90°. To get the 45° cuts they then made equal cuts either side of the 90° cut. This then allowed them to cut timbers fairly accurately to form a mitre joint. The method, however, limited them to cutting timber the height of the box and of course to its width.

A hand-operated compound mitre saw can cut timber at many angles and with great accuracy. The saw is quite long and operates in metal guides which increase its accuracy. Another useful tool is the mitre guide. This is particularly useful because one can cut wide planks of wood, not only at 45° but to any set angle. A metal swivel upright with a precise slot to hold a backless tenon saw is fixed to a base plate. This is attached to the timber so that it doesn't move. Swivel the cutting guide to the desired angle, tighten the guide screw and you can cut timber as wide as the saw is long.

A proprietary jig can be bought which is simply a metal base with holes on the surface that takes nylon rods. These, in turn, hold the wood in position for sawing through the metal guides. You actually alter the position of the wood and not the saw to get your different angles.

Nowadays, you can buy a sophisticated mitre cutting device, discussed in a previous section, which can replicate any angle, internal or external, to be cut with the hard back saw provided with the kit. It has a hinged template which is held first of all against the wall and locked in position at that angle. Two arms are then located on to the moveable jig which is locked off. You'll get a professional finish every time so you can throw away the filler!

Board the ceiling with plasterboards after cutting through a ceiling joist to form a hatch and lining the inside of the hatch with prepared timber. The liners should be proud of the joists by the combined thickness of the board and the plaster skim.

Worm, rot and damp

Worm

It has been estimated that up to half the houses in the UK are affected to some extent by woodworm, even if it is only brought in in furniture bought from an antique shop. The tell-tale signs of woodworm are tiny holes surrounded by wood dust. Woodworm can cause a great deal of damage to the timber in any house, so you've got to make regularly inspections to check for signs of attack. Carry out any necessary treatment as soon as you discover any trouble because you wait at your peril! In older houses check particularly in attics. If you find widespread attacks in structural timbers, you must consult with a wood preservation company. Estimates for treating woodworm are usually free and any treatment carried out is given a 20–30 year guarantee. However, if there is only superficial damage to the surface of timbers, the affected area can be removed and the new timber and its surrounding area treated with a proprietary woodworm fluid. A number of insecticides and fluids, specially formulated for this problem, are sold in all DIY stores. If you have a largish area to cover use a spray. A pump action garden sprayer that holds three or four litres (five or seven pints) and has a long probe is ideal to give a coarse spray to cover a wide area. To reach difficult corners you might need an extension lance. The manufacturers will provide specifications and recommendations for the use of their product but it is essential to saturate all the joints, crevices and end grain surfaces and to extend beyond what is the apparent edge of the infestation. Don't use a fine nozzle because the liquid may vaporise to float in the air and not do its work. And be very careful not to drench the area, the fluid could run down timbers to soak and stain the ceiling below.

Woodworm treatment
After about three years boring through timber, the grub eventually emerges as an adult beetle (as shown much magnified in the drawing). The holes will be clearly visible. DIY applications are available for minor attacks.

Woodworm have a life cycle during which the grubs make a tunnel through the wood and emerge through exit holes (or flight holes) after two or three years as fully grown adults. You can treat the infested area at any time of the year. Always wear protective clothing, a fume mask and protective spectacles. Professionals I know always rub barrier cream on any exposed skin and wear leather gloves because they know that rubber can possibly be damaged by the fluid.

It is normally only necessary to surface spray furniture that has a minor attack of woodworm. Softwood furniture does not necessarily need to have the fluid injected into the flight holes. However, do use the injector and the fine nozzle for any affected hardwood furniture which will benefit from the extra penetration achieved by injection. You don't need to do every hole because you can get the best results by injecting about every 8–10 cm (3–4 in). Treat the insides of drawers and the backs, feet and undersides of furniture, paying special attention to the area around joints. Plywood is very susceptible to woodworm attack so the back panels of older wardrobes and cupboards need to be looked at very carefully. Furniture that has been treated can be kept free from further attack by applying an anti-woodworm polish. This can also be applied to the insides of drawers and the backs of wardrobes to provide added protection. Keep checking any areas where you've had a problem to make sure that you've killed off eggs and grubs. The following year you might just find a small attack again, because some grubs have dodged your treatment, but treating areas again in early summer should solve the problem.

Specialist treatment   If woodworm infestation requires specialist treatment, approach two or three companies to obtain estimates and specifications to compare. The estimates will arrive with full recommendations for necessary treatment. The specialist company will locate every source of infestation and flood it with an insecticide. They will inspect roof timbers, and if these are covered they will expose them to inspect the structural timbers. They will check under stairs and lift floorboards to examine between the joists. They will also inspect all vulnerable furniture, especially unpainted furniture, and if there is a cellar they will look at all the timbers there as well. You will be told which structural timbers have been permanently damaged and given their recommendations regarding the replacement of those timbers. On the other hand, they might only suggest that the affected timbers are strengthened.

If a lot of wood needs spraying, the area will have to be cleared as much as possible. All insulation material will have to be moved to expose the timbers. Importantly any cold water storage tanks will have to have total protection to prevent contamination of your water supply to bath and handbasins. Water tanks are often insulated with expanded polystyrene and this, too, will have to be protected. Polystyrene and rubber can disintegrate if sprayed with the insecticide. Joists at the eaves cannot be reached by spray, so the specialist team will use a deep penetration paste which will be absorbed by the end grain of the timber.

If floors need treatment, you will find that they lift every fourth or fifth board in order that the lance at the end of their spray hose can reach every part of the undersides of all the boards and the sides of the joists. Once the boards are replaced the top surface is then treated. It will take at least a week for the insecticide to dry but quicker if there is a movement of air through the house. You'll have to wait before the floor coverings can be replaced!

Remember, the specialist team will need to look at all the timber in the area where there is a woodworm attack. If in a floor, for example, they will look underneath a door to see if it has been protected by paint. Now that you've got the general picture, you can relate this to any other part of the house where you might have an infestation and realise that it is quite a major event to overcome this problem using a specialist firm. However they do provide a guarantee, and just as importantly, you will have peace of mind.

Mould

Fungal attack The experts say that it is the relative humidity that determines whether mould grows and wood decays. It sounds simple? Well, it is really if you think in terms of keeping your house warm and dry with no condensation to feed the spores which are ever present. Mould will only develop if spores are allowed to feed in warm, damp conditions. Tiny black specks first appear and these join to form the nasty black mould which we hate! We don't like it because the development of mould can have an adverse effect not only on the structure of our homes but on our health too.

Condensation occurs when warm moist air meets a cold surface, and the levels depend on how moist the air is and on how cold the surface of the building is. So you have to prevent moist air spreading to other rooms, from, say, the kitchen and bathroom, and then provide ventilation to those rooms and use heating sensibly. Boiling potatoes in the kitchen produces an enormous amount of moisture. If the kitchen door is left open, the moisture permeates the rest of the house. The secret is to leave windows open (or to have an electric extractor fan working) but to keep doors closed. Some parents tell their children, after a bath open the door, don't let the bathroom steam up! It's a mistake. A shout goes to the person who is drying clothes, 'Leave the door open, the room is steaming up!', but that too will cause condensation and damp problems throughout the house.

In older houses ventilation occurs naturally through fireplace flues and draughty windows. It is uncomfortable in cold weather to have too much ventilation and it also wastes heat, but some ventilation is absolutely essential both for the fabric of your house and your health. Modern flats with double glazing, and housing with up-to-date and complete draught proofing, will certainly suffer from insufficient ventilation. Ventilation in your home is essential for a reasonable time each day and for nearly all the time that a room is in use.

Walls that have suffered a breakdown of the damp-proof-course (DPC), or where there has never been a DPC, will have signs of rising damp. A tidemark can creep as high as 6 ft in a porous wall on damp ground. A silicone liquid can be injected to solve the problem.

It has been worked out scientifically that condensation is produced in frightening amounts when a portable paraffin or flueless gas heater is used. For each litre of fuel used, the equivalent of about a litre of liquid water in the form of water vapour is produced to spread around the house. Airing cupboards can also be a problem unless they are properly ventilated. Homes left unoccupied and unheated during the day get very cold. If possible it really is best to keep some heating on, even at the lowest level. It takes a long time for floors and particularly walls to warm up, so remember that it is better to have a small amount of heat on for a long period than to have short bursts of whole heat. In bungalows and flats that have a lot of outside wall area, condensation is a very likely hazard. It is very useful to have an inexpensive thermometer to check temperature levels in various rooms. Even if your home is well insulated and has reasonable ventilation, it is best to keep all the rooms at not less than 10°C (50°F) during cold weather in order to avoid condensation. When rooms are in use their temperature should be about 20°C (68°F).

If you spot any sign of mould growth, you will need to solve the condensation problem. Heating, structural insulation, ventilation, or all three, will need your DIY expertise. Extra heat and ventilation is called for during new building work of brick or stone. Plaster, especially, takes a long time to dry out and litres of water vapour from a newly plastered room will spread around the house. Consider hiring a dehumidifier which will extract the condensation and moisture from the air and convert it to water. This is discharged through the machine into a bucket. You'll be amazed how quickly the bucket fill up!

It is essential to have a constant air supply in any room with a gas or solid fuel appliance. If you propose to fit an extractor fan, or to change the ventilation in that room in any way at all, obtain advice from a professional, that is the Gas Board or the Solid Fuel Advisory Service. You need to know about the risks of drawing toxic fumes back into the room.

A powerful fungicidal solution, preferably with detergent properties, is needed to clear black mould, mildew and other fungi from interior surfaces and leave them clean and free from contamination. Look for a product which has been tested by the Department of Environment Research Establishment. For hard and non-porous surfaces such as tiles, use a clean cloth, well damped with fungicidal wash, to wipe away all traces of mould. Continue the cleaning and rinsing process, working in an area of about a square metre (square yard) at a time. Finally, leave a film of the fungicidal solution on the surface to protect against recontamination. Allow the film to dry overnight. The instructions on the container will tell you that it is not a primary skin irritant but sensible precautions must obviously be taken during use.

Mould on wallpaper can be treated by applying a low-cost acrylic clear emulsion which can be used on most paper finishes. It dries in just two hours to a clear, semi-matt, colourless film. It will also give long-term protection against further mould attack and can be used as a fungicidal sealer prior to any wallpapering. This clear emulsion, properly prepared and applied, is durable and fully washable so it can be applied to most surfaces to give protection. You can even use it outside your home to clean and protect exterior decorations in areas worst affected by mould and growth.

Restoration If you have mould in a localised area, say between the edge of the bath and the wall tiles, there is an alternative treatment. Make a solution of diluted bleach, one part of bleach to twelve parts of water. As usual, use gloves and take all other precautions. Leave the solution on for half a day, then the mould should come away quite easily. It is a growing organism so you'll need to wrap it in newspaper and burn it. Apply a second solution and leave it overnight. This will sterilise the area but you'll need to neutralise it with plenty of running water. If mould has affected the grout lines between the tiles, apply the same solution but leave it for a shorter time. Alternatively, there is a grout removal tool which will take away the mould at the same time. Yet another treatment for use after you have regrouted between the tiles is a proprietary grout revival product which comes in a squeezy container with a felt applicator. Simply squeeze the bottle and apply the solution to the grout line and leave overnight. The liquid will penetrate the grout to form an impervious seal but it will wash off from the tiles. It also has an anti-fungicidal compound to prevent further contamination.

You might want to remove the silicone sealant from around the bath if it is so badly affected that it's going to take many successive treatments. To do this you will need a bathroom sealant kit that has a scraping tool for removing the old sealant. Alternatively, apply a sealant remover over the length of the silicone sealant. This begins to work immediately. It destroys the sealant's adhesive qualities between the tiles and the bath so makes it easier to peel off. When you reseal and, in fact, when you regrout, always use products that have anti-fungicidal properties in them.

Mould on chimney breasts is usually caused by condensation within the flue. Once you've eradicated the cause of the damp, you need to tackle the mould which has crept through the brickwork and on to the decorations. Hopefully, it has occurred only in a small area so you can hack off the plaster which will only be about 18mm (¾in) thick. Patch plaster, as described in the section on 'Plastering', before applying the new one-coat plaster. Liberally paint on an anti-fungicidal solution. Allow it to dry before proceeding. Make good the patch before stabilising with a PVA solution. Let it dry completely and then paint or paper to match. An alternative is to clean off the chimney breast back to the plaster, then cover the chimney breast using rolls of foil instead of wallpaper. Hang this with a paste and pasting brush just like wallpapering. Add a layer of lining paper and then either paint or wallpaper to match.

Wet rot

Identification Wet rot is caused by a combination of dampness and lack of ventila-

tion, so, when you think of it, wood that has not been totally protected can be liable to it. Wet rot is almost certainly restricted to wet timber. Think of the areas that could be subject to wet rot in and around your house: the roof, the attic, bathrooms, kitchens, certainly cellars, fence posts, garages and wooden sheds. One problem associated with spotting wet rot is that all the damage may be taking place under what appears to be a sound surface. The bottom of an outside door post might just have the signs of cracking paint. Check it with a sharp knife and you might find that the skin of paint collapses and you discover crumbling timber underneath. A post which has been installed when still damp, subjected to rain and then painted before it dried out, has been subjected to the conditions under which wet rot will survive and demolish timber.

Wet rot is revealed in its early stages by discolouration around decayed wood. You'll see yellowish-brown streaks or patches which later on becomes lighter in weight and brownish-black in appearance. Fungal strands may grow in a fern-like shape on the surface of the timber and often a thin, olive-green fungus is seen. As the wood dries it will shrink and crack along the grain. Often there is cross-cracking resembling cubes and, in very bad cases, the wood will crumble between your fingers.

Removal of timbers Once you have recognised the presence and extent of the wet rot problem in your home, you now have to take appropriate action. That means cutting out and replacing the damaged timber! Of course you have to correct the cause of the damage but first apply a fungicide over the whole area. Once you've identified the central part of the area check all the timber around it to a distance of 2m (6ft). It's as well to look at the plaster, masonry and building materials because you might find evidence of decay and spreading which will have to be dealt with at the same time. You have to take a tough line here and cut away all timber showing signs of attack and go beyond the centre of the attack, but obviously you must make sure you are not weakening any other part of the building.

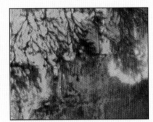

Wet rot fungus mycelium on the surface of damp brickwork, caused by being soaked in water. Cut away the rot to good wood, burn the rotten material, treat the whole area and renew with treated timber.

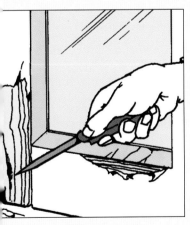

Identifying wet rot
Wet rot is a form of decay prevalent in damp climates. It develops from fungal spores carried into cracks and open joints in timber, and thrives on damp from rain and condensation. Flaking paint and cracked putty are sure signs of potential problems. Probe with a screwdriver for soft timber.

Treating wet rot
Use a three-part DIY treatment. Rake out the soft timber, apply the hardener and fill with the two-part cellulose filler after inserting wood preservative pellets into drilled holes. The pellets will slowly be absorbed by the surrounding timber to give protection from further attacks.

Dry rot is the most insidious of all fungi and should be treated immediately it is discovered. This shows a typical neglected area, where dry rot has been allowed to spread. The fungus (Serpula lacrymans) attacks and weakens floor timbers. The red fruiting bodies make the spores that are released into the atmosphere. Call in a specialist firm.

Once you've corrected the cause of the dampness you can start the next part of the treatment. You must allow the timber to thoroughly dry out and only then will the fungus die off. That's very important to remember! Once you've cleared the crumbling timber, prod all the surrounding timber with a sharp knife until you detect sound timber. You must collect all the attacked timber, dirt and debris, and burn it. And, of course, when replacing timber remember to use well-seasoned and pressure treated wood.

Cut the replacement timber to size but before you fix it in place, because you've exposed new wood, give it a generous coat of a proprietary wood preservative, even though it has been pretreated, and then treat all adjacent timber and even bricks, concrete and block, with a good coating as well. The ends of timbers that are hidden, for example, the ends of joists being replaced, should be painted with bituminous paint. To replaster any damaged wall areas you must finish with anhydrous wall finish plaster.

Preservation Now that you've seen how wet rot can hide and grow insidiously behind a coat of gleaming paint or in a quiet unobserved corner, I am sure you'll be ready to pounce on any suspect area with the tiniest crack. But because you are now aware that wet rot develops only under certain conditions, you'll be more vigilant and help your house from further attack by a preservation treatment.

Spray a fungicide in and around all the area that you have reinstated in order to sterilise it. Lightly spray all walls, partitions, sleeper walls, concrete, remaining timber, even steel and pipework, within a radius of 2 m (6 ft) from the furthest extent of what was the infection. Check any tiny cracks and if you find any signs of wet rot, kill it before it spreads! So, for example, if paint on a wooden windowsill has the tiniest amount of rot, hack it out, use a wood hardener, backfill with a wood filler treatment, wait for it and the surrounding wood to dry completely, and then begin the sterilisation process for the preservation of the area as you did before.

Dry rot

Dry rot is insidious. Damp, dark areas, cellars or underneath stairs are the perfect environments for dry rot to spread. Dry rot hates daylight and turns bright yellow if it comes into contact with it. A treacherous fungus grows on damp wood and then spreads, if not destroyed, throughout the whole building. The first sign is a covering of matted fungal strands spreading on the surface of timber and even into walls. The strands have a silvery-grey appearance and some have splodges of purple or yellow. Dry rot grows very quickly to takes on the appearance of cotton wool. It eats in and around the wood which then takes on a darker colour but becomes lighter in weight and will even crumble between fingers.

If you see a mushroom-like growth, called a fruiting body, you'll know that this is an advanced case. It will be pale grey in colour but white around the edges. In fact it does have a strong mushroom smell and can send out a covering of rust coloured spore dust. This is awful and a hazard to the respiratory system and so to one's health. You might also see pencil thick water-carrying roots which send out more roots going further afield, even through walls, to find timber elsewhere on which to feed. Every part of the house has to be examined, even chimneys, rain water pipes, pointing, rendering (especially if it's blown or cracked), and masonry. If you haven't checked the air vents below the level of the ground floor, now is the time to do it and clear them if they are blocked. Look for damp patches on walls inside the house because this might indicate that the damp proof course has broken down and damp is getting to the timbers beneath the ground floor. You must lift some floorboards near the source of damp to check for discoloration of timber and the finger-like strands travelling across joists. Anywhere that you find mushroom-like fruiting bodies or spore dust, call in a specialist firm. It does mean that it has been there some time and has travelled considerably.

Central heating

Radiators

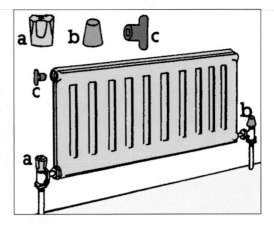

Radiators
The control wheel (a) opens and closes the control valve at the inlet side of the radiator. The plastic cover (b) on the locking valve can be pulled off so that the control wheel can be used to open or close the locking valve. If part of a radiator is cold it is probably due to an air pocket. Air can be released by opening the bleed valve at the top with a special radiator key (c).

Cold spots A cool patch in the centre of an otherwise warm radiator can only happen in a system that has been running for some time. A chemical reaction takes place within the system between the water, copper pipework and steel radiators. This produces deposits of corrosion at the bottom of the radiators in the form of a black sludge. The longer the system has been running with no protection from corrosion, the heavier the deposits will be. The water circulation in the radiators is restricted which in turn produces the cool and warm patches. This is a problem that can be solved by introducing a proprietary corrosion inhibitor to the water. Do it as soon as you spot the symptoms because if it is allowed to build up, the sludge can clog the pump and reduce the heat output of the radiators by partially blocking them.

Glue foil to a piece of card and pop it behind a radiator to reflect heat to the room.

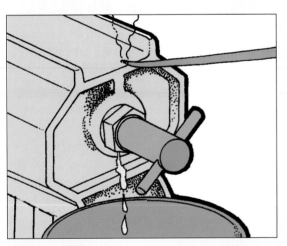

Venting a radiator
An airlock in a radiator will prevent the water circulating properly. You can rid a radiator of an airlock by turning a key (supplied with the radiator) in the bleed valve. If you find that you need to do this frequently it is probably because of corrosion within the system. Make a simple test before adding a special solvent to remove possible sludge. Taking all the necessary safety precautions, hold a lighted taper in the air escaping from the valve. Hydrogen is produced when corrosion takes place so you'll get a blue flame if it is present.

When a central-heating system is first installed, an inhibitor should be introduced following the manufacturer's instructions. It is so simple to do at that stage by pouring the liquid into the water tank and allowing it to circulate in the system. However, it is not too late to add it at a later date, provided the system is still operating! The instructions will tell you all you need to know about draining and refilling the system. If you are getting cool patches in more than one radiator you will need to drain the entire system (see the section entitled 'Fitting thermostatically controlled valves') by draining and refilling repeatedly until the water runs clean from the hose into the gully. If, however, the problem is slight and only one radiator is affected, then all you need to do is to drain off enough water to empty the feed and expansion tank and some water from the pipework. Drain about 23 litres (5 gallons). The manufacturer's instructions will tell you to pour the inhibitor (about 5 litres (1 gallon)) for most systems but the amount will depend on the size of your boiler and the type of system) into the tank and to restore the water supply.

When you switch on the circulating pump once again, the inhibitor will be distributed throughout the pipework and the radiators, and the protection process will have started! It is now worth going round each radiator in turn checking that there is no air left in them by using the vent (bleed) key and that there are no leaks anywhere. If there are, make the necessary adjustments. Finally, check that the draincocks are closed.

Fitting thermostatically controlled valves
In the UK the majority of owner-occupied homes have a central-heating system. At some time, a high percentage of homeowners are likely to be confronted with a central-heating problem which can be solved by a competent DIYer. The common faults that occur in a gas- or oil-fired central-heating system should not require the services of an engineer to put them right. If, however, it is a gas-related problem then it is your statutory obligation to call in a Corgi-registered engineer.

We all know and appreciate the comfort that a central-heating system gives us. We should also be fully aware of how the system operates. When it is needed, water is heated in the boiler, flows around the system, through the radiators and returns to the boiler to be reheated. A small, silent electric pump ensures that the water continues to flow steadily and evenly. An electrically controlled room thermostat senses the temperature of the room and controls the output of heat in the system. Each central-heating system has to be separately designed. A heating engineer has to take into account the heating needs of each part of the house and the rate at which the heat is lost from the building. Obviously the construction of walls, floors and ceilings, and the insulation in them, are important factors. The temperature to which each part of the house is to be heated must also be taken into account. The required radiator sizes and boiler can then be determined.

The addition of thermostats, a zone controller and a temperature/time programmer means that you can have a high level of control over where you want the heat and when you want it. Unfortunately, many older central-heating systems were installed with just one room thermostat, usually located in the hall. This means that there is no separate control on individual radiators, but, depending on circumstances, it is sometimes necessary to lower the heat in one room, whilst boosting it in another. Now, with step-by-step guidance and an inexpensive thermostatic radiator valve (TRV) this problem is

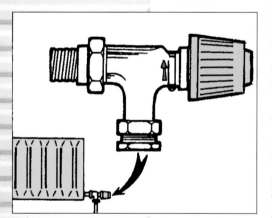

Heating – radiators

Thermostatically controlled radiator valves automatically and reliably keep a room at a set temperature and can save fuel. They must only be connected to the flow connection. To check which this is, start the system from cold by turning off all the radiators. Turn on each radiator in turn and note which connection warms up first. This is the flow pipe.

easily solved! This is one of the easiest of DIY jobs. No solder or heat is necessary, only spanners for the compression joints on the radiators. The TRV must be fitted to the flow inlet side of the radiator. This is often the side with the 'on/off' turning wheel but it is not always the case so you should do a 'warm pipe' test – turn on the radiator, from cold, to find out which pipe gets warm first. Simple isn't it? Most radiators are fitted with two valves, one called a hand wheel or control valve and the other a locked valve or locked shield valve. At the top of the radiator is a vent (bleed) valve which can be opened to release air trapped in the system.

Now turn off the central-heating system because you will need to drain it. Locate the drainage valve, which is located at the lowest point in the system.

If you suck water into a straw and put your finger over the top of the straw, the water will be held in the straw and will not flow through the open bottom end! Something similar can happen when you try to drain a central-heating system because air cannot enter the radiators preventing the water from escaping. You will need to break the seal by opening the radiator bleed valves to allow air to enter as the water drains out. Start at the top of the house and work downwards in the system, opening each of the vent valves in turn. Allow time for the water to drain away. Check outside at the gully to see when the water stops flowing.

In some houses with solid concrete floors, it might have been necessary to loop pipes up and over door openings creating what are now called 'inverted pipe loops'. If you find one in your house you'll find that it also has its own draincock. These must be drained separately after the water has stopped flowing from the main system.

You'll need to choose the TRV to suit your particular system. Check the size of pipe (it is probably the standard 12 mm (½ in)) and whether you've got a one-pipe or a two-pipe system. Now comes the interesting part – fitting the TRV. Make sure that you read and follow the manufacturer's instructions, but basically all you need to do is remove the control valve (by undoing two compression nuts and lifting it off) and replace it with the TRV. You won't need any force to remove the control valve but make sure that you support pipework so that there is no risk of joints being forced apart below the floorboards. A small threaded joint (the union tail) is now left in the radiator. Unscrew this and remove it, using a spanner with a square shank or the squared end of a pair of pliers, and replace it with the new one that comes in the TRV package. Before fitting, wind some plumber's joint sealing tape (PTFE tape) on to the thread making sure that it runs in the same direction as the thread. This helps to make a watertight seal. As part of the compression joint on the original control valve, you'll see a tight copper ring (olive) left on the pipe itself. The instructions will ask you to cut the pipe just below that ring and clean the pipe (especially of paint). Drop the new nut over the pipe, then the new olive and add a smear of sealing compound around it.

The new valve can be very simply fitted in place. Don't over-tighten the nuts because any leaks encountered when the system is refilled can be overcome by tightening them a little. Remove the green cap, but keep it safe to fully shut off the radiator in the future. You'll find a sensor which simply pushes on to the valve body, make sure that the marker points upwards, then just tighten the adjusting band. Having accomplished what might have seemed a daunting task, sit down, have a cup of tea and go through the instruction leaflet again. You now have a better understanding of how to fit a TRV so the installation of the others will be easier. When you've finished take away the hosepipe and close the draincock, and in sequence, go to each radiator and check that you've tightened all the nuts and closed each air vent valve. Now restore the water supply to the feed and expansion tank in the attic. As the radiators fill up, air will be trapped in the tops. Wait until the water stops running and then, starting at the bottom of the house this time, open the air vent valve in each radiator in turn. Hold a rag against the valve key and when all the air has

escaped and all the hissing has stopped, signs of water will appear. Now close the valve.

Allow the system to warm up before making a final check of all the draincocks and air vent valves for signs of leaking. Gently tighten where necessary, and I mean gently as that's all you'll need. A simple but very effective test for leaks is to put your finger underneath the joint and if there is a leak the tip of your finger will glisten. Leave the pump running for a while before checking that all radiators are warming up.

Now you have full control of every radiator adding to everybody's comfort in the home! The thermostats automatically and reliably keep the room temperatures to the level of comfort that each individual wants. A simple adjustment of the easily read calibrations on the thermostat will allow a change of setting and temperature.

Another advantage of TRVs is that you will save fuel by bringing your central-heating system under complete control – a Department of Energy recommendation. This will obviously save on costs too. It is claimed each 1°C reduction of the temperature of the home will take eight per cent off your heating bill. Radiator thermostats also prevent over-heating by automatically regulating the room temperature to the level that you set. Another interesting factor is what is called 'free heat gain'. Having a thermostat in every room enables one to save fuel by utilising this free heat gain from sources such as sunshine, domestic appliances and even people!

A leaking radiator requires drastic action. If a spot of rust is seen, remove the rust back to clean metal. Apply rust-resistant primer and matching paint.

Joints

Fortunately all new houses built these days will have a central-heating system installed. New owners of unmodernised Victorian houses in which central heating has not yet been installed will soon discover how chilly the interior can be. In homes in the UK where central heating has been installed, it will probably be one of two types, either a 'wet' or a 'dry' system, and it will be of a type that is easy to install and to maintain. The wet system is very simple in that it has one central boiler to which is connected inlet and outlet water pipes and a source of energy, that is, heat. This can be either solid fuel, electricity or gas. A pump circulates the heated water through pipes to each radiator in the system. It is, in fact, a continuous circle because the water circulates throughout the system and is pumped back to the boiler for reheating.

A dry central-heating system is different in that rooms are warmed by heated air being ducted to each room. Typically this type of installations is found in blocks of flats, large office buildings and institutions. We also class electric storage heaters and underfloor heating as central heating, although, in these cases, there is no one central source, for example, a boiler, to provide the heat for those systems.

A more expensive central-heating system, which requires specialist installation, is the 'sealed' system. As the name suggests the system is totally sealed so there is no expansion tank to supply water to top up and there can be no corrosion problems. As the system is totally watertight, special components, like a safety valve, an air release valve, an expansion container and a filling system with a non-return valve, are essential and why this system calls for specialist engineers.

So let's deal with what the majority of people have as a central-heating system: the wet system. Now comes another consideration. Is the system a 'one-pipe' system or a 'two-pipe' system. In the one-pipe (or single pipe) system water flows from the boiler through one pipe

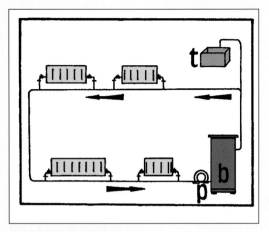

One-pipe heating system
The sketch shows a one-pipe 'wet' central heating system. The arrows indicate the direction of hot water flow from the boiler (b). The pump (p) can be located either side of the boiler but the feed pipe must also continue up and over the tank (t) to discharge any hot water that builds up excessively. This is the safety factor in this type of system where a vent pipe is open to discharge expansion of hot water due to over-heating. Note that the flow and return pipes of each radiator are connected to the same pipe, hence 'one-pipe' system.

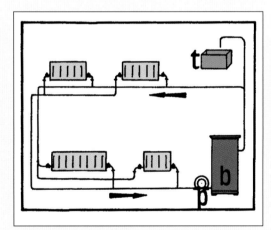

Two-pipe heating system
Water is heated in the boiler (b) and forced by the pump (p) through the pipes to all the radiators before it is returned to the boiler for reheating. The tank (t) keeps the system topped up and safely takes any expansion of water through the open vent pipe. Note that the hot water flows along one pipe and into each radiator but is returned to be reheated through a separate pipe, hence 'two-pipe' system.

only and back to the boiler to be reheated. On its way around the pipe the hot water is diverted into and out from radiators. In theory the last radiator in the circuit is going to be cooler but there are sophisticated controls which can be installed in the system to alleviate this problem. The two-pipe system has a flow pipe from the boiler taking the hot water to the radiators. A separate return pipe takes the cooled water from each radiator back to the boiler. High technology controls, by way of thermostats, zone controllers and programmers, mean that you have a higher level of automatic control over where you want the heat and when.

Because water is flowing past so many joints in the system it is possible, due to vibration and contaminants, for leaks to occur. The three most common forms of 'connectors' in a system are (a) a compression joint, where a nut has to be turned with a spanner to compress a small ring of copper (the olive) making a watertight seal; (b) a 'capillary' joint, where heat is applied to melt solder which then solidifies when it's cooled to form a watertight joint; and (c) the 'push-fit' connector for use with copper pipes and plastic pipes.

Unless a leak is very obvious, one sure way of detecting a leak in a joint is to place your finger underneath the joint, wait a couple of seconds then look for signs of moisture. No shine means no leak! However should there be a leak, a repair can be made quite simply depending on its location and the type of joint. The ease at which the repair can be made also depends on how easy it is to isolate the joint. This means turning off the water supply. A compression joint is the easiest, because you simply undo it, wrap PTFE tape (plumbers' sealing tape) around the thread and retighten. A capillary joint needs heat to soften and loosen the joint, and then it has to be resoldered. It's always best, in this instance, to clean up both ends of the copper, using flux and solder, following the instructions on the flux container, to produce a new joint. A push-fit connector is unlikely to leak, however if it does there is no option but to change it and install a new one.

Panel radiator and brackets

By closing both valves it is possible to undo the compression joints and lift the radiator off its brackets.

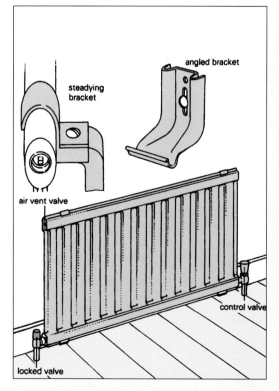

angled bracket

steadying bracket

air vent valve

control valve

locked valve

Sludge

If a chemical reaction has taken place within the central-heating system and one radiator has a cool patch in the centre of it, this indicates the presence of sludge at the bottom of the radiator. To remove the radiator and drain the sludge is not a difficult job but it does require two people. First close the control valve by turning the plastic control wheel clockwise. The central holding screw can then be released to lift off the control wheel. The plastic cover on the locking valve at the other end of the radiator can now be pulled off and the control wheel pushed on in its place. Use it to turn off the locking valve. It is important to count the number of turns required to close the locking valve. The same number of reverse turns will be needed to open it later on because the radiator was at one time correctly balanced and it needs to be set again. A pipe wrench or an adjustable spanner can be used to gently turn the large compression nut holding the control valve to the radiator. Once you've opened the vent at the top of the radiator with the special square key, water will begin to drain off. You can now control the flow of water by opening and closing the vent. Prop something underneath the radiator to support the valve and the copper pipe to prevent distortion. Otherwise your able helper can do this! It doesn't take long for the water to drain off. Leave the vent open and when the water has stopped running, turn your attention to the valve at the other end of the radiator. This is the locked valve. Release the compression nut completely. Some water might still flow out, so be ready with your container.

With the radiator still supported, disconnect the control valve completely and spring out the valves from the radiator to lift it off its brackets. You'll need to be very quick with the rags because you have to cover both holes whilst carrying the radiator outside. Take great care because the sludge can permanently stain the carpet! With a hosepipe in one end and the outlet over a gully, flush it out until water runs clear. If a great deal of black sludge is present ask at your DIY store for a corrosion inhibitor.

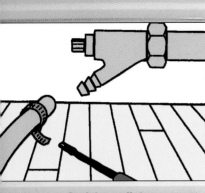

Draining radiators

After the system has cooled down, switch off the pump and turn off the water supply to the feed and expansion tank. Now drain the system. The main draincock is located at the lowest point of the system near to the boiler. Tighten one end of a garden hose onto the outlet of the draincock and run the other end to a gully outside. Open the draincock with a special key or wrench. As the water runs away, open each of the radiator bleed valves, starting at the top of the house, to prevent water being kept back in the radiators.

Full instructions on introducing this into the system are supplied with it.

To refit the radiator, first clean out the couplings in the valves and on the radiator to remove any debris that might be left behind. Gently lift the radiator back on to the brackets and check with your partner that it is sitting properly and that the valves are exactly in line with the compression joint. Tighten each nut by hand, then use an adjustable spanner. Remember at all times to support the valves and pipework as if it is not in line you could end up with leaks. Now open the control valve which allows the radiator to fill. Open the vent a little and you will hear air being expelled as the radiator fills. It's best to hold a rag to the vent until the air is expelled and a little water is seen. Close the vent and open the locked valve to get the warm water circulating. Have you remembered about the number of turns? Look at your notes and open with the same number of turns used to close it previously. This time use the finger test for leaks on the joints. If there's any trace of moisture on your fingertips, gently tighten the compression nuts and check again.

Draining and refilling

Draining   There is another reason for draining the system. If you leave your house for any length of time, especially during winter, it is advisable to drain the central-heating system. The boiler and radiators are supplied with water from the expansion tank. Therefore if you stop the supply to the expansion tank, you can drain all the water out of the system. The means of escape for the water in the system is always at its lowest point. Either you'll find a draincock at the base of the boiler or you will see that one has been provided at the lowest point of the run inside or outside the house. If it's outside the house, make sure that the water has a clear run to a gully.

Find the expansion tank which will probably be high up in the attic. Turn off its stopcock, which will shut off the supply of mains water to the tank. Then go to the draincock. If it's inside the house, you'll find it has a hosepipe connector as part of it. Insert the end of a hose into a jubilee clip before pushing it on to the hose connector. Tighten the jubilee clip to prevent accidents as the hose takes the water to the nearest gully. Turn on the draincock and wait until the system drains out. This will take a little time. You can seal off any switches to the central-heating system with sticky tape. Make a note of what you have done, so that when you have to refill the system you do things in reverse order.

If you're not sure about the stopcock to the expansion tank, you can always tie up the ball-cock so that it won't drop with the water level. This means that you've effectively stopped the water entering the tank and, as a consequence, the system. If the central-heating system has been on allow the water in the system to cool

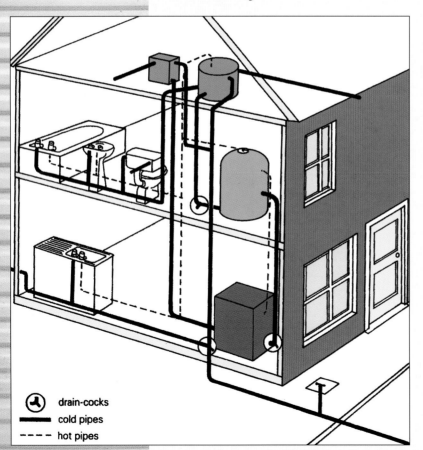

drain-cocks
cold pipes
- - - - hot pipes

Draining a central-heating system

If you leave the house for any length of time, especially in winter, it is advisable to drain the central-heating system. The boiler and radiators are supplied with water from an expansion tank. By stopping the supply to the expansion tank you can successfully drain the whole system. The draincock is always at the lowest point in the pipe run.

At the lowest point in the pipe run of a central-heating system you will find a drain-off valve, useful when for any reason the whole system has to be drained down. Attach a hose, open the valve, then open the air vents on each radiator.

If an old stove works well using smokeless fuel and it has a back boiler to supply hot water, there is no need to dump it! This one has been in use for more than 70 years and still provides radiant heat and comfort in a kitchen/ dining room.

before opening the draincock. One more thing – you have to turn off the pump before opening the draincock. To turn the square shank on the draincock use the key that came with your system, or simply use an adjustable spanner.

So that the water flows out of the system you will have to allow air to enter it. All you do is allow air to enter the tops of each radiator by carefully opening the radiator air vent (bleed) valves. These vent valves are easily controlled with a small square key. Start at the top of the house. As you work downwards in the system, opening each of the air vent valves, allow time for the water to drain away. Check outside at the gully to see when the water has stopped flowing.

Sometimes central-heating designers met what seemed to be an insurmountable problem where solid concrete floors were already laid in a house. In many cases, the problem of running a pipe across a door opening has been solved by looping it over the top. This creates what is called an 'inverted pipe-loop'. This creates its own problem, but the drainage of each loop was simplified by providing it with its own draincock. This must be drained separately after the water has stopped flowing from the main system.

Refilling Restore the water supply to the feed and expansion tank in the attic by either untying the ballcock arm or by undoing the stopcock. Having checked that all the vent valves are closed and that the draincock is also closed, you have to start your checks at the bottom of the house. Starting at the lowest radiator open the air vent valve a little to expel the air that is inevitably drawn into the system when it has been drained. Open each air vent valve on each radiator in turn. Hold a rag against the valve key and when all the air has escaped and signs of water appear, close the valve. You might even find that the pump is not performing as it should, which means that there is a possibility of an airlock in the pump itself. The symptom of this is that even though the pump is running, the radiators don't seem to be warming up properly. You can solve this

problem very simply with a screwdriver or a vent key. The pump is usually located next to the boiler. There will be an air vent on the side of the pump (usually it is labelled) especially for bleeding it. Switch the pump off before you open the valve. Be prepared for a slight spillage of water after the air has escaped, then fully close the valve. Switch on the pump again and the problem should be solved.

Checks Allow the system to run for a short time and then start making your checks from the bottom up.
- Check each air vent valve to ensure that you have tightened each one and that there is no water escaping.
- Check each of the bottom valves by the finger 'shine' test!
- Check that there are no cold spots in any part of each radiator.
- Check that the pump is running silently.
- Check all controls including the thermostatically-controlled valves on each radiator, the programmer and wall thermostats. Each of these can be switched on and off to give you control of the system while you do your tests.

Fireplaces

installing
An attractive Victorian fire surround is worth restoring, but if the fire place is removed and the front blocked up, insert a small vent so that condensation won't occur in the flue.

215

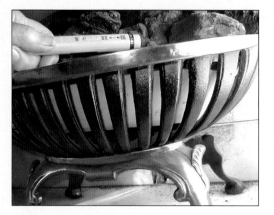

Open fires

Entering a house and seeing a live fire in a living room gives a sense of comfort to most people. The emphasis is then on 'home' rather than 'house', with the invitation to be at ease! The fire is the very heart of a home and gives it life. It is a focal point. The desire for warmth (and the need to cook food) is primeval and basic to survival. No wonder more and more house owners are opting for a 'living' fire.

How we have changed! From an open air fire to one in the centre of a primitive structure with a hole in the roof, then to an enclosure with a flue and now the sophistication of electronic remote control, instant heat and flame-effect fires. All to match the architectural and cultural style of any age too! Even if you live in a renovated Victorian or Georgian house and opt for a restored fireplace, you now have the added advantages of modern technology. At the press of a button,

a warm fire can spring to life. A gas 'coal-effect' fire can be more efficient and attractive than a badly installed solid-fuel fire (but it must be installed by a 'Corgi' registered engineer).

For years solid-fuel fires have, however, not only provided room comforts, but with a back boiler they have been a source of hot water for domestic use and for central heating. It is perfectly possible to reinstate, renovate or rebuild a fireplace to incorporate all technological advances, but the very basics of the well-proven essentials for high efficiency, from the hearth to the throat opening to the wide 'gather' and up the narrower flue to the top of the pot, all remain important to understand.

Renovation In the 1960s fireplaces were often 'boxed in' to meet the demands of minimalistic designs! This was sometimes done without knowledge of building principles so that an important vent was omitted. It is extremely important to allow air to circulate within the flue, by means of a grille or vent at a low position, to prevent condensation. Remove the flimsy box structure and you might reveal an attractive Victorian iron fireplace. Mind, you'll now probably have to remove the remnants of birds' nests, soot and debris in the fire basket and you'll certainly need to have the flue cleaned!

You'll need only a basic tool kit to fit a prefabricated fire-surround kit. All the instructions are clearly illustrated and the dowel joints easy to glue together. Use a laser line generator to get a level top shelf and true vertical side members.

Ornamental fireplaces were often painted over but the problem of restoring them to their former glory is quite simple. Use a thixotropic paint stripper, following the instructions carefully, to remove most of the paint. Paint in the incised pattern and stubborn paint marks on the main uprights are best removed with an old toothbrush and a small wire brush. Leave the stripper to activate for the recommended time, then use a paint scraper and a shave hook to remove the paint from the larger areas. Deposit the old scraped paint on a newspaper for disposal in a plastic bag. Rub over the surface with fine steel wool, then neutralise the stripper with the recommended solvent before using dry steel wool to prepare the surface for the old-fashioned look that is so redolent of Victorian fireplaces.

Clean up any tiles on the surrounds, especially on the angled sides, with a more fluid stripper that is soluble in water and will not harm the grout or filler between the ceramic tiles. Afterwards rub with fine wire wool and wash with warm water and a little detergent to make the tiles sparkle.

After this preparation you can give the fireplace a traditional black finish. Lay protective sheets on the floor and use masking tape on the adjacent walls. Wear protective clothing, goggles and gloves and have a bucket of water ready in case of splashes from the 'jelly-type' paint-stripper.

For the genuine Victorian look you will need to use a graphite-based product which comes in a handy tin and is easily applied with a shoe brush or cloth. Although it has a slight smell and gives off a vapour when first applied, it is not toxic, but, of course, ensure adequate ventilation. The paste is the consistency of soft putty. Don't rub it in too hard, but work it gently in the same direction up and down. It can stain wallpapers and carpets so check that the coverings are firmly in place. Leave it for five to six hours to dry before buffing. A cordless drill with a buffing pad attachment will save aching arms, but start the process with a clean, hard brush before the final polishing stage.

Soot

An open fire is part of our heritage! It is inviting, provides a focal point and is a real comfort when it is lit. However, inherent in its design are problems to overcome. The most obvious of these is soot, so it makes sense to have the chimney swept as often as is necessary to prevent down draught and lessen the chances of flue fires.

There are laws to help improve the environment by preventing the burning of certain fuels, so we must burn only recommended fuels. Of course, there is the option of having a gas, coal-effect open fire that does not cause a soot problem.

Years ago, the friendly, soot-covered face of a chimney sweep was a common sight. With a hand cart, protective sheets, a huge bristled brush and rods, and pan and brush, they were to some people figures of fun. However, they played a very important part in cleaning the environment and preventing serious chimney fires. Later on came the small white van, the vacuum system and the cleaned-up 'sweep-operative'!

Soot is a hazard – a serious one that could, if allowed to build up in a chimney, create blockages in a flue that could easily catch fire. A build up of soot, particularly on a 'dog leg' bend can restrict the flue opening, which in turn will cause down draughts and smoke-filled rooms. You need to regularly sweep your chimney so that these problems don't occur. How often you sweep will depend on the number of times you light the fire. A regular fire user will need to have the chimney swept at least twice a year.

Fortunately all the equipment necessary to sweep your own chimney flue is available for hire. A number of canes, each about a metre (a yard) long, come with screw ends, one a socket screw end and the other a bolt screw end, so that you can extend the brush to sweep the highest chimney flue. Check outside before pushing the brush up the flue! Is there a directional cowl or a 'capping' on top of the pot? Often it is difficult to locate which pot serves which flue and fireplace! If you don't know, have someone light a piece of rag, safely guarded, in the fireplace so that you can check from which pot the smoke emerges.

Use your common sense when chimney sweeping because all the soot you dislodge will come down the flue to the fire opening where you will have to bag it. You will have to stop all the soot and dust from spreading into the room. Remove all the fireplace fittings to give you space and fix a heavy duty sheet around the fire opening (either weight it down or stick it with low-tack adhesive tape) before carefully feeding the rods up the chimney by extending the length one section at a time.

Don't be tempted to twist the rods in any direction as they might become unscrewed and you don't want to leave the brush stuck half way up the chimney! If the brush is difficult to push around a 'dog leg' bend or if it meets an obstruction, gentle persuasion up and down will eventually get the brush passed. Once you've got to the top of the flue, start to extract the rods one at a time by unscrewing them as they appear. When the brush appears, remove it and have a cup of tea. This is time well spent as you have to allow the soot to completely settle into the grate. Keep windows and doors closed when you remove the covering cloth from the fire surround as any draught is likely to scatter the soot! Take care when removing the soot. It's best to do it in small amounts with a pan and brush for safe disposal in a plastic bag.

For those of a low-activity disposition, there is an alternative. It is not as effective as a thorough brush sweep, but it will clear the flue of smaller amounts of soot and help to prevent soot being deposited in the flue in the future. You can buy a special substance with soot-destroying properties. Sprinkle it on to the fire when it is lit and shortly afterwards you'll see fine deposits of soot crumbling into the fire to be burned. It's all non-toxic, so it is safe! If you choose to use this slightly more expensive method, always have a door or window open to help create a good updraught to take away all the gases created by the chemical, which in turn mix with the solid fuel gases to be expelled through the chimney pot to the outside air.

Blowback

To solve the problem of blowback (smoke being annoyingly gusted back into a room) you first have to understand how a fire and chimney work. Blowback can be the result of turbulence above the chimney pot or it may be caused by a fireplace opening that has been changed. Many standard design features were originally intended to ensure the efficient operation and burning of solid fuels in an open fire. For example, the opening was constructed with splayed sides and the lintel chamfered to divert the flow of air from the room over the grate (to help burning) and then up the flue. The height of the opening over the fire was 700–750mm (28–30in) because this height proved to be the most effective. Heated air and smoke from the fire is guided through an inverted funnel construction, built just above the fireplace in the 230mm □ 230mm (9in □ 9in) flue, as you'll see from the illustration. It is also very important to retain the narrow throat just above the knee of the fireback. It is essential, for an efficient and effective fire, that there is a properly designed means of escape for the gases and smoke and that there is also a good supply of air with oxygen to feed the fire. We all know that heated air and gases expand and rise as they become lighter than the surrounding air so the flue depends upon certain properly built-in features for it to be effective.

Hopefully there should be no problems in a well-designed system, but if there is blowback, the first thing to look at is the chimney pot. The best and most effective method of ensuring an updraught is by installing a directional cowl. These often look like a Roman gladiator's helmet and fit standard sized pots by being securely held with lugs. Manufactured in galvanised steel, the cowl has an open side and opposite that a fin which swivels it in the wind either on ball-bearings or in a container of grease. If the chimney opening has not been altered and you've swept the flue, the addition of a directional cowl will solve the problem of blowback.

We all demand comforts at home! One of those comforts is not being bothered by draughts to

Firebacks usually come in separate pieces to be assembled in situ. The intense heat generated at the hottest point will sometimes crack the top section, but it is not difficult to repair with a proprietory fire cement.

Rake out the crack before dampening, ready for the fire cement to be forced in to the cracked fireback repair. Allow the specified time for the repair to cure before lighting a fire.

Having allowed the fireback repair to cure for a couple of days, a fire may be lit so that the comfort and warmth associated with a 'living' fire can then be enjoyed!

spoil our evening reading or television viewing. Consequently, we draught-proof our windows and doors but this does something that could contribute to blowback. The lit fire is now being denied its necessary supply of air, and particularly oxygen, and it is necessary to install a vent somewhere in the room. Underfloor ventilation is a good idea but it does take some installing. You will have to lay a duct from an outside airbrick to a small circular vent just in front of the hearth. The duct can be as simple as a 50 mm (2 in) waste pipe with the appropriate connectors. The floor vent can be as small as the pipe and be located just in front of the hearth so that the fire, and not you, is getting the benefit of the fresh air.

If it is obvious that a fire opening, that is the open area just inside the fire surround, has been enlarged at some time, this could be another cause of blowback. It is possible to solve this problem by reducing the height of the opening to assist the smoke and heated gases to escape more readily up the flue. By reducing the height of the opening by as little as 100 mm (4 in) you can effectively help the smoke to properly clear up the flue. Have a piece of armoured glass cut to fit the width of the opening by the desired height and seal it into the opening with fire cement. First, though, support the glass with two galvanised brackets screwed either side of the opening.

Firebacks

Cracks   If a fireback shows signs of cracking, wait until the fireplace has cooled then use a wire brush to clean the area. Do it vigorously to ensure that you reveal whether the cracks are superficial or serious. Vacuum all dust and debris before commencing repairs. It is necessary to undercut any crack before filling. A bolster chisel and a club hammer are recommended, but use them gently as further cracking could result if harsh tactics are employed! Old firebacks become brittle, so it might be a better plan to use an old screwdriver or file to gently rake out smaller cracks. The

raking out process is simply to ensure that the fire cement is pushed in far enough to hold without falling out, hence the need to undercut, which means that the back of the crack is wider than the front. Use only fire-clay cement, available from all DIY stores, for the repair work. The instructions that come with it will tell you to splash the area with plenty of water so that the cracks are thoroughly soaked. Load and press in the fire-clay cement with a trowel or an old knife and point it up as you go along. Be certain that the crack is well filled and dampened before any subsequent filling. This is a very easy and satisfying job and the repair will last for years if correctly carried out. Drying out takes about a day, then you can enjoy an evening in front of your usual warm fire.

Replacing   The radiant heat that provides the warmth that we love also heats the fire basket and the firebrick. Firebacks usually come in separate pieces and the intense heat can cause the lower part of the fireback to expand while the upper part remains fairly static. Four-piece versions are available with separate side pieces. In order that the fireback can expand without cracking, the separate pieces are slotted together to rest on a non-combustible tape. If you are confronted with the problem of replacing a fireback, it is not too difficult to lever out the broken pieces and the rubble behind. Most firebacks are stamped with a maker's name or mark which solves the problem of deciding what to order as a replacement. If you cannot find any marks, take measurements of the height, width and depth and ask for a replacement which complies with British Standards and has a high knee. The knee is the protruding part of the fireback facing you (it will cause problems if it is too low!). Before fixing the new fireback in position, offer the lower half into position to check that it sits centrally in the opening. Pull it forward so that the sides sit behind the fire insert. Check also that there is room for the top to sit comfortably on the lower half. Lift off the top half and begin filling behind the lower half of the fireback. Professional installers use a layer of corrugated cardboard between the back infill material and the fireback itself. Use either vermiculite mix or rubble, mixed with one part of lime and two parts of sand, as the infill, because cement used in a mixture like this would be too strong and cause further cracking. Once it has set, and the heat has destroyed the corrugated card, an expansion joint has been formed. If vermiculite is used, add one part of lime mixed with water. A non-inflammable rope or tape is used between each of the pieces to allow for expansion. The top

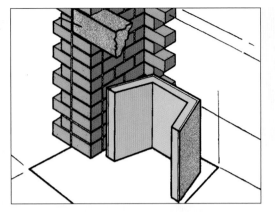

Replacing a fireback (1)

The drawing shows how the first piece of the new fireback is positioned. The forward position is crucial so carefully follow the manufacturer's instructions.

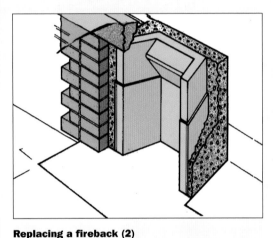

Replacing a fireback (2)

Slot the top half of the new clay fireback onto the lower half with it sitting just behind the chamfered lintel – another crucial position. Now mix cement-mortar and vermiculite to fill the void behind the two sections

Replacing a fireback

New fireplaces usually come in two halves separated at the knee. The lower half must be eased on to the back hearth and swung around to sit comfortably behind the front surround. Insert packing between the fireback and the surround. This is compressed by a mix of four parts of vermiculite and one part lime behind the fireback. As you build into position the second piece of the fireback, continue to backfill with a similar mix.

The diagram shows a typical fireplace construction with a lintel (l) and the wide gather narrowing to the flue dimension (g to f). The fireback sits behind the fire surround which is fitted last of all.

The cross-section of a typical fireplace clearly demonstrates the relationship between the component parts. The lintel (l) is angled to help the flue gases escape. The narrowing of the throat (t) opens up into the flue (f). Notice that the knee (k) and the lower half of the fireback are backfilled with a vermiculite mix which has been levelled off at the throat. The flaunching is formed as a triangular shape to run smoothly into the gather.

Repairing cracks in firebacks

Firebacks often crack but it is not always serious. Rake out and undercut surface cracks to provide a key for the fire cement. Always rake out and clean up all the debris before dampening the whole area. Never use ordinary cement but use a proprietary brand suitable for fireplaces. The illustration shows the crack before being raked out (a) and the inverted-V key (b).

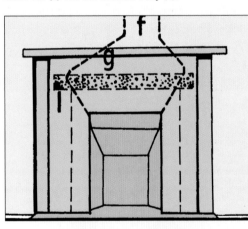

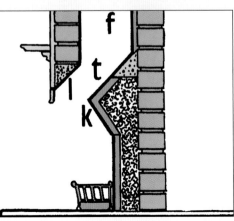

half must on no account overhang the lower half, but should be set back by at least 3 mm (⅛ in) to prevent its lower edge being subjected to excessive heat. Fill in behind the top half with the same mix and level the infill to the top of the fireback.

With a mix of four parts of sharp sand to one part of lime and rubble, fill the space around the top of the fireback. Slope it to about 45° upwards towards the back of the chimney opening. There should be a smooth line, with no protrusions, from the back of the knee up to the back of the flue. Allow three or four days drying-out time before you light up again!

Replacing a fireback (3)
Build up the slope above the fireback to match the slope of the front lintel and to meet the back of the flue. This is the 'throat' which guides smoke and gases up the flue.

Removing a fireplace (1)
A hearth is a separate unit. Lever this out first using any long, strong, steel bar. It will come away in one piece because it has reinforcing bars holding it together.

Removing a fireplace (2)
Prefabricated tiled fireplaces were popular in the 1940s. They were easy to install so they are easily removed by a DIYer. Drill out the screws from the lugs after removing the plaster at the top corners.

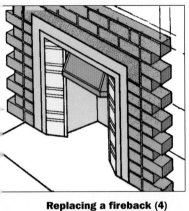

Replacing a fireback (4)
Make good the joint behind the fire surround and your new work with fire-cement. Make sure there are no gaps left for smoke to escape.

Renewing

Removing In the three decades after the 1920s, period properties, especially Victorian ones, suffered at the hands of 'improvers'! Beautifully moulded dados were ripped off walls, delicately moulded panelled doors were insensitively covered with hardboard and, perhaps worst of all, exquisite Victorian fireplaces were ripped out and dumped. Mostly they were replaced with a small, simple, tiled fire surround and tiled hearth. Fortunately, over the whole country, a reappraisal has taken place and proper restoration is being carried out. An appreciation of the older designs is evident not only in cars, buildings and furniture, but also in fireplaces! However, you might be confronted with one of the replacements and want to remove it. Now that you have some knowledge of how a fireplace is fitted in the first place, this will make the job of taking it out fairly easy. Obviously take precautions, clear as much of the furniture as is practicable from the room and roll back the carpet. Use dust sheets and wear a dust mask for your own protection. The hearth is usually fixed in position last of all after the existing surround has been fitted, so it needs to be levered away first. If you're working on a solid floor, you'll need to bring the level of the hearth area up to that of the floor. A bag of ready-mix concrete is ideal for this job. Mix it following the manufacturer's instructions. Pour it into the uneven

Removing a fireplace (3)
Use a trimming knife to score into the plaster around the outer edge of the fireplace. Lever the top unit, but place a protective blanket or an old mattress under it. Be prepared for dust and soot! Block in the fire opening but build in a louvred vent to prevent damp and condensation.

hole that is left and level it by simply drawing a batten across the top. The edges of the existing floor will act as a level guide.

If you're working on a suspended wooden floor, the hearth will rest on a concrete infill but the edges of the floorboards and possibly some joists will be exposed. A heavy timber called a 'trimmer' runs parallel with the hearth and is located just underneath the front edge of it. This is supported by two joists at either end and its purpose is to support the intermediate joists which have been cut short. It is extremely important to examine as many of these surrounding

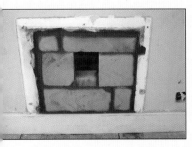

Having removed a fireplace and fireback, sweep the flue and block up the opening. It is essential to leave a hole to take a vented louvre.

joists as possible for worm or rot. Probably none will be found, nevertheless treat as much of the timber as you can with a preservative. Take care not to spill it on to the lath and plaster or plasterboard ceiling below. It would only create another DIY job! Bring the base of the new hearth up to the level of the floor as before.
A fire surround is fixed in position with as few as four fixing points, but sometimes even only two! A small piece of metal with a hole in it is already fixed to the back of the fire surround at the top, protruding so that a fixing can be made through these lugs. Nails or screws could have been used to secure the fire surround. Sometimes lugs were located at the bottom of the side columns or at the inside position at the base of the columns. Tiled hearth and tiled surrounds were actually cast in separate pieces and each section tiled by the manufacturer. Lightweight reinforcing steel bars would have been used in the construction. However, it is possible to break up these with a sledgehammer or even a club hammer.

Remove as little plaster as possible to locate and release the fixings. Use penetrating oil to release screws and a small wrecking bar is the best tool to lever nails, metal fixings and eventually the surround itself. Use an old mattress or similar padding on the floor before lowering it. Incidentally, a second pair of hands is useful at this stage.

Repair any broken plaster with a DIY tub of one-coat plaster available at all DIY stores. Remember to dampen the area before applying the plaster! While the plaster is drying, you've got time to clear away all the debris and prepare for fixing your new fire surround.

Replacing The demand has been so great over the past years that manufacturers have reproduced many authentically designed fire surrounds. Replacement marble fire surrounds made in four pieces can be carried home in the boot of a car. For the enthusiastic DIYer, it will take less than a day to fix a surround in place. Victorian cast-iron surrounds are just as easy to fix but, of course, are heavier to handle. Pine surrounds manufactured to simulate Georgian

and Victorian pieces, can be purchased inexpensively from specialist suppliers. A new wooden surround will have some form of protection from the direct heat of the fire, usually metal inserts. A marble surround has two separate columns, which are fixed first. Usually a mix of cement and rubble is dropped into the base of the columns but the manufacturer's instructions for fixing will be precise. A special two-part cement-adhesive supplied by the manufacturer is used on all marble joints. Slip the horizontal 'facing' piece into position and rest it on the shoulders fixed to the back of the columns. The columns will have cappings or scrolls, the tops of which line up with the vertical facing piece. A bed of the cement-adhesive spread over the whole of the top surface will hold the mantelshelf in position. If the mantelshelf is a deep one, with a lot of overhang, it is advisable to chop away a channel of plaster in which to insert its back edge. Accurately cut and chisel the channel using a trimming knife so that the shelf goes into a cleanly cut slot. Apply a coat of diluted PVA to make a bond for the one-coat plaster, which is also used to secure the marble mantelshelf.

If the fire surround is in two pieces, follow the maker's instructions, installing and fixing the inner part first and making a good seal between that and the existing opening. Sometimes the inner part has splayed sides, either in cast-iron or a tiled finish, designed to help the flow of air into the grate. It is important that this first piece is fixed properly and very securely. Check whether nuts and bolts are used for fixing cast-iron parts. Whatever the fixing, ensure that no cracks or gaps are left to spoil the efficiency of the burning process. Never use ordinary cement for sealing around the fireplace, only special fire-clay cement. It's as easy to apply as spreading butter on toast and readily available in tubs in all DIY stores! If your fire surround comes in one piece and the inner splayed part is still in existence, ensure that a tight fit is obtained between the two parts. The instructions for fitting your new fire surround will deal with the problem of sealing where one meets the other. It could be that a metal 'trim' is supplied to fill the space

Although it is a very dusty and dirty job to remove an old fireplace, it is not difficult if it's done in stages and safely. There are no structural problems, providing the original fire-opening brickwork is not disturbed.

between the surround and the fire opening, so read the instructions carefully. Obviously, a non-combustible material must separate the fire and the wooden surround and 'expansion joints' must be filled with non-asbestos rope and fire cement. Incidentally, if you have to remove old asbestos rope, the first thing to do is to spray it with water to soak it thoroughly. Only then is it safe to rake out. Seal it in a plastic bag and dispose of it through your Local Authority.

Finishing   Once the new fire surround has been properly installed and the surrounding walls made good, you are now ready to carry out the manufacturer's instructions for 'finishing'. This simply means painting, sealing or coating the new fire surround, but to complete the job you might find it necessary or desirable to renew the skirting boards either side of the surround on the face of the chimney breast. Matching skirting boards are available in all types and sizes at either your local DIY store or a sawmill. The external mitred corners are easily cut at 45° using a mitre tool. It is best to cut the mitre ends first, then measure accurately from the ends for the 90° cut where the new skirting board meets the fire surround. Drill, countersink, plug, drive in the screws and then use wood filler to hide the head of the screw. Sand and paint to match.

To solve the problem of downdraughts, fit a directional cowl with a fin or an open cornered cowl. These use the force of the wind to blow in and over the pot pulling out gases and smoke with it.

Prefabricated fire surrounds constructed in wood, will have had either a sealer finish or a primer finish applied to protect the timber. This will need to be sanded or smoothed with fine wire wool before any 'finish' treatment. If a wax finish is your desired choice, it's best to ensure a good seal first, which means a mix of 50 per cent white spirit and 50 per cent yacht varnish. Allow the wood to absorb the sealant and to dry completely before applying furniture wax. The more you apply and the more you burnish, the better will be the finish! To obtain a professional paint finish, always sand between coats, starting with a priming coat, undercoat and a top finish coat. Leave the recommended time between each coat and ensure that there is no dust to spoil the finish.

Chimney pots

Unused flue   It is inadvisable to remove a chimney pot from a flue that is no longer in use. If the fireplace has been blocked up there are certain essentials to be done to prevent condensation and rainwater problems. If a chimney pot serving that particular flue does not have some form of protection from penetrating rain, problems inside the flue can occur. A blocked-up and unventilated fireplace can also cause problems because there is no heat to evaporate moisture. A chimney pot or a chimney stack opening must have either a capping or a tilted clay tile cemented on to allow air to escape but keep the rainwater out.

Capping   Attractive chimney pot cappings are available and they serve a very serious purpose. For various reasons, tar stains can occur and show up on wallpaper above a fireplace, used or unused. Unfortunately, the burning of logs, vegetable waste and recommended fuels, creates gases which cool and condense, more often than not half way up a chimney flue. The more that is burnt, the more condensation soaks into the mortar between the bricks, breaking it up. A revolving cowl helps minimise the problem and also stop penetrating rain. Obviously, use all the precautions when working on a roof as described in the section entitled 'Roofs and safety'.

Venting   Now you know about some essentials when dealing with a blocked-up fireplace, there is one other absolutely vital DIY job to be done – you have to get rid of static air which causes condensation and instead introduce a through draught by providing ventilation! This is accomplished quite simply by fitting a proprietary plastic vent into the wall or a 'hit-and-miss' vent into the boarded covering of the fireplace. A hit-and-miss vent is simply a metal vent that can be opened and closed at will. With a vented cowl on top of the pot and an air vent at the bottom of the flue, you will successfully overcome any condensation problems.

Condensation Kitchens

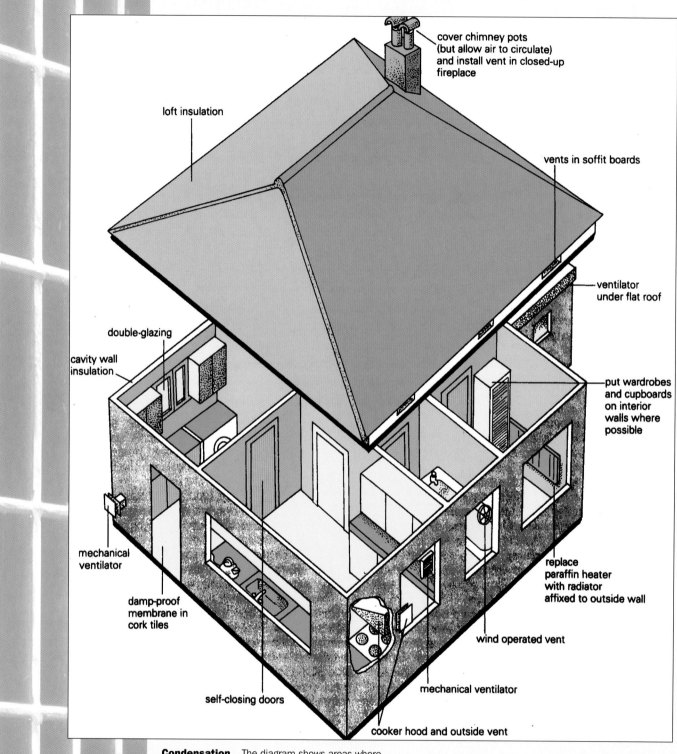

cover chimney pots
(but allow air to circulate)
and install vent in closed-up
fireplace

loft insulation

vents in soffit boards

ventilator
under flat roof

double-glazing

cavity wall
insulation

put wardrobes
and cupboards
on interior
walls where
possible

mechanical
ventilator

replace
paraffin heater
with radiator
affixed to outside wall

damp-proof
membrane in
cork tiles

wind operated vent

self-closing doors

mechanical ventilator

cooker hood and outside vent

Condensation The diagram shows areas where condensation is produced and ideas for solving the problem in different parts of the house. Your local DIY store will be able to give you helpful literature about every form of condensation and the methods of overcoming problems of mould in cupboards.

Source The relative humidity in houses determines whether mould grows to destroy decorations. Their presence adversely affects not only the structure of our homes but also our health. Pollutants in the air also destroy our buildings and our well-being. A temperate climate such as ours brings many advantages

Clear out air-bricks at ground level to stop musty smells under a wooden floor.

Don't use a paraffin heater if condensation is a problem – they produce water vapour!

Hiring a dehumidifier will dry out damp plaster – but not cure recurring damp!

but black mould, moss, fungi, lichen, algae and bacteria seem to thrive on damp conditions and short bursts of sunshine. Airborne spores fly in enormous numbers and variety all around us. Tiny organic particles, too small to see or feel, are all the time feeding on the moisture.

Condensation – which is practically pure water – provides a constant source of food for the these unwanted organisms. Dry up the source and the offenders will die. However, a certain amount of humidity is essential to our health and to the fabric of our homes so a balance has to be struck.

Stagnant, unmoving air can be held in corners of rooms that have cold external walls. This is because of a lack of ventilation. Black moulds are often most severe there. Cupboards and wardrobes against external walls, particularly 230mm (9in) solid brick walls, provide ideal breeding grounds for moulds and mildew. Condensation occurs when warm moist air

Dehumidifiers
A dehumidifier will extract moisture from building materials and furnishings. It combats condensation by drawing moisture-laden air into the unit where it is condensed. The dried air is heated and released back into the room.

meets a cold surface. For example, if you breathe on a cold window your breath condenses causing water rivulets to run down the glass. When condensation occurs depends upon how moist the air is and the coldness of the surface of the building. Of course, both of these depend upon how the building is used, so get to the source of the problem first of all to prevent moist air spreading to other rooms. Provide ventilation to all rooms and use heating sensibly. Cooking potatoes in the kitchen provides an enormous amount of moisture.

If the kitchen door is left open, the moisture permeates to the rest of the house. The secret is to leave the kitchen window open, or if we prefer our comforts and warmth, the thing to do is to provide an electric extractor fan either in a window or wall. But remember to keep the doors closed as you don't want to allow the condensation from the kitchen to cause damp problems throughout the rest of the house.

Extractor fans You can now see how important it is to get rid of steam before it condenses and causes problems on walls and possibly to one's health. However, new buildings will not suffer this problem because electrically controlled extractor fans have to be installed as a statutory requirement of the building regulations. We know that hot air rises, so the best place to fit an extractor fan is high on a wall and opposite the source of replacement air. The reason for this is simple, the whole room gets a change of air as the steam is sucked outside. If you choose to install an extractor fan in a wall, visit your local DIY store and check all the ones available. There are different types for different sized rooms. Some come with a graduated switch to control the speed of extraction and others automatically switch off after a certain period of time. Most extractor fans have external flap shutters to prevent wind blowing back into the room when the fan is not in use.

If it is difficult to build in a wall vent in a kitchen then a window vent will do the same job. Read leaflets to help you decide on the appropriate fan, which needs to be calculated based on cubic capacity of the room, the usage and the air change rate.

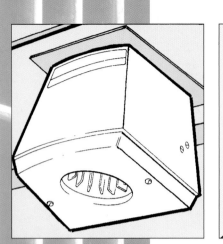

Ceiling extractor
Fit a canopy type extractor in a kitchen. Check that you have the correct size fan for taking away fumes, steam and smells effectively. Ideally, 15 air changes an hour are required for an average volume kitchen.

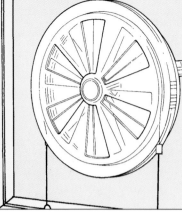

Self-activating fan
The position of a self-activating fan is important as it operates as a result of the pressure difference between indoors and outdoors. Once the correct hole is cut in the glazing this type of fan is easy to mount.

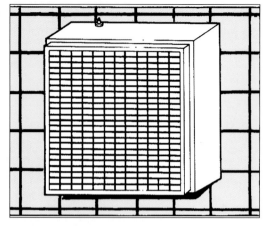

Bathroom fan
A wall fitting centrifugal extractor fan can be installed directly in a hole in the bathroom wall or it can be ducted to an outside wall.

Under-unit heaters Most kitchen floor units have what is called a 'toe-kick' recess at the bottom of the base units. The top of the toe-kick is usually level with the bottom of the door and level with the bottom shelf. Toe-kicks are usually clipped on to the legs and the void that is created behind the toe-kick gives plenty of space to install a specialist under-unit heater. The toe-kick is removable so a slot can easily be cut into it using the template supplied by the manufacturer. This hot air heater is easily installed by a DIY enthusiast provided that the instructions are fully understood and followed. Two of these heaters opposite each other in the kitchen will provide comfortable heating, which can be controlled, to warm the whole of the kitchen as the warm air rises. It obviously helps lessen the potential damage by condensation. Before embarking on a search for under-unit heaters, check at your local DIY store, read all the pamphlets on those available and then make your choice.

Bathrooms

Source Possibly more black mould is found in bathrooms than in any other room in the house. This is for one main reason: most steam is produced in a bathroom ready to condense on colder walls. Spores that produce black mould feed and multiply in damp conditions, so if bathroom tiles are not dried after every shower or bath the damp will contribute to black mould. If there is no extractor the warm moist air will remain static and will produce even more condensation.

Wall vents You can buy a range of extractor fans, mainly for bathroom walls but also for bathroom ceilings. Their installation requirements differ so the manufacturers give detailed specifications and instruction books to give information on the type and size of the room in which it is to be fixed. The information will also tell you about any ducting that will be necessary. Most essentially of course, because it is an electrically powered extractor fan, you need to be absolutely certain of the correct procedures otherwise you must seek the advice and services of a fully qualified electrician who is an approved member of the NICEIC (National Inspection Council for Electrical Installation Contracting). Remember – SAFETY FIRST, DIY SECOND – which means that if you do know what you're doing electrically then you know that you must switch off at the mains before attempting any wiring.

Window vents Window vents in bathrooms are not an ideal solution to extracting steam-filled air because a hole has to be cut in the glass and more often than not a cracked

Anti-condensation paint on a cold surface warms it so overcomes the problem of damp.

pane will result. This means that the best idea is to install a new pane of glass with the pre-cut hole. In this case the logistics have to be worked out carefully. Precise measurements of the window have to be taken and the appropriate size of the right gauge of glass cut.

By following the instructions on reglazing given in the section entitled 'Glass and glazing', you'll be able to take out the old pane and replace it with the new one with the hole already cut into it. Part of the job of installing the extractor fan will have to be done from the outside. This means thinking in terms of SAFETY FIRST, DIY SECOND! Most window vents have a circular holding flange on the outside which screws into the body of the extractor fan located on the inside of the window. If you're not sure about the electrical installation after reading the manufacturer's instructions, please consult with a qualified electrician and get him or her to do that part of the work for you. Make sure that the electrician is a member of the NICEIC. You should, as a precaution to your-self and to your family members, only contract with an approved member of the Council. After the installation is complete check that the fan is running properly and that the flap shutters close to stop air blowing back into the room when the fan is switched off.

Solve mildew in cupboards by lining walls (with polystyrene) and drilling holes top and bottom.

Cupboards

The air around us always contains water in the form of vapour. We can neither see it nor feel it and when we are out of doors we are not aware of its effects. Indoors though, where the damp air comes into contact with a cold surface, some of the water vapour will condense into water, resulting in visible condensation. The amount of water vapour that air can hold depends on its temperature. Warm air can hold much more than cold air, so it follows that because we keep our rooms warmed we run the risk of increased condensation. We've all been encouraged to try and improve the insulation of our homes. This, combined with the use of central heating, means higher temperatures in all our rooms. In turn, warmer air means the amount of water

vapour present is increased. Without adequate ventilation your home will almost certainly suffer from condensation.

This is no more evident than in a cupboard that is built against a cold outside wall of a house. When a cupboard has been left unopened for any length of time and static warm moist air inside is in contact with the cold outside wall, you'll get mildew on leather coats and any shoes and boots that are kept there. This is a fact of life. In Victorian and Edwardian homes where there was no central-heating system, it was often necessary to leave the doors of cupboards open where they were built against cold outside walls. However, advances in technology have produced the materials and techniques for us to overcome all of these problems.

Insulation

If you can eradicate the two causes of condensa-tion, warm moist air and cold surfaces, then you can eliminate the results, mould and mildew. There are paints available on the market which are specially formulated to warm up any cold wall. These 'anti-condensation' paints are simply painted on as normal, but they contain micro-scopic beads of polystyrene. Once painted on a cold wall and allowed to dry the wall becomes warm to the touch.

If you are preparing to wallpaper a room, then a very effective way of dealing with condensation on a cold wall is to use rolls of polystyrene that look and are hung just as ordinary wallpaper. This gives added insulation to the wall and certainly prevents condensation from forming so there'll be no more black marks caused by mould.

By far the most effective way of preventing condensation is to install dry-lining. This simply means fixing a damp proof membrane to the wall, which can be a plastic sheet. Then nail foil-backed plasterboard on to pretreated battens. An added refinement can be introduced by cutting polystyrene sheets to fit exactly between the

227

battens. If the battens are 25mm × 25mm (1 in × 1 in) you can get polystyrene sheets of the same thickness. These are lightweight, inexpensive and effective both for keeping the inside wall warm and to give some form of sound insulation in addition to the plasterboard.

Gyproc® is a thicker version of polystyrene sheet. It is a sandwich of compressed polystyrene between two boards. The sheets can be cut with a saw and fixed directly to the wall with blobs of special adhesive supplied by the manufacturer. Otherwise use blobs of ordinary plaster.

Chimneys

Mould on walls Mould on chimney breasts is usually caused by condensation within the flue. Once you have solved the ventilation problem you need to eradicate the mould which has crept through the brickwork and on to the decorations. Hopefully, it has only occurred in a small area so that you can hack off the plaster ready for patch plastering to make good. Before applying a one-coat plaster, liberally paint on an anti-fungicide solution and allow it to dry. Plaster and stabilise with a PVA solution. When the repair is dry you can paint or wallpaper.

Alternatively, clean the chimney breast back to the plaster and then cover it using rolls of foil applied in the same way as wallpaper. Add a layer of lining paper and then either paint or wallpaper to match.

Blockages Most blockages can be cleared by sweeping the chimney using conventional methods. However, if a serious blockage has occurred like a dislodged brick, this can be serious. No fires should be lit until the repair is made. Locate the height of the blockage with screwed-in rods and prepare to open up the wall in the room at that level. This is a messy job but can be done by a DIY enthusiast. It does mean that either you or a contracted builder will have to open up the chimney breast sufficiently to remove the offending brick and rebuild the hole you've made.

If you block up a fireplace, vent the flue with a grill to stop condensation.

Blocking in a fireplace will give condensation problems if a vent is not fitted. A properly sized plaster vent is simple to fit with coving adhesive after the wall has been plastered. Seal the louvred vent properly to the wall with a mastic gun after the adhesive has dried. Decorate to match the surrounding wall so that it fades into the background!

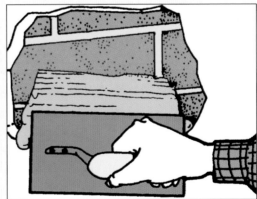

Patch plastering
Chisel away the patch of blown plaster to a hard edge. Dampen the lower undercut edge and firmly apply the plaster to it. Key the plaster into the undercut edge. Build up the whole area so that it is slightly proud of the wall surface. Use a straightedge in a scissor movement to flatten the patch. Leave the plaster to stiffen. Use a damp sponge over the almost dry plaster and then polish the surface with firm strokes of a steel float (trowel).

Thermal Windows

Glue mineral fibre tiles directly to a ceiling to insulate it for heat and sound.

Stop a rattling sliding sash by moving the staff beads closer to the sash.

If a sash joint is loose, drill two holes diagonally 50 mm (2 in) apart and glue in dowels.

Double glazing When I think about thermally insulating a house, I'm always tempted to think that it's like wrapping myself up warmly against the cold on a winter day! This analogy is actually quite sound, because with a woolly hat on I stop heat loss from my head, just like insulating the roof space on the top of a house! Then you can work down with scarf, woolly, overcoat, gloves, warm trousers and fur-lined boots. You can equate this with wall insulation, double-glazing, draught-proofing, pipe lagging, foil reflectors and polystyrene underfloor insulated slabs.

In autumn, when swirling copper-coloured leaves fall and a nip in the air produces rosy cheeks, we all feel the need to protect ourselves. As winter draws closer and the weather worsens we protect ourselves more fully against the ravages of frost, snow and biting winds, and, as I've just suggested, what we need to do now is think about the essential protection of our own homes in the same way. The saying 'Having a roof over one's head' means more than just having somewhere to live. It means having a feeling of security, a psychological feeling of protection, especially if the roof is sound and insulated.

But it doesn't stop there. The rest of the house must be soundly maintained too. Make a check list of what has been insulated and add to it as various problems arise. Check in the attic for 'total' insulation – well, except under the cold water tank and for ventilation at the eaves!

Check for air gaps around windows, doors, floors, cat flaps, air vents, fireplaces and, surprisingly, electric sockets in the cavity wall construction. If you have windows which are 'fixed', that is, they never open but are still letting in air through gaps or cracks around the edges, there is a simple solution to this problem. Those edges letting in the air can effectively be sealed using a clear liquid product, and of course we all know about the special brush seals and plastic strips to seal

windows when they are closed. Ideally, to maintain warmth in a room windows should be double-glazed. There are so many specialist firms advertising their wares these days that it is not difficult to find one locally to supply a carefully measured unit that you can fit into an existing frame as a DIY job. The one consideration is that the 'rebate', or recess that holds the glass, is deep enough to accommodate both the double-glazed unit and the putty. A double-glazed unit is simply two sheets of float glass, that is ordinary glass, with an air gap between that acts as an insulation layer. This 'sealed' unit has a protective aluminium self-adhesive tape around the outside edge to help the seal and to protect the edges of the glass. So long as the rebate is deep enough to take the thickness of the panes and the air gap, together with the putty, then refer to the section on 'Reglazing' for tips on the easiest way to fix the unit in position.

There is one further consideration you will need to take into account. Check with the double glazing supplier that their units comply with the new building regulations that stipulate the thickness of the air gap and thermal reflectivity properties of the glass.

Secondary double-glazing

Providing that secondary double-glazing has been fitted as recommended by the manufacturers of the kits, then you'll have thermal insulation almost as good as more expensive double-glazed units. A plastic sheet, or a separate pane of glass, is tightly fixed on to the window to effectively seal the gap between the secondary glazing and the existing windowpane. One of the most common methods of solving this problem is to use a kit that incorporates double-sided sticky tape and a sheet of plastic film. If, for example, you have a window comprising two casement openers and one fixed 'light', that is, a matching window between them, this is what you have to do. Before fixing secondary double-glazing, you have to overcome any problems of gaps and cracks around the main window frame and the opening 'lights'. Then use the double-sided sticky tape, not around the main frame but around each opener and the fixed light. Full instructions come with the kits making installation one of the easiest DIY applications. Once the film is securely stuck to the tape, trim around to remove the excess plastic film, cutting tight to the outer edge of the tapes. Then you'll find some wrinkles in the film, which is normal. The instructions will then tell you to use a hairdryer, held about 30 cm (1 ft) away from the film to remove the wrinkles and tighten the film so that it is quite taut. There are other suggestions that the manufacturers make, which are fairly obvious but worth mentioning. These are to clean the windows first and to dry the inside of the frame and the glass before applying the film.

Various other interior secondary double-glazing units and methods of application are also available. Extruded sections of moulded aluminium or heavy duty plastic are available in lengths ready to be cut to exactly the dimensions that you require for your particular job.

In this instance you can either use a roll of plastic film or some kits come with sheet plastic. You will keep most secondary double-glazing in place throughout the winter, to be removed and stored in spring or summer, ready for installation the following year. One very important thing to mention is that secondary double-glazing must never ever be used where it will prevent safe and easy escape in the case of an emergency. So, obviously, don't attach a full secondary double-glazing unit around the total framework of a window.

Sealing A distorted metal casement window frame might touch the frame only in one place. This will leave a gap somewhere else along the touching edge letting draughts creep in. One way of overcoming this, is to use a self-adhesive foam strip. However, it could be that the foam strip will touch where the casement edge is closest to the frame, but still leaves a gap elsewhere. So a manufacturer has come up with the idea of a foam strip that actually expands to fill the gap. However, for years, professionals have been carrying out what I call a DIY gap filling application! It works like this: overfill the gap by first spreading a bead of silicone sealant on the frame. Before closing the casement against it, spread Vaseline® on to the edge of the casement window. This means that the grease-covered edge will not adhere to the silicone sealant. Close the window and lock it so that the residual silicone sealant squeezes out either side. Clean this off whilst it is still possible and then wait

Double glazing
A simple and effective DIY method of secondary double glazing allows a separate pane of glass to be fitted in an aluminium frame inside an existing window.

Use fixed double glazing on the fixed light and hinged casements held by twist clips.

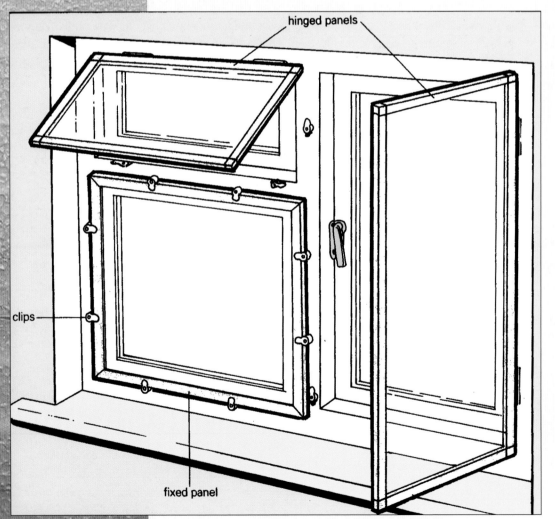

hinged panels

clips

fixed panel

for the silicone sealant to cure. You'll have to read the instructions on the cartridge to get the curing time. When it has cured and you open the window, simply clean off the Vaseline® from the edge of the casement window and you will have a perfect, draught-free joint!

The range of draught-proof strips and foams available in DIY stores is such that every conceivable joint in any shaped window can be made draught-proof. There is an abundance of literature available at the DIY stores and experts are there to guide you and to save an exhaustive search through the maze of products.

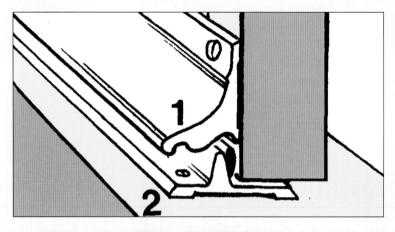

Front doors

Thresholds

On one of my television programmes I calculated and demonstrated that a gap of about 3 mm (⅛ in) around a front door and with a 6 mm (¼ in) gap at the bottom, adds up to about the size of a normal house brick! The obvious conclusion from this is that on a cold winter night, if there is no draught excluder around the door, then you could have the same amount of cold air entering the house as if a brick was missing in the wall! However, through wear and tear and taking into account the number of times the front door is banged each day, there are probably larger gaps around it. A conventional uninsulated front door could cause one-tenth of the total heat loss from your house each year, so it makes sense to insulate it well. Any form of insulation will pay for itself by cutting your heating bill. Obviously the length of the 'pay-back' period will vary, but as it is comparatively inexpensive to draught-proof a front door it's bound to be quick.

Start with the threshold area. There are a number of under-door draught excluders on the market which deal with pretty well any situation. Obviously, there has to be a small gap at the bottom of the door to allow it to open properly but there are many cleverly designed excluders available to fill the gap and prevent draughts. A trip to your local DIY store will prove profitable because you can read all the specifications and instructions to find the one best suited to your particular problem. One important point here is that for a front door you have to look at weatherproof threshold excluders because of potential problems with rain as well as driving wind.

Threshold draught excluders, to be effective, have to make a continuous seal with the side excluders that you've chosen. Amongst those that you'll find available is a spring-loaded type that lifts automatically as the door is opened. As you close the door the draught excluder is forced against the floor by a separate 'stop' fixed to the frame. The plastic or rubber strip fits tightly to the floor and closes up slight indentations or discrepancies in the level of the floor. Another type, perhaps more fitting for a floor that is very uneven, is the brush excluder which has long sets of bristles fixed firmly into an aluminium strip. This is screwed into a set position at the bottom of the door. The bristles slide effortlessly over carpets or wooden floors and give good draught protection. Yet another, that is not actually fixed to the door but to the floor underneath the closed position of the door, forms a seal as the door closes over on to it. It is ideal for fixing to a wooden threshold underneath the door but not if the threshold is constructed of concrete. These arched draught excluders have a vinyl or neoprene insert which gently 'gives' to the door, sealing gaps against rain and wind. One more good idea is a combination of a rubber-backed weather strip screwed to the floor and a concave weather bar fixed to the bottom of the door. Two things are accomplished here. The bottom of the outside of the door closes tightly to the rubber strip and the weather bar screwed to the bottom of the door covers it and throws rainwater off (just like the larger Victorian wooden version).

Icy winds can blow into the hall through a letter-plate. Fit an inexpensive brush-strip excluder to stop these. It will still seal even when a newspaper is held in it. Even more effective is one with an inside flap as well.

Lofts

Government statistics are always telling us how much heat is lost through uninsulated walls and attics. Of course, the figures that we read about are for a 'typical' building and individual houses vary in the way they lose heat depending on what they are built from, but it is claimed that the typical heat loss through a roof over one year is over £100 in a terraced house. No two families have similar life styles and no two households are alike in the way they spend energy. Government and Building Research Establishment figures cannot include the cost of energy used for cooking, lighting and washing, but, of course, no amount of insulation will reduce these figures. Other energy saving methods are needed to reduce your bills for these activities, but there is a lot you can do to reduce your heating bills.

I once met a man in Petersfield brushing the snow from the path in front of his house after a heavy shower. As I looked up I saw that all the roofs in the street were covered with snow except his, which was absolutely clean. Surprisingly, he said to me, 'Look at that, I'm not going to get problems with melting snow causing wet problems in my attic'. Little did he realise that he was paying a lot of money to not

Insulating an outside door
The cheapest and easiest draught insulation to install is foam strip. You can remove it in the summer and replace it in the autumn. Fix it to the doorstop on the opening side and to the frame on the hinge side.

Front door edges
Front doors often have very uneven gaps around them, sometimes as much as 12 mm (½in). Fit a rigid excluder with a rubber or neoprene seal to take up the variations. Cut the aluminium or plastic excluder carefully.

Letterboxes A letterbox, or a 'letter-plate', without an inside draught-excluder, allows icy wind into the hall and therefore into the house! This again is a problem that is easy to remedy and inexpensive. You only need to fit a brush-strip excluder, which is held by two screws. The great advantage of this type of excluder is that when a newspaper is left in the flap, the brush strip will hold tightly against it, so preventing draughts. An even more sophisticated one has an attractive inside flap as well.

Edges Before fitting an effective draught excluder around the sides and the top of a front door make a carefully check the gap sizes. You'll find this much easier when the edges of the door and the frame are clean! In any case, if you choose a self-adhesive foam strip excluder then you'll certainly have to clean off any dirt and grime otherwise the foam will only stick to the dirt and soon part company with the door and become ineffective. If the gap is uniform then draught proof around the door with a foam strip. There are different thicknesses available and different qualities, so check carefully and get one that is going to solve your particular problem. Full instructions come with the foam strip. Notice particularly that the strip is fixed to the doorstop, or 'rebate', on the leading edge side of the door at the top but on the doorpost on the hinge side. This is because the door effectively squeezes against the foam as it closes making a good seal. If the gap is uneven or is extra large then you'll need to think in terms of a solid strip of either aluminium or hard plastic with a rubber or neoprene insert. This is either screwed or nailed to the door frame when the door is in the closed position. Coloured versions are available to match the existing decor.

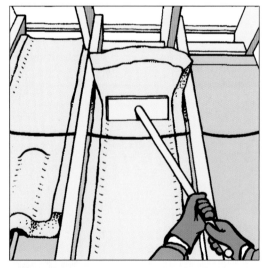

Loft insulation
When thermally insulating a loft, wear gloves, protective clothing, a mask and goggles. Lay the material between the ceiling joists. You must ventilate the roof space so don't push the material tight into the eaves. Allow for the material thickness. Cover pipes but not cables. Check with your local authority about the availability of grants.

Check pipes in attics and against exterior walls are insulated with split foam.

All exposed pipes must be protected from frost. Attics must have ventilation and are, therefore, exposed to possible freezing conditions.

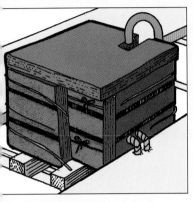

Tanks

A cold water storage tank must be insulated to prevent water freezing in winter. Do not insulate underneath it! Allow any warmth rising from bedrooms to help prevent freezing.

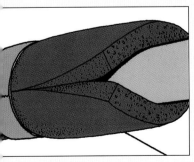

Pipes

Lag every pipe in the attic. Split foam tubes are best but secure them with tape. Cut the foam at 45° to lag 'elbows' (right-angled corners in the pipe run).

only melt the snow but to warm the air above his house. I asked him what sort of insulation he had in his attic. His reply did not surprise me. He said, 'None mate, I never go up there'. So I guess the 30 per cent that Government figures give as heat loss through an uninsulated attic could go up to 40 per cent in his case! I went straight to the Local Council offices and asked them to send him advice on attic insulation.

To insulate the attic thoroughly it's imperative that you lay a thick blanket of mineral fibre absolutely tight to the joists and abide by the Government recommendations for the thickness.

Government Building Regulations stipulate that there must be ventilation in attics. Pamphlets which contain the details are obtainable from your Local Council. However, ventilation will not prevent the insulating material doing its work because air gaps or air vents are placed at the eaves, outside the area covered by the insulation material between the joists. An alternative to fibreglass is a loose-fill insulation (that is, granules of insulating material) but it has one disadvantage. Any disturbance caused by moving air or wind will move the pieces very easily, and, of course, they could, if allowed to, flow down inside a cavity wall. To avoid this, block off each gap where the joists meet the rafters in the narrowest part of the roof void. You have to spread the granules evenly using a board notched at both ends to run along the tops of the joists. Your DIY store will give you a pamphlet with advice on protective clothing and how to crawl about safely in the attic. If there isn't a floor, you'll have to use a set of 'crawl-boards'. Remember to insulate the back of the board covering the attic opening; it's easy to stick a sheet of thick polystyrene to cover it. Then you'll have to clean off the 'stops' on to which the door lays before using foam strip insulation.

One piece of advice, when handling glass fibre or mineral wool, it is advisable to wear gloves, a dust mask and goggles. Wear old clothes that can be shaken out and easily washed. You might come across electric cables and

plumbing runs in the attic. Ideally, electric cables must lay on top of the insulating material or be secured to the sides of the joists using cable clips. Electric cables covered with insulation could get too hot!

Once you've insulated an attic that has been cold for a long time, you'll notice the warmth on the landing and in the bedrooms. The change is quite dramatic.

Pipes and tanks All pipes must be covered with tubular pipe insulation at least 25 mm (1 in) thick and fixed with special adhesive tape. All elbows (right-angled corners) must have the foam strip mitred to ensure that the insulation is total and complete. This is quite simple to do and in fact a lot of people use a serrated bread knife for this job because the insulation is a similar consistency to bread. All stopcocks must be insulated right up to the handle. Lag every pipe in the attic. There are various forms of insulation, not just foam tube, which, incidentally, has to be the right diameter to fit a particular pipe. Also available are mineral-fibre rolls and strips of blanket insulation, but what you don't want to do is compound any potential problem by insulating with a material that holds water!

The cold-water storage tank must be insulated to prevent the water in it freezing in winter. Either use sheets of 50 mm (2 in) thick expanded polystyrene or buy a ready-made tank cover. If you choose polystyrene, the pieces can either be skewered together or fastened with tape or string. Whichever method you choose, don't insulate under the tank, as this will prevent heat rising from the house which helps to stop the water freezing.

Skylights Most skylights these days are already double-glazed, so if you are dealing with a skylight that is, for example, in a Victorian house and is in its original condition, it might be worth considering having it replaced with a double-glazed unit. Alternatively, fix a secondary double-glazing unit to the skylight frame. Don't cover the outer window frame, otherwise you'll neither

be able to open the window nor have easy access to the open window in an emergency. If, over the years, the timber or metal frame has distorted, it is possible that the skylight is letting in a lot of air around the edges. Sometimes it is difficult to ascertain just exactly where the draught is coming through, so here's a little trick to help. When you are outside and you want to find the direction of the wind, you wet your finger. In this case, wet the palm of your hand and move it around the frame. You'll feel the draughts quite easily. For insulation, I always use foam strip in these situations, because I can renew it every year. It is a cheap but effective draught excluder that is really worth renewing, for example, every time you paint.

Walls

Yet another set of figures tells us that in a typical uninsulated house, approximately as much as one-third of the heat loss is through the walls. But before you begin the process of keeping the heat inside your house where you need and want it, it is useful to understand the ways in which heat is lost from the house and particularly through the walls. Check whether you have 23 cm (9 in) solid brick walls or 33 cm (13 in) cavity walls, and whether the exterior is covered in some form of thermal insulation with a decorative finish such as cladding. Insulating boards can provide effective insulation when used on the insides of external walls. Check the paragraph on 'Panelling walls' and you'll see that there are two main methods of fixing boards. In houses with solid walls, as is the case with more than half of the houses in the UK, this is almost the only way of providing insulation. Boards can be fixed directly to the wall and the boards can either be plasterboard with foil backing or specially manufactured 'sandwiched' boards that have a compressed polystyrene core. The alternative is 'dry-lining'. This is simply carried out by fixing boards to a series of battens attached to the walls. In bedrooms, where a board is not likely to suffer too much rough treatment, and providing that the walls are sound and flat, decorated insulating board may be stuck directly on to the wall with impact adhesive. There are denser, standard or medium boards, with a tougher surface that can be used in a child's bedroom. These provide heat insulation when fixed to a framework of battens because you are creating an air gap between the wall and the back of the board. Before fitting the boards, either line the cavity with aluminium foil, as described in the section on 'Wallpapering', or as I've already said, use foil-backed plasterboard.

Cavity filling Energy conservation is as important as the comfort we get from a warm house. As part of ongoing developments and improved technology in house building, new houses under construction have a layer of insulation 'batts' built into the cavity between the inner skin and the outer brick skin. This is a very simple measure to increase the thermal insulation of the house that is relatively inexpensive for the builder and adds little to the final cost of the building work. However, it does increase, somewhat, the saleability of the house and, more importantly, increase the comfort of the inhabitants by reducing heat loss.

Nowadays, to meet national demand, companies have set themselves up as cavity wall insulation experts. After drilling a series of holes in the outer skin or 'leaf' of a house, they pump expanded foam in through the holes to fill the whole of the cavity, so reducing heat loss. This is not usually a DIY application and therefore you should look for a company that belongs to the National Insulation Association. It is better still if the contractors are also registered with the British Standards Institution and approved by the British Board of Agrément. These are your protections to ensure that the job is done quickly, cleanly and professionally.

There are a some provisos that you must be made aware of before hiring a contractor to carry out this type of work. A professional survey of the walls must be made to ensure that there is no failed pointing and that there are no gaps to allow water penetration which will affect the insulation. After the survey an application has to be made for Regulation Approval. If you live somewhere like West Wales or the

Plymouth area, anywhere where your property is exposed to salt-laden, westerly winds, you must seek advice about the suitability of whatever is recommended as an insulation material because it could be affected detrimentally. You must ask about a long-term guarantee, and check that the material, once it is cured, becomes inert. You must also be guaranteed that it will not shrink or flop (settle)!

Mastic

We've all experienced sitting near a door or window in a warm room, totally engrossed in conversation, but then becoming aware of a nasty draught of cold air around the back of our necks. Doors and windows can effectively be draught-proofed to eliminate this problem. However there's another source of cracks and gaps around doors and windows and that is between the frame and the brickwork. Older houses had cement pointed into the gap between the frame and the 'reveal'. This has always caused problems because wood moves, and cement doesn't, so it cracks and falls out. To remedy this problem it's very easy to apply a mastic bead right round the framework to fill the gap. A cartridge of matching exterior silicone is inexpensive and so is the skeletal gun that is used to apply it. In fact gaps in brickwork and even render can be filled with an exterior mastic.

All door frames and window frames must be sealed to the exterior reveal. Mortar filler cracks and falls out so use a flexible mastic sealant. It completely seals, despite inevitable movement in the fabric of the building.

With a temporary coating of Vaseline® on the facing frame or the casement, apply a generous coating of silicone sealant to the main frame where the two will meet when closed. Close the window and wait for the sealant to cure. Open the casement, wipe the grease away and the hardened sealant will have formed a perfect seal filling all the gaps!

Floors

Gaps

Draughty floors usually have bare floorboards and are at ground level. If you have wooden floors that have gaps between the boards, you'll be losing a great deal of heat. Floorboards are fixed to strong timbers called joists and it's at this level that you'll find ventilating grilles or vents on the outside wall of the house. This source of fresh air, as has been described previously, is essential to maintain the fabric of the house beneath the floor level and to prevent rot, but you have to stop that cold air entering the room through the floorboards. If you want to retain the beautiful grain of the wood, there are a couple of ways of overcoming the cold air problem. If the flooring is made of tongue and grooved timber, draughts are likely to be present if the tongues have split, if the timber has shrunk to give oversized gaps, or if the timber itself has split. Check also round the skirting boards where you might find undulating gaps caused by movement of separate floorboards. You may in fact find one long gap along the whole length of the floor. This could be caused by the floor dropping or by shrinkage in the skirting board. If the floor is sanded and sealed and there are only a few gaps to fill, a mixture of sawdust and transparent wood adhesive can be made into a very good filler. This is an easy DIY application because

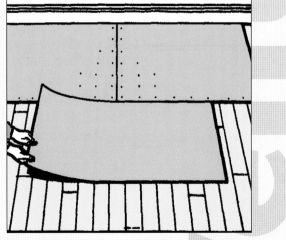

Floorboard gaps
To cover gaps in floorboards and to provide a flat surface for a cushioned vinyl or carpet covering, lay hardboard sheets first. Dampen them and lay so that the joints are staggered. Use a nail gun (every 15cm (6in)).

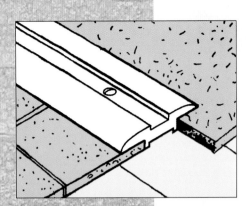

you simply press the mixture into the gaps, leave to dry and only then sand it down so that it is level with the adjoining floorboards. After finishing with a fine grade sandpaper, apply another coat of seal into the joints only to start with. It will be absorbed by the mixture and form its own seal along the length of the joint. Then sand again, vacuum the residual dust and clean with a rag dipped into white spirit. A further coat of seal over the whole area will complete the task.

If the gaps are simply around the edge of the floor between the skirting board and the floorboards, glue and pin a special moulding to the skirting board itself. Small sectioned decorative moulding can be bought with a thin rubber strip glued its underside. Cut to size and then press the rubber side tightly down to the floor, apply pressure to it and only then pin it to the skirting board.

Timber merchants and DIY stores sell laths of different thicknesses and widths that will fit larger gaps between floorboards. Where the gaps taper you'll have to use a smoothing plane to get a better fit. Use a good wood glue, so that when it is dry you can plane the slightly protruding laths down to the level of the existing floor. This ensures that you have a good professional looking finish.

An alternative to filling gaps is to lift the floorboards carefully and relay them. This is not such a tiresome task as it might at first seem. Lifting floorboards is described in detail in the section on 'Timber floors'. The tools are simply a claw hammer, a bolster chisel and a small crow bar or wrecking bar. You might have to cut off all the tongue from the a tongue and grooved board in order to more easily prise it up. The rest will follow without difficulty. It is obviously easier to lift flat-edged boards. After removing the nails from all the boards, check that the joists are free of woodworm and that all screws and nails are removed or sunk beneath the level of the top of the joist before

beginning the relaying process. Now you can either hire a floor clamp or make your DIY floor clamp with a batten and two wedges. This again is described in the section on 'Flooring'.

If you're dealing with a floor at ground level, you might even consider an added barrier of insulating material between the joists underneath the floorboards. There is a traditional method of literally 'hanging' the insulating material on plastic garden netting stapled between the joists. Simply lay the netting in small areas at a time. Lay it over the first joist and staple it. Let it hang down about 13 cm (5 in). Staple it to the sides of the joist. Bring it across the opening, up the other side of the adjacent joist, staple it there. Over the top of that joist, down the other side and so on and so on. Now you have a series of 'hammocks' to support the 'sleeping' slabs of insulation material!

Use the secret nailing method if you're refixing tongue and grooved boards. This means that the nail is hammered into the tongue. Alternatively, a powered nail gun makes this very easy. For flat-edged boards, use the traditional method of nailing or screwing about 13 mm (½ in) from both edges into each joist. If the boards are not to be covered, use a proprietary filler over the nail heads or insert plugs over the countersunk screws.

If the ground floor is to be carpeted then you don't necessarily have to move boards together if there are gaps. There is a proprietary floor gap filler available which comes in a cartridge and used with a cartridge gun. Alternatively, you can nail hardboard to the floor first, but the slight extra height might mean that you have to take a little off the bottom of doors that open in to the room. You can then cover the surface with either vinyl, cork tiles or carpet. Before laying the hardboard dampen it slightly so that it expands and then nail it down every 15 cm (6 in), either conventionally with a hammer or with a powered nail gun which is far easier, speedier and gives a more professional finish. When the hardboard dries it will slightly contract so there will be no undulations or bumps to contend with.

Gaps and cracks

There are many surprising places around the house, such as pipe holes, where irritating gaps allow wind to whistle in through walls, roofs and floors. Overflows from WC cisterns, header tanks, cold water storage tanks and waste pipes should all be backfilled to prevent this not immediately apparent problem. If the back-filling has dislodged, or has not even been done properly in the first place, then it has got to be tackled as a matter of urgency. Cracks around frames that are sealed to the brickwork open-ings for doors and windows, must always be checked and given an extra bead of mastic where necessary.

One potential location of cracks that often escapes detection is underneath the windowsill. Inescapably, there is always movement in the fabric of a house. This can cause the cement pointing between the underneath of the sill and the brick wall to dislodge. So again you need to use your mastic gun to solve this problem.

If you can't get to a high point where there could be a problem – for example, where an overflow pipe goes through a wall to the outside – you might be able to backfill the hole from the inside with a can of 'expanded' foam. Underneath the kitchen sink you can often see where the waste pipe goes through the wall – often with a large hole around it. Typically this is where neglect or oversight can result in a lot of cold air entering the kitchen. Check behind the removable back of the kitchen unit hiding this irritating source of cold air. A word of caution – don't overdo the expanded foam treatment because it really does expand to fill gaps and can overflow. However, there's no cause for alarm. It can be trimmed with a knife, planed, filled or sealed and painted. Another place to check is where a 100 mm (4 in) soil connector pipe goes out through the wall from the back of the toilet. Often this is overlooked because it's out of sight, partly hidden by the skirting board!

A plaster repair kit comes with thin gauge self-adhesive tape (woven like netting), a circular sponge for feather-edging the repair, an appli-cator made of plastic but similar to a steel float, and one-coat plaster. This is an ideal solution for filling cracks and gaps around ceilings and walls. Sometimes the only sign of a crack being present in plaster, say near a skirting board or a window reveal, will be the sign of dust that has blown in by cold air. A gap between a plaster ceiling and wall will not be too apparent to start with but because of movement in the fabric of the house, the gap might increase sufficiently to allow cold air through. The kit, formulated to produce a professional finish, comes with full instructions. Follow these and you'll find that it is one of the easiest of all DIY tasks. Yet another tape and filler kit is available that is similar to the tape and filler used by professionals to fill the chamfered gap between plasterboards. First, apply a layer of the filler, then bury the tape into it with the plastic wide-based spatula. After allowing it to almost cure, use a damp sponge to feather-edge and smooth flat the subsequent covering to the tape. Then, as with all new plaster work, you'll need to seal it with either a stabilising solution or a diluted PVA solution.

Filling gaps and cracks
Expanding filling and fixing foam comes in pressurised containers. It is an excellent filler around pipe holes, and it also acts as an insulator stopping draughts and damp from penetrating. It is waterproof and will not shrink, crumble or rot.

Electrical tool kit
Store these tools near the main consumer unit in case of electrical emergencies:
(1) mains test screwdriver with easy-to-see neon indicator;
(1a) plastic socket tester;
(2) plug and socket terminals screwdriver (with safe handle and insulated shaft); (3) small, slim-shafted screwdriver for intricate work; (4) carpenter's screwdriver with insulated handle for mounting boxes, ceiling roses, etc.;
(5) electrician's pliers with insulated handles; (6) trimming knife with retractable blade; (7) wire stripper for stripping insulation, cutting wire to length and for separating the two halves of twin flex; (8) card of correctly rated fuse wire (see text); (9) spare correctly rated cartridge fuses (see text);
(10) powerful torch that is diffused to minimise shadows, with a means of attaching to keep your hands free for working or a support stand. Keep a spare bulb and set of batteries handy, and wear rubber gloves and rubber soled shoes if you have any doubts.

Stripping wallpaper? Mask around sockets and switches.

Switches

Electricity is not the mystery that most people believe it to be. It does not take an engineer to understand the wiring in a home, but it does help to have some knowledge of the basics to make the best use of it and to maintain uncompromising standards of safety.

Arriving home on a cold winter evening, we expect to be warmly welcomed by bright lights at the touch of a switch. We also expect instantaneous hot water from our shower, a warmed room, a hot drink and a favourite television programme (remotely controlled, of course!). We take all this for granted. Electricity is produced at power stations for immediate use. Immediate is the operative word because electrical energy cannot easily be stored and it does not burn like gas, coal or oil when it produces light, heat or power. A large number of power stations are located around the countryside to

supply different areas, but also to cope with sudden extra demands in wintertime when engineers have to switch on additional generators.

Loose connections   Loose connections or any other problems with switches must only be tackled after you've switched off at the mains! This means that you first of all have to check which circuit that particular lighting switch is on and you can do this by leaving the light on and then either taking out fuses or switching off at the consumer unit until the light goes out. Label the fuse or breaker so you readily identify the circuit if you need to isolate it again in the future. If it's a removable fuse, take it with you and put it in your pocket. Otherwise tape up the switch and put a label on it to say that you're working on that circuit. A switch face plate is just a covering to the switch mechanism. There's absolutely no danger in undoing the two holding screws and releasing the face plate to look inside provided that you

Electricity – bad practices

Lazy and potentially lethal practices include: (A) overloading the socket with adapters; (B) cable insulation in poor condition; (C) kinks and knots in the cable; (D) extension lead fixed to the skirting to provide an extra socket trailing on the floor; (E) plug only half way in a socket; (F) cable running under a carpet; and (G) loose, live cables snaking around a room.

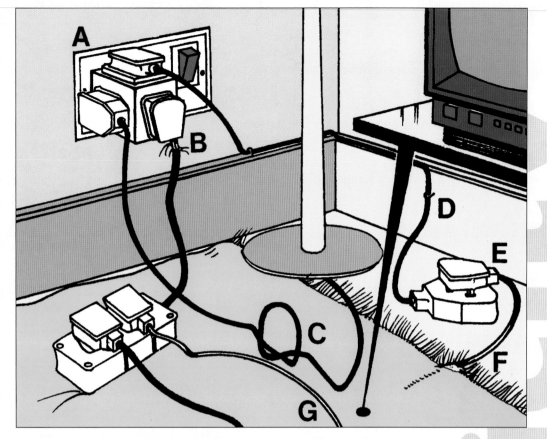

have isolated that particular circuit. A simple DIY device to check that it is absolutely safe to work on any circuit is an electronic mains-voltage tester. These really are essential, inexpensive and should be in every home. First of all check on a circuit that you know to be live, to make certain that the tester is working properly. It really is a simple device. One probe goes on to the live terminal to be tested and the other on to the neutral terminal. You'll see a little window with a bulb showing, lit up for on, and no light when no current is flowing in the circuit. Always test a second time between the earth terminal and each of the live and neutral terminals to reassure yourself that you're working on a circuit that isn't live. Manufacturer's instructions are always printed on the tester, so familiarise yourself with them before starting and then follow them step by step.

If there is a problem with a loose connection in a particular switch, use a magnifying glass and a torch to ascertain whether or not any of the fine filaments that make up the core wire are loose and touching other parts or other terminals. It could be that the tiny screws holding the

core wires in the brass terminals are loose. This will cause intermittent power and could possibly cause heating in the switch too. If there is any blackening around any of the terminals or the back of the switch plate, then it's time to buy a new switch and plate. You might even choose now to swap a plastic one for say a brass plate. I always advise that you make a sketch of the box through which the main cable comes and the back of the switch plate with the correct colour coding clearly marked.

You might have a dimmer switch already installed or a two-gang switch (two separate switches on the front of a single face plate. Often this happens where you have a light operated by one switch and the second switch operating a two-way system. Another switch that you might encounter is a simple two-way switch. But the most common is a simple one-way switch but this could have two terminals one above the other or it could be a two-core-and-earth cable. Whatever you see and whatever coloured insulation covers the core wires, the replacement switch must be connected absolutely exactly the same. The connections to the new switch must

Plastering around a switch or socket (1)
Use a filling and fixing foam to repair perished plaster. Use only a little at a time because it expands.

Plastering around a switch or socket (2)
Once the foam has cured and expanded to almost fill the cavity, use a one-coat plaster to bring the new surface in line with the existing. Redecorate to match.

After wiring switches and sockets with the current off, make final checks on every terminal. Let nobody into the room, switch on and use a mains tester. Always keep SAFETY FIRST, DIY SECOND in mind as you screw the cover plates back on.

have the same coloured cables going to the same terminals as the old ones.

Loose plates If you discover a loose switch plate immediately tighten the holding screws. Movement in a switch plate could be the cause of a flickering light and the possibility of over-heating. As you tighten the holding screws you might find that one or other continues to turn. In this case the thread has gone and the screw needs replacing. Replacement screws cost pennies so you should keep a supply of them in your toolbox just in case! If you've changed a switch, you should always try to use the original screws because they will have eased themselves into the threads on the wall box.

It is possible that a loose plate could be caused by an insecure wall box. In this case you'll need to go through the same procedure of switching off at the mains and ensuring that the circuit is not live, before tackling the refixing of the box. Whenever you take a face plate off from a switch box, the first thing to do is to check that the live, neutral and earth wires are secured firmly in their terminals. First of all, check the screws holding the box to the wall and check that the plugs are not loose in the predrilled holes. It could be that there's insufficient plaster surrounding the box to hold it firmly in position in the hole that has been chopped out from the plastered wall. Again testing that the circuit is not live, use a dry mix to backfill behind the box. We all know that water and electricity are not good together, so allow the plaster to dry overnight before checking and reconnecting.

Replacing with a dimmer switch

Dimmer switches are ideal for easily and cheaply changing the lighting effects and atmosphere in bedrooms, sitting rooms and dining rooms, by enabling you to change the light effects from subtle to bright at the touch of a button or turn of a knob. It is perhaps inadvisable to use them in workshops, separate WCs, bathrooms and kitchens. Note that you can only use one dimmer switch to control each set of lights.

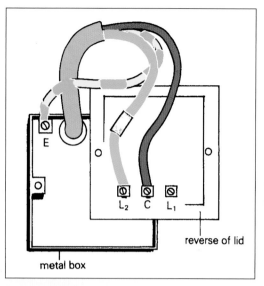

Dimmer switch
Switch off the mains power to the circuit you are going to work on. Double check with a circuit tester. Read the dimmer switch installation instructions and keep them to hand as you do the change over. The coloured core wires and the terminal markings will be the same on the old and new switches – make a sketch of the layout before you disconnect the wires.

You don't have to go to a specialist electrical store to buy a dimmer switch, most DIY outlets have a large selection of the best on the market. You may buy them as a simple kit with full, illustrated instructions. All you have to do to install one is to replace your present switch cover with the same sized dimmer switch cover.

Most modern switch plates are held to a wall-mounted box by two screws. The size of plate and the screws are standard, making replacement with a dimmer switch quite simple. The single standard switch must, of course, be replaced by a single dimmer switch; a single dimmer switch cannot be used in place of a double or multiple switch. Now, having switched off the power and checked that you're working on the correct circuit, take out the two retaining screws on the switch plate and you'll find that the plate hangs down 5–8 cm (2–3 in) on the cable. Place the dimmer switch instructions in front of you, alongside the dimmer switch (face down). Refer to the instructions and double check that you know which cable goes to which terminal. The markings on the dimmer switch will be similar to those on a normal switch, although they could be in a slightly different position. Before you disconnect the wires to take off the existing switch plate, check that you have understood which wire is live and which is switched. Your instructions will tell you. The live connector is red and connected to the 'common' terminal, marked 'C'. The switched wire is black, maybe with a red sleeve, and is connected to the terminal marked 'L'. Loosen the terminal screws (but not too much or they'll fall out and you'll lose them) and disconnect the wires. Now connect the wires in the dimmer switch. The red live conductor to the common terminal and the black with red sleeve conductor to the other terminal. Make sure that the end of each wire is not damaged and that no stray bits of copper stick out. Tighten the terminal screws and then give a little tug on each wire, just enough to ensure that the wire is firmly trapped in the terminal. Lastly, if there is a fuse in the dimmer switch and it's more than 3A, change it. Gently ease the back of the dimmer switch into the box, pop in the retaining screws and tighten up. All you have to do now is to replace the lighting circuit fuse (or switch on the power) and wait until evening to show off your modification and dramatic improvement to your lighting!

Enjoy the luxury of dimmed lights to create your own particular mood by fitting a dimmer switch to replace your standard switch.

One thing to note is that if, when you first take off the existing switch plate and look inside the box, you find two cables connected to the switch; this means that the switch is wired into a second switch. One cable will have three cores and the other one four. The four-cores will be a 'real' live conductor, a blue conductor, a yellow one and a green/yellow earth conductor. It is obviously slightly more complex than the simple dimmer switch wiring and you must refer to the specific manufacturer's instructions for two-way wiring. Obviously a standard wiring diagram does not exist since there are so many variations from dimmer to dimmer. So remembering SAFETY FIRST, DIY SECOND, what you have to do is make no cardinal errors! So double check everything, then you'll get it right. Only by following the instructions will you do it properly and, more importantly, safely.

There are two popular types of dimmer switch. The more sophisticated and expensive type is the 'touch-control' dimmer. It appears to have

no switch but, as the name suggests, the square switch plate is sensitive to the touch and the light is controlled simply by putting your finger on it. Switching on and off is operated simply by touching a panel and the amount of light varied by finger pressure.

The cheaper and more popular type is the rotary dimmer. This is turned on and off by turning the central knob. The brightness of the light is altered by further turning the knob. Some manufacturers provide an on and off switch at the side of the dimmer control knob.

One important point for you to consider, however, is the mode of lighting in that room. Most dimmer switches are not suitable for controlling fluorescent lights, they're only suitable for normal tungsten light bulbs. Manufacturers supply DIY stores with leaflet telling you all about dimmer switches. All the essential installation details are included, as well as their power rating, expressed in watts. The usual maximum rating for a dimmer switch is 400W, but this figure can vary between makes.

If you want to be ultra-sophisticated and make use of advanced technology, there are some amazing innovations on the market. Lights can be dimmed with remote control units by installing an infra-red beam system. Time-delay switches are available for dimming the lights at a set time. You can also buy dimmer switches which can be fixed to plugs so that standard and table lamps can also be controlled. A great model is one that incorporates an automatically timed fading device. Its soporific effect makes it ideal for a bedroom, especially when children are going to sleep!

Sockets

The electricity supplied to your home is the electricity company's responsibility as far as the meter and sealed main fuse. These are nearly always situated near to your consumer unit. From your consumer unit, wires and cables of different thicknesses carry the supply to the

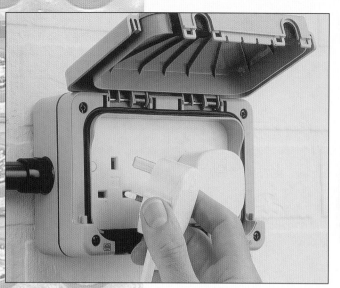

This award-winning socket has been designed for use indoors or outdoors, and in areas exposed to dust and splashing water. As the plug goes in, the socket actually seals around it making it very safe.

Plastic socket boxes installed in a shed or workshop won't last too long! This metal-clad, impact resistant socket is specifically designed for such environments. Note the conduit safely enclosing the cable.

various outlets in the house. A 1 mm^2 or 1.5 mm^2 cable, for example, supplies all the lighting point, whilst a 2.5 mm^2 one runs to all the power sockets. Heavier cables are used for such things as cookers.

Probably the most important factor in any electrical installation is 'earthing' and this is our own responsibility. It is a safety factor if a fault occurs in the circuit, such as the damage to cable cores, perhaps by a nail or screw piercing a cable when driven through a floorboard or into a wall. In the past, most earthing in an electrical installation was linked to the cold water supply pipes, so that current passed out along the metal water pipes into the ground in which they were buried. Improvements in technology have meant that this has had to change. Flexible underground pipes are now being used and these are not made of metal so they do not conduct electricity. However, all metal pipes in your home, whether they are water or gas, must be cross-bonded, that is, connected and linked to the clamp on the service cable sheath so leakage current runs straight to the earth. The earth clamp, installed by your electricity company, is a very important safety connection and therefore should never be removed. This ensures that all appliances, all light switches and particularly socket outlets are 'earthed'!

Whether you have a switched or an unswitched socket outlet, the wiring will be the same. Only work on any socket after switching off at the

mains and checking that the circuit is no longer live. Some sockets are surface-mounted but most will be flush to the surface of the wall. Some surface mounted types have round corners, others square, so any replacement will have to be compatible with the existing. Having switched off the power and tested, remove the fixing screws from the face plate and gently lift the socket out of the box. Now check the wiring. If you are replacing a damaged socket you literally just have to make sure that the coded core wires go into exactly the same terminals as the existing. Use the existing holding screws because they will fit perfectly into the threaded lugs of the box. After firmly fixing the face plate, switch on and test it. An inexpensive ring main socket tester can be used to check that it is properly wired and that there are no faults. And it can be a life-saver! It looks just like an ordinary plug but has three neon lights on the face. After plugging into a socket various faults can be detected by looking at the lights. All wiring problems in a faulty socket can be detected and it can identify what is wrong. In fact it only takes a few minutes to test every socket in the house.

Adding a spur If you've never installed an additional power point before, your best plan is to add a single power point to an existing single power point and use the shortest possible run of cable. Make certain that there are no pipes or wires buried in the wall. The easiest socket to mount is one that is screwed to

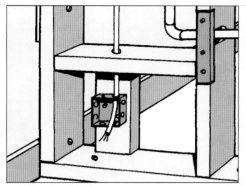

Dividing a room – sockets and pipes

To run a spur socket to a stud dividing wall, drill through the centres of the studs and noggins. Fix an intermediate timber to hold the socket box at the correct position for the plate to finish on the surface of the plasterboard.

Run pipes away from the edges of the studs and protect them with a batten let into the edge of the stud. This will also reinstate the strength of the notched timber.

Additional power point

Use an existing socket on the same floor as the spur that you are going to connect. Remember SAFETY FIRST, DIY SECOND so switch off at the mains and double check with a mains tester before doing any electrical work.

the surface of the wall. There are areas of thinner plastic marked on the socket box and you'll need to knock out one to push the 2.5 mm² cable through. Run in the new cable, then fix the new socket in place. Release the screws on the new socket terminals (which are marked 'E' for earth, 'N' for neutral and 'L' for live) and then strip back the correct length of the outer insulation with wire strippers at the correct gauge setting (see page 246). Insulation strippers are calibrated to take off exactly the length of insulation that you want and to strip

both the outer insulation and the inner core insulation. Remove about 1 cm (³/₄ in) from the cores. Use a green and yellow PVC sheath on the earth wire before connecting it. Check that the cores are into the correct terminals and that the insulation goes as far as the terminal holes. Screw the socket plate to its box. Either surface mount the cable using cable clips or run the cable through conduit chased (or embedded) in the plaster. Leave sufficient cable to make the connection to the existing power point.

The branch or 'spur' that you now have in position has now to be connected to the electricity supply via a convenient socket. Unless you live in a old house, the socket will be on a

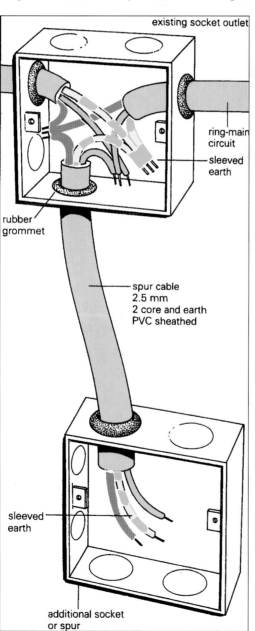

existing socket outlet

ring-main circuit

sleeved earth

rubber grommet

spur cable 2.5 mm 2 core and earth PVC sheathed

sleeved earth

additional socket or spur

A 'clip-in' socket box for a spur, showing the wiring arrangement and colour-coded wires. The insulation on each wire covers each one as far as the terminals. Switch off at the mains before tackling any electrical job.

Wiring a 13 A socket which is protected by a current-operated earth leakage circuit breaker (ELCB) is as easy as wiring an ordinary socket. There are just three wires – neutral, live and earth. Please remember to follow instructions carefully – safety first!

The face plate of a sentry socket shows the layout with the pin holes at the left side, the switch at the centre and the all important test button at the top right. Press button T to trip and then reset by switching off, then on.

Don't overload a socket with adaptors!

Every appliance is marked with a fuse rating – stick to it.

ring-main circuit. At the consumer unit, switch off the power to this ring main and make sure that you test it. Older houses may have a radial circuit and you might even find round-pin plugs! Now, if any spurs have already been added to the ring-main circuit, you must find out how many. You cannot have more than four spurs.

When you open up the existing socket you should find two cables entering the box (if there's only one, it has already been converted to a spur). Your new cable can enter the box by removing a 'knock-out' piece of thin plastic. Remove the outer insulation and the coloured insulation to the cores as previously indicated. Release the screws in the terminals to allow another wire of the same colour to be added to each terminal. Sleeve the earth wire with a green and yellow sheath. Double check that the terminal screws are holding the three wires firmly and that they are not twisted together as they go into the terminal. You need to push the connections inside the box without having to force them in with the socket plate. Fit the plate with the retaining screws. Now switch on at the mains. Again test with your ring-main tester. You should find that it is wired correctly if you followed the instructions that come with the additional spur unit.

Overloading   It is pretty obvious, but it's worth saying – overloading a socket outlet with a number of adaptors is dangerous! You obvi-

ously need more sockets if you have to use a lot of adaptors. Read the previous paragraph to familiarise yourself with the simple DIY task of installing an extra socket on a spur. Overloading means one thing – overheating. Overheating can cause fires, so this means simply don't overload a socket! You might be tempted to think that using a trailing socket extension with four outlets is safe just because it's some distance away from the socket outlet. It still adds to the build-up of heat around the socket itself. Please remember SAFETY FIRST, DIY SECOND because it isn't only you who is involved in this decision making. Think of the consequences to other people in the house.

Plugs

Fuses   There is a mistaken belief that a fuse will prevent electrocution. The main purpose of a fuse is to protect the wiring, not you! The thinnest wire in any circuit, the fuse, is the safety wire. Without the protection of a fuse, wires could overheat and cause a fire. If too much current flows through a cable or flex it is the fuse wire that melts or breaks, cutting the current immediately. Fuse wires, or cartridge fuses, have, for safety reasons, to be of the correct rating. Each circuit in a consumer unit or fuse box is protected by a particular fuse or miniature circuit-breaker. By taking out a fuse carrier you'll find a single- or double-bladed contact at each end. If the fuse wire is present, it

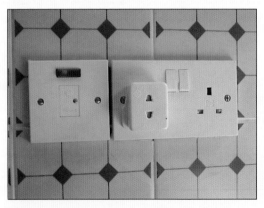

The left side fused connection unit has a cartridge fuse to protect any appliance connected to it. A neon indicator will show when the connector and socket are live. The fuse allows you to safely disconnect from the mains.

You should see no bare wires inside a plug – for safety's sake!

Wiring plugs

Only buy plugs that conform to British Standard BS 1363 and periodically check that the wiring in them is secure. It is important that a correctly rated fuse is fitted. An appliance rated up to 720W takes a 3A fuse and one rated 720–3000W takes a 13A fuse.

Sketch A illustrates a post-terminal plug. Sketch B shows a clamp-terminal plug where the core strands are wound clockwise around the studs. In both types of plug check that the cable's outer insulation, and not the three core wires, is held securely by the cord grip.

has got to be of a certain thickness relating to its current rating (the amperage). A lighting circuit is governed by a 5A fuse, an immersion heater by a 15A fuse, storage heaters by 20A fuses, the power or ring main by a 30A fuse, and a cooker over 12kW by a 45A fuse. The fuse carrier will either have a cartridge fuse, just like those in an ordinary plug though of the different size, or a rewireable fuse which is a thin wire held at each end by a screw in a terminal. Never ever be tempted to use anything other than the correct size of fuse wire or the correct cartridge fuse. Hair grips, paper clips or even nails must **never** be used as an alternative – a fire will certainly be the result.

A square-pin plug has a cartridge fuse meant only for a standard 13 A plug. Check all your plugs and make sure that any appliance up to 720 W is protected by a 3 A fuse. Appliances rated 720–3000 W should be protected by a 13 A fuse.

Safe, high quality plugs are available to give you peace of mind: safety plugs with guards to reduce the risk of touching live parts; durable plugs for harsh conditions; and tough plugs made from impact resistant plastic that is coloured too!

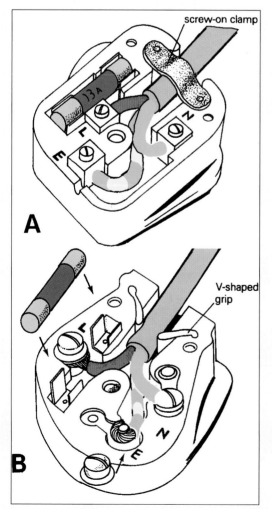

A screw-on clamp

B V-shaped grip

A cheap plug should never be used. Plugs marked with the British Standards number BS 1363 are the only ones that you should ever use in your house. It is the duty of everyone capable of wiring a 13A plug to learn how to do it safely. A screw located between the pins holds the cover to the body of the plug. Inside are three terminals and the fuse holder. Strip the outer sheathing of the flex to about 50mm (2in) without damaging the insulation to the separate conductors or wires using a wire stripper as described on the next page. Hold the flex at the position of the clamp so that you can cut each of the core wires exactly to length. These should lie

without twists in the correct grooves. The green/yellow or green wire is secured to the earth terminal, marked 'E', which is usually in the centre of the plug. Be sure that the insulation covering of the core wire extends to the terminal. The brown core wire is secured to the live terminal, marked 'L', which is the one connected to the fuse. The blue wire must be connected to the terminal marked 'N' which is the neutral terminal. Double check that all the wires are held securely in the terminals and that no 'whiskers' (stray strands of bare wire) are left unconnected to the terminals which could cause problems. There is a clamp where the cable or flex enters the plug which should grip the outer insulating sheath and not the three separate wires!

A double-insulated appliance will have only two core wires (without the green and yellow earth). In this case connect to the plug using only the live and neutral terminals.

Electrics

A mains test screwdriver with an easy-to-see neon indicator should be used before working on any appliance, even if the power has been turned off. Use it to test mains power cable, sockets, switches, lampholders and other circuits. Other features are a fully insulated hand grip and shaft, and a non-roll protective profile.

You should also keep in your toolbox a calibrated wire stripper so that you can remove exactly the right length of outer insulation and core-wire insulation.

Trimming mains cable

For everyone's safety, make sure you know the difference between new and old flex codes, and how to trim the wires correctly.

Stripping cable Whether you are wiring to a bell installation transformer, stripping telephone cables, wiring a shower unit, stripping $1.5\,mm^2$ lighting circuit cable or $2.5\,mm^2$ power cable, it is essential that the outer insulation and the core wire insulation are properly and safely stripped to the correct length. 'Properly stripped' means only cutting the insulation and removing the sheath without nipping any of the filaments of the core wire. You can only do this professionally by using a proper wire stripper, now specially designed and manufactured for the DIY enthusiast. This means that it is less expensive and does exactly the same job – again, safely and properly. When you open what is called a 'plug top', that is, take off the top plate from the plug body, you'll see three wires. But they're all of different lengths. Each of those core wires must have their own insulation sheath completely protecting the wire as far as the terminal, which means they have to be cut accurately. A wire stripper will do this for you, expertly and accurately. The

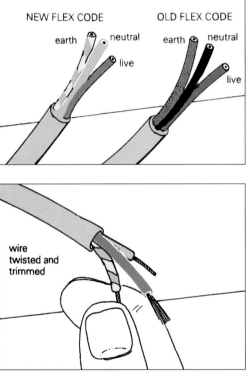

NEW FLEX CODE   OLD FLEX CODE

earth   neutral   earth   neutral

live   live

wire
twisted and
trimmed

outer sheath must be trimmed so that it is securely clamped by what is called the cord grip. Never ever be tempted to cut the outer insulation short so that the three core wires are held dangerously by the cord grip.

After ascertaining the correct length of insulation to remove, hold that particular wire in the calibrated jaws of the wire stripper. A gentle squeeze on the trigger and the core wire is gently cut at the correct length and removed with no damage to the core wire itself. Repeat the process for all the other wires and then push the outer insulation into the cord grip before feeding the ends of the core wires into the correct terminals (see illustrations on page 245).

Circuits

Testing continuity If something goes wrong with the electricity in your house, like the lights going out, the kettle doesn't boil, or maybe the radio stops working, lots of people's reaction is to say, 'Oh! A fuse has blown'. So a fuse is replaced and the power switched back on. The lights, however, could go out again! The reason is simple. The fault is still there and it's imperative that it is traced. It really is the duty of us all to know something about electricity, because it's dangerous not to. To many people, electricity is something of a mystery and something that they fear.

Ask yourself these questions. Do you really know how to wire a plug correctly? Do you know the correct colour coding? Do you know the correct fuse for the different appliances? And do you know about continuity testers? This all adds up to awareness of the fundamental principles of electricity. So, treating electricity with circumspection means that you will become more aware of what you can and cannot do when dealing with wires, sockets and appliances.

Think of it this way – electricity flows through wires and if something goes wrong it is likely that something has stopped, or is interrupting, the flow. If you still have power, but it is intermittent, you need to turn it off, first, at the nearest power point or socket and then at the consumer unit or fuse box. You then need to make doubly sure that the mains is off and that the circuit is not live by testing with a mains

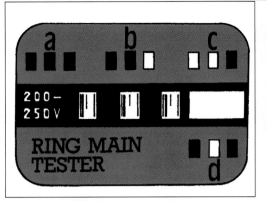

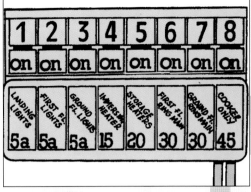

Ring main tester

It only takes a few minutes to test every socket in a house with a ring main tester. The back looks exactly like a plug with three square pins for fitting into a socket. Three neon lights indicate any faults such as an earth fault, a neutral fault or that live and neutral are reversed.

Consumer unit

In an emergency you should know exactly which fuse or breaker governs which circuit, so label them accordingly. Mark the fuse ratings as well where appropriate. To determine which fuse or breaker applies to which circuit, first switch off the power. Take out a fuse or switch off a breaker and then switch back on the power. By going around the house, switch on the lights to see which ones don't work – they'll be on the circuit you switched off at the consumer unit. Repeat this process by taking out different fuses or switching different breakers. You can check which sockets are affected by plugging in a table light. Remember to check that all the fuses are correctly rated.

This is a brilliant tester that decides whether a socket is safe to use or not! Plug it in any socket and note the sequence of the three neon indicators: all lit – correct wiring; centre and right lit – no neutral; right lit – live and earth reversed; left lit – live and neutral reversed; centre and left lit – no earth!

voltage tester – an inexpensive but essential part of your DIY tool box. There are always easy to follow instructions which will keep you safe and ensure that the circuit is not live and that it is safe to work on.

Correct cables
Every lighting system and power circuit in our homes must have a fuse box, or what is now termed a 'consumer unit', installed within the circuit. Technology has brought about a doubly safe consumer unit, fitted with miniature circuit breakers connected to each circuit in the house. These circuit breakers are so sensitive that as soon as there is a leakage or a fault in an appliance, the current is instantaneously switched off. They are similar to the residual current devices (RCDs) you use when protecting yourself against faults

with outdoor appliances. From the consumer unit separate circuits, or wiring systems, are run around the house. Each lighting circuit uses a 1–1.5 mm² cable and is rated at 1200W. In other words it should supply no more than twelve 100W light bulbs. Each ring main or power circuit using a 2.5 mm² cable should not serve a floor area of more than 100 sq m (120 sq yds). Cookers with a load greater than 3000W must have their own radial circuit using a 10 mm² cable connected directly to the consumer unit and a 45A fuse protecting them. This applies also to immersion heaters, but the circuit can be run in 2.5 mm² two-core and earth cable. This must be protected by a 20A fuse. Storage heaters are run separately in 2.5 mm² two-core and earth cable to their own consumer unit.

Cable or flex in domestic wiring is made up of three wires. The live (or line) wire, colour coded red or brown, carries the electricity to the appliance. The neutral wire, colour coded blue or black, carries the electricity back. And the earth wire, colour coded green, or yellow and green, is the safety wire. Every earth wire in every part of the electrical insulation is linked to a common earth point at the meter position. In turn this is connected to the earth terminal provided by the electricity company, which is also bonded to all metal water and gas pipes. Together with circuit breakers, the most important factor in an electrical installation is earthing.

Connections   The earth clamp, installed by your electricity supply company, is a very important safety connection, and therefore should never be moved. All metal pipework in the home should be connected to the earth terminal in case one of the live conductors (wires) in the house should accidentally touch a pipe at any time. Nowadays a new consumer unit will have its own miniature circuit breakers connected to every circuit in the house. In the event of a fault in any circuit, the miniature circuit breaker will trip to the off position, isolating that particular circuit. Open the consumer unit lid to find the faulty circuit by switching on again. If it will not stay in the on position, carry out the following tests to

find where the fault is. Each miniature circuit breaker is marked and numbered, so begin by unplugging all appliances on the faulty circuit. This is to ensure that this particular circuit is not overloaded. If the circuit is still faulty the probable cause is a loose wire in a socket outlet or light fitting. Switch off at the mains and inspect each one. A loose wire touching one of the other wires, another terminal, or perhaps the outer casing, can be the cause of this short circuit and loss of power.

Power   If a circuit is not working at all, you must unplug everything or switch off lights in that particular circuit. To test which appliance or light is faulty carry out the following test. After having unplugged everything or switched off all lights, replace the fuse or switch on the miniature circuit breaker. Switch on the appliances or lights one by one until the fuse trips or blows again. Remove the faulty appliance and restore the circuit to live. This means that you've restored power.

Don't ever be tempted to take on an electrical repair job that is beyond your capabilities. Remember, electricity can be lethal! Don't take risks. If in the slightest doubt, phone a qualified electrician. And qualified means one who has been recommended and is a member of an acknowledged electrical contractor's association.

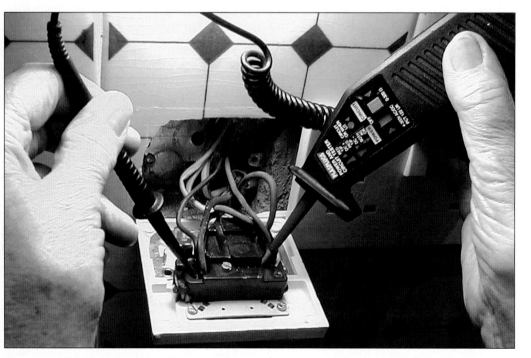

A DIY circuit tester will check electrical continuity, but read the instructions before carrying out the test. Use the probes on designated terminals to check that it's safe to work on the appliance.

Doorbells Replacing

So many people tell me that one of the most satisfying DIY tasks in the home is to take out something old and replace it with something new, but it has to be easy, quick and inexpensive! Typical of this simple and satisfying DIY job is refitting an inexpensive battery-operated doorbell.

Carefully unscrew the bell push from outside the house and extract the wiring, taking care with the cable clips so that you don't spoil decorations. Then comes the job of removal of the bell unit or chimes. Having chosen a new kit, which will include everything that you need to fit the doorbell, make some notes for your own guidance. Stand outside your front door and decide on the best position for the new bell push. You might want to use the existing hole that was drilled for the original bell wire. Remember it is better that the bell wire has the shortest possible distance to run to the bell chime box. Full instructions come with every kit and these will help guide you to locate the bell in the best possible position. Remember that it is better if the bell wire can be effectively hidden. The box housing the batteries and bell chime can be installed at a convenient position but should not be fitted over a radiator. Usually you will be able to hear the chimes all over the house if you locate them in the entrance hall. If you have to make a new drill hole through a window or door frame, you obviously don't want the problem of splitting wood so measure the distance that the drill bit has to go through, but don't drill more than 6 mm (¼ in). Then have someone hold a piece of timber tightly against where the drill is to emerge so that the drill bit continues to drill marginally into the timber block. This will prevent any splitting of the timber frame so no redecoration will be necessary.

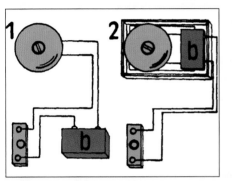

Wiring a doorbell

If the battery is separate from the bell, run the bell wire as shown (1). The job is even simpler if the battery (b) is housed in the bell box (2).

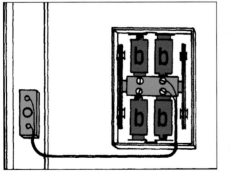

Wiring door chimes

Either wire can go to either terminal, but the batteries (b) must be inserted correctly.

With your wire strippers trim off the insulating material from the copper core wire to be able to fix the two wires to the terminals of the bell push. Check that the screws are tight before locating the bell push over the hole in a level position. Fix it firmly with two small brass screws supplied. Take the cover off the bell chime box and hold it in your chosen position to mark the screw holding positions. Nothing looks worse than a lopsided fitting, so use a spirit level and mark the positions on the wall by pushing a pencil through the screw holes in the back of the box. Check for pipes or cables in the wall before using a masonry drill bit as recommended by the manufacturers to match the plugs and screws supplied. If the box is fitted to timber, obviously first use a wood drill bit of a smaller size for a pilot hole.

With the back of the bell chime box screwed in position the next stage is to pin the bell wire into position using tiny staples. The fine insulated bell wire is only two-core for a battery-operated door bell. It is usually white and can be run unobtrusively under dado rails, up behind door architraves and over the tops of door frames.

Connections When you have installed the wire all the way to the box, cut the wire to enable sufficient of the outer insulation to be trimmed back to fix the core wires to the terminals to make the correct connections. Instructions on the box will tell you exactly how to do this. Also take note from the instructions of the positions of the batteries. Even though it doesn't matter which wire goes to which terminal, it does matter how the batteries are installed. The attractive cover is usually held by integral clips and only needs a push to click it into position. So simple to fix and as simple to operate!

Now check it works by pressing the outside bell push. This action activates an electromagnet or a solenoid, which causes a metal striker to hit the bell or chimes. Chimes and bells make a pleasant change from the harsh banging of a door knocker, are inexpensive to install and will give years of service.

Outside lights

The increased visibility and the dramatic effect created by a front door or patio light, is certainly worth the effort of installing one. First of all, find the best position to give you the most light on a dark evening. That position should also be convenient to a lighting point indoors. You'll need a light-fitting that is specially manufactured for use out of doors and it must be earthed. Instructions for wiring an exterior light are included with the product. Unless advised otherwise, the easiest method of installing one is to run a length of 1 mm² twin-core and PVC-sheathed cable from it to the hall light by connecting to the terminals matching the coloured wires, having first switched off the power – remember SAFETY FIRST, DIY SECOND especially where electricity is involved. Somewhere you'll have to drill through the wall and you should try and find the most inconspicuous run for the cable. You might drill in a position just above the floor upstairs and be able to pull the cable to the ceiling rose position under the floorboards. Now switch on the power and test.

Electricity and water are dangerous together – always keep them separate!

Change ordinary light bulbs to 'energy saving' ones – they will last years!

Light fittings, light shades, power points, sockets, anything electrical that is used outdoors must comply with strict regulations for everybody's safety.

Wiring regulations will specify what particular cables are to be used. Exterior installations must be protected by a residual current device. All light fittings, such as the one shown, must be manufactured for use outside.

Thread the cable down through the ceiling rose and make your connections as follows. Sleeve the earth wire and connect to terminal marked 'E'. The red wire should go to the outer two-terminal block. The black wire to the outer three-terminal block marked 'N'. You've now made the necessary connections so that your new light can be switched with the existing hall light. The instructions that come with the exterior fitting will give these details but more explicitly. What you've done has now saved the introduction of a terminal joint box, extra cable, an extra switch and a great deal of disturbance to decorations. You'll have to carry out exactly the same operation if you want to put a light at the back of the house.

Fittings
Junction boxes

Installing a new junction box into your domestic lighting circuit gives you the opportunity to add an extra light, even an exterior light, which can be controlled automatically by dawn and dusk light levels. To fit a new junction box and connect it to the existing lighting circuit is not too difficult for a DIY enthusiast. Switch off the power, remove the fuse or tape up the trip switch for that particular circuit. Test once again that the circuit is not live.

One easy place to install a four-terminal junction box is above the hallway and to do this you simply need to remove a couple of floorboards above it. Screw the junction box to a joist and then read the instructions that comes with it. You will have to cut the existing lighting circuit cable – this is where your DIY wire stripper comes into its own once again. The live, neutral and earth conductors are then connected to their respective terminals. Having fitted your new exterior light in its prepared position and run a 1 mm² cable from it as far as the junction box by the best way possible (through conduit or chased into the plaster) you're ready to connect it to the junction box. Connect its red conductor to the switch terminal, its black conductor to the neutral terminal and the earth conductor to the earth terminal. Professional electricians always identify the black conductor by wrapping a piece of red tape around it! But that's only to show that it is connected to the switch terminal. Remember to check that all the core wires are firmly fixed into the terminals and that their insulations go as far as the terminals.

With the junction box securely screwed to the side of the joist and the wires connected, you can then securely screw the cover in place and you're ready to test your electrical installation work. Switch on at the consumer unit or replace the fuse and ensure that the mains power is on once again. The final thing to do is to enjoy the benefits of your work when darkness falls!

Second stage of cutting the circular holes in a plasterboard ceiling for downlighters. The rotating arm accessory creates a perfect circle and the drill-cutter gives a clean hole.

Ceiling roses

When you unscrew the rose cover of an existing ceiling light, don't be surprised to find that a red tape might be wrapped around one of the wires. This is only there to identify the switch wire. You might find only one red and one black wire, in which case the rose is already on a junction box and so will not have a red tape on a wire because there is no switch cable. Having switched off at the mains and either removed the circuit fuse or taped up the switch of this particular circuit at the consumer unit, now test with a mains circuit tester to ensure that the circuit is no longer live.

Replacement is simplicity itself because all you do is wire the new one to operate in exactly the same way as the existing. Note that if you're dealing with very old wiring there are probably wires running into three-terminal blocks. In this case there will be a black wire with a red tape around it indicating that it is the switch return wire. The first terminal block will have all red wires, that is obviously the 'live' block. The next is the neutral terminal block which has the black neutral wires and the blue flex wire. And then comes the black conductor with the red tape and a brown flex wire. Also note that all earth wires will run to one terminal on the back plate. If you don't see any earth wires then you have no alternative but to get in an experienced electrician.

Replacing a ceiling rose flex (1)

A ceiling light flex can be weakened by wind blowing through an open window. It can also deteriorate from the heat from the light. A short circuit can result if the flex is not in good condition.

Switch off the power at the mains and unscrew the rose cover. Double check that the circuit is not live.

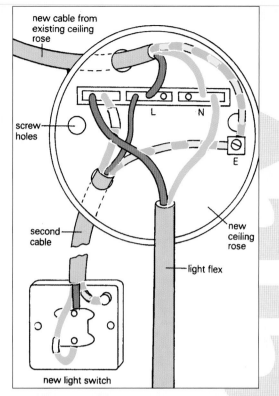

new cable from existing ceiling rose

screw holes

L N

E

second cable

new ceiling rose

light flex

new light switch

Adding an extra light

The diagram shows the correct wiring both if the new ceiling rose and the new switch. Use 1mm² two-core and earth PVC sheathed cable. Make a sketch of the existing ceiling rose connections before disconnecting the wires. Drill 13 mm (½ in) holes above the new light and new switch positions (you may need to lift floorboards to do this). Drop cables through the holes to reach the switch position and the new light position – check the diagram to see how to make the connection to each. Use a piece of red PVC sleeving on the black wire (a statutory regulation). Cover the earth wires with yellow and green sleeving.

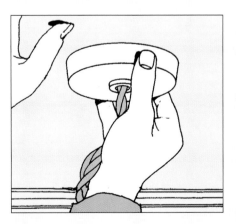

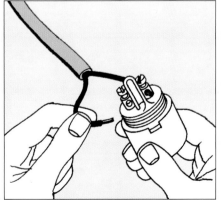

Replacing a ceiling rose flex (2)

Cut a length of the correct type of flex (round PVC-sheathed twin-core for a plastic lampholder, three-core if it's metal). Disconnect the old flex, noting which wire goes to which terminal. Connect the new flex using the core supports on the plastic moulding.

Replacing a ceiling rose flex (3)

Thread the flex through the rose cover and connect it to the rose terminal block making sure to connect the wires exactly the same as the original flex. Double check your notes on the connections before screwing on the rose cover and switching on the mains.

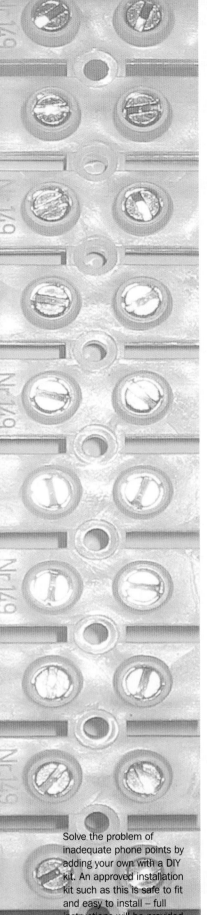

Wall lights

Having learnt how easy it is to install a new junction box, you're now in a position to fit and fix new wall lights into your lighting circuit, and the best way of doing this is first to isolate that particular circuit by switching off at the mains and testing that the circuit is not live. Then you can chase the cable into the wall, preferably in a plastic conduit, and run the cable into the void between the ceiling and the floorboards.

When you buy the wall light or lights make sure that the fitting has an integral backplate that encloses the wires and cable connectors quite comfortably. Wiring Regulations are very specific about new wall lights in that the metal box mounted in a recess cut into the plaster must accommodate the connections and be of a non-combustible material.

Some wall lights have integral switches whereby the light can be individually switched on and off. The instructions will tell you to run a 1 mm^2 two-core-and-earth cable from the junction box to each of the wall light fittings. Within the mounting boxes the earth wires will have green and yellow sleeving and these need to be connected first of all to the earth terminal which is marked with the letter 'E'. Follow the instructions to connect the red and black wires to a block connector inside each light fitting. A one-way switch is all that is necessary for all the wall lights in your room, although it is possible that each light will have its own integral pull switch. Check every connection before switching on at the mains. Check that the lights are working. To complete the job, make good the plaster work around the light fittings before redecorating.

Telephones

Extension sockets   Did you know that you are allowed to install an extension cable and telephone socket in your home and that inexpensive kits are available for the DIYer? You don't have to know anything at all about electricity or about the technology of telephones! Normally there are six colour-coded insulated wires in a telephone low voltage cable, but the one that comes in the kit only has four wires which are just pushed with a special slotted tool that secures the wires into the terminals.

First fix the new socket in the location of your choice. This is simply screwed to a skirting board or screwed to plugs into predrilled holes in the wall. I find it easier to run the tiny white cable along the top of the skirting board, held in place with the use of a glue gun. You can of course run cable, under floorboards or tucked between a carpet and a skirting board, but it is best not to run a telephone cable in close proximity to a mains electricity cable. The instructions will tell you exactly how to make the connection between your new cable and the master socket.

Fixing   Run the cable to the extension socket, fixing it by either using cable clips or a hot glue gun. Glue guns nowadays have transparent hot melt or coloured glue sticks to match existing decor. Having fixed the extension socket into position it is now a simple matter of running the cable, cutting the ends, trimming the insulation, and with the slotted insertion tool, pushing the exposed wires into the marked slots. The wires are held in place without terminal blocks or screws because they are sprung clamped. Screw back both covers and the job is complete.

Testing   New telephones with either 'tone' or 'pulse' dialling all have standard rectangular plugs to fit master sockets and socket extensions. Even though they're rectangular one end is slightly curved so that no mistake can be made when inserting the plug into the socket. It's best to test your new socket by plugging in your existing telephone before buying a new one.

Residual current devices (RCDs)

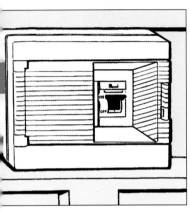

Residual current device (RCD) (1)
Protect all of your house with an RCD fitted close to your meter. It must be installed by a qualified electrician.

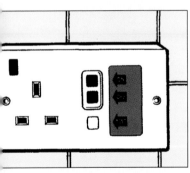

Residual current device (RCD) (2)
Install a wall-mounted socket with RCD protection.

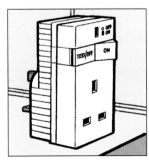

Residual current device (RCD) (3)
A portable three-pin socket adapter with an RCD can be moved from socket to socket.

Powered tools

The use of electrical equipment outdoors need not be the hazard that it was. With the protection of a residual current device (RCD) plugged into the socket indoors and the appliance plugged into that, any leakage or fault that occurs will, in a split second, cut the flow of electricity. It can be a life-saver. As an extra protection, always wear rubber-soled boots when working with electricity outside.

If you're thinking of running an extension lead for a temporary light in the garden – don't! Cables for all external leads must be of the correct size and suitable for outside use. Plugs and sockets used outside must be sealed and manufactured especially for that purpose like the relocatable garden lights that you can buy. The specially sealed fitting has a non-conducting spike on the end of it to secure it into the ground. If you use such lights, or external lights at Christmas time, then the power supply must be protected by an RCD. Small submersible pumps for powering fountains are inexpensive and very popular. These too must be protected by an RCD. To safeguard you, your family and friends, and your pets, you must read the instructions and fully understand them before starting any installation work.

When using an electric-powered lawnmower for cutting the lawn, there is always the danger of severing the cable. To prevent this you can even buy a shoulder holster for gripping the cable whilst mowing the lawn, but there is nothing as safe as an RCD when using any powered tool outside the home.

I recommend the use of an RCD even when working indoors with a powered tool, particularly in outside buildings like sheds and garages. In outside locations like these, it is possible that moisture has been around long enough to affect the electrical connections in a powered tool. The only sure protection against unwittingly using a suspect powered tool is an RCD.

Never plug an RCD into an extension lead, only into a protected socket outlet indoors. RCD adaptors, which can be moved from socket outlet to socket outlet, depending where it is needed most, are just as effective as a permanently wired RCD. Sockets with a built-in RCD can be installed into a power circuit and protected from weathering, but I suggest that if you intend to have one of these fitted, you should seek the help of a qualified and professionally trained electrician. However, if you know what you're doing and understand how a spur can be run from an existing socket, then that spur can have a built-in RCD to comply with Wiring Regulations. These regulations are specific in that they say categorically that a socket in a conservatory or garage that supplies power to powered tools and garden tools, must have an in-built RCD.

If a power tool or appliance fails but the plug is fine, call in an expert.

Always unplug electrical equipment before changing any accessory.

It is of utmost importance to plug any powered tool being used outside into a residual current device (RCD). Plug the RCD adaptor into a socket indoors for total protection. The RCD will instantaneously cut the power if a fault occurs (like cutting a mower cable) so that you are not harmed.

Pipework   Leaks

Use wire wool to clean a copper pipe before making a joint. Centre is an in-line valve (stopcock). From top right clockwise – a capillary coupling (solder), a capillary elbow (90°), a T-joint compression (spanner), a drain-off valve and a bath tap connector.

I've always maintained that, in the case of plumbing and drainage, a little knowledge is not a dangerous thing! For example, knowing where your main stopcock is located means that you can turn the whole of the supply to the house off in the event of a leak or an emergency. Make sure that your main stopcock is in good working order by turning it on and off at least three times a year. Your local water authority has a statutory duty to supply all domestic properties with drinking water. As cars and lorries trundle over the main roads, our drinking water is flowing along pipes under those roads and to our homes – but water is flowing the other way too! Soil water and waste products are taken from our houses by means of soil pipes which connect to the main drainage system. This in turn connects to a network of sewers underneath our roads. Once clean mains water has passed the main stopcock and entered the house, it passes through pipes direct to the drinking tap in the kitchen and to the cold water storage tank in the attic. From the storage tank water is drawn off at baths, handbasins, bidets and WCs.

Don't be confused by the different runs of pipework in your home, some of which might be copper of different sized bores (diameter) whilst other runs will be in plastic ranging from 10mm (½in) for an undersink water softener to

a 5cm (2in) waste pipe and up to 10cm (4in) for a soil pipe. Each and every one of these runs must have joints along the way. Sometimes the choice of joint or coupling is at the whim of the plumber! In, for example, a 15mm (½in) copper pipe system you could possibly find compression joints, capillary joints or 'push fit' joints. All pipework is meant to be held semi-rigidly by clips so that there is no 'shudder' or movement along the run. For different reasons couplings and joints are vulnerable to movement, and therefore to leaks, so it is a good idea to learn something about the different couplings you may encounter.

A compression coupling joining two pieces of copper together comprises three main components. The joint body, the cap nut and a soft copper ring or 'olive'. This type of joint needs two spanners to secure it tightly over both ends of the copper to be joined. The hexagonal cap nut is slipped over the pipe first, followed by the olive. Liberally smear the outside of the tube and olive with a joint paste (to give an extra safeguard against leaks). Then insert the tube end into the joint body as far as the shoulder or stop. Use your fingers to screw the nut as tight as you can and then, holding the joint body with a spanner, give the cap nut a complete turn with another spanner – it's best not to use a wrench or you may over-tighten the nut. One turn should ensure that the cap nut compresses the olive against the tube wall to make a watertight joint, then repeat the process with the second piece of copper pipe to be coupled. As well as a straight (in-line) coupling there are elbows to make 90° joints, T-junctions to break into a straight run for an extra run at 90°, and tank connectors to connect the supply pipe to, for example, a ball-valve. So if a leak does occur in any of these copper fittings it should be easy to solve the problem with the use of a spanner and gentle tactics, without the need to turn off the water supply. If however the leak persists, you'll need to turn off the water supply, drain down that part of the system, open the fitting and apply a couple of turns of PTFE plumber's tape which will solve the problem when the cap nut is tightened up again.

Plastic pipe can be joined by a number of methods but the two most commonly used are solvent welding and push-fit jointing. Plastic pipes, for drainage and for cold water supply, are light, easy to handle, long lasting and much cheaper than copper pipes. However, there is one disadvantage and that is they can't be used for hot water supply. They can, of course, be used for waste pipes from sinks, baths and handbasins. Another advantage is that plastic tubing comes in long lengths which can eliminate expensive couplings.

Underneath sinks, traps and elbow joints are made using compression joints. These are recommended for use with waste and drainage systems by the manufacturers because of their ease of fitting and disassembling for maintenance. But of course this makes it easy to solve the problem of leaks too.

Hard plastic (PVC) pipes can be joined by three methods: by compression joints, as you'll see on most traps, by solvent-welding or by ring-seal jointing. For a cold water supply, solvent-welded joints should be used, while for waste and drainage systems the three methods are often used together. Solvent-welded joints are usually used for small bore waste pipes and ring-seal joints are used for larger diameter waste and drainpipes.

Leaks from plastic compression joints are fairly easy to overcome because the problem is solved simply by an extra tightening turn of the compression cap-nut. Leaks can occasionally occur in that area because hot water and then cold water is passing constantly giving rise to expansion and contraction of the pipes and the compression joints.

Solvent-welded joints are put together after first roughening the inside of the socket with medium abrasive paper. Clean the area with a coat of approved spirit cleaner and degreaser and apply the solvent cement evenly to the tube end and the interior of the socket. If a leak does occur it's simply a matter of applying an approved solvent cement to bond the two parts of the pipework together.

A ring-seal joint has an advantage over the others in that it allows for expansion of a waste pipe resulting from the drainage of warm water from sinks, baths and basins. Initially a joint is made by inserting the tube end into the ring-seal socket as far as the pipe stop which is a shoulder just inside the tube. Then insert the sealing ring into the ring-seal socket, before lubricating the tube end with a little petroleum jelly and pushing it firmly home passed the joint ring. A leak in this area will probably necessitate a new rubber ring, but do take the original so you buy a replacement of the correct diameter and size.

Soldered joints There are two ways that copper pipes are joined by soldered capillary fittings: integral ring fittings (also known as Yorkshire joints), which incorporate sufficient solder to make the join, and end-feed fittings into which solder wire has to be fed along with flux to make it run more easily. The secret of success in making soldered capillary joints is thorough cleanliness. Deburr and clean the cut end of the copper pipe and insert it into the capillary joint. Apply heat either side of the joint and then gently to the joint itself. When a bright ring of solder is seen all around the mouth of the fitting, the joint is complete and becomes, when cool, watertight. If you need to remake a joint for any reason, then reverse this process – applying heat to the existing joint, after the water has been turned off, will allow the fitting to be pulled apart.

Soldering is normally a professional plumber's job, so if you are not too sure of how to accomplish this task there might be a risk because a flame is used – circumspection is needed! Please remember SAFETY FIRST, DIY SECOND and in this instance it might be prudent to call in a plumber.

Push-fit joints Push-fit connectors come both in plastic and brass, but both have a rubber seal inside each end of a coupling. The design of a push-fit coupling ensures that a pipe pushed into it will remain there, secure and watertight. When you assemble a push-fit joint in a plumbing run, first slightly roughen the pipe and apply a recommended lubricant to the end so that it then slides into the fitting without damaging the sealing ring. Push it fully home but ease it back about 3 mm (⅛ in) to allow for expansion when hot water flows through the pipe. Full instructions come with each push-fit fitting and so if one leaks you can fit a replacement quickly and easily.

In an emergency, you can stop a leak in a joint or actually in a pipe itself, no matter what material the pipe is made of or what it's used for, with a plastic putty kit. Epoxy resin plastic putty comes in a stick about 25 mm (1 in) in diameter and 75 mm (3 in) long, but in two parts: the outer, which is the hardener, and the resin core. Cut off a small piece about 6 mm (¼ in) long and knead it so that it becomes one constant colour. It then becomes slightly warm and is ready to apply to a leaking pipe. You can use this product to solve many leaking problems. Once cured and hard it can be filed, sanded and painted. Although often used in emergencies, it certainly can be used as a permanent repair.

Valves

Non-return valves

I suppose we've all suffered the inconvenience of wet feet messing up the kitchen floor, buckets slopping water or even a hosepipe trailing over the kitchen sink. But not if you have an outside tap fitted! A bib tap with a hose connector is virtually essential for the gardener or car owner. Proprietary garden tap kits are fairly inexpensive and easy to fit. But to comply with by-laws, a non-return valve must be fitted into the pipework between the tap itself and where it joins to the rising main to prevent contaminated water being drawn back into the mains water system. Fitting one is as simple as fitting an ordinary compression coupling. They are about 75 mm (3 in) long and must be fitted into the system with the arrow pointing in the

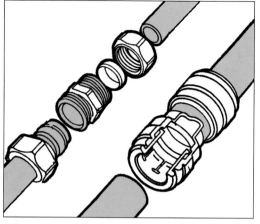

Pipe joints
Compression joints (left) are simply joined by tightening nuts at both ends of the coupling. Brass push-fit joints (right) make watertight couplings because of their grab ring and rubber seal.

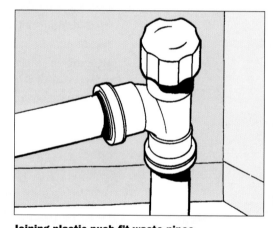

Joining plastic push-fit waste pipes
Cut the pipe ends square and take off any burrs with a file. Smear silicone grease on the pipe ends and push into the fitting. Ease back about 2 mm (¹⁄₁₆ in) to allow for expansion. The rubber seal in the fitting makes it watertight.

direction of the water flow. Compression joints hold the fitting to the two ends of the copper pipe. This means that water will pass along the pipework but cannot flow in the opposite direction. Explicit instructions come with the non-return valve, very easy to follow, and as simple to install.

In-line check valves   Often a cry goes up, 'It's under the kitchen sink, turn off the water for goodness sake!' This can happen when a WC cistern is overfilling, or maybe a tap on the handbasin begins to leak. This indicates to any sensible person that each and every appliance, WC, handbasin and bath, should have their own separate isolator or stopcock.

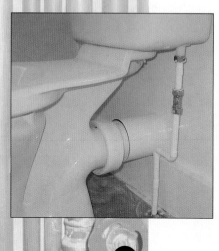

An in-line control valve (stopcock) will isolate the cistern for repairs. A screwdriver is all that's needed to turn the valve off and on.

Overcome banging in pipes by replacing washers.

Banging in pipes could be due to too much pressure – try turning down stopcock.

Separate valves are absolutely essential so that a problem can be dealt with immediately. An in-line valve can be fitted, for example, 300 mm (12 in) from the entry point of the water supply to a WC cistern. It is similar to a non-return valve in length and size and also has compression joints at both ends, but in the centre is a small slot into which a screwdriver fits so that the operation of opening and closing the valve is as simple as half a turn.

A smaller stopcock, called a mini-valve, is usually fitted just before a ball-valve or below a basin tap. Again a screwdriver or even a coin can be used to turn the slotted screw. When closed, the water supply to the tap or ball-valve is interrupted so that you can replace washers without affecting any other part of the plumbing.

Gate valves A gate valve can be used where it is necessary to have an uninterrupted flow of water and where the water pressure is low. It is ideal for bathroom cold water taps, especially when located immediately below the cold water storage tank. A gate valve is identified by the wheel which is used to open and close the valve. They are not directional like stopcocks, so you can fit them either way round. However, they must be the same size as the pipe into which they are fitted. Always keep a gate valve fully open. Often an airlock in a hot water cylinder is caused by a gate valve on the supply pipe (from the cold water system) not being fully opened. A gate valve is fitted into the pipe run with compression joints either side of the valve. Keep them free by turning them off and on a couple of times a year.

Noise

Water-hammer Banging or steady drumming noises in pipes or in cold water storage tanks are often the result of a worn washer in a ball-valve. The incessant drumming noise that is often heard after hot water has been drawn off, happens when water flows in to refill the tank. As water rushes into the tank, ripples are caused on its surface. These can cause the ball and valve to bounce. When the valve bounces on its seating, it produces hammering noises. Sometimes a banging noise is heard in pipes when a certain tap is turned on. In this case, the cause is probably a worn tap washer not closing properly on its seating. It might also be that the metal 'shoulder', or seating, is worn and needs a DIY reseating tool to level it. This is a very simple job carried out with an inexpensive reseating tool which comes with full instructions.

If the water-hammer problem cannot been solved by replacing the washer in the ball-valve, then the problem of fluctuating water pressure can be overcome by replacing the valve itself. The valve is held securely in the cistern body and connected to the copper supply pipe by inner and outer fixing nuts. The first nut on the supply pipe is called a tap connector and this needs to be unscrewed with a spanner to disconnect it from the valve stem.

Ball-valves are manufactured specifically to suit different water pressures and are marked LP, MP or HP (low, medium or high pressure, respectively). If the cistern is fed from the

An in-line valve is an important part of any plumbing run to an appliance. One must be fitted on the supply pipe so that the appliance can be immediately isolated for maintenance and repairs.

Loose pipes
Pipes laid in notches cut in joists will inevitably cause problems. Expansion and contraction in the runs will cause noises. Expanding filling and fixing foam will solve this problem.

mains, an HP valve is essential. However, most WC cisterns are fed from a cold water storage tank, in which case the pressure is low and an LP valve should be fitted. If you have to solve the water-hammer problem by replacing a washer, close the stopcock to stop the supply of water to the cistern. After loosening the tap connector, as described previously, remove the float arm and unscrew the outer fixing nut so that you can pull out the valve. It's always a good idea to replace the washers either side of the cistern body. Push the new valve into position and reassemble the tap connector and tighten all fixing nuts. Double check that the tap connector and the valve are all aligned and all nuts tightened.

Although fitting a new washer or a new valve can possibly solve the water-hammer problem, there is yet one more preventative measure that you can take to stop water-hammer happening in the future. Water falling from the supply pipe and splashing into the cistern was often a source of annoyance. Sometimes a rigid plastic pipe was screwed into the valve so that the water was discharged below the water level in the tank. However, there is the possibility that contaminated water could be back-siphoned through this 'silencer' tube, so rigid tubes were no longer manufactured and were replaced with flexible plastic collapsible tubes. But people noticed that water-hammer ceased when a silencer tube was in position! So by using the permitted flexible tube fitted to the valve to introduce the water beneath the surface, the result is no ripples and no water-hammer!

Airlocks   There are a number of ways in which air can enter a water system to form an airlock (a blockage caused by a trapped air bubble). For a direct cylinder hot water system, with no central heating, it's quite a simple job to overcome the problem of an airlock and to avoid the possibility of airlocks forming in the future. Whilst the system is filling, connect one end of a hose to a cold water tap on a mains supply and the other end to the draincock on the hot water system. Open both the draincock and the tap and, as if by magic, the system will

fill from the bottom and air will naturally be pushed in front of the rising water.

If a plumbing system has been poorly designed, a pipe of too small a diameter might have been used to feed the hot water storage cylinder. It should be 22 mm (¾in) and at this bore (size) replacement cold water will not be allowed to fall in the vent pipe when hot water is drawn. If the level is allowed to reach the horizontal supply pipe in the hot water system, air will be drawn into the pipe and an airlock formed.

If a full system is being refilled, when all taps and draincocks are closed and the mains stopcock opened, check that there are no sluggish ball-valves. This can be another reason for trapped air in the system. All these reasons can be checked and put right but the symptoms are all the same – a poor flow of water, bubbling and spluttering from a hot water tap and the possibility of complete failure of the system so that no water is available when the tap is turned on. Now, all this sounds as if it's a job for a professional plumber's bag of tricks, but it need not be! It is a simple DIY job for you armed with a length of garden hose! The trick is to use mains pressure from your cold tap over the kitchen sink to blow the air bubble out of the system. Firmly secure one end of the hose to the kitchen sink tap or any other tap on mains water pressure, and the other end to the affected problem tap. Open both taps and in a short while the higher pressure from the mains water will force out the air bubble. You might have to repeat this two or three times to get all the air out of the system. Remember that a long length of hose can contain a lot of water, so take care when removing it!

Loose pipes   There are a number of reasons why you should make one big check on all the pipework whether it's domestic water or central-heating water pipes. Because of different temperatures both inside the pipes and outside and around them, all pipework expands and contracts. Often central-heating pipes running alongside joists underneath the bedroom floor will be noisy as the central heating switches itself on or off. This can be quite alarming (or funny!) when an unsuspecting guest hears a 'tap tap' in the middle of the night. This problem is easily remedied. Simply screw more pipe clips around the pipes at strategic positions to hold the pipes more firmly to the sides of the joists.

Loose pipes can cause leaks! As has been stated, all joints in pipework are vulnerable to excessive movement. Eliminate any possibility of joints working loose through movement by getting the correct diameter saddle clamps or pipe clamps to hold the pipes more firmly. Sometimes pipes are loose because they are too far away from a fixing for a normal sized pipe clip. However there are clips available with longer arms. And if the pipe is still loose within the longer type clip, cut a piece of rubber to wrap around the pipe to give it a cushion inside the clamp.

Pipes that run through notches cut into the tops of joists are suspended between the joists and only have support at the notches. Again because of contraction and expansion, notches are usually cut much wider than the diameter of the pipe itself with obvious disadvantages – the main one being that the pipes are not 'anchored'. A simple DIY solution to this problem is to use expanded foam. A little of the foam from a pressurised canister is sufficient! As it expands to fill the notched gap it also encapsulates the pipe, holding it firmly but still allowing for expansion and contraction. In order that the expanding foam does not harden to potentially cause problems if the floorboards ever have to be replaced, use the following trick to keep it level! Liberally smear petroleum jelly on to a piece of board or stiff card and hold it down over the gap before injecting the expanding foam. It will then spread only as far as the board but will not adhere to the petroleum jelly surface. It will expand either side of the joist but that really doesn't matter.

Wherever a water pipe is adjacent to an exterior wall and, more particularly, if it is bedded in the wall there is an inherent danger of an ice plug forming. Do not use a flame gun – the gentle heat of a hair drier will melt the ice plug.

Frost

Ice-plugs Even though you feel that you've fully protected your house and the plumbing system against severe winter weather, under certain conditions water pipes can still be vulnerable to ice and frost. Attics and lofts are the most likely place for bursts to occur because they are the coldest part of the house.

If, in wintertime, your problem is lack of water when you turn on a hot tap, then an ice-plug has probably formed in part of the hot water system. There is risk of an explosion if it is allowed to go unchecked and the immersion heater or boiler is not switched off, so switch it off immediately! Copper piping is an excellent conductor of heat, so apply some form of heat along the pipe away from the tap. Leave the tap open to encourage the flow of water when the plug of ice melts. I recommend gently using a hot air gun or a hair dryer, but never ever a butane or other type of flame gun. The warmth will travel along the copper pipe some distance to melt the ice and clear the blockage. Leave the tap running for a while to warm up the whole length of the copper pipe. Try to find the source of the cold air and use an insulating material to prevent it happening again! Now switch the boiler and the immersion heater back on.

Quite often a waste pipe running through an external wall has its trap very close to the wall where an ice-plug can form in the water in the U-bend designed as a seal to prevent foul smells entering the house from the sewage system. A symptom of this is that water does not run away when it is freezing cold outside. If it is left standing for a long time in winter, it is very likely that it will freeze. These days, most traps and waste pipes are made of plastic and hot air or a naked flame will melt them. The ice must be melted by the application of

Put salt in traps and U-bends to stop them freezing when you leave your house in winter.

Winter protection

Long before winter comes make sure that your house is fully protected against severe frost. It is too late when you have to repair burst pipes in the freezing cold! Start with the mains water pipe. If a burst happens, turn off at the mains and open all the taps to drain the system.

The diagram shows the likely danger spots for frozen pipes.

Never use a blowtorch to cure an ice plug in a pipe – use a hairdryer.

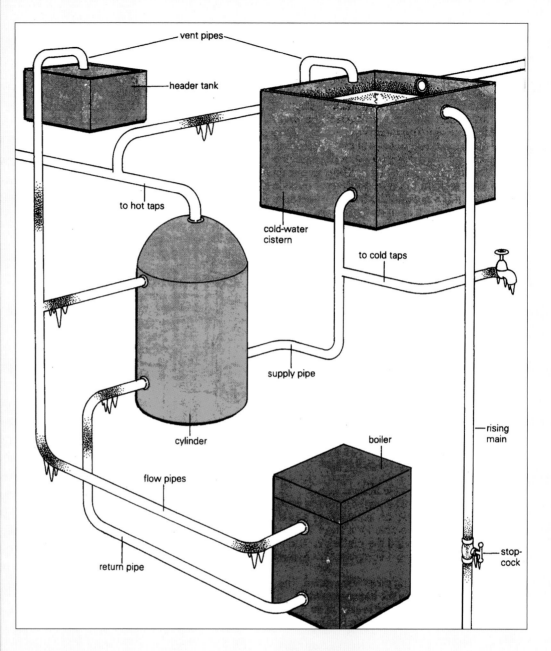

vent pipes

header tank

to hot taps

cold-water cistern

to cold taps

supply pipe

cylinder

boiler

rising main

flow pipes

return pipe

stop-cock

warmth so the problem is solved by wrapping hot towels around the trap and waste pipe. As soon as the towels are cool, replace them immediately and repeat the procedure until the ice melts.

As soon as the water flows from the basin, leave the hot tap running to warm up the rest of the waste system. Add salt to the water in the trap to stop this reoccurring in cold conditions and especially if a sink or basin is infrequently used. Check also that the waste pipe going through the exterior wall is completely sealed. If it isn't, use a mastic sealant outside and a squirt of expanded foam to completely seal the joint inside.

Burst pipes   If you are unlucky enough to experience a burst pipe this is how to solve the problem. Don't rush to find the location of the burst but go immediately to the mains stopcock and turn it off. If this is difficult, tie up the ball-valve in the cold water storage tank. You simply lift the arm, which stops the flow of water into the tank, and tie it to a piece of wood laid across the top of the tank. Get everybody to turn on all the taps in the house and if one does not run then you've located an ice-plug position. Flush the WCs; if the cistern does not refill quickly the burst is in the supply pipe between the storage tank and that WC.

Burst pipe

To make a quick and effective temporary repair to a burst pipe use either a two-part resin-based mix or a steel clamp as shown. A pipe clamp should be kept handy in case of an emergency. It can be used on pipes of different sizes and reused once a permanent repair has been made. A rubber gasket seals the split in the pipe and a butterfly nut and bolt tightens the clamp to make the repair watertight

Split copper pipes

Epoxy-resin plastic putty is easy to use but read the instructions! Resin repair kits come in stick form. Cut off sufficient to do the repair. Knead together the inner core and outer skin to make a compound and wrap this around the split to make an immediate repair.

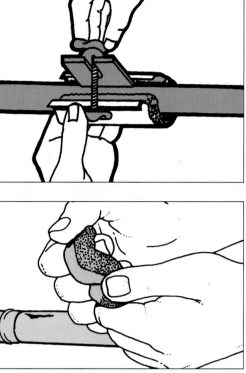

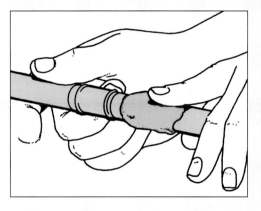

If water is dripping through a ceiling, take great care because it could have entered a junction box or a light fitting. Having turned off the taps to prevent serious flooding, there might still be a pool of water lying just above a plasterboard ceiling. You'll need to turn off the electricity supply before checking in the loft. Never use candles or matches in an emergency but use your standby torch. In the room underneath the rapidly staining ceiling place a plastic sheet and buckets on the floor and poke a pointed stick through the centre of the wet patch. Once all the water has drained away, carry out a temporary repair to the pipe.

Burst pipe repair kits are available at your DIY store, so buy a few different types and sizes to keep for an emergency. A steel clamp with a rubber gasket to seal over the split is a quick and efficient temporary repair aid. It is particularly useful because it can be used on different sizes of pipe. Once a permanent repair has been carried out, put the clamp away, hopefully never to be used again!

Another useful emergency repair kit is a two-part resin sealant which sets rock hard around the split – it's an incredibly versatile repair kit! Couplings are available, which are easily inserted after the split part of the pipe has been cut out. If a joint has been affected by ice expansion it's probably not actually split but just pulled apart. Water expands when it freezes so that's why longitudinal splits occur in copper pipes and also it's the reason why an ice-plug will push apart a copper joint. Manufacturers have been made much more aware of the demands of DIY enthusiasts and have produced replacement repair kits with compression joints and also with push-fit joints.

Dripping overflows When water runs continuously from an overflow pipe, it can cause many problems. Walls become damp, mould and algae grow, soil can become eroded and worst of all nasty accidents can happen when it is allowed to freeze on a path or patio. With the thought of upheaval and disruption well to the back of one's mind, it is so easy to put off calling in a plumber. However, not only are most WC systems or storage tanks easily accessible, they are also not difficult to repair and service. So to solve this particular problem is actually a very simple DIY application.

Understanding the basic design features of a ball-valve cistern and how it operates will help you gain confidence to tackle the replacement of a washer, a diaphragm in a modern cistern or a float valve. Ball-valves supply and maintain the level of water in WC cisterns, cold water storage cisterns and expansion tanks. The ball or float is connected to the valve by an arm. It's a very simple piece of engineering which works efficiently most of the time. When the water level falls in the cistern or tank, you'll see the ball or float falling with it opening a valve that allows water to gush in to fill the cistern or tank. When the water reaches a prescribed level, with the floating ball has lifted the lever and this action forces the valve mechanism to close, stopping the supply of water. If the inlet valve does not shut off the water will continue fill the tank until it reaches the overflow outlet – the tank's safety device. Without the overflow pipe, water would continue to rise over the edge of the tank and cause very serious problems. Water dripping outside from an overflow pipe usually indicates a faulty ball-valve.

The diagrams (on pages 265–6) show the difference between an older ball-valve, such as a Portsmouth valve, and a modern diaphragm ball-valve. If yours is the older type with a brass body, it's quite easy to replace the small washer housed in the flanged washer cap. Constant opening and closing of the slotted plug which houses the washer causes a great deal of wear and the washer will need to be replaced from time to time. Start by closing the stopcock to shut off the water supply. There should be one located close to the storage tank. You might sometimes find a screw-on cap at the end of the valve body and this must be removed. A split pin holds the float-arm to the body of the valve, which must also be removed, enabling the cranked end of the float-arm to be pulled clear of the slot in the plug. The plug (piston) can now be pulled free of the body of the valve. By holding a screwdriver through the slot in the plug you can unscrew the cap which holds the washer. Use a pair of pliers, but protect the brass from the jaws of the pliers with a piece of cloth. Ease out the old washer from the cap and clean the piston, especially where the pliers held it, with fine wire wool. If the plug does not have a removable cap housing the washer, use a sharp skewer to pick out the worn washer. It isn't difficult to wriggle the new washer underneath the flange in the plug. Smear the plug with Vaseline® and carefully clean the inside of the valve body. Do this by wrapping a piece of fine abrasive paper around a pencil and use it to remove any corrosion or hard water scale. Reassemble the parts in reverse order.

After restoring the water supply you'll probably have to adjust the ball-valve arm in order to maintain the water at the level indicated on the inside body of the cistern. Having replaced the washer in the ball-valve, you might be lucky enough to find that another source of annoyance, the problem of 'water-hammer' has also been eliminated!

Fitting a garden tap? Install a double-check valve to stop contamination.

Taps
Washers

Replacing   Most people think that the only cause of water dripping from a tap is a worn washer that needs replacing. However, check that the water is not leaking from beneath the head of the tap when it is turned off. Drips from the spout may also be caused by a worn shoulder or 'seat'. The washer sits on the shoulder and is compressed when the tap is turned to stop the flow of water.

The stains that have been left on a bath or sink by a continuously dripping tap are easily removed by a proprietary brand of bath cleaner. Apply it with a brush, leave it for the recommended time, then wash it away and the stains disappear.

The two most common types of taps are pillar taps (also called bib taps) and reverse-pressure taps. A more modern type of pillar tap is the shrouded-head tap.

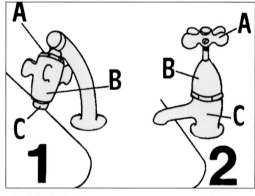

Plumbing – taps

Tap 1 is a typical reverse-pressure tap. You do not need to turn off the water supply to replace the washer. Only one retaining nut (A) needs to be unscrewed. The body (B) will then drop down to expose the jumper and washer which will fall out when the nozzle (C) is tapped on the floor. Tap 2 is a common pillar tap where the mains water must be turned off to open it up. (A) is the capstan head, (B) the shroud or sheath and (C) the body.

Pillar taps   Replacement washers for all types of taps are fairly standard and it makes sense to keep a stock handy. Before dismantling and repairing a pillar tap, turn off the supply to the tap, put the plug into the waste outlet and a

Plumbing – repairs

Remember to turn off the supply and plug the waste before you start. To replace a washer, unscrew the shroud (B) taking care to protect the chrome. With a spanner, loosen the head-gear nut just above the main body of the tap (D). This will release the whole assembly including the jumper (E) and washer (F). Unscrew the small holding nut (G) which allows the washer to be prised off and replaced. If it is rusted on, it's probably easier to replace the jumper and washer with new ones.

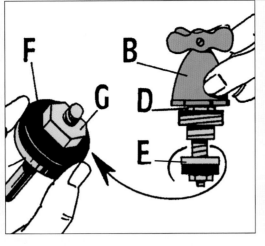

thick towel in the sink or handbasin. Drain the pipe feeding the tap and then open up the valve as far as it will go as if turning on the water. A pillar tap will have a domed cover which has to be unscrewed first. A strap wrench is the ideal tool for this but there are also some great tools on the market that have protective jaws so that the chrome dome is not scratched or damaged. The head-gear nut, just above the main body of the tap, can then be unscrewed and the whole of the head-gear assembly lifted out. You'll find the washer fixed to a jumper, which in some cases comes away with the head-gear, but in some taps will be lying inside the tap body. The washer is either held securely by a nut or pressed over a rivet-like end of the jumper. Occasionally the nut can't be unscrewed without damaging the jumper, in which case replace the jumper and washer together. Separate parts and washers are available at most DIY stores. After the new washer has been replaced, screw up the retaining nut. Lower the head-gear back into the base of the tap, tighten the head-gear nut and reassemble the chrome cover.

Reverse-pressure taps

This upside-down tap or 'Supatap' is sometimes called the DIYer's gift because there is no need to stop the supply of water to the tap when the washer has to be replaced! These taps are actually turned on and off by turning the nozzle of the tap. Replacing a washer in a reverse-pressure tap is easy, because a water-valve closes automatically as the tap body or outer cover is removed.

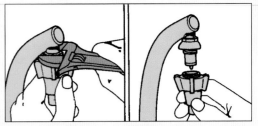

Replacing a 'Supatap' washer (1)
This is the easiest tap to repair because you don't have to turn off the water supply!

Open the tap slightly and release the retaining nut at the top of the nozzle. Start turning the tap to increase the flow of water. Suddenly the water will stop as the check valve slides into place. The nozzle will then come away in your hand.

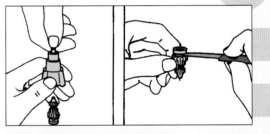

Replacing a 'Supatap' washer (2)
Tap the nozzle on a hard surface (not one that will crack) to loosen the anti-splash device. The washer and jumper are inside. Turn the nozzle upside down and the anti-splash device will drop out. Remove the washer and jumper as shown, and insert new ones.

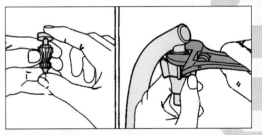

Replacing a 'Supatap' washer (3)
Replace the anti-splash device and reassemble the tap. The nozzle screws back on with a left-hand thread.

You'll find a small holding-nut at the top of the nozzle, which has to be unscrewed. Now turn the tap on and keep on turning, as if you were opening it. The water will flow and, at first, increase but suddenly the check-valve will be activated, stopping the flow of water. A few more turns of the nozzle and it will come off in your hand. Hold the nozzle in your hand in its upright position and tap it on a hard surface (but not on a breakable handbasin!). Now, turn it upside down and you'll find that the anti-splash device, which holds the washer and the finned jumper inside it, will fall out. Gently prise the washer and jumper from the end of the anti-splash device. You'll now see why this is one of the easiest of DIY problems to solve – the replacement simply presses into the finned device. To reassemble the tap is child's play!

Shrouded-head taps
A more modern type of pillar tap is the shrouded-head tap. Instead of the traditional capstan-head, this tap has a neatly designed cover which does not conduct heat. The cover is normally held to the head-gear by a small retaining screw underneath the label disc. If this is not the case in your tap you'll find a tiny screw in the side similar to the retaining screw on a pillar tap. Once you've removed the cover, the head-gear is easily unscrewed and the procedure is then exactly the same as for the pillar tap. At the top of the head-gear of the tap is a gland nut and gland packing. Some modern shrouded-head taps have a rubber O-ring seal instead of a conventional gland. They are designed to be trouble-free but if there is any water escaping up the spindle, renew the ring.

Reseating
Don't feel that you've failed if a tap continues to drip after you've fitted a new washer! It probably isn't your fault at all but suggests that the valve-seating might be scratched, so even fitting a new washer is not going to result in a watertight seal. Although there are reseating tools available, the cheapest and quickest way to deal with this problem is to use a seating kit with a new nylon washer. Instructions are supplied with the kit. The nylon seating is placed on to the scratched brass

seating, and a new washer and jumper are inserted into the head-gear of the tap. When screwed down, the valve seating is forced into position. Don't try to change the seating on Supataps without using a special reseating tool, available from the manufacturer or DIY stores.

The shoulder, or 'seat', against which a tap washer is forced to stop the supply of water from the spout, can get pitted or worn over a long period of time. This is an easy problem to solve because special threaded steel tools are available with different sized cutters to suit different taps. All you do is simply turn off the water supply, screw in the standard threaded tool after removing the head-gear and gently grind the seat flat by turning the handle gently to and fro. Normally the seating is manufactured in brass, so you will have a small residue to clean off or wash away. Some tool hire companies have reseating tools for hire.

Leaks

Glands
The sight of water coming from the top of a tap can be disconcerting. If the tap can also be turned on and off very easily with the fingers, then the cause is certain to be gland failure. It's most common on a conventional tap and can often be stopped just by tightening a nut.

To do this, take off the capstan-head by removing the retaining screw. The shield or protective cover of the tap must come off next.

Leaking taps – glands (1)
Turn off the mains supply. Unscrew the upper nut, anti-clockwise, after taking off the cover. Stop the leak by tightening the upper (gland) nut. Otherwise renew the gland packing.

Leaking taps – glands (2)
Replace the gland packing with strands of wool coated with petroleum jelly. Pack this well down into the tap. Don't over-tighten the gland nut when replacing it as this will make the tap stiff to turn.

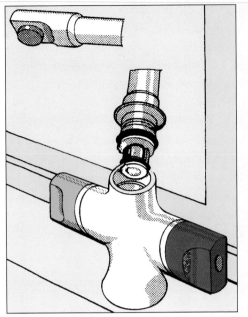

Leaking taps – O-ring mixer
Remove the small retaining screw at the back of the tap. Twist the spout to the right, parallel to the taps. Now pull the spout upwards to remove it. Replace the O-ring and reassemble. Full instructions come with O-rings when you buy them.

The adjusting nut, which you need to tighten, will be the first nut through which the spindle of the tap passes. Trial and error will give you the correct adjustment. If all the allowance for adjustment has already been taken up then you'll have to remove the gland packing and replace it. Take off the nut completely to remove the greased packing material. Repack the void with string or wool and Vaseline® , filling it completely before replacing the nut. Reassemble the tap, open the stopcock and you've successfully completed yet another DIY job.

O-ring/mixer taps

The mixer tap on your kitchen sink is just as easy to repair as a conventional tap. When working on taps, to prevent losing anything down the plughole, put the plug in and use a folded towel to protect the bottom of the bowl. Mixer taps are differently designed in that the gland packing is no longer present but you will find a rubber O-ring in its place. Before you take off the domed or shrouded head you'll find a circlip which holds the spindle in place. Remove the circlip and the spindle so you can then prise the old O-ring out of a groove in the spindle. You can then easily slip on the new O-ring but use a silicone grease to lubricate the parts. Reassemble in reverse order. Whether the leak is from the top of the shrouded head or from the central base of the swivel spout, replacements of any of the parts are easily available. However, always take the old O-ring with you when you buy the replacement one. You'll find a retaining screw at the base of the spout which holds it in position. If water seeps from this junction turn off the hot and cold and undo the screw. Inside you'll find an O-ring, or perhaps a washer, and because of the constant swivelling action of the spout, this obviously is subjected to wear. After fitting the replacement and with the swivel spout pushed back into position, the only tool that you'll now require is a screwdriver!

Tanks
Valves

Renewing a float The two most common faults that occur in a cold water storage tank or a WC cistern are water overflowing or that it does not fill properly. Regularly check that the level of water in the tank and in the WC flushing cistern is maintained at a constant level. The mechanism to achieve this is a float fixed to a movable arm which, in turn, pushes a washer or diaphragm to seal off the water supply. When water is drawn off the float falls and the arm opens the valve. When water rushes in the float raises the arm which in turn seals the water supply. Modern float-valves are small and non-corrosive but the older types of ball-valve have a washered metal-plug to control the flow of water.

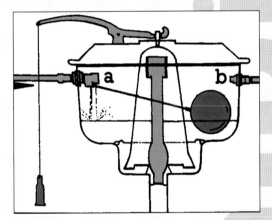

Cisterns
The sketch illustrates an older type of ball valve in a cast-iron cistern. The flushing action starts when the bell is raised by pulling the chain and water is forced inside as it falls. The water level rises to cover the inside stand pipe and siphonic action starts as the water rushes down the flush pipe to the pan. The ball-float falls and the arm opens the valve (A) allowing water to refill the cistern. A fault with either the valve or the ball-float could allow water to continue to run until it reaches the level of the overflow pipe (B) – the safety factor in all cisterns and storage tanks.

Problems with too little water in the cistern? – Adjust the arm upwards. Water overflowing? – Adjust the ball-valve arm down.

Plumbing

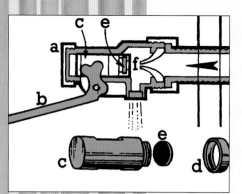

Replacing a washer

Overflowing pipes are often the result of faulty valves. The Portsmouth valve (illustrated) was used for many years until the 'diaphragm' was introduced. To replace a washer, turn off the water supply at the stopcock, unscrew the end cap (a) and pull out the split pin so that the arm (b) can be detached. Slide out the piston (c) and unscrew the cap (d) in which the washer (e) is housed. Renew the washer and reverse the procedure. The washer seals by pressing against the valve seat (f).

As I have described in the sections on 'Pipework' and 'Water-hammer', disassembling the various parts of a Portsmouth type of ball-valve (similar to the Croydon ball-valve) is a fairly simple operation. However, there are times when a new unit (float-valve) will have to be fitted.

You'll need to turn off the control or stopcock before replacing a float-valve. These will be connected to the pipework just before the water supply pipe enters a WC cistern or a cold water storage tank in the attic. On the outside of the casing you'll find first of all a washer, then an outer fixing nut and a connector. All of these will be 'in-line' with the supply pipe outside the tank and the float-valve threaded stem on which is a washer and an inner fixing nut. Undo the connector nut on the outside of the tank first, and then the fixing nuts, so that you can pull out the valve. Fix a matching replacement valve, working in reverse order, before tightening the fixing nut to hold the valve in a rigid position to the casing of the cistern or tank. The installation instructions will always tell you to turn the water supply back on, which is pretty obvious, then to adjust the float arm to get the correct level of water in the tank.

Replacing a flap-valve

A more modern WC cistern, a one-piece siphon system, is one that has a perforated plastic plate at the bottom of the mechanism. As the lever is pressed to flush water, the plate rises but the perforations are closed by a plastic, flexible diaphragm called a flap-valve. This movement releases the water up and over a U-bend and starts the siphoning action, when all the water is discharged. The float then drops with the water level which in turn opens the float-valve to refill the cistern. After a time wear in the valve will cause a lot of noise during filling which can also be slowed down.

To replace the flap-valve you'll need to isolate the cistern by closing a valve or tying up the float arm to a piece of wood across the top of the cistern to close the water supply. Get rid of the water in the cistern by flushing it through. Underneath the cistern you'll find a large nut, similar to a compression nut, which holds the water flushing pipe to the underside of the cistern. You'll then be able to lift the siphon out of the cistern but, as it's a delicate piece of mechanism, be very careful. Then it's an easy job to remove the diaphragm from the metal plate and reassemble with one of a matching size. Reconnect the handle hook to the spindle that lifts the plate and completely reassemble it but, before tightening the retaining nut

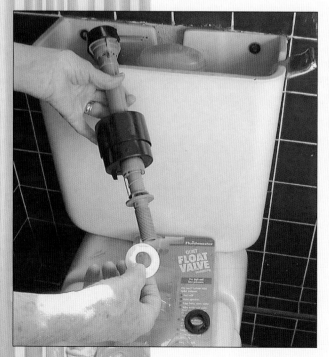

The old floating ball and metal arm has been superseded by the more simple float-valve that is easy to install. No bigger than a cricket ball, the float literally glides up and down on the supply pipe!

After installing a new float-valve, make a few important adjustments. The water must meet the correct level marked inside. An adjusting nut is at the end of the arm. The float must be free of the sides and all the joints tightened.

underneath the cistern, wind a few turns of PTFE tape around the threads to ensure a leak-proof joint.

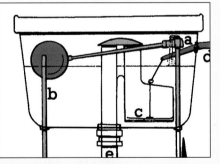

Replacing the diaphragm
The ball-float activates the pivoted end of the arm (b) on which is fixed a plastic disc. This 'presses' a plug (c) which closes the water supply by firmly pushing a diaphragm (d) against the valve seat (e). The water supply pipe (a) is located in the cistern base. To replace a faulty diaphragm in a modern cistern, first turn off the water supply at the stopcock, Unscrew the large retaining nut (f) so that the old diaphragm can be removed.

Adjusting the ball arm
A modern direct action WC cistern is flushed by pressing a lever or handle (d). A perforated metal or plastic plate is raised inside the siphon tube on which there is a thin plastic diaphragm or flap valve (c). Water is forced over the bend and down the flush pipe (e). Both the supply pipe (a) and the overflow pipe (b) are located in the base of the cistern. If the ball-float is faulty, or the arm is not properly adjusted, water will rise up over the overflow pipe causing problems outside the house.

Diaphragm valves

The diaphragm valve in a WC cistern is made mostly of hard plastic, it is smaller than most of the other types of valves and it is probably the easiest to replace. The design of a diaphragm valve is really quite simple. The arm which moves up and down as the float rises and falls, simply presses against a quite small piston which in turn pushes a rubber diaphragm to seal the small end of water pipe. The only part of the valve that you will never need to replace is the diaphragm itself. After turning off the water supply and unscrewing the large retaining cap which holds the two pieces of the unit together, simply slide them apart. You'll find the diaphragm in front of the piston and close to the water inlet. Now you can see how easy it is to lift out the diaphragm and replace it with a matching one. Reassemble in reverse order and have great satisfaction once you've turned the water supply back on again.

Replacing a valve washer

There are various types of valve available, some still in use from many years ago. The Portsmouth valve, for example, has been in use for many years and even though washers might have been replaced, provided that the piston has not seized, it could still be in working order today. Replacing a washer in this valve has been dealt with in a previous section. There are information sheets available from builders merchants and DIY stores to help you familiarise yourself with the fitting in your own storage tank. By reading and understanding the specifications and instructions for installing your own particular brand of float-valve, you can then assess the type of washer needed when you need a replacement.

Water

Maintaining level

A house's storage tank is usually sited on strong battens in an attic or loft so that it can feed water to appliances, handbasins and baths by gravity. That is the reason for them being as high up in the building as possible. For our convenience we get cold water from a storage tank simply by turning on a tap. We expect it as our right! However, there are working parts within the tank – the ball-valve system. If, without knowing or realising it, a valve becomes stuck or there is a blockage, the water level will drop drastically. As more water is drawn off, eventually by opening a tap, air will be sucked into the pipe instead of water. Only then will you realise that something is wrong. Maintaining ball-valves in good condition is paramount.

The opposite situation to this is when too much water is allowed to enter the tank forcing the valve arm too high. This will exert too much pressure on the washer. At the extreme the water will be allowed to enter the overflow pipe, which is the safety feature built into all storage tanks. Some arms have a stop-fitting to adjust the level of the arm to exactly what it should be so that the water level is just below the outlet pipe. An older type ball-valve fitting will have a flexible metal pipe, strong enough to be held in position but easily bent to maintain the perfect water level. To maintain the level of water, which should be about 25 mm (1 in) below the overflow pipe, some ball float arms have a 90° cranked end to which the ball float is held with a butterfly nut. This means that it easy to adjust by sliding the ball float up or down and tightening the holding screw until you reach the correct position to maintain the best water level.

Noisy filling

There can be a number of reasons why water refilling a storage tank in an attic is more noisy than it should be! Storage tanks have to be located as high as possible in a house, and this unfortunately is usually above the bedrooms. Consequently, it's not during the day that one is disturbed by a noisy tank, but at night! So check first of all the area that separates bedrooms from the attic space above. Is the floor of the attic adequately insulated and is the hatch door insulated with sound as well as thermal protection? Another thing to look at is the tank itself. For thermal and sound insulation it should have a heavily padded insulating jacket. Pipes can even transmit sound, so make sure that they are protected too, right as far as the tank itself.

Running water hitting the water in the tank is obviously going to make a noise. This is normal, but if the pressure is too high then the noise will be excessive. Try turning the stopcock to the ball-valve just sufficiently to make less noise but not to cause interference in the filling of the tank. The valve itself could either have debris lodged in it or a worn part. If this is the case, the water could be spraying out instead of being a steady jet and this would cause a 'hissing' sound which obviously can be very annoying.

Continuously running If the ball in a ball-valve system inside a cold water storage tank is allowed to ride too high on the surface of the water, it's going to let too much water into the tank causing the water level to rise above the overflow outlet. This is wasteful and so must be dealt with as a matter of urgency. By lowering the ball-valve arm, you can adjust the level that is will cut off the supply and therefore the problem will be solved. However, in some cases, despite the fact that the ball and the ball arm are aligned properly, water can still flow into the tank over and above the ball and out through the outlet pipe for another reason. If the diaphragm, or in a ball-valve system, the washer, is worn or it is prevented from sealing the water inlet, then water is going to flow through. In this case you have to either replace the valve itself or deal with the washer or diaphragm. This has been described in a previous section.

Pressure Water pressure varies from area to area but not enough to cause a real problem! However, if the water pressure is fairly high in your area and you have a wrongly rated valve installed in your cold water storage tank, then this might be another cause for the valve to leak continuously. There are three different types of float-valves made especially for different water pressures: LP, MP and HP, for low, medium and high pressures, respectively.

WC cisterns should not be connected to the mains supply! These are always fed from the cold water storage tank and therefore the valves in cisterns must be low pressure valves (LP). Without a valve of the correct pressure a cistern may take a very long time to fill. Sometimes it's necessary to fit an MP valve in a WC cistern when the height of the storage tank is more than 14 m (45 ft).

If you're uncertain about what pressure valves are in the various tanks in your home, go to a builders merchant or DIY store and check the specifications on the ones similar to yours. Ask for a copy of the installation instructions which will include a list of all the parts. There are so many variables governing valves that it is important to get to know what you have and to replace any with matching parts. Some modern valves are manufactured so that you can alter the pressure by simply replacing the seat inside, but if the valve is an old Portsmouth or Croydon type and it is of the wrong pressure, then you have no alternative but to change it for another one of the correct rating.

Cold water storage

These days, most cold water storage tanks are made from high density plastic. They are formulated and manufactured to last for years and come in all shapes and sizes, some are round, others are square or long oblongs. What one doesn't want to have happen is for debris and polluted dust to fall into the tank so a protective cover is essential. These are available with holes for overflow pipes that discharge into the tank itself from elsewhere. These pipes from hot water cylinders and central-heating systems are meant purely to provide some measure of safety.

The tanks are all pliable, so that they can be lifted through a normal sized hatch to get it up

The water level in a cold water storage tank has to be maintained at the correct level to prevent overflows! One method is to carefully bend the ball arm to lower the level to about an inch below the overflow pipe outlet.

into the attic, but this means that it is necessary to reinforce the entry holes cut into the tanks for flow and return pipes. It's at these points of connection that you have to be aware of potential problems. All connections, whether they are plastic or brass, should be given the finger 'shine' test periodically and, obviously, because you're dealing here with flexible plastic, absolutely no heavy-handed tactics! An eighth of a turn might be sufficient to stop a leak but a quarter of a turn might spell disaster. If you have to open a connector to make a repair then you must drain the tank by stopping the flow of water through the valve. At the same time it's always worth inspecting the inside of the tank and giving it a thorough clean. Any chemicals left behind after cleaning will contaminate the water which tells you the obvious thing: use nothing that is toxic. Once you've made a repair and cleaned out the tank, flush it through for a couple of hours to neutralise any cleaning agent. All connectors are available, are inexpensive and, as you've read from the previous sections, quite simple to replace. Valves and overflows have already been dealt with, but when you do any work on the tanks themselves, and especially on pipes running between floor joists, take care with any insulation material, especially if it is old fibreglass. The fibres can be a hazard so it's

This old storage tank contravenes current by-laws. Replacement of the tank is overdue because of pitting, deposits, no protective lid, inadequate insulation and a leaking valve!

always best to wear a filtered mask, goggles and protective clothing. Take care to lay the fibreglass back over pipework, if it has been disturbed, but electric cables have to be laid on top because of the possibility of overheating.

By-laws The supply of water into all habitable properties comes under the heading of 'Services'. By-laws exist that state that all domestic properties must be supplied by a water authority with drinking water to a kitchen tap.

The mains pipe also has a diverter which takes water to a cold water storage tank at a high point in the house. Water from the storage tank, by statute, has to feed WC cisterns, handbasins and baths. Other pipes feed hot water cisterns and yet another one for central-heating boilers. This is a simplified version of course. Copies of the water by-laws governing plumbing regulations are available for you to see at your local council offices or you can obtain a copy from your water authority. They will tell you what you can and cannot do with your plumbing system and how it can be connected to the water authority's rising main.

A cold water storage tank in an attic must be properly supported, usually on boards at right-angles to the lay of the joists. For an ordinary domestic dwelling, a tank can store 230–370 litres (50–80 gallons) of water and must be high enough to exert the pressure needed to give sufficient 'head' (which means pressure) of water to supply all the fittings and appliances.

Another requirement of the by-laws governing the installation of cold water storage tanks is 'By-law No. 30', which has been in existence for some little while. This particular by-law has a requirement that a kit includes a lid with a deep overhang to stop light getting in on to the water and of course to keep insects at bay. In the water authority's information leaflet it will tell you about the 'screened breather' and a sleeved inlet for the vent pipe. The sleeved inlet takes the vent or overflow pipes from hot water cylinders and boilers and the screened breather allows air to circulate around the void above the water level. It is also recommended that the overflow pipe has a special screened assembly to stop creepy-crawlies getting into the tank. As well as this a reinforcing plate must be fixed to the tank wall just outside the float-valve. We've already talked about the insulating jacket which these days is mandatory.

Blockages

Never pour hot fat into the sink waste – it'll coagulate and block it!

Traps

There are millions of traps or U-bends in daily use in the UK, each holding small amounts of water in order to prevent unpleasant smells from entering our home! Baths, basins, sinks, showers, WCs and yard gullies, plus more, all need to be maintained in pristine condition to safeguard our health and to keep appliances running properly. But blockages can occur from time to time!

It's not difficult to fit a trap underneath a bath because most have a built-in access panel especially for this purpose. Sometimes you'll find that a bath has a shallow trap and doesn't have a good fall (or gradient) for the waste pipe to quickly take away the bath water. In this case grease and hair can easily accumulate in the trap and build up to become a minor blockage. Eventually the bath water will start to run away quite slowly. Now is the time to inspect the trap. This is not a difficult job, although, if the access panel is small, you'll have to be a bit of an acrobat to get to the knurled nut that releases the trap. A slight complication is that you'll probably find a flexible hose connected to the trap at one end and to the overflow outlet higher on the end of the bath at the other end. You might also find a cleaning eye at the back of the trap which, when unscrewed, can be used to clean out small blockages.

Basin traps can either be a bottle type or a U-shaped trap. Each is easily dismantled for regular cleaning, but always have a bucket ready underneath the basin, especially if a blockage has already occurred and the basin holds a certain amount of dirty water.

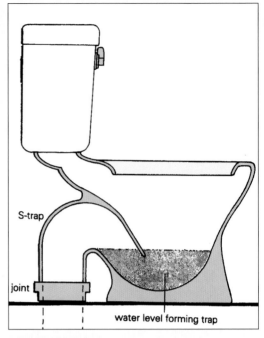

Lavatory blockages

The diagram shows the S-trap and ideal water level.

If the water level rises to the rim when you flush there is some sort of obstruction for you to clear. An 'instant drain opener' with a WC rubber disc attachment will solve the problem.

If an outside waste pipe is blocked you might find that a ground floor lavatory could get a 'back-up' of water. Wearing gloves and a mask, start at the manhole and use a series of rods to unblock the waste pipe. Use plenty of disinfectant and flush the lavatory a couple of times to clear the system.

In institutions up and down the country where sinks and basins are in constant use 24-hours a day, there is a proprietary 'instant drain cleaner' available for whenever a blockage occurs. It is CFC-free, non-acidic and is non-poisonous but is effective in clearing most blockages with one press of the cylinder into the waste outlets of baths, basins, sinks, etc. The tool works by blasting an air wave along the pipe to dislodge the blockage. It has been designed to be powerful enough to move any blockages without damaging the joints.

The tempting aroma of a joint of roast pork or lamb may activate the taste buds, but the resulting coagulated fat can spell disaster for the waste system below the kitchen sink! Greasy roasting trays and dinner plates should be allowed to cool and the residual fat scraped off and disposed of in a plastic bag rather than swilled down the kitchen sink. Hot water only

Plumbing – blockages

Use a flexible drain auger (A) to clear blockages well down a waste pipe. This is a length of coiled wire which will pass through small diameter holes. Crank the handle (B) to turn the corkscrew end and dislodge debris. Pull and push the auger and run water to free the pipe. Use a 'force cup' (C) to clear a blocked trap, but remember to cover the overflow with a damp cloth.

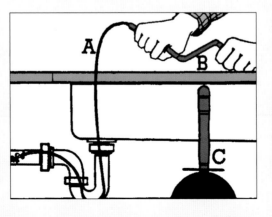

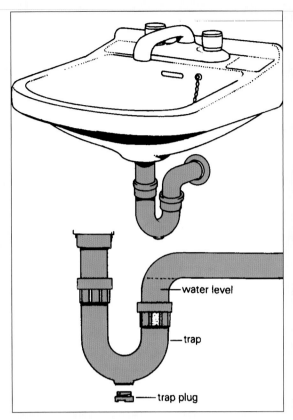

Blocked traps

It is easy to unscrew the compression joints in a blocked trap. Some traps have a trap plug at the base of the U-bend making cleaning easier.

melts the grease and fat momentarily. Once it hits the cold water in the trap, it hardens and stays there. Other debris will build up until a serious blockage occurs. If you find that less and less water is draining away as the days go by, then a complete blockage is not far away. This should never be allowed to happen but if it does, reach for the 'instant drain cleaner'. A 'force cup' can usually be found, in many homes, underneath the kitchen sink, together with the cleaning materials, bucket and collection of plastic bags. These sink plungers have been used since Victorian days! The plunger is a rubber or plastic cup mounted on a wooden handle. Tightly hold a cloth over the overflow outlet and with the rubber cup held firmly over the plughole and with 75–100 cm (3–4 in) of water in the sink, pump the handle up and down until the water begins to clear. This usually works for small blockages.

Modern plastic traps can be either of the screw type or have joints that push and fit together held tightly by a rubber ring. Each is easy to dismantle, so when you disconnect a trap the water that had been trapped in the sink will flow through the waste outlet into a bucket. After cleaning out the trap, reassemble it, but remember to test for leaks.

We are taught at a very early age what should and should not be flushed down the lavatory! If the water rises in the pan and subsides only slowly, it is most likely to be result of somebody's carelessness or neglect. You might have already in the house a larger plunger similar to the sink force cup and this can clear a part

blockage, but if the obstruction is preventing water running away then resort to the 'instant drain cleaner'. Rubber gloves and a disinfectant are an essential part of this operation!

Yard gullies get blocked by debris, earth and leaves being washed down by the rain. Most yard gullies have deep seal traps and are very easy to clean. It is always better to lift out any earth and debris in a yard gully rather than rake and hose it through to cause a problem further on in the sewage system. With a protective sheet to lie on and a tough plastic garden refuse bag wrapped around your arm, it's quite an easy job, although tedious, to scoop out the debris. Dispose of it in the plastic bag. It's also a good idea to pour in some disinfectant before commencing the job!

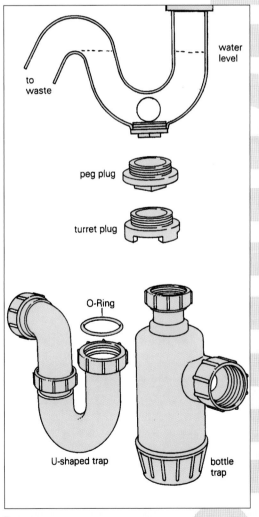

Traps

The diagram illustrates a one-piece traps and alternative plugs (top), a two-piece trap (bottom left) and a bottle trap (bottom right).

A blocked drain is a nuisance but solving the problem is really quite simple. Whether the blockage is in a kitchen sink, a bath, basin or WC, this pressurised cartridge device, used in institutions all over the world, will clear it. It is non-toxic and will not harm pipe joints.

Put your hand in a plastic bin bag to clean out yard gullies annually.

Waste pipes

Cleaning eyes Cleaning eyes are found along waste pipes at strategic positions to give access for rodding and cleaning. A flexible drain auger is the best tool to clear a blockage in a waste pipe with a very long run to an manhole. The auger's length of coiled wire will pass through the smallest diameter hole and by twisting the crank handle the corkscrew end will dislodge debris which can be pulled or pushed as you run water through the pipe.

Underfloor Waste pipes that run under floors are usually in long lengths and only accessible for cleaning from a cleaning eye at one end or from the trap. If there are bends in the run they will be 'slow bends' rather than right-angled elbows. This makes it easier to use a small gauge coiled auger to clean through the length of waste pipe.

Indoor runs Unseen and usually unheard, waste pipes can run in every direction – under floors, behind walls, in specially built ducts and through cupboards – but if well planned each and every one will be accessible and a compression nut or a push-fit connector will give access for cleaning with a coiled spring auger.

Exterior There should be a boss with a screwed stop-end, to be used as a cleaning eye, on all exterior waste pipes at every bend or elbow. This means that every short or long run can effectively be kept clear of obstructions. If for some reason a solid obstruction is preventing any flow of water, which is then backing up to the house, you'll have to call on the help of the 'instant drain cleaner' once again. However, in order that the blockage is pushed in the direction of the manhole, it is essential to plug or block the end of the waste pipe that is closest to the house. Wherever a blockage has occurred and a successful clearance is made, allow hot water to run down the pipework system to complete the clearance successfully.

Manholes and inspection chambers

A hive of activity in building and manufacturing was created in the UK during the Industrial Revolution and in subsequent years. The government and local bodies then proceeded with a programme of providing a system of public sewers in many urban and suburban areas. Unfortunately, there has not been a great deal of renewal of the original sewer network since then. Local Authorities are still finding that they have to find considerable sums of money to upgrade existing sewers.

At a similar time there was a great deal of speculative domestic housing built in most British towns and cities but sanitation and the discharge of waste was not then a priority. Health hazards were soon recognised and very soon the building of civic waste systems was seen to be important. Improvements continued throughout the twentieth century and building regulations came into force to ensure that builders complied with statutory requirements. Drains had to be laid in straight lines, they had to slope downwards so that they were self-cleaning, they should be adequately ventilated, they had to be protected from damage which might arise from subsoil settlement, there must be an inspection chamber at the junctions of branch drains, and finally, that all changes of direction in the system had to have a means of access to enable blockages to be cleared.

Many houses built during the surge of activity in the Victorian era will have systems constructed of glazed stoneware pipes that run in straight lines between manholes. When you lift a inspection cover you'll find at the bottom not a solid pipe but a half-channel. This might have branch openings running into it discharging from other outlets. At both ends of the half-channel there is solid pipe and it is through these that you can remove any blockage by a process known as rodding, for which you need a set of flexible drain rods.

A yard gulley, usually a back-inlet gulley with a trap, will have to be regularly cleaned to prevent flooding. Leaves and soil are the main reasons for a blockage.

Blockages
Use a heavy-duty bin bag wrapped around your arm to lift out the debris, but use plenty of disinfectant. Clear the area and hose down, allowing the water to wash through the system.

This shows an important development in the construction of mains drainage. A circular inspection chamber can have as many branch channels as are wanted.

Clean the side inlet into the trap, again using a heavy-duty bin bag wrapped around your arm. Scrape off and brush clean the iron (or plastic) gulley top. Then check that your plant pots are not overspilling with too much compost!

Before you can clear a blocked straight-run drain, you need to know where the blockage is. Raise the covers of the inspection chambers, one either end, and if the chamber nearest to the house is flooded but the one nearest to the boundary is clear, the blockage must be situated between these two points. You can remove the blockage by lowering one end of a set of two or three rods into the flooded chamber and feeling for the drain entrance. When you've found it, push the rods towards the blockage, screwing more on as you need them. Always twist in a clockwise direction. This helps the rods to move along the pipe. When you reach the blockage, which will be obvious, one or two sharp prods will usually clear it. There are special tools available which can screw on to the ends of rods to help clear difficult obstructions.

Intercepting trap An intercepting trap is similar to a trap built into a plumbing system underneath sinks, baths and wash handbasins. It holds water to prevent unpleasant odours returning into the house. In an manhole system the trap is built at the lower end of the half-channel. The top outlet of the intercepting trap has a stopper which can be removed and the open end is then available as a rodding eye. If all the inspection chambers are flooded and the drainage system has an intercepting trap, it is likely that it is the site of the blockage. To clear it, screw two drain rods together with a 100 mm (4 in) rubber disc or drain plunger on the end. Lower the plunger into the chamber, feel for the half-channel at the base and move the plunger along it and downwards until it reaches the point at which the half-channel descends into the intercepting trap. Sharply plunge down three or four times to remove the blockage. After clearing a blocked drain remember to run the household taps to flush water through the drain and to wash down the sides and the mortar benching of the chambers with hot water and washing soda.

The remaining length of drain from the manhole, with an intercepting trap, to the public sewer is our own responsibility. So it's worth checking periodically that the stopper has not fallen out into the water in the trap which could cause a partial blockage. This could possibly result from back pressure from the sewer. If this happens and waste material starts to back up, you are sure to get complaints from either members of the family or neighbours about an offensive smell!

Sewer pipe Cast-iron pipes and salt-glazed stoneware pipes were the only two types of pipe used in the construction of a sewage system for Victorian houses. Both used a spigot and socket method of connection. One end of each pipe was constructed slightly wider so that the normal end could be inserted in the next pipe and then caulked with lead, in the case of cast-iron. Cement mortar completed the joint in a salt-glazed stoneware system. It was common practice early on to lay the pipes directly on to the earth, but this was regarded later as a defective arrangement and pipes then began to be laid on a bed of concrete – one can begin to appreciate how, in earlier buildings, seepage was possible through joints opened by movement.

Rodding underground pipework with damaged sockets can be either a heartache or a joy. In the worst case it might even mean that the antiquated system needs to be renewed with a modern smooth plastic flexible system. Ring-sealed joints are used to connect the long lengths of underground robust UPVC pipes. Drain pipes of this kind will move or give slightly to accommodate any ground settlement and do not need to be laid on a concrete bed. Smoother internal surfaces and a reduction in the number of joints means shallower gradients and less chance of blockages. If one does occur it is far easier to rod the blockage away in this system.

Tie a label to your main stopcock and stop it seizing by regularly turning it.

Appliances

Washing machines

Plumbing in a kitchen appliance sounds tricky! 'Plumbing' suggests a big bag of plumber's tools, pipe benders and blow torches, but when you think about it, all you're doing is pushing a self-contained box of tricks into a space beside the sink. Firstly, connect the water supply, as you would a garden hose. Secondly, help the dirty water out to the gully. Thirdly, plug the appliance in to the power supply, then set the automatic controls and switch on. Whether you're going to plumb in a washing machine or dishwasher, manufacturers supply illustrated instructions for their installation. These are easy to follow and the illustrations show the simplest methods of making connections.

Having checked that the size of the available space in your kitchen will take the machine and fittings, check where you will take the water supply from. Some machines take hot and cold water, so you must be certain that there is sufficient pressure in the hot supply to match the cold. If the machine takes only cold water, this should come from the domestic cold water system or from the mains. The installation instructions will tell you which.

If you've not yet purchased a washing machine, it's worth noting that you might like the advantage of a faster washing cycle which is provided by a machine that uses hot water only. Obviously check all the literature first! Also be sure to check that there is sufficient water pressure because if you live in the upstairs of a converted house, there has to be enough 'head' of water to give the required pressure. Now the last thing to check is whether the manufacturer recommends that the appliance is installed in the conventional way or if you can use a saddle clamp with a self-bore valve. The first of the alternatives is as follows.

Find a convenient pipe from which to take the supply and turn off the stopcock so that you can drain the water from the supply pipe. Cut a 20 mm (¾ in) length from the 15 mm (½ in) copper pipe and put a compression T-joint in its place. Make sure that the cut ends are

This simple tap valve is all you need to successfully plumb in a washing machine or a dishwasher. And you don't have to turn off the water supply. Simply connect the saddle clamp, then the handle is turned to cut into the water pipe. Everything is sealed, so no leaks!

square, and clean the pipe ends and the olives with steel wool. Put on a cap nut and then the olive. The olive has a long and a short slope to each side and the short side should face the cap nut. Before inserting the pipe into the joint, apply boss white to the pipe ends and the olive. Make certain that the pipe ends are against the shoulders inside the fitting. Thread on the caps and tighten up but do not use strong-arm tactics! Connect a short length of 15 mm (½ in) pipe from the outlet of the T-joint and then fit a special washing machine hose attachment called a 'running tap'. Washing machine stop-cocks are available which have back plates that can secure your pipework to the kitchen wall. The inlet hose from the appliance has a screwed connector and, with the washer in place, tighten up the compression joint to the running tap. Keep the machine's control knob in the 'off' position until you turn on the mains stopcock again.

A flexible hose at the back of the appliance takes away the waste water. You can, if it's convenient, hook it over a sink to discharge the water, but of course it's neater to install a stand-pipe outlet and keep the hose hooked perma-nently into it. This is hidden behind the machine. It should be larger in diameter than the outlet from the machine and a trap at the base will ensure that no smells come back into the room. The plastic tube from the trap is taken through the wall of the house to discharge outside.

You'll probably use one of two methods to join the plastic pipe: solvent welding, which is cheaper, or push-fit, which is easier. In either case, to obtain a square cut on the pipe itself, first of all wrap a sheet of paper around the pipe to overlap squarely. The top of the paper forms your square cutting line which will be at 90° to the length of pipe. There are various cutting devices on the market but a junior hacksaw will do just fine. Then, with a fine file or sandpaper, chamfer the edge of the pipe so that it easily pushes into the joint. For solvent welding, roughen the end of the pipe a little and also gently abrade the inside of the fitting. Clean off all dust and apply the solvent cement

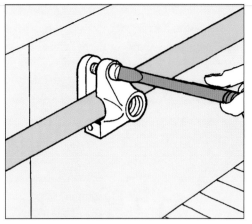

Plumbing in a washing machine (1)

A two-part self-cutting tap can be installed without having to turn off the water supply. First, fix and tighten the saddle clamp around the supply pipe.

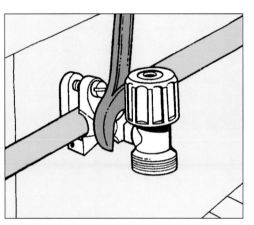

Plumbing in a washing machine (2)

Screw the tap with its cutter into the clamp. As you tighten the tap it cuts a hole in the supply pipe which is sealed with a rubber insert.

Plumbing in a washing machine (3)

Finally, connect the inlet hose from the appliance and connect it to the tap with a the standard compression fitting. Turn on the tap and check for leaks. Be careful not to kink the hoses when you push the appliance back into position.

to the end of the pipe and to the inside of the fitting, using a small brush. After gently pushing the pipe into the fitting add a smear of cement around the joint. In less than a minute it will have bonded.

When using a push-fit joint slightly roughen the pipe as for solvent welding. A rubber seal between the fitting and the pipe completes the joint. Use a recommended lubricant on the end of the pipe so that it slides into the fitting without damaging the sealing ring. Push it fully home and then ease it back about 3 mm (⅛ in) to allow for expansion when hot water flows through the pipe.

If convenient, the two vertical pipes supplying a kitchen sink with hot and cold water can be the source of hot and cold to a washing machine by cutting and fixing the T-joint in those runs. And it always makes sense to be able to isolate an appliance with an in-line valve. Water hoses at the back of washing machines have a standard threaded compression nut. It's a simple matter to connect each hose to a (disconnecting) miniature valve. This in turn is connected to the water supply with a compression nut and olive.

If you live in a hard water area there is one more fitting that is going to be a boon to the household –an in-line, magnetic device, which softens the water. Once installed it's there for good, needs no maintenance, doesn't add anything to the water but is active immediately and from then on!

The alternative and much simpler method of connecting an appliance to the water main is by a saddle clamp with a self-bore valve but check that this is suitable for your particular appliance. It is simplicity itself and it has a great number of advantages. The first one is that you don't have to turn off the water supply in order to install the connector. Where a supply pipe runs close to a back wall, find the most suitable place for fixing the back plate of the saddle clamp to the wall with two screws. The principle involved in the self-bore valve is that when tightening up the second part of the fitting a cutter bores a hole into the supply pipe but a rubber seal prevents any leakage. With the tap part of the valve in the off position and the two parts of the saddle clamp bolted together, attach the hose connector to the threaded end of the tap. Open the tap and you have an immediate supply of either cold or hot water. The valves are colour coded so you can't go wrong! This self-bore valve is larger than, but similar to, the self-bore tap used in conjunction with a water purifier cartridge installed underneath a sink unit.

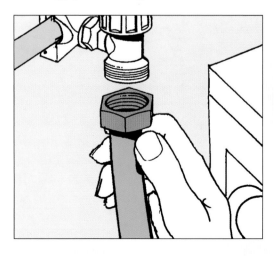

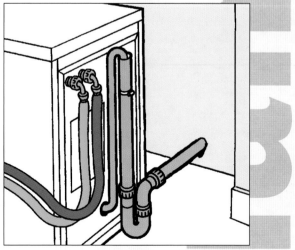

Plumbing in a waste pipe

A washing machine waste pipe for discharging dirty water should be at least 40 mm (1½ in) in diameter. The flexible hose from the machine must discharge above the level of the drum or it will empty by siphoning.

Alarms and detectors

Burglar alarms

In practically every police station in the UK a Crime Prevention Officer (CPO) is available to give free advice, not only on crime prevention but more especially on the system of home security most suitable for your home. They will visit you by appointment and spend time looking around the inside and the outside of your property. Their advice and knowledge of all security devices will prove invaluable and when you consider that more than a million homes a year are broken into, it is certainly worth considering a burglar alarm kit suitable for a DIY installation. The CPO will have pamphlets illustrating how any possible entry points can be protected. Before you consider any type of installation the officer might ask you to take into account the following considerations: a burglar alarm system that you install yourself is not likely to be acceptable by your insurance company; whether you have a cat or a dog which is normally left indoors whilst you're away and which could accidentally trigger the system; whether you are happy to secure all the doors and windows every time you go out, even for a short while; whether you are willing for a neighbour to hold spare keys for the alarm and for your house (if not, alarms could ring for long periods unnecessarily); and that the local police must have your and your neighbour's addresses and telephone numbers.

By the time you are ready to make your choice of the system most suitable for your home, be it a house or a flat, you need to assess all the available information. You can either fit a wired circuit into the mains electricity supply or fit separate home security, an internal electronic door and window alarms.

The mains circuit alarm system has a number of components: an outside bell, an inside bell, a control box, a number of activating sensors and a separate panic button. When the key is turned and the alarm is set, an intruder will disturb one of the sensors and the alarm will sound. (It is also possible to link the system direct to a police station.) The security of your home can also be assured by fitting internal electronic

door alarms. This separate system gives you great flexibility in that you can choose door alarms suitable for any door in the house.

There is also a very wide range of door and window locks available: door security bolts, window stay locks, lockable window handles, door chains and push bolts.

Modern technology has brought the burglar alarm system into the DIY market. All DIY stores now stock alarm systems. Collect a few brochures on different systems so that you can decide more easily on the one most suited to your home. The more sophisticated systems installed by specialist firms can be connected to a local police station but are expensive. DIY systems are reliable, but remember that even though it might make you feel more secure, it is not a substitute for unopenable doors and windows. The best DIY alarm systems are fairly easy to install and come fully illustrated with instructions but make sure that the one you buy complies with British Standard BS 6707.

Do all your own investigation work before talking to a CPO and familiarise yourself with the information contained in the leaflets. You've got to be conversant with your requirements and with what the systems available provide so that you'll fully understand the CPO's detailed discussion and advice.

There are two main types of system for you to think about, but the officer will probably tell you that a passive system is most likely the best to install in a home. This system has a number of sensors that detect the presence of anyone moving around inside the house after you've activated the system and left the property. The alternative system is one that detects all likely means of entry, like a small WC ground floor window, a small first floor side window approachable from a flat roof, and so on. However, there are systems, just as easily installed, that combine different security measures to protect the whole of the house. Manufacturers are more than ever determined to help us secure our homes and to give us peace of mind. Because of this, we are spoilt for

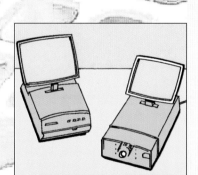

Home security system
Video surveillance systems are available that do not need to wired in making it easy for the DIYer to install.

choice because the number of systems on the market are so varied and competitive. The choices available will enable you to get a reliable burglar alarm system to suit both your pocket and your property.

First of all then, visit your local DIY store. Get as many pamphlets and instruction leaflets that are available, then go back home. You now have to work out the number of pads and sensors that you'll need for the doors and windows. You might also need to cover entry points in outbuildings, conservatories, garages or even garden sheds.

Whether you install a wireless alarm system or one wired to the mains, the basics are similar. A number of PIR movement sensors are fixed strategically around the house to cover every vulnerable area.

Wired circuit systems
In a wire system tiny magnetic pads are fixed to doors, windows and frames. These are magnetic switches (the most popular device for use in a wired circuit system). The alarm sounds when the system is switched on and the door or windows are open. This is the type of burglar alarm most popular with the DIY installer. One advantage of using magnetic switches between a door and its frame is that the two surface contacts can be as much as 10 mm (½ in) apart and even movement or rattling of a window by the wind will not break the contact. (Once switched on, the alarm system will be activated whether a door is opened accidentally or by force, so it is important that all catches on doors and windows fitted with surface contacts can be securely closed.)

Contacts can also be put under carpets or mats, where an intruder might have to step to get into a room. You'll obviously have to think carefully about where you locate the contact – if your pet dog is used to sleeping at the foot of the stairs, you'll have to take this into account!

All alarm systems carry full fitting instructions. Read them as many times as you need, so that you know exactly how and where to fix them. A panic button, for example, can be fixed by your bedside. Or you might consider it more important to have the button close to the front door, but if you do have an unwanted visitor, a door-chain will bar entry for enough time to allow you to make full use of the panic button located elsewhere. When you fix the wiring, take extra care with the connections. Loose wires or faulty connections can result in false alarms. The contacts placed under carpets must have no wires showing and the wires and the contacts must not be allowed to move. You can secure the mats with double-sided sticky tape. Hide the control box so that it is not immediately visible, but is easily accessible to you. The outside bell should, of course, be on view to everyone!

Electronic door alarms
This alarm is suitable for exterior and interior doors and flush fitting windows. It is well designed and unobtrusive when fitted. The two parts are simply fixed with four screws. When switched on, the loud battery-operated alarm will be activated if the door is forced open. Even if an intruder closes the door, the alarm will continue to sound. To stop the alarm, the switch has to be turned off.

Front door security
Fit a magnetic switch to a front door. The two parts fit on the door and post. When the door is opened an alarm is sounded.

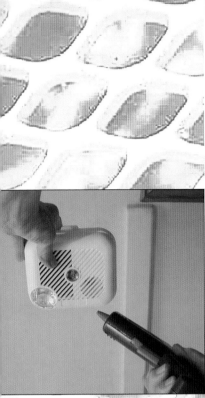

Statistics compiled by Government agencies and by the Fire Service prove that lives can be saved by installing smoke-alarms. We owe it to ourselves and particularly to our families to fit them in our homes. Look for alarms that also have an additional life-saver in the form of an escape light. It comes on when the alarm sounds.

Check the instructions for the best location for a smoke alarm. Fitting more than one, linked together, is best. You don't have to use fixing screws, often it is easier to use a cordless glue-gun.

To comply with British Standard BS 5446 smoke detectors must have a test button. Test your detectors frequently, they could save a life.

If you live in a block of flats or if you're a student in rooms in a communal block, this extra front door protection is ideal. Some of the battery-operated front door alarm systems can be as small as a pack of cards. Some even have a self-adhesive pad which gives a very strong fixing to a door and frame. The alarm is fail-safe and will still operate even if a door is forced because an electronic contact is broken to sound the alarm. Some of the devices have a key to switch it on or off, others have buttons with a secret code.

Wireless systems   The great advantage of these systems are that they are 'wire-less', which of course means that there are no wires to install. However, the control box, the heart of the system, needs to be reliable and tamper-proof. The instructions will tell you that it needs to be accessible but protected. The system is very simple in that it sends radio waves, if a contact is broken, to trigger the alarm to indicate an intruder. This type of burglar alarm system is relatively easy to install, understand and, of course, should you move, it's easily dismantled so that you can take it with you.

Smoke alarms

Statistics show us that too many people are dying in house fires and many because they have not been made aware of what is happening by the installation of a smoke alarm. Many people still think that smoke alarms have to be 'wired in'. Even if you're not capable of climbing a stepladder to screw it to a ceiling, all you have to do is ask somebody to do it for you. Nowadays you don't even have to screw it to the ceiling. Glue guns, adhesive pads and cartridge adhesives are all suitable because of the high 'grab' quality of modern-day adhesives.

Smoke alarms are obviously life-savers and can cost little more than a few litres of petrol! Fire-fighters tell us that smoke alarms can prevent many of the tragedies that they have to witness.

House fires often break out when the residents are asleep. Before the fire itself reaches the bedroom, it's possible that the sleeping occupant could be overcome by smoke because there was no warning of the imminent danger. Smoke alarms can provide this crucial early warning, by sounding a piercing alarm. The Fire Prevention Officer in charge of giving advice at your local fire station is always there and advice is free. Flats and bedsits need special attention so if you don't have a smoke alarm installed make a phone call now. The officer will also have copies of the free booklet 'Smoke Detectors in the Home'.

One of the things that the officer will tell you is that you must buy a reliable model of smoke alarm. It should meet British Standard BS 5446 Part 1.

Battery-operated models are reliable, but do follow the instructions for changing batteries, which should be at least once a year. It's a good idea to test the alarms regularly, say monthly, and put it in your calendar to remind you! Some people even check the alarm's sensitivity by holding a smouldering taper or cigarette under the alarm.

Your alarm will be useless if you cannot hear it when you're in the bedroom. It is worthwhile testing to see if you can hear the alarm before your fit it! Ask someone to set off the alarm while you are in the bedroom, with the door closed and the radio on. Can you hear it? If not, move the alarm closer to the bedroom or fit two linked alarms, one near the likely fire source, the other near to the bedroom. If you're fitting only one alarm, the best place is between the bedroom and the living room or kitchen where fires are most likely to start. In a traditional two-storey house, this usually means on the hallway ceiling at the bottom of the stairs, not high up in the stairwell where access for testing and maintenance is difficult and dangerous. In houses on one level, fit your alarm in the hallway or corridor between the living and sleeping areas. And another thing: it's worthwhile taking time to plot your escape route just in case fire does break out and make sure everyone in the house knows what to do if the worst happens. In fact, make it a game. Practise getting out in the dark!

Here are some tips. Don't fit alarms in kitchens, bathrooms or garages. Don't fit them where steam, condensation or fumes can set them off. And never install one above a heater. The last important point – some time ago, polyurethane foam was banned in the manufacture of furniture. The foam burns quickly and toxic fumes are emitted. Night fires involving some foam furniture can be lethal. The legislation that came into force has obviously saved a lot of lives, but there could be foam furniture still in use in the home today. If you suspect that you have this filling and you haven't got an alarm fitted, don't you think you owe it to yourself and your family to install one?

Linked alarms Fitting just one alarm will increase your security, but for extra protection, have several at strategic points around the home. All types of alarm can be powered individually by battery, and you might want to install a number of smoke alarms linked by cable, so that if one alarm senses a fire, they will all sound the warning. Linking battery alarms is a relatively simple DIY job. Always follow the maker's instructions. Take care though – not all models are suitable for linking. If you can afford it, and you don't object to the look of the smoke alarms, fit them in all rooms where fire may break out. Mains-powered alarms (with battery back-up!) are also available. You can find out about these from the officer at your local fire station.

Locks
Main doors

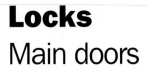

Five-lever mortise locks
The strongest lock for a front door is a mortise dead-lock because it fits in a slot cut in the door edge so becoming an integral part of the door. Always use one meeting the British Standard BS 3621 – it will be pick-proof, resist forcing and the bolt will be made of hardened steel. However, there is little point in fitting security devices like a five-lever mortise lock to a front door that is weak and likely to be broken down easily. Exterior doors should be at least 45 mm (1¾ in) thick and made of stout hardwood.

The front door is usually the most vulnerable door because it is the one you use to leave your house and therefore cannot be bolted from the inside. Even though it can usually be seen from the street, a large percentage of all break-ins occur from the front of private houses. Many front doors are fitted with old-fashioned rim locks but for your added security and for insurance purposes, you must fit a mortise lock.

The principle of the modern mortise deadlock is that 'detainers' or levers are brought together in pre-selected positions by a key which only fits that particular lock. When properly fitted, a mortise lock is designed to be stronger than a

Rim lock
Choose a rim lock that can be deadlocked and requires a key to open it from the inside. Fit a security chain just below the lock.

Mortise lock
Fit a mortise deadlock in a slot cut into the edge of the door. Make sure it is to the BS 3621 standard which is pick-proof, resists forcing and is made from hardened steel.

You should change door locks in any house that you move into.

timber door. This means, in the event of a break-in, the wood itself would fail before the lock. The locking bolt is enclosed inside a steel box to prevent the lock being picked. Some have up to three anti-picking devices as well. The bolt itself is often enclosed and reinforced with steel rollers which rotate to prevent a thief cutting through the bolt. Once the bolt is locked, it is secured automatically.

Manufacturers differ in their suggestions for methods of fitting. As a rule the lock is placed along the central rail, which, on a panelled door, is slightly lower than halfway down. The instructions will be very precise and tell you to position the lock on the inside of the door and to draw around it. Then you have to drill holes into the edge of the door centrally, so that the mortise hole can then be chiselled deep and straight. The recess for the front plate and keyhole have to be made, their location marked by holding the lock body in the appropriate position. Once all holes are made, the striking plate recess is marked and chiselled out ready to take the striking plate which is fixed securely with screws. Fitting a mortise lock should offer no problems to the DIY enthusiast, with one proviso – as long as the manufacturer's instructions are carefully followed!

Cutting a mortise hole is a great challenge to all students in woodwork classes! The banging on the end of a mortise chisel with a wooden mallet gave great satisfaction especially when the resulting hole was straight and true. Nowadays that exercise is totally dispensed with by the invention of the mad-bit. This is a bit that not only drills but cuts in all directions. Whereas a mortise hole cut accurately into the edge of an oak door could take half an hour, with the mad-bit it can take as little as five minutes! Not only does it drill faster, pulls out the debris quicker, but it then proceeds to cut sideways in absolute straight lines. The curved ends to the slot make no difference because the front face (fore-end) of the lock will cover the hole when it is screwed into the recess. This latest development in drill technology makes it a boon to tradespeople and makes life easier for the DIYer resulting in a more professional finish.

Door viewers   A door viewer is a great idea enabling you to take a look at visitors to find out if they are welcome or not before you open the door! But a door viewer (peephole) is not much good if all you can see is a dark outline, so you need to buy one, the best that you can afford, with a wide angle so that you can see the whole of the person. Viewers come in two parts with the screw-in half fitted from the inside. You can buy viewers to fit most thicknesses of conventional front doors.

The instructions will tell you the size of hole to drill for the viewer you've purchased. They will probably tell you to drill right through the centre of the door at a comfortable eye level to suit most members of your family. And it will recommend a 'spade' bit as many people have complained that either the front or the back of the door has been split by the drill bit! Solving that problem is very simple. When the point of the bit appears on the opposite side to where you're drilling, somebody must shout 'Stop!'. You simply then drill from the exit hole and make a clean hole from the other side which meets the original drilled bore. The barrel is then inserted from the outside whilst from the inside use a coin in the slot provided to drive home the telescopic viewer piece. It really is as simple as that to bring a feeling of added security and a feeling of satisfaction with a job well done.

Door viewer
Simple and unobtrusive, a viewer gives you added security. Drill a hole in the door with a flat bit, but don't go all the way through as this will damage the wood. As soon as the point of the bit appears, stop and drill through from the other side. Insert the thread lens from the outside and secure it with the threaded collar on the inside.

Rack bolts are as strong as locks, but only take minutes to fit to any door.

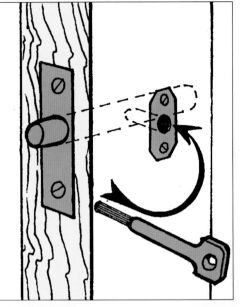

Rack bolt
The rack bolt is an integral part of the door and so is very strong. Fit these as extra security to all doors and some windows.

Rack bolts The rack bolt is an extremely simple device to fit but since it is let into the door edge, it is powerful and strong. It is a simpler form of a mortise-deadlock in that it becomes integral with the door. These are unobtrusive and yet can be fitted as extra security to all doors and some windows. A key has a pinioned end to activate the racked bolt which can then only be undone with the same key. So obviously keep this in a safe place. Rack bolts are so inexpensive that, I think, it is worth fitting two to any door or window.

For most rack bolts, you will need to drill a 15 mm (⅝ in) hole into the leading edge of the door after having marked the position by laying the bolt against the face of the door. With the door wedged open (wedges both sides of the door are best) drill the hole to the correct depth, horizontal and absolutely central to the door. Taking into account the thickness of the face plate, measure back for the correct position of the keyhole. The instructions will tell you what size drill bit to use for the keyhole. With a bevelled edge chisel clean out the recess for the face plate. Now screw the locking plate into position after having drilled the hole for the bolt and correctly marked and cut the recess for the plate. And remember two is better than one!

Hinge bolts The hinge bolt is very similar in principle to the rack bolt, but it is much smaller and has no moveable parts. The principle of a steel bolt interfacing with a steel plate is the same. Place the bolt near the hinge of a door and fit the hinge edge into the back edge of the door. Drill the recommended hole for the static bolt. Drill a matching hole into the frame which is also recessed to take the locking plate. This added protection to the back edge of the door prevents forcing with a wrecking bar in an area that might otherwise be quite vulnerable.

Sheds and garages

Double locks If you keep tools or other important possessions in a shed or a garage, you have to be certain that you've given the building the best possible protection from a break-in. Many garage doors are fitted with old non-deadlocking rim locks, which offer low security. Bolts and locking devices on outside buildings should never ever be fixed and held with ordinary screws. Always use bolts with the nut on the inside of the door. Now that you're thinking about upgrading the security locking systems on outbuildings, when you go to your local store ask for leaflets on: a padlock bar; a heavy duty padlock; a combination padlock; an angle padlock bar; and an upright padlock bar with closed shackle padlock. It would be prudent to fit any two of these to any outbuilding door.

A shed, garage or other outbuilding that has two doors must have extra protection. A garage that has a second exit door should have the main doors fitted with locks extra to the outside ones, on the inside. This means that you exit from a side door and then secure it behind you. And don't forget that you can chain together and padlock items of value so that they become either too heavy for a thief to remove or too much trouble to release.

Solvents
Keep all solvents and chemicals safely away from children and pets. Keep the product in its original container so you know exactly what it is. Keep them in a cupboard or shed that has a child-proof lock. Remember SAFETY FIRST, DIY SECOND!

Window locks Window locks in sheds and garages should be in pairs. These can usually be seen from the outside fitted between the opening casement and the frame. But a would-be thief seeing two at either side of the window will be less determined because it means that it would be necessary to try to crawl through a broken window pane rather than try to force a second window lock. Think of this – the most secure locks are those that can only be opened by a key that you take with you! So always choose this type of lock even though it might be slightly more expensive. View the very large number of window lock devices that are available at your local DIY store and read all the relevant literature.

You'll find that the two parts that make up the locking device have to be properly aligned so that the catch or bolt has a chance to do its work properly. The lock body, that's the biggest part of the unit, is screwed to the window or casement and a small hole has to be cut into the frame for the catch or bolt. Metal windows can be protected by a similar device.

Padlocks I suppose there were not so many villains about many years ago when two eye-hooks, one in a door post and one in the door itself, served as a locking device with a bolt dropped into them as they met. Sometimes a very small and inappropriate padlock linked the two hook-eyes together! It is essential that a heavy duty, pick-proof padlock is used in conjunction with a hasp, which is a metal fastening consisting of a hinged strap with a slot that fits over a staple and is secured by the padlock. The hasp (or padlock bar) must be fixed to the door with bolts with the nuts countersunk inside. A closed shackle padlock is one where the shackle (the curved metal bar) is completely enclosed except for the part that goes through the eye. This makes it less vulnerable to forcing or sawing.

Always choose a heavy-duty padlock with a shackle that is only just long enough to go through the staple of the padlock bar.

Windows

Sliding sash bolts When sliding sash windows were originally installed, it was then thought that the central latch device was sufficient to stop rattles, prevent draughts and secure the window from forced entry. However, some swivel catches, when only partially operated, can be slid fully open with a penknife. A means of locking and securing had to be found which was simple and unobtrusive. The simplest method and probably the most effective, was to insert two bolts at either side of the meeting rails. With the rails in the closed position, holes were drilled through both meeting rails in line. Then metal 'receivers' were fixed into the holes. The closest one went right

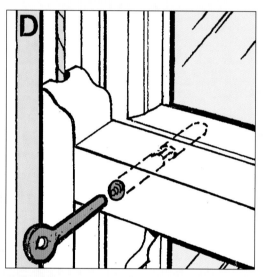
Sash lock
Sash window locks hold the meeting rails securely. Two sleeves are inserted into drilled holes into which a bolt is screwed with a key.

Fit two centrally located screw-in locks to stop sliding sashes being opened. Two brass bushes are inserted into predrilled holes. The threaded bush in the outer meeting rail locates only half way to receive the bolt that is screwed in from the inside.

through the meeting rail but the furthest one only partially. This meant that a bolt with a special key could be inserted through the first to be screwed into the second meeting rail. This proved to be exceedingly effective and has been in use for years.

There is another advantage to this method of securing the sashes in the closed position. Slightly higher in the outer frame but in line with the bolts, another bolt receiver can be fixed about 75 mm (3 in) above the meeting rails. This means that the sliding sash windows can then be locked with the bottom sash just raised by this distance. This is obviously a great advantage where the bottom of a sash window is low in the room and is dangerous to young children.

Casement locks
In principle, although there is a variety of casement lock devices on the market, they are all quite similar. A casement window is one that opens on a hinge and is swung open to be held by a window stay. When closed, casements need to be secured with more than just a cockspur handle, despite the fact that a cockspur handle can itself be locked by screwing an extending bolt to the frame below the handle and operated by a removable key. At the top and bottom of a wooden casement window, for extra security fit either a two part casement lock or an automatic self-lock. A base plate and catch unit are screwed to the edge of the openable casement and the unit has a bolt that is thrown into the locking plate by a catch on the front of the body of the unit. Once the bolt is inside the recess of the locking plate a removable key safely secures the device.

The difference between this and the automatic self-lock is that the body of the lock is securely fixed to the window frame and not to the casement. With the casement in the closed position, the lock is positioned close to it and about 50 mm (2 in) up from the sill (or from the soffit, if one is being fixed at the top of the frame). A metal stud is screwed into the correct position on the opening casement which locates with the locking device at the back of the automatic self-lock unit. A turnkey is provided to secure the casement to the lock.

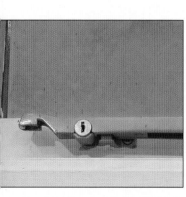

Top-hinged casement windows are easily protected by a window stay that has an integral keyed lock built in to the moveable stay. Remember that you'll need easy access to the key in an emergency.

Older type casements were secured with keyed locks either on the stay or the latch. Modern equivalents are more sophisticated with locks as an integral part of the framework.

If a casement window on a ground floor is not secured by lockable window devices, it's easy for an experienced thief to break the glass to open the catch. Two window locks are a big deterrent. The range of window security devices is wide and plenty of leaflets are available at your local DIY store to help you choose which is the best for your own windows. Preventing easy access and causing as much obstruction as possible to an intruder is the aim here. And it is worth fitting these to all the windows in your house, even to those which are above the ground floor. Fanlights should also be protected, as should small permanently shut windows.

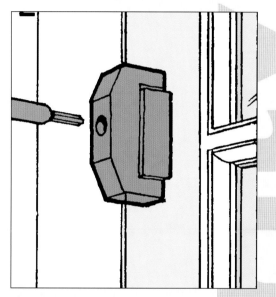

Casement lock
A casement window lock is an alternative to a rack bolt. Separate parts are screwed to the frame and sash. A special key secures the holding bolt.

Stay catch
Many locking devices are available for locking the casement stay. The simplest form is a key-operated bolt.

Rack bolts After making a plan of window locations and noting the size and type of each window and its existing fittings, check how frequently windows are usually opened! Casement windows, for example, that are not opened very often, should have two rack bolts fitted top and bottom – refer to the fitting of rack bolts to doors earlier in this section. The fitting is no different.

Patio doors Patio doors provide an almost uninterrupted view of a garden, giving the impression that the garden is part of the house. A room can appear brighter because of the area of glass in the doors. Doors are available that require minimum maintenance since the frames are made of extruded aluminium or UPVC, which will not rust or warp and need never be painted.

However, in the earlier designs of patio doors there was a vulnerability which needed to be overcome. The aluminium inner frame with sliding channels top and bottom was screwed and sealed to the outer wooden frame. The sliding panels were first inserted into the deep top channels, lifted up and then dropped into the bottom channels. Now you can see the weakness. Usually one locking device was fixed at the centre of the meeting verticals, so if that was forced a panel could easily be lifted out. Since these early days, great strides have been made and there have been improvements in design and technology. However it is still worth fitting extra locks top and bottom to stop the possibility of the sliding panels being lifted out of channels. With full instructions these are very simple to install providing the security to give you peace of mind.

For extra security at a vulnerable balcony window, fix laminated glass to the casements and long-bar locks to the doors. These specialist locks have a metal vertical sliding bar, which locks securely into mortised keepers in the floor and upper frame.

Glass in louvred windows is easy to prise out, so superglue each one.

Glass
Safety

Inside doors In a new-build, or where restoration or renovation is taking place under the supervision of a building control officer, safety glass has to be used in certain situations; for example, only safety glass should be used where low-level windows are being restored or installed. It is a statutory requirement that glass hardened by means of reinforcement or a toughening process is the only glass that should be used in this situation. 'Safety glass' is mandatory in glazed screens, large interior windows, even shower screens.

All glaziers carry a stock of safety glass and will advise you on safe transportation and installation. Glass has very sharp edges and therefore, remember SAFETY FIRST, DIY SECOND. Please use leather gloves, never rubber!

A normal size door that is between two rooms and is panelled with glass must have safety glass held in place on a cushion of putty by wooden glazing beads. These are best fixed with a powered nail gun using tiny panel pins. Safety glass is best ordered cut to size from your local glazier. Take care when measuring for the glass to allow for either a bedding 'bead' of rubber strip or putty. On no account measure so that the glass is a tight fit. Any slight movement in the frame of the door will cause future problems.

Toughened Ordinary sheet glass or 'float' glass is produced by a process in which the molten material is 'floated' over a tank of molten metal, producing large clear sheets of consistent thickness. The most popular thicknesses are 4 mm ($^1/_{16}$in) and 6mm ($^1/_4$in). Large sheets of polished plate glass produced by this process can be up to 6 mm ($^1/_4$in) thick and for special installations thicknesses can go up to 15mm ($^1/_2$in)! Victorian glass, still seen in well-maintained houses, often contains blemishes which are absent in the modern material. These occurred because old-fashioned sheet glass was produced by blowing the molten material out into a hollow cylinder. The ends of the cylinder were cut off and a straight cut was made longitudinally down the tube, which was then put in an oven and flattened out under the influence of heat. After manufacture, the sheet glass was sorted into classes according to quality. Much of the poor quality glass was installed in speculative housing and is often still found in such housing today. Objects take on a wavy or broken appearance when viewed through the windows of a Victorian house.

Because float glass was so easily broken, a 'tempered' glass process was invented. This new heat-treated glass gives five times the strength of ordinary float glass of the same thickness. A great advantage, when the float glass undergoes this treatment, is that if and when it breaks it does not produce dangerous shards but shatters into fairly harmless tube-like granules.

However, you can't go into local glaziers and buy a piece of toughened glass so that you can cut it at home. You cannot drill holes in it either. It will merely shatter. An order must be made for a particular size and predrilled holes in requisite positions carefully measured so that the float glass can be prepared before it is given the toughening process.

Laminated   Laminated glass really is a brilliant idea. I've demonstrated on television just how tough laminated glass is! With a piece in a steel frame, and me kitted out in protective clothing, gloves and protective goggles, I've whacked it half a dozen times with a baseball bat and only succeeded in crazing it like a spider's web!

Laminated glass is two sheets of float glass with a very tough piece of plastic bonded between. Looking through a piece of laminated glass is the same as looking through ordinary window glass. There is no difference and no distortion. There is also no risk of flying fragments of glass because the sheets of float glass adhere to the plastic sheet in the bonding process. It is the ideal material to glaze a vulnerable, obscured window, say a WC window at the back of the house.

Burglars hate laminated glass – buy it cut.

This piece of laminated glass has had a number of blows with a hammer. It still has not shed one piece of glass and it has been impossible to make an opening. Fit laminated glass where you have a vulnerable window to add to your security and safety.

Laminated glass
Laminated glass, being safe and tough, is suitable for vulnerable windows. The glass will not shatter even if hit with a hammer several time. If the rebate (recess) is deep enough, fitting it is a DIY job! However, you fill have to specify the shape and size of any pieces needed as it has to be made to order.

Lighting
Security

Porches PIR sensors   In an earlier section I described how important it was to give extra security by fixing a viewer (peephole) in a front door. This is fine for daylight hours but what about at night time? If a porch or the front door does not have a light fitting near to it, then the viewer is ineffective after dark. Where an exterior porch light exists or if you have to fit a new one, the important thing is that it should be connected to a sensor so that the light is activated when a person approaches. To fit an outside light please refer to the section on 'Safety' and 'Exterior lights'. This will give you full instructions on the type of fitting to buy and the method of installation.

However, there is one additional fitting that is a simple DIY application and converts an ordinary porch light into one that switches on as

PIR sensor
The PIR sensor will detect movement in the zone covered by the detector and sound an alarm.

Fix childproof latches to cupboards containing white spirit and chemicals.

anyone approaches the front door. The detector fitted is a passive infra-red (PIR) system that can be positioned above the front door to detect anyone approaching it. It is smaller than a closed fist, often black and therefore very unobtrusive. This is simply linked to the ceiling rose so that the light is activated when the sensor picks up anyone within range. It stays on for only minutes at a time. PIR-controlled lights are also useful in deterring cats or other animals which activate them! Instructions come with this very easy to fit security device.

Exterior
You can also install passive infra-red (PIR) detectors on roofs and high walls. Exterior light fittings can be purchased with built-in detectors which make them very simple to install. The instructions will tell you simply to mount the fitting high on a wall or on a gable roof timber so that a whole area will be lit when you or an intruder trigger it at night. A floodlight is, of course, the best light for a large area. These are available with built-in detectors and can be wired to the nearest junction box. Take extra care to read the instructions, which will tell you that only exterior fittings are to be used and how the wiring is to be run for complete safety. Most built-in infra-red detectors are electronically controlled so that they are not activated by small animals or by trees moving in the wind. You also don't want the light to be switched on every time a car passes your house, so you have to be careful and, by trial and error, get the right tilt to the sensor. Take care, excessive heat, such as from a gas flue outlet can activate a sensor, so read the instructions and fit accordingly.

Interior Lamp holder sensors
These days even ordinary lamp holders are being made with a sensor built into them. A lamp holder doesn't even have to be wired in. With a bayonet cap push and twist connector, the lamp holder adaptor can be mounted into any standard light fitting. This can be a ceiling fitting or a wall fitting or even a batten holder (a basic fitting with a lamp holder attached to a plate that is screwed directly to the wall or ceiling). Batten holders are very useful where an attractive shade is not important but where it is

important to have a light fitting with a sensor to activate the light in an emergency.

Time switches
Another brilliant gadget is the time switch. This is a plug and socket set about twice the size of an ordinary plug that you plug into a conventional socket outlet. One type of time switch has a series of plastic push pins around a dial graduated to correspond with the minutes and hours in a 24-hour day and which turns as the time passes. The face of the switch looks like an ordinary three pin mains socket and you can plug a table light, or any appliance, in to it. You can set the times that you want the light to come on and off by inserting the push pins at the appropriate time. The cycle will continue even if, say, you are away for a month! The timer adaptor can also be used in connection with a dual adaptor so that lights can be used together on long leads, one upstairs and one downstairs.

Today, you can buy time switches that are electronic rather than mechanical. This means that you can set the time, the on time and the off time by using a conventional 24-hour clock display.

Safety
Features

Fire extinguishers
When you take account of the potential damage and loss caused by any fire in the home, then the relatively small cost of a fire extinguisher must make it worthwhile buying one, if not two. You should certainly keep one in the kitchen and, ideally, one on each floor of the house. You must take every precaution to protect yourself, your family and your property.

There are various types of fire extinguisher available for controlling different types of fire, as well as other devices to help you to escape from any part of the house. To reassure yourself, telephone or visit your local fire station and ask for advice. Fire extinguishers are not as unwieldy and confusing to use as they might at

Fire extinguishers

Only buy a fire extinguisher that is suitable for its purpose in your house. Different extinguishers can be used on different types of fire. Each holds a particular compound and is classified according to capacity and intended use.

Fire extinguishers and a fire blanket are absolute essentials in any kitchen. Your local Fire Prevention Officer will give you all the information that you require.

Find the most convenient position in your kitchen to hang your fire blanket. It needs to be as near the cooking area as is practicable. Hanging tabs are pulled to release the blanket. Read the instructions, so that you know how to prevent oxygen getting to the source of the flames.

first appear. Go to your local DIY store and ask the staff to help you decide which is the best and the most effective for your own purposes. They will have easy-to-follow pamphlets which will tell you all you need to know about siting, handling and safety.

After ensuring that you have extinguishers of a correct capacity and rating, the speed with which you attack a fire is the next most important factor to think about. All extinguishers have simple operating instructions printed large enough to read easily even by short-sighted people. Make yourself read through the instructions until you are thoroughly familiar with them. Test each member of the family, so that they too know and understand the operating instructions. A valuable half minute can be lost trying to find out how to operate the extinguisher in the event of an emergency. If a fire, even a small one, occurs in your home or you smell burning, dial 999 and

summon the fire brigade immediately. Having an extinguisher in the home is no substitute for the professionals but don't underrate its effectiveness. If used quickly and properly, it can keep damage and loss to a minimum. If a fire is too large to tackle yourself, then leave the house as quickly as you can and wait for the fire brigade. Your first consideration must be to save lives. Fire can be prevented from spreading too quickly by shutting all doors and windows. If there is dense smoke and it is difficult to see or breathe, get away as speedily as you can by crawling. Often, the air near the floor is easier to breathe and the smoke will be less dense.

A personal fire extinguisher is small enough to be carried around and simplicity itself to operate. You will have your own reasons for carrying one in any particular situation, but it is particularly useful when near or working with inflammable liquids. There are particular fire extinguishers with special compounds for dealing with particular fires. When carrying out your research, pay particular attention to ones that you ought to buy for particular areas of your house. Check the relative merits of extinguishers that can be used for electrical fires, cooking oil fires, furniture foam fires and wood fires.

If you keep inflammable liquids in a store or in a garage, then a woven glass fibre blanket in a flat wall-pack should be hung close by. A kitchen fire-blanket on the other hand is ideal to smother a fat fire on a stove and it is sensible to keep one near by. Never ever use water if your chip pan catches fire or if electricity is the cause of a fire.

Hot fat is the commonest cause of fires in the kitchen. There are some simple precautions to take:

1 Never turn up the heat to full.
2 Never tip wet food into fat.
3 Never leave oil or fat unattended when cooking as it will start smoking and burst into flame.
4 Never move an oil or fat pan that is on fire.
5 Smother the fire immediately with a fire blanket.

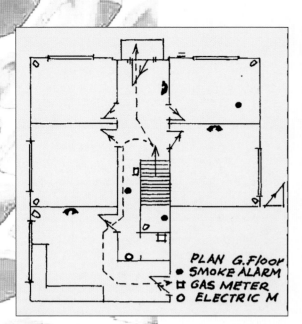

Escape routes
Draw a plan of your house marking alarm sensors, gas and electricity meters, telephones, and escape routes in different colours. Show windows suitable for exits, flat roofs and portable escape ladders if you have them.

Use the Omnitron gas leak detector regularly on your gas stove and gas hob. It detects natural gas and LPG, giving an audible and visual warning.

If an electrical appliance catches fire, switch off the source of power. If you can't get to the socket, switch off at the fuse box or consumer unit. The most suitable extinguisher for use on a fire caused by electricity will contain dry powder, inert gas and vaporising liquid. The contents of all extinguishers are very clearly marked and by reading the pamphlets at your DIY store and by talking to the professionals, you'll be able to find out which sort of extinguisher to use on which sort of fire.

Gas detectors

Carbon monoxide detectors are life-savers. The simplest form comes as a stick-on device that is located in a position determined by the location of the appliance and as specifically recommended by the manufacturers. This device simply changes colour when gas is detected. However, a more sophisticated type of device will actually sound an alarm warning you to immediately turn off the gas supply at the meter. If you suspect that a gas tap at the hob or at a gas fire has inadvertently been left on, check this immediately, but not before you've extinguished all flames. Remember not to operate any electrical switches. The next thing to do is to open all doors and windows so that you have a through draught. Then call the gas company who will immediately send out an emergency service.

Before you buy or install any gas detector, check with your gas company the type of gas that is being used in your home and what type of detector they would recommend. One type is wired directly to an unswitched fused connection unit with a 3A fuse. This provides the power for the built-in alarm. Check also with the company the British Standard number of the detector that they recommend.

Escape routes

We've all read the emergency procedures in blocks of flats, hotels, or any type of building that has lifts and know the escape route is always the stairs. In our homes, we should take a leaf out of these regulations books and determine for ourselves the best emergency escape route. Moreover, each and every member of the family and any visitors should be made aware of it. Nowadays, owing to Government-run campaigns and television documentaries, we are made much more aware of the need to provide ourselves with every facility to guard again loss of life in the home. These include rope ladders that can be hooked on to an upper storey window sill and dropped down to provide an immediate means of escape in case of a fire.

If a fire escape already exists, it is probably at the back of your building and because it is out of the way, probably few people will have bothered to investigate the best way down. Do it, it's worthwhile! In large buildings, check that escape route windows that open on to flat roofs, do actually open. They might be your only means of escape if you are prevented by flames from using a front entrance.

I've already mentioned two very important people that you should contact. Each is important in our daily lives and each is available to give free advice to help us in our goal of living a more comfortable and worry-free life. One is the Crime Prevention Officer at your local police station and the other the Fire Prevention Officer at your local fire station.

Regulations

For most of the work described in this book you will not need planning permission or building control approval. However, taking down an interior wall or making structural alterations might. So consult with your local council for advice. It's free and could save money and time. Check the departments which advise on loft conversions, double-glazing, garden plumbing and building extensions.

Nails, Screws and Tools

Nails

The quickest and easiest method of joining two pieces of wood together is by nailing. Add glue or a modern adhesive and the joints will be considerably stronger. There are many different types of nails available, so make certain that to solve your particular problem, you use the right type and size for the task you have to do.

Harry's DIY tips for correct nailing

The first thing to remember is 'SAFETY FIRST, DIY SECOND', so wear protective gear.

When joining two pieces of timber of different thicknesses, the length of the nail used should be just under twice the thickness of the thinnest piece. Drive the nail through the thinnest piece into the thicker piece at a slight angle. This increases the strength of the joint. Try to nail on a firm surface or hold a heavy block against the back of the joint. Drill a pilot hole to avoid splits in hardwood, chipboard and plywood, but make it slightly smaller than the diameter of the nail. When nailing into softwood, avoid driving nails close together in the same line of grain as you'll encourage the timber to split! Oval nails are good for softwood, but use them with the longer sides parallel to the grain. You'll often see carpentry with nails close to the end of timber and no splits. The secret is simple – the timber is left oversize, the nails driven in and then the wood is sawn to size! It's also worth tapping the point of a nail to blunt it, again to avoid splits.

Angled nailing gives a remarkably strong joint. One nail is driven in at an angle of, say, 45° and the second nail at the same angle from the opposite direction.

Clench nailing is used for rough timber that is eventually hidden. Round wire nails, an inch longer than needed are best, driven in from either side. Bend over the ends showing and drive them flat into the timber to give a very strong joint.

Panel and veneer pins are difficult to hold and generally have to be located more carefully than larger nails. There are a number of proprietary 'tack-holders' which help to overcome the problem. Alternatively, simply push the pin through a small piece of card. This will allow you to use the flat side of a pin hammer on it to get started without hitting your fingers!

For some decorative work, and to hide the head of a nail, lift a sliver of wood with a sharp chisel and drive in the nail underneath it. Punch in the nail, taking care to avoid knocking the hinged sliver. Glue the sliver of wood back into position, place a weight over it and sand it when it has dried. The nail will be hidden! An alternative is to drive the nail below the surface with a wood punch – use only matching wood-filler and sand it when dry.

Veneer pin   This small and fine pin is used for delicate work such as fixing mouldings. Punch it home and fill the hole.

Panel pin   This is used for beadings and cabinet work. The ideal tool for this pin is the 'push-pin'. This magnetic, hollow steel tool holds the pin while you push it into the wood. Size: 12–50 mm (½ in).

Oval nail   This is most suitable for joinery work where appearance is important and for fixing architraves and skirting boards. They are good for nailing into end grain. They are easily punched below the surface and less likely to split wood. Size: 12–150 mm (½–6 in).

Round wire nail   A large round-head nail mostly used in rough carpentry, stud-work and shuttering, where appearance is not important, but strength is essential. Size: 20–150 mm (¾–6 in).

Galvanised round wire nail For fencing and all outside work, where rust would affect ordinary wire nails. Size: 12–100 mm (½–4 in).

Plasterboard nail This galvanised nail has a wide head for holding plasterboard to timber without breaking the paper skin. It has a rough shank to give a good hold. They come in various lengths and head sizes depending on the materials used.

Annular ring nail A flat head nail with a rough shank that is difficult to remove once driven home. It has a strong grip, so is used mainly for holding down plywood or hardboard on a floor prior to laying floor coverings or tiling. They come in various sizes.

Masonry nail These are toughened steel nails, hardened for nailing directly into brick, breeze-block and most other types of masonry. Different gauges are available with lengths from 18 mm to 100 mm (¾–4 in).

Blued tack These small tacks are specially designed for carpets and fabrics, and have very sharp points and large heads. Size: 18–32 mm (¾–1¼ in).

Cut floor brads These are rectangular in section but with an L-shaped head for holding floorboards to joists. Size: 12–150 mm (½–6 in).

Clout nail Most of these are galvanised for outside use, particularly for fixing roofing felt. The extra large head prevents the felt from tearing. Size: 12–50 mm (½–2 in).

Coppered hardboard nail The diamond shaped head almost disappears when driven in. It has good holding-down qualities for thin materials. Size: 9–38 mm (⅜–1½ in).

Cut clasp nail A favourite of Edwardian carpenters for fixing skirting boards. Rectangular in section, they are difficult to remove and provide a very strong fixing in predrilled masonry. Size: 25–150 mm (1–6 in).

Screws

Screws can be wrongly used around the home, largely through a lack of knowledge. All screws can be driven in by hand providing the appropriate pilot hole and shank clearance hole have been drilled and countersunk properly. However, it is easier to use a powered driver.

Harry's DIY tips for driving screws

The length of the screw should be about three times the thickness of the workpiece being fixed. Make sure the pilot hole is slightly shorter than the screw. The gauge is the diameter of the shank (the unthreaded part). Information about the head type and pre-fixing comes on the packet, as does the size of bit to use. Cross-headed screws are better suited to power-drivers.

When using brass or chrome screws, first insert a steel screw of the same size. This cuts a thread for the softer screw, limiting the chance of it snapping off. For difficult screws coat with candle wax or wax polish to make entry much easier. When using conventionally slotted screws, make sure that the screwdriver blade fits perfectly square and tight into the slot to avoid a slip and damage to the workpiece.

Countersunk screw These screws are available in steel and brass, and are used for fixing countersunk components. These may have a predrilled recess, as with hinges or brackets, or the recess may have to be prepared, (for example, for timber joints). Ensure that the screw head is the same size as the counter-sunk recess.

Dome head (mirror) screw These decorative screws are used to hold mirrors. They come in chrome and brass with a special dome head that screws onto the head of the screw. Once the screw is driven home the dome is then added for effect.

Raised head screw Look at your door handles or other decorative fittings – you'll probably find raised head screws holding them. They come in in brass and chrome. Make sure that the screw goes in at precisely 90°, otherwise the edge of the dome will not be level with the fitting.

Self-tapping screw If you ever work with sheet metal, you'll doubtless have the need for these special case-hardened screws. The thread is coarse enabling it to cut and grip the metal.

Multi-purpose wood and chipboard screw Look at one of these closely and you'll see a twin thread; The screw is made from hardened steel, so it's suitable for all timbers, including chipboard. The bright zinc-plated screw is protected in damp conditions too. With a recessed cross-head, it is threaded for three-quarters of its length. Shorter ones are fully threaded.

Round head screw The slight head of the dome protrudes decoratively when used on flat surfaces. Use black, japanned round heads on brackets and wrought-iron door furniture, or choose brass or chrome to match a fitting.

Coach bolt Use a coach screw or bolt for hanging heavy radiators, fixing heavy timbers to walls and for very heavy work in the garden. They are available in black steel or plated and can have square or hexagonal heads. You'll need a spanner or a socket driver to drive one of these home.

Pan head screw This screw is very similar to the round head and has the same good fixing pressure on flat surfaces, but it has a lower profile with a flattened dome. It can also be used as a self-tapping screw and this type of head is found on metal thread screws.

Tools

A small bolster chisel, a hammer and a cold chisel are useful for removing old floor tiles but the cutting edges must be kept sharp throughout the job. Use a portable clamp, with a small grinding wheel attached to your drill.

Use a variable speed, safe, cordless drill/driver to drill pilot holes, to countersink for screw heads.

Don't skimp on the essentials; you really should buy the best you can afford. A cheap screwdriver bought on a market stall will soon lose its 'flat'; 'Never-to-be-repeated', bargain-price tools are simply not a good idea. We are all limited to a financial budget, but the need to become equipped for the tasks involved in maintaining our homes has never been more evident than in today's economic climate. What we all need in order to carry out routine maintenance, repair and improvement jobs is a basic tool kit.

Ten important points for you to consider first:

1 Always buy the best that you can afford.
2 Choose good, household-name brands.
3 Decide on a place for each tool, whether it's a carpenter's box, a wall rack or a cupboard.
4 Use each tool for the purpose for which it was designed.
5 Learn the correct way of using each tool and always read instructions when provided.
6 Handle tools carefully and properly.
7 Always handle power tools with special caution.
8 Make sure that tools are returned, after use, to their designated place.
9 Keep all tools sharpened and in good repair.
10 Don't buy expensive, sophisticated tools when you can hire them.

Standard screwdrivers are designed specifically for driving in or removing screws. Don't be tempted to use them for opening paint tins, forcing up bent nails or chipping off hardened cement. Buy a screwdriver that feels right for your hand. Slightly more expensive is a pump screwdriver with a range of interchangeable bits. This will cope with electrical work and 'Posidrive' screws with cross slot heads, as well as slotted screws, although you can, of course, buy separate screwdrivers for the different types of work.

A steel tape, apart from its job of measuring, serves as an excellent conversion device for imperial to metric measures. Buy one up to 16 ft (5 m) long, which is ideal for measuring rooms, carpets, curtains, wallpaper and for the job of measuring before cutting wood. Do buy a steel tape that has a little arm which locks off the tape to any measurement.

As you get more experienced, some of the tools that you'll be seeking to use will probably be: a steel combination square, a spirit level, a tenon saw, a smoothing plane, a flat file, a pointing trowel, a try square, and a brace and bit (or hand brace) with some auger bits for drilling larger holes in wood. (Remember that those bits need to be kept separately from the electric drill bits which come housed in a plastic case.)

All tools, of course, need to be maintained properly and it's no use owning a plane or chisel without having sharpening facilities and knowing how toy use them. A double-sided oilstone with an inexpensive honing guide is a must. The hardest job that you will have to do in order to get an accurate cutting edge is to set the blade into the guide!

Sharp tools are safe tools, so keep bevelled edge chisels sharp for jobs like paring recesses in door edges for hinges. DIYers need to be able to maintain equipement, not least because it can cost as much to get a router bit sharpened as the original cost of the cutter. Sharpening your own adds years to its life.

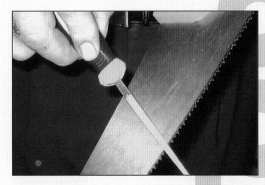

Save time and money by sharpening your own saws. Follow instructions to get correct angles because different saws have different settings and numbers of teeth.

A powered nail gun can be used to fix vertical boards to form panelling between a dado rail and the skirting board.

A pipe and cable detector can be a life saver! Switch on, sweep it over where you want to drill and it will tell you if you are in a danger zone, audibly and visualy.

A screwgun attachment drives in at least 20 screws a minute, all automatically!

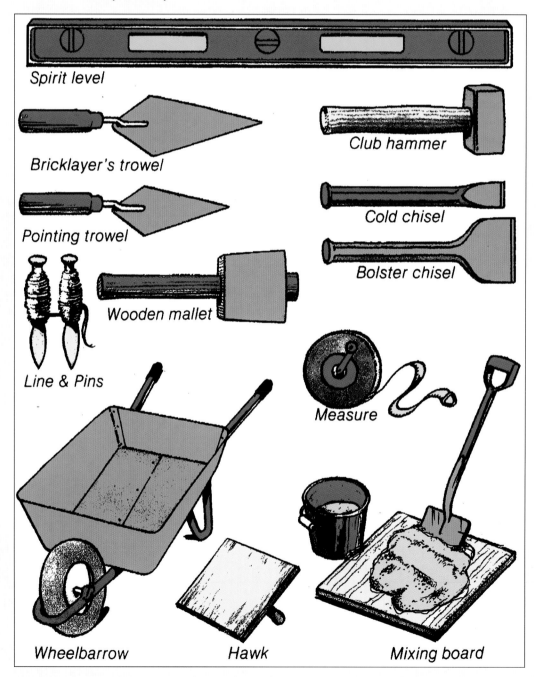

Spirit level

Bricklayer's trowel

Pointing trowel

Line & Pins

Wooden mallet

Club hammer

Cold chisel

Bolster chisel

Measure

Wheelbarrow

Hawk

Mixing board

Garden tools

Tools used in the garden for patio laying, walling, pointing and repairing.

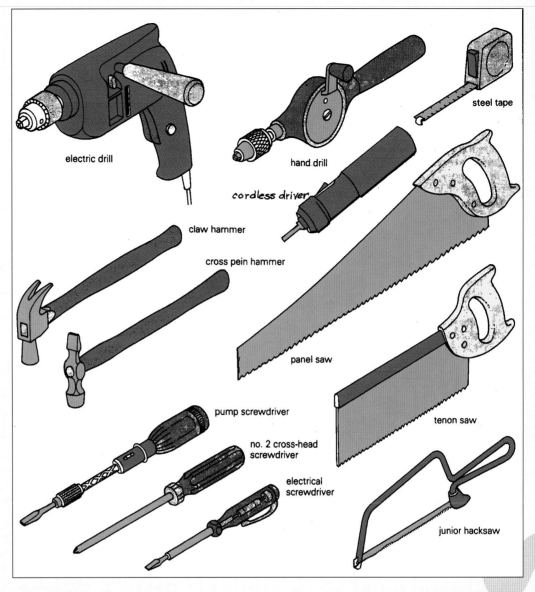

steel tape

electric drill

hand drill

cordless driver

claw hammer

cross pein hammer

panel saw

pump screwdriver

tenon saw

no. 2 cross-head
screwdriver

electrical
screwdriver

junior hacksaw

A basic tool kit

Start with the basic tools and add to them as you need others.

Choose a versatile electric drill which is much less work than a hand drill. Make sure that you read and fully understand the instructions before using a powered drill and its attachments. A hand drill is useful for small spaces that are inaccessible with an electric drill, although a flexible drive shaft (a bendy extension for drilling in awkward places) is available.

A hammer's first job is to bang in nails, but a claw hammer will also pull them out. If a nail is too deep for it to be drawn out, try tapping it in further using a bigger and blunted nail, and pulling it through the opposite side with pliers. If the opposite side is inaccessible, tap the nail as far in as it will go and fill the hole with putty or plastic wood. If you are afraid of damaging the wood by drawing a nail out, use a small piece of wood against the nail head as a sort of wedge. The nail will come out with very little effort. For light jobs that need precision, not strength, use a smaller cross pein hammer instead.

The first saw you buy should be a 550mm (22in) panel saw, which will suit your general needs. It should have eight points (the number of teeth to an inch). Always

hold the saw with your index finger pointing along the direct of the blade – this will give you better control when sawing. Always use the whole length of the blade but never force with undue pressure. Let the saw do the work, applying light pressure on the downward stroke only. A junior hacksaw is a handy tool for cutting wire, cable and small pieces of metal, and for cutting of nails. Use a tenon saw for fine work where accuracy is important.

Standard screwdrivers are designed specifically for driving in and removing screws. Don't be tempted to use them for opening paint tins, forcing up bent nails or chipping off hardened cement. Buy a screwdriver that feels right for your hand. Pump screwdrivers are slightly more expensive than the standard type, but they do come with a range of interchangeable bits. Use one for electrical work, cross-head and slotted screws, although you might prefer to buy a range of screwdrivers to cope with all the options.

A steel tape, apart form its job of measuring, serves as an excellent converter between imperial and metric units. Buy one that is 5m (16ft) long, which is ideal for rooms, carpets, curtains, wallpaper and wood, and that has a lock.

pincers

pliers

bradawl

multi-purpose
trimming tool

aluminium
step ladder

bevelled-edged chisel

trimming knife

staple gun

portable
work-bench

Extras to a tool kit

Pliers are ideal for holding small items such as a nut while you unscrew a bolt. Long-nosed pliers are especially useful for electrical work, but make sure that the handles are insulated. A pair of pincers are similar to pliers. Never use them for cutting and stripping wire – use a pair of wire strippers instead!

The multi-purpose trimming tool is available in lots of sizes. Blades are held by only two screws making replacement easy.

A bradawl is a useful tool for starting holes for small screws. Make absolutely sure that you cut into the wood at right angles to the grain to avoid splitting the wood.

Don't buy a chisel with a wood handle as your first. Buy one with a plastic shatterproof handle that will withstand banging with a hammer or mallet. A 20 mm (³⁄₄ in) bevelled-edge chisel is ideal. Make sure that it has a plastic cap to protect the blade.

A trimming knife with a retractable blade is also an essential part of your toolkit. You can use one to cut through thin plywood when used with a straight steel edge, or for marking timber to get a more accurate saw cut. It will also cut carpet, vinyl and cork.

The modern equivalent to the hammer and tack is the staple gun. It is invaluable for small upholstery jobs, mounting thin ply or card on the back of pictureframes, holding down carpet underfelt, fixing roofing felt to the underside of rafters, and many other fixing jobs.

Keep to hand an aluminium stepladder (with an open leg-lock and non-slip feet). Make sure that it is high enough to reach your highest ceiling or a loft hatch. A paint tray that locks on the top of the ladder is a useful accessory.

The traditional work bench is heavy and cumbersome. Nowadays, lightweight, portable and strong versions are available. If you get into the swing of DIYing, it is probably worthwhile investing in a DIY work bench.

Electric power saw

It is quick and easy to use a powered saw to cut all types of board such as for loft flooring or for a loft hatch. Clamp the board, mark it and use a fence guide to get parallel straight cuts.

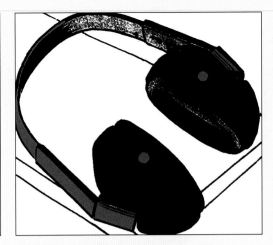

Ear defenders

Wear ear defenders for all DIY jobs involving large drills, high-powered saws, floor sanders, chain saws, hedge trimmers, routers, and other similar powered tools.

Hand saw

Despite the convenience of a powered saw, a good quality, sharp panel saw with about nine teeth to the inch is useful in many situations, such as for sawing timber of all sizes (especially joists and noggins). Keep the saw vertical as you cut and remember to saw against your marked line and not on it! Gently push on the forward stroke only.

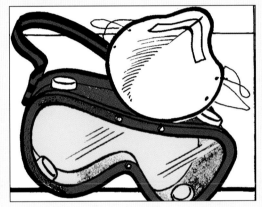

Goggles and masks

Eye protection is essential when you work with glass. Similarly, wear goggles for chopping wood, concrete and stone, or for any job where there is a risk of eye injury. Wear a mask to protect you from harmful dust when sanding, drilling, grinding, etc., or from dusty materials such as cement, filler, etc.

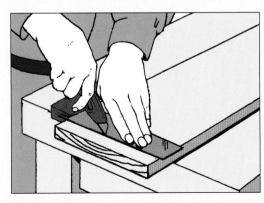

Marking knife

A scored line made with a marking (or trimming) knife and metal square ensures that a saw cut will follow the correct line. Use only retractable blades which are safe when you aren't using the knife. The tool is versatile and you can use it for trimming, cutting, paring and many other tasks.

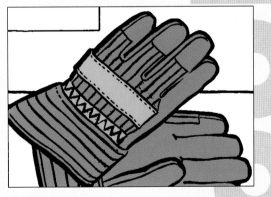

Gloves

Jobs in the garden can be hazardous, especially to your hands. Stones, bricks, slabs, heavy timbers and powered tools, etc., could cause injury, so wear suitable protective gloves. Wear them also when working with liquid paint stripper and solvents.

Index

Index

Index